Recycling and Reuse of Sewage Sludge

Proceedings of the International Symposium organised by the Concrete Technology Unit and held at the University of Dundee, Scotland, UK on 19 - 20 March 2001

Edited by

Ravindra K. Dhir
Director, Concrete Technology Unit
University of Dundee

Mukesh C. Limbachiya
CPD/Consultancy Manager, Concrete Technology Unit
University of Dundee

Michael J. McCarthy
Lecturer, Concrete Technology Unit
University of Dundee

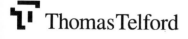 ThomasTelford

Published by Thomas Telford Publishing, Thomas Telford Ltd, 1 Heron Quay, London E14 4JD.

URL: http://www.thomastelford.com

Distributors for Thomas Telford books are
USA: ASCE Press, 1801 Alexander Bell Drive, Reston, VA 20191-4400, USA
Japan: Maruzen Co. Ltd, Book Department, 3–10 Nihonbashi 2-chome, Chuo-ku, Tokyo 103
Australia: DA Books and Journals, 648 Whitehorse Road, Mitcham 3132, Victoria

First published 2001

Also available from Thomas Telford Books

Sustainable construction: use of incinerator ash, edited by Ravindra K. Dhir, Tom D. Dyer and Kevin A. Paine, 2000, ISBN 0 7277 2861 X
Sustainable construction: use of recycled concrete aggregate, edited by Ravindra K. Dhir, Neil A. Henderson and Mukesh C. Limbachiya, 1998, ISBN 0 7277 2726 5
Recycling and reuse of glass cullet, edited by Ravindra K. Dhir, Mukesh C. Limbachiya and Thomas D. Dyer, 2001, ISBN 0 7277 2994 2
Recycling and reuse of used tyres, edited by Ravindra K. Dhir, Mukesh C. Limbachiya and Kevin A. Paine, 2001, ISBN 0 7277 2995 0
Recovery and recycling of paper, edited by Ravindra K. Dhir, Mukesh C. Limbachiya and Moray D. Newlands, 2001, ISBN 0 7277 2993 4

A catalogue record for this book is available from the British Library

ISBN: 0 7277 2992 6

Printed and bound in Great Britain by MPG Books, Bodmin

PREFACE

Varying degrees of environmental impact by sewage sludge disposal alternatives, present challenges for waste management. Many regulating bodies throughout the world are implementing measures which actively promote environmentally sustainable and economically viable routes to convert this waste into a valuable resource. Indeed, with increasing international awareness of the importance of these issues, it is likely that such policies will become widespread in future. These provide opportunities, but at the same time, given the nature of the material and obstacles that may exist, require that responsible and proven practices are followed.

This International Symposium is the first of its kind held in the UK and is contributed to by some of the World's leading experts in the field of recycling and reuse of sewage sludge. The proceedings contain thirty-two papers presented under four sessions: (i) Generation, Handling and Treatment of Sewage Sludge, (ii) Main Disposal Routes and Environmental Impact, (iii) Material Recovery and Reuse in Value Added Applications and (iv) Way Forward and Developing the Sustainable Use of Sewage Sludge. Thus, they comprehensively summarise the state-of the art in recycling and use of sewage sludge.

The Symposium Opening Addresses were given by Sir Robert Alan Langlands, Principal and Vice Chancellor, University of Dundee, Professor Stan Dagg, Chairman of the Scottish Environment Protection Agency, West Region Board and Mr Sam Galbraith, MSP, Minister for Environment, Sport and Culture, Scotland. The Opening Keynote paper was presented by Dr Tim Evans, Tim Evans Environment, UK. The Closing Keynote paper was given by Mr Andy Johnson, Terra Eco Systems, UK.

The Editors would like to thank Dr A Stenger, INRA, France, Dr C E A Carlson-Evkall, Swedish National Testing and Research Institute, Sweden, Dr E H Bryan, National Science Foundation, USA and Dr P B Clark, W S Atkins Water, UK for chairing the Symposium sessions.

The Symposium was sponsored by Dundee City Council, Recycling Market Development Scotland, Scottish Enterprise, Scottish Environment Protection Agency, Scottish Executive and Valpak Ltd. All sponsors are gratefully acknowledged for their invaluable support of the Symposium.

The Symposium was run concurrently with three other International Symposia to promote recycling and reuse of Glass Cullet, Paper and Used Tyres.

The proceedings have been prepared directly from the camera-ready manuscripts submitted by the authors and editing has been restricted to minor changes where it was considered absolutely necessary.

Dundee
March 2001

Ravindra K Dhir
Mukesh C Limbachiya
Michael J McCarthy

CONTENTS

PART THREE: MATERIAL RECOVERY AND REUSE IN
VALUE ADDED APPLICATIONS

OPENING KEYNOTE PAPER

THE JOURNEY TO SUSTAINABLE TREATMENT AND USE OR DISPOSAL OF WASTEWATER BIOSOLIDS

T Evans

TIM EVANS ENVIRONMENT

United Kingdom

ABSTRACT. Sustainable - action today that does not compromise the options of future generations. This goes beyond merely complying with legal obligations but the balance sheets of those that operate the due diligence that is implied by sustainable development are much safer than those whose objective is just to operate within the limits set by regulators. Treating wastewater so as to protect the quality of receiving waters into which it is discharged is an important part of sustainable development, and it results in biosolids. The wastewater collection system is open to a range of chemical and biological hazards. The principle of controlling hazards at source is well established and its operation has resulted in a dramatic increase in the safety of biosolids as regards chemical quality. Attention has turned to biological hazards, especially the emerging ones. In some cases these can be controlled at source and for others a control point has to be operated during biosolids treatment. There are several ways in which biosolids can be treated or destroyed, new methods emerge periodically and there is a continual flow of variations on existing themes. The facility for innovation is important. Biosolids contain organic matter and plant nutrients that have been concentrated out of the wastewater, these can be very beneficial to sustainable use of land. Many believe that having got these constituents (particularly phosphorus) into the anthroprogenic cycle it is imperative that they be conserved. The paper will discuss the whole of the biosolids process in the particular context of sustainability.

Keywords: Appropriate technology, Biosolids, Climate change, Competition, Disposal, HACCP, Indemnity, Phosphate-recovery, Recycling, Sustainability, Treatment, Use, Wastewater.

Dr T Evans, is trained as a soil scientist in England and USA and has own consultancy specialising in recycling, composting, HACCP, etc. He launched Thames Water's first environmentally controlled biosolids recycling. He moved to business planning and performance indicators for clean and dirty water and biosolids again to design and manage clearance of 4 million m^3 of stored biosolids from the site that will become Heathrow's 5th terminal. He has developed a range of peat alternatives based on composted biosolids and achieved nation-wide retail distribution. He worked with insurance/risk-management to enable strict-liability latent-defect insurance for biosolids producers and treated land.

INTRODUCTION

The collection, treatment and safe disposal of wastewater is one of the greatest contributors to improving public health. Biosolids are an inevitable consequence of treating wastewater. When we debated updating the title of the then "Sewage Treatment and Sludge Disposal Panel" of the Chartered Institution of Water and Environmental Management we decided it would be a tautology to refer to biosolids because correct management of biosolids is essential to proper operation of wastewater treatment works. Instead we opted for the title "Wastewater Management Panel".

Biosolids contain constituents from the wastewater that have limited solubility in water, that are sorbed onto the solid phase or that are incorporated into microbial biomass during treatment. The most soluble remain in the aqueous phase. This is an immediate difference from residuals that have not been conveyed by water. The solid phase has been eluted with water. Biosolids comprise organic matter and mineral matter from the wastewater and biomass that was grown during the treatment process. The typical ash content of untreated biosolids is about 20% in UK. It is higher where there is combined sewerage (i.e. surface and foul water are collected together) and lower where surface water and infiltration are minimised.

Some of the microbial content of untreated biosolids is pathogenic. This is often exaggerated, for example in an urban catchment the content of *Salmonella* is generally low because most of the people, most of the time, do not have salmonellosis. However it is important that procedures should be in place in case the system is challenged. In some catchments there is a predictably greater input of pathogenic organisms as will be discussed later.

Phosphate is one of the constituents concentrated from wastewater into biosolids. In the context of sustainability it is very important that we give special consideration to this element. The economic life of the world's reserves of phosphate have been estimated at about 100 years at the present rate of extraction. Phosphate is fundamental to biochemistry, we cannot substitute another element for phosphorus in biological processes. Phosphorus bonds strongly with iron, aluminium, calcium and magnesium, these elements are abundant in soil. Thus the natural chemistry of soil tends to convert phosphorus into forms that are of limited availability to plants so farmers have to use fertilisers, manures, biosolids etc. to maintain the content of plant-available-P at an adequate agronomic level. Just as inadequate plant-available-P in soil can limit the growth of agricultural crops, so it can be the limiting nutrient for algae in water. With this in mind P-removal targets have been applied to many wastewater treatment works to prevent eutrophication of the receiving waters and algal blooms. The Swedish government has taken a lead in sustainable use of P and set an environmental goal of recirculating 75% of phosphate by 2010. This will become a challenge for the wastewater industry. Will other governments follow this precedent?

The waste management hierarchy is

- Avoidance and Minimisation – we can manipulate the diets of farm animals to minimise excretion but that is not likely to be a vote-winning strategy if suggested for humans; instead processes are being researched that minimise biosolids production,

- Reuse and Recycling – for biosolids this is generally regarded as the Best Practicable Environmental Option, it conserves organic matter and completes nutrient cycles, but this option requires an appropriate culture if it is really to be sustainable,
- Disposal with energy and resource recovery – for special situations this may be appropriate,
- Disposal by incineration or landfilling – this is regarded as the least preferred option.

There is no universal solution. As people consider climate change and carbon credits the goal posts are likely to continue to move. Perhaps one certainty is that continuous improvement, which means continuous change, will remain a necessity.

HAZARDS

Life is not risk-free. Hazard is the potential to do harm, risk is the likelihood of that harm occurring. Safe is a 4-letter word that is open to interpretation or mischief. Airlines do not advertise themselves as being "safe", they might say they are punctual, favourite, comfortable, etc. but not safe, because they know that there is an element of risk and journalists can pick at this and jeopardise confidence. Communicating and evaluating risk are difficult and subtle. The Financial Times quoted Sir John Krebs (Chairman of the UK Food Standards Agency) on 28th October 2000 – "People have a lot of common sense and should be allowed to make their own judgement about what risks they are willing to take. It's like riding a bike on a busy road. My wife knows the risks and won't do it. I know the risks and do." Table 1 summarises the hazards associated with wastewater collection and treatment and with the use or disposal of treated water and biosolids. These hazards need to be considered for each catchment and effective risk management strategies developed that are appropriate to need.

RISK MANAGEMENT

Inputs of hazards can be considered as 'point-sources' and 'diffuse-sources'. Generally the former are easier to control provided that having identified the source(s) you have the capability to influence the discharge. Wastewater operators in the UK have considerable powers to control discharges from point sources to the wastewater collection system, but this is not true for all countries. Possession of such powers and operating them are essential for sustainability.

Heavy metals and other chemical pollutants in biosolids are to some extent part of mythology. Control of inputs from industrial sources has been so effective that concentrations in wastewater are now a fraction of the historic values. But one of the first questions from the uninitiated is often "How do you get the heavy metals out?" to which the answer is that we don't let then get in in the first place.

Figure 1 illustrates the effectiveness of active source control over many years for two large urban domestic/industrial catchments (Mogden and Deephams in London, 1.8 and 0.8 million p.e. respectively). Each has combined sewerage, primary settlement, fine bubble activated sludge and mesophilic anaerobic digestion. A similar trend applies to other elements that are regulated by the sludge use in agriculture regulations and would be seen at most other works.

Table 1 Summary of hazards

FACTOR	HAZARD
Chemical	Damage the fabric of the collection system or treatment works, or adversely impact the treatment process, employees or off-site receptors via emissions
Litter	Impair the treatment process by fouling plant etc. and/or contribute 'aesthetic pollution' t emissions
Sand & grit	Impair the treatment process by silting up vessels and reducing retention time or abrading equipment
Pathogens	Transmission of diseases (phyto- and zoo-) via wastewater, biosolids, air-emissions or effluent; in addition to domestic inputs there may be inputs peculiar to the catchment
Water pollution	Either of groundwater or of surface-water as a result of leakage from tanks, etc. or run-of from stored biosolids
Saline intrusion	Excessive salinity in biosolids resulting in adverse effects on soils or crops
Odorants	Odour complaints about the works or the biosolids. Odour compounds might result from industrial discharge, they may form during treatment, or they may result from inadequate treatment. Because of the large number of people affected odour is probably the greatest threat
	Failure to comply with legal or voluntary obligations
	Failure to make biosolids that are fit for the intended use or disposal
Nutrients	Excessive enrichment of soil and/or water
Propagules	Transmission of [pernicious] weeds

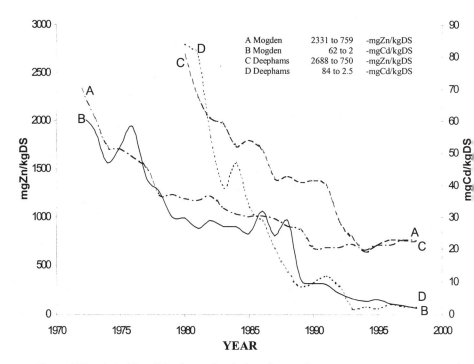

Figure 1 Trends in biosolids zinc and cadmium for two large wastewater treatment works

Other potential pollutants have been controlled by legislation regulating the use and disposal of dangerous substances (Table 2).   However an impression persists that the urban wastewater collection system is an open door for pollutants, which end up in the biosolids. Alternatively there is the idea that less is better and that it should be possible to continue to reduce the input of potential pollutants but here we run into diffuse inputs.   Copper dissolved from pipework is one example of a diffuse input.   Some water supplies appear to be more cuprosolvent than others.   Cuprosolvancy decreases as pipework gets older probably because of protective scaling.   The answer to further reducing copper in wastewater in some areas would be to reduce the cuprosolvancy of the water, or substituting a different type of pipework.   Recent evidence [1] suggests that copper pipework has significant bactericidal effect that is protective of human health.   Slime growth is much less in than in plastic or stainless steel, pathogenic bacteria such as *E. coli* O157 can grow protected by these biofilms. When it is recognised that there is widespread deficiency of copper and other trace elements in crops then the aspiration for ever-lower concentrations in biosolids may appear questionable.   However this is an aspect that is subject to regulation and the choice of where to set limits is ultimately political.   Strategies are necessary to ensure compliance.

Table 2 Dioxin analysis for biosolids from Moden wastewater treatment works.

DATE	ΣTEQ (ng/ kgDS)
1942	18
1944	36
1949	61
1953	127
1956	402
1958	229
1960	166
1998	4.2

Pathogens are often thought of as a diffuse-source hazard, but there may be point sources. Sewage contains pathogenic organisms, that is why its collection and treatment has been so beneficial to public health.   In UK most of the people, most of the time, are not excreting virulent pathogens but the risk may be increased on occasions as a result of outbreaks of infectious disease.   In some other countries the human burden of parasites is so high that there may be 10^5 viable helminth ova (or more) / gram dry solids in night soil or sewage [2].

With the emergence of new pathogens animal manures have become a significant risk.   Cattle can have symptomless infection with verotoxigenic *E. coli* including O157:H7 (also called VTEC or EHEC strains) – 9% of cattle were estimated to be infected in UK in 2000.   For humans these pathogens are highly infective and the symptoms are severe, even fatal in some cases.   Apart from disease outbreaks, VTEC *E. coli* will not be significant in human sewage, but some catchments may have inputs of animal manure (abattoirs, markets, and even farms).

There are other point sources such as premises processing hides imported from countries where anthrax is still endemic.   There was one case where a potato processing factory imported from a country where Brown Rot was endemic. Infected material was not captured by import inspection and the disease organism ended up in the factory's effluent. It was transmitted it to solanaceous weeds on the riverbank, which became a reservoir, and to commercial crops via irrigation.

The above illustrate that inputs of risk materials to the sewerage system vary from catchment to catchment and from country to country. Wastewater undertakers may actively manage them, or they may be controlled through general legislation. However there is a due-diligence responsibility on wastewater undertakers to have knowledge of the discharges and connections so as to consider the likely hazards and control their risks.

HAZARD ANALYSIS AND CRITICAL CONTROL POINT

Hazard Analysis and Critical Control Point (HACCP) was developed by the Pillsbury Company in the 1960s to assure the safety of food for the American manned space-flight programme. End product testing had been proved unacceptable as a method of control because by that means it was only possible to be confident in all of the production by testing all of the production, which was clearly impracticable. HACCP has proved so effective that it has been widely adopted [3]. It has also been employed in non-food manufacturing to improve product reliability.

HACCP was introduced to the water industry in the UK during discussions with the British Retail Consortium, which led to the agreement on how biosolids should be treated, applied and used in farming [4]. This agreement is not the destination on the journey to sustainable use, much work is continuing, but it is a very significant milestone.

HACCP demonstrates due diligence and does not inhibit innovation. It is a structured, transparent, pragmatic, non-prescriptive and proactive approach to preventing hazards becoming unacceptable risks in the final product by identifying points in a production process where these hazards can be controlled. These are called Critical Control Points (CCP). Each CCP is operated at Critical Limits (e.g. time, temperature, and pH) which control the hazard. Thus by recording the operating parameters of the CCPs there is a trace of the risk control. The validity of the CCPs may be verified by end product testing, but it should be noted that within HACCP this is no longer a control, it has become a verification. Another important feature is to establish Corrective Actions that shall be taken if a CCP fails. HACCP is complimentary, and not an alternative, to Quality Assurance (QA). Having worked with QA for more than 10 years I find it hard to understand how anybody can expect to achieve compliance with legal and other obligations consistently if they do not have a QA system. HACCP is a technique for designing a process, it is entirely applicable to the Biosolids Process. It also has the merit that it is a methodology that has the confidence of the food industry.

Figure 2 illustrates the 'Biosolids Process' where biosolids are used on land. The details of other use or disposal routes would differ in some details. Some think of HACCP as only being applicable to the sludge treatment step of the process, but it is equally applicable to every other step. As discussed above, sludge treatment does not control the risks of all of the hazards about which we are concerned, and failure to control any could be damaging to the programme. It is quite clear that source control is the CCP for many chemical hazards.

Preliminary treatment is a CCP for litter, grit and screenings, though the CCP for litter may be screening at the start of sludge treatment. Effective liaison with the public health authority is important in the pathogen control strategy for giving warning of a disease outbreak. This is not the place for a detailed discussion of HACCP, but I hope that its potential is obvious.

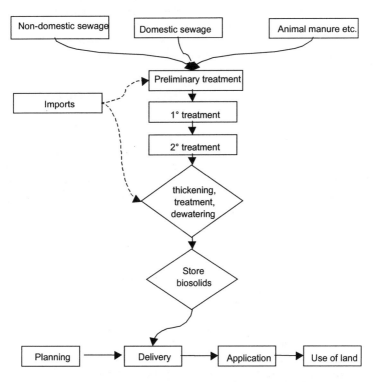

Figure 2 Biosolids process diagram for use on land.

SLUDGE TREATMENT

Mesophilic Anaerobic Digestion (MAD) is the most common treatment process in UK in terms of the quantity treated (Table 2) [5]. A total of 53.8% of sludge was treated by MAD in 1996/7, and 42% of that total was subsequently dewatered. The figures will have changed significantly since this survey because of the agreement between Water UK and the BRC and the ending of disposal at sea. Biosolids producers agreed to end the use of untreated biosolids on grassland by 31st December 1998 and on arable land by 31st December 1999, except for 'industrial non-food crops' which could continue until 31st December 2001).

MAD involves bacterial conversion of organic matter into methane (about 60% v/v) carbon dioxide and water at a temperature of about 35°C in the absence of air. Typically digesters are fed with liquid sludge at 5-6%DS, although some at feeding at 7-8%DS [6]. This results in the Loss on Ignition (LOI) decreasing from about 80% to between 60 and 50%; that is a reduction in total solids of between 50 and 60%, however the change in water content is trivial so the change in mass is negligible. As a generalisation, the greater the LOI the easier the digested liquid is to dewater and the lower the risk of odour nuisance associated with the cake.

The anaerobic digestion breaks the peptide links of proteins resulting in ammonium ions in solution, which makes the product a more readily available source of nitrogen for uptake by plants or loss by volatilisation. It also releases phosphate from biomass especially where there is biological phosphate removal during wastewater treatment. This can become a problem when dissolved carbon dioxide is released if the ammonium : phosphate : magnesium ratio is right for formation of struvite, which forms a low solubility intractable scale that can block pipes and machinery. However this solubilisation of P can also be an opportunity to recover some of the P in a form that is useful to the chemical industry and narrow the N:P ratio in the biosolids to one that more-nearly matches agronomic needs.

MAD with managed liquid storage (called secondary digestion) in batches can achieve the 2-log reduction capability required for 'Conventional Treatment' [7].

Table 3 1996/7 sludge quantity (tDS/y) and treatment processes [5].

WORKS SIZE	NOT SPECIFIED		p.e. < 10k		10k<p.e.<150k		p.e. <150k		TOTAL	
MAD liquid	12680	31.4%	7540	15.8%	117451	32.8%	210123	31.4%	347794	31
MAD dewatered	7049	17.5%	1992	4.2%	36055	10.1%	207374	31.0%	252470	22
TAD liquid			51	0.1%					51	0.
TAD dewatered			295	0.6%					295	0.
Composted			318	0.7%	15074	4.2%	3952	0.6%	19344	1.
Lime stabilised	3300	8.2%	48	0.1%	24410	6.8%			27758	2.
Unstabilised liquid	8070	20.0%	27720	58.2%	82302	23.0%	173798	25.9%	291891	2(
Unstabilised, dewatered	3158	7.8%	6342	13.3%	66257	18.5%	43077	6.4%	118833	1(
Liquid storage for 3 mths	6077	15.1%	3362	7.1%	9554	2.7%	2287	0.3%	21280	1.
Thermal dried treated					1030	0.3%	3787	0.6%	4817	0.
Thermal dried untreated					94	0.0%			94	0.
Other [1]					5730	1.6%	25393	3.8%	31123	2.
Total	40334	3.6%	47668	4.3%	357957	32.1%	669791	60.0%	1115750	
Number [2]	94		935		524		126		1679	

[1] incineration was sometimes classified as a treatment rather than as a disposal route

[2] there are about 4k additional small works and facilities that 'intersite' to these 'larger' works

Methane production and power generation is becoming an increasingly interesting benefit of anaerobic digestion as the Climate Change Levy (and other financial instruments to achieve Kyoto commitments) become apparent.

Thermophilic Anaerobic Digestion (TAnD) has not been favoured because it is considered to be unstable but it appears that this may be the result of misinformation that has become part of the industry's mythology. Several large installations in North America have converted MAD to TAnD in order to achieve higher pathogen removal, greater gas production and better dewatering.

Controlled heating of the liquid feed to digesters (called pre-pasteurisation) has been practised in Switzerland for about 12 years as standard practice required by law. It is starting to appear in UK in order to achieve the 'Advanced Treated' status [8]. Some processes use short retention autothermic thermophilic aerobic digestion to heat the sludge, with backup supplemental heating, others rely on external heating. The process is claimed to increase solids destruction, improve gas yield and dewatering and to eliminate the need for heating the MAD because the daily input of hot liquid sludge satisfies the heating requirements for the MAD.

Thermal hydrolysis (Cambi) is another adaptation of existing MAD to achieve Advanced Treatment. It was developed in Norway. The first installation in UK was at Chertsey where it boosted treatment capability of the existing digesters from 100k p.e to 270k p.e. [9]. It is being installed at Aberdeen and Dublin. The first step is to dewater the raw feed to about 14%DS (about 2.5 times the feed of conventional MAD). This paste is cooked at about 160°C (6.5 bar) for ½ hour, which reduces the viscosity to something that looks like conventional 6%DS sludge. The process sterilises the sludge, disrupts cells and makes the sludge (especially secondary sludge) more digestible. The hydrolysed liquid is cooled and then fed to conventional MAD which yields about 40% more gas, ½ of which is used for raising steam used for the process. It seems to eliminate the problem of digester foaming. The digested liquid is very easily dewatered to greater than 30%DS at low polyelectrolyte dose and the cake has low odour and is easily stacked. Cambi has high capital cost but often wins on whole-life DCF analysis. It enables existing assets to be sweated, which may create an opportunity arising from implementation of the Landfill Directive [10] and Biological Treatment of Biodegradable Waste.

Treatment of secondary sludge with ultrasound also disrupts cells and increases digestibility and gas yield but has negligible disinfection effect. The resulting digested liquid should have the improved dewaterability discussed above. The challenge has been to develop suitable horns to deliver the radiation [11].

A further variation on the MAD theme is to separate the two phases. The first phase of MAD is performed by acidophilic bacteria that convert large organic molecules to simple organic acids that are processed by the second phase (methanogenic) bacteria. In 2-phase digestion there is a short retention preliminary digestion where phase-1 bacteria predominate, a longer retention methanogenic reactor follows this. The process has been around since the early 1970s and claims 'Advanced Treatment' capability. There is interest on both sides of the Atlantic.

Lime stabilisation has increased significantly since Table 2 in many cases as a 'quick-fix' interim solution to phase out untreated biosolids. The addition of lime to raise pH with controlled increase in temperature can reliably achieve the 6-log reduction requirement of advanced treatment if it is engineered properly. Disinfection is effective. The mechanism is a bit complicated because there are four factors at work in combination; they are pH, temperature, ammonia and contact time. Time for installation is rapid, the footprint is small and the capital cost (which scales down well) is moderate, however the operating cost is high because of the cost of alkaline additive. Excessive alkaline hydrolysis can create powerful malodorants. It appears this can result from high doses of very reactive quicklime, which gives a fierce reaction. Some alkaline additives also contain potassium, which is a very useful agronomic feature. One process uses moderate alkaline addition to raise pH to about 10.5 and electrical heating in a feed through reactor with controlled retention time to balance the requirements for sanitisation with the cost of lime addition [12].

Stand-alone Thermophilic Aerobic Digestion (TAD), and Autothermic Thermophilic Aerobic Digestion (ATAD) can achieve 'Advanced Treatment' if the time and temperature are right. However they are high energy and frequently result in a treated liquid that is difficult to dewater and becomes anaerobic and septic unless retention is long enough to achieve high solids destruction.

Composting is another autothermic thermophilic aerobic stabilisation process but conducted in the solid phase. There are many proprietary processes, some with high capital cost. The essential features are an adequate supply of moisture, air, carbon and nitrogen to feed the microbial biomass. The composting mass self heats over 2 to 3 days to 55-65°C. Some systems exploit pyrophilic bacteria that operate at 75°C. After about 3 weeks the high-rate decomposition phase tails off and a slower stabilisation phase (called maturation or curing) starts. Odour emission risk peaks between day-7 to day-14 of the primary phase. Windrow composting (turned or static) can achieve Advanced Treatment but it is more prone to odour emission and being stalled by excessive rainfall than in-vessel systems; fabric covers can mitigate these risks. Although the process appears simple and natural it must be actively managed if a quality product is to be assured. The product seldom exceeds 3%N (even 3 is high) because excess nitrogen is lost as ammonia, but plant-disease suppressing properties have been demonstrated and are being verified continually.

Vermiculture uses worms to process the biosolids. It uses varieties of worms that are adapted to high organic environments. Worms feed on organic matter and mix it with the medium in which they live. If it is excessively hot, cold or dry they curl up and go into a resting state until more favourable conditions occur. They breathe through their skins and will drown in excessively wet conditions; they are also sensitive to ammonia, which can be lethal. If anybody has seen dead worms on the surface of a field surface applied with liquid digested (MAD) biosolids it was because ammonia killed the worms near the surface. Survivors from deeper in the soil would have multiplied as a result of the extra food when the ammonia nitrified or volatilised. Although the basics are simple, the process needs to be managed if it is to be continuously successful. Vermiculture can provide a low-tech solution for small works [13] and it has also been engineered to provide a high-tech solution for large works [14]. Lotzof and Trafford [14] reported the development of a system that is processing 50,000 tonnes per year of biosolids and greenwaste and consistently achieving Advanced Treatment status. This has involved significant investment in research and development to perfect the engineering and understand the process and product.

Reedbeds, if they are thought of at all, are probably thought of for treating liquids, but they can also be used for biosolids [15]. They are simple to operate and need about 0.2-0.5m² per person. An installation near Copenhagen that serves 125,000 p.e. occupies about 4ha. Liquid biosolids can be applied at about 50kgDS/m²/year. The reed roots exhale oxygen into the rhizosphere, which supports aerobic bacteria that stabilise organic matter in the biosolids and treat BOD in the drainage water. A stabilised peaty medium accumulates at about 5cm depth per year so (depending on the freeboard of the original construction) beds need not be emptied for 10 or 20 years. Effective treatment apparently continues through winter but in Denmark the rate is 15-20% slower than in summer.

Thermal drying is favoured by many in the wastewater industry. It results in a 95% mass reduction compared with liquid sludge, or 75% compared with cake, but dewatering alone results in an 80% reduction compared with liquid. It is capable of producing Advanced Treated biosolids that are dry to handle and are particulate. In their physical form they therefore superficially resemble the mineral fertilisers that farmers are used to using. However fertilisers have about 10-times the nutrient content and are available in a range of plant-nutrient ratios; they also have high specific gravity and impact resistance which means that the "fly" well to the full width of farming tramlines when spread with a fertiliser spreader. Few dryer operators or manufacturers appear to have given much consideration to these product features. Unavoidably dryers user a lot of energy, this could be a penalty with the Climate Change Levy. There has also been a history of 'uncontrolled thermal events' in dryers but this is avoidable [16].

USE AND DISPOSAL

The use and disposal routes for biosolids in the UK in 1996/7 are compared with the operators' predictions for 2000/1 and for 2005/6 in Table 3 [5]. The opportunity to dispose of sludge at sea ended 31st December 1998. Some of the sludge that used to go to sea is now treated and used on land, and some is incinerated. For the longer term it can be seen that some companies anticipate that use of biosolids on land is going to become too hard and are pinning their hopes on gasification. However the largest proposed scheme (Bran Sands) has been concluded non-viable at present in comparison with use of thermally dried and pelletted biosolids on land which has proved far more reliable than consultants had predicted at the planning stage. It will be interesting to see how the situation develops.

Incineration is expensive to build and to operate, it is generally regarded unfavourably by the public which means that considerable effort is necessary to gain planning approval. In some countries public opposition has caused operators to close incinerators. If sludge is not dewatered to an 'autothermic' condition, where the heat from combustion is sufficient to dry the incoming dewatered cake so that it ignites, then supplementary fuel is needed. A large part of the operating expenditure is due to flue gas cleaning to comply with emission standards. Modern fluidised bed incinerators comply with the most stringent emission standards. Ash is generally landfilled but there has been work on using it in construction materials. Co-combustion of cake or dried sludge in coal-fired power stations, cement factories and brick-works is another way of burning sludge without risking the stigma of building an incinerator. This can be considered as energy recovery and may benefit from carbon credits when the method of applying them has been agreed. Co-combustion is threatened within the EU by the Incineration Directive, which would require emission monitoring of any facility burning waste, this could be an undesirable burden on the facility, depending on the value it receives for burning the sludge. It is perhaps worth noting that DG Environment of the European Commission is opposed to incineration and co-combustion.

Table 4 Use and disposal routes in UK in 1996/7 and predictions [5]

SOURCE	1996/7		2000/1		2005/6	
Sea	176800	19.2%	0	0.0%	0	0.0%
Incineration	90800	9.9%	247900	20.9%	291900	24.2%
Agriculture	477200	51.8%	721300	60.9%	608600	50.4%
Dedicated	38900	4.2%	36100	3.0%	38100	3.2%
Landfill	58900	6.4%	54800	4.6%	26800	2.2%
Reclamation	62800	6.8%	52600	4.4%	71200	5.9%
Silviculture	1000	0.1%	2000	0.2%	2000	0.2%
Horticultural Compost	13500	1.5%	13900	1.2%	2000	0.2%
Gasification	1400	0.2%	55100	4.7%	167000	13.8%
TOTAL	921300		1183700		1207600	
On Land	554500	60.2%	789800	66.7%	683800	56.6%
Energy	92200	10.0%	303000	25.6%	458900	38.0%

Oil From Sludge (OFS) has been in development for about 18 years and is now operational in Australia processing all of the sludge (25tDS/day) at a 300k p.e. works [17]. Bridle [17] reported the costs of this plant as Capital £8M; Power & Carbon Credits £0.4M; Net Operating & Maintenance £0.9M. Dewatered sludge is dried and then thermally and chemically converted to oil in a dual stage reactor at 450°C under reducing conditions at atmospheric pressure. The first stage produces hydrocarbons that are condensed to oil similar to diesel in the second stage. 50% of the energy content of the sludge is converted to oil. The remaining 50% is char and non-condensed gas that are burnt to power the dryer. Oil can be easily stored until it is needed (for example to generate high tariff electricity) or exported from site. All of the metals are reported to be conserved into the ash where they are present as oxides and silicates, which are non-mobile in leaching tests. It has been judged to have a CO_2 credit of $1.4kgCO_2/t$ sludge processed. Presumably the economics would depend to some extent on how the oil is used and on how it is taxed, since diesel from oilseed rape is taxed like diesel from fossil sources in UK it would be surprising if this OFS diesel were taxed differently. However if it were burnt on site to generate electricity then presumably it would escape tax, but this is an additional step.

Gasification is the remaining emerging thermal process. There are about 150 suppliers, each claims their technology is unique [18]. To date there are no fully-commercial sludge-only gasifiers but there are some in Japan and USA that use sludge as part of their feedstock. Several UK water companies have looked at the technology but most have postponed plans to proceed; Anglian Water ordered a commercial plant late in 2000. Gasification does not share the stigma of incineration amongst the public or politicians.

Use on land as a nutrient-rich soil improver is considered by the European Commission and national governments (including the UK) to be the Best Practicable Environmental Option

(BPEO) in most circumstances. The largest market opportunity is agriculture, followed by land reclamation, amenity horticulture and then gardeners. This is a sales and distribution exercise, where customers with real choice have to be persuaded that they want the product. This is in contrast to most of the customer interaction of water undertakers where they are dealing with captive consumers. There are too few that have really accepted in their souls that they need to understand the features and benefits of biosolids and how they can be fitted to customers' needs.

Farming has been changing fast. UK farming incomes are reported to have decreased by 90% in the period 1995 to 2000 through a combination of falling world prices and support, a strong £ and weak €. In response farming operations have effectively consolidated through acquisition and even more often through contract farming arrangements. The retailers have also consolidated and increased their buying power. The wholesale markets have declining influence on prices in UK and the large retailers and processors buy directly from farmers. In an attempt to avoid further food scares these retailers and processors demand that the produce they buy should be grown and reared according to their protocols. That is why the BRC agreement is such a milestone. If farmers did not have that assurance that the saleability of their produce would not be jeopardised by having land treated with biosolids, they would have refused biosolids, even though they knew from experience that it improved profits. Landowners are concerned that there may be something in biosolids that might damage the value of their assets and have asked "If you are so sure that biosolids are safe you won't mind indemnifying me will you?". Water companies in UK have so far refused to give strict liability indemnity, which has triggered the response "If they think the risk is too great for them to give me indemnity, why should I take the risk?". In Germany there was a voluntary levy of DM20/tDS that accumulated in a fund to indemnify landowners and farmers, on 1st January 1999 the federal government took over the fund and the levy is now compulsory. Biosolids generators in France have asked their government to operate a similar scheme but this was declined saying it was a job for insurance. Strict liability latent-defect insurance has been enabled in UK to those who operate their biosolids processes according to good practice standards based on the principles of HACCP.

Undoubtedly biosolids are good for farmers. They substitute for mineral fertilisers and correct trace element deficiencies. They improve soil structure and can reduce the susceptibility of crops to disease infection. They bring life to soils that have been in continuous arable cultivation for many years. However competition is going to increase. There are going to be greater controls on the use of manure which, will mean that they will be spread at lower application rates over larger areas of land. Biodegradable waste is going to be treated (in order to implement the Landfill Directive) with the intention of using the product as soil improver. The amount of biodegradable municipal waste (BMW) going to landfill has to decrease to 75% by 2010, 50% by 2013 and 35% by 2020 all compared with the 1995 quantity. The quantity produced is reported to be increasing at 6% per year. By 2010 there might be 1 million tonnes of composted BMW on the market. In order to maintain market share in this increasingly competitive market biosolids recyclers are going to have to be better than the competition. They have the advantage of being first to market, but their product carries a stigma and like all established manufacturers when competition emerges they are at risk of complacency. Now is the time to increase the integration of biosolids into farming practice, to increase the awareness of biosolids features, benefits and value and to publicise the good news about biosolids.

Land restoration is a very different market from farming. Jobs can have a long lead time, there may be several decision makers, and when work starts large quantities of biosolids may be needed during a very restricted time window. Once again those trying to sell the biosolids need to understand how they can satisfy customers' needs, and they need to make life easy for their customers [19].

Some argue that high value markets such as gardening and amenity land are in the "too hard" category. That although they are high value they are low volume. A counter argument to this is that they give members of the general public opportunity to experience products based on biosolids. If perception is reality, and negative perception is a threat, which many believe, then this is the market segment that gives the greatest opportunity to manipulate perception. Again it is very different from farming or land restoration. The amateur garden market is the fast moving consumer goods market where you are selling to a retailer, not to the final user. It therefore becomes necessary to give the retailer a reason to start to stock this new product, in addition to developing a product that meets the competition on price, performance and consistency [20]. The venture can be profitable, from the point of production (pre-packing and distribution) when distribution has been built to a sufficient level. The opportunity value of protecting the bulk recycling markets from negative ill-informed perception is immeasurably greater.

APPROPRIATE SOLUTIONS

The above discussion of treatment technologies and options for use and disposal should be considered in relation to the local situation for which they are intended. Experience in Cairo is a dramatic (but regrettably not unusual) example of people who sold their 'conventional' technology and did not consider the local situation. Cairo is growing rapidly. Gabel El Asfa will be the largest wastewater treatment works in the world. It is built on the conventional European model with primary settlement, activated sludge, 60 concrete MAD reactors and 30 belt presses. The annual cost of polyelectrolyte will be more than US$1 million in hard currency. The sewage arrives at the works black and part-digested because of the length of the sewers and the high temperature. Part of the specification for the biosolids strategy was to include consideration of how to stop people stealing the biosolids – because they are so valuable to the farmers. The city and irrigated land are to one side of the works, the desert starts on the other side. Gabel El Asfa was designed and constructed without considering the local farming and assuming that there could be a fully monitored biosolids recycling operation, but when you look at the farming it is in small plots and mostly by hand. Monitoring and mechanical application would be impossible. The parasite burden in the raw sludge is enormous, reflecting the health of the human population. Fortunately the content of potentially polluting chemicals in the sewage is low. Field trials showed that crops were immensely responsive to biosolids.

Therefore in order to fit the farming scale and practices biosolids must be prepared so that they can be sold for unrestricted use. It happens that there is air-drying of untreated liquid sludge at a satellite facility out in the desert. Drying conditions are severe with high temperatures and negligible humidity. Microbiological examination showed complete absence of viable helminth ova in the dried product – which was also low odour. By harnessing the local situation and designing a managed system for solar drying with quality assurance procedures, storage of the dried biosolids and a positive release scheme it would have been possible to make inherently safe biosolids fit for purpose. This would have eliminated the capital cost of the digesters and dewatering halls and also the operating costs, which at the end of the day make conventionally treated biosolids that are not fit for the local situation.

COMMUNICATION

If people don't understand the risks, benefits and sustainability arguments for using biosolids and organic residuals of suitable quality, then it is largely our fault as objective professionals for not communicating adequately. The annual cost of using biosolids in agriculture in the EU is about €400 million. What would be a reasonable communication budget for a €400 million turnover business? The answer is - a lot more than we are spending at present.

Effective communication of how biosolids treated land should be used is also an important part of the biosolids recycling process. Although biosolids producers don't farm the land, they have a responsibility to communicate acceptable cropping and grazing to those that do. This extends to checking post-application, counselling farmers that have not followed the rules, and ultimately not supplying those that persistently refuse to comply.

CONCLUSIONS

Biosolids treatment, use and disposal are changing continuously. Implementation of the Urban Wastewater Treatment Directive has increased the quantity. The nature has changed at some works where nitrogen or phosphate limits have been applied to the consents for effluent discharge.   For sustainability and cost effectiveness it is important that wastewater management, including the use and disposal of biosolids, is viewed holistically.

The opportunity to dispose biosolids in landfills, even if they were operated as biogas reactors, has been curtailed in the EU, because leakage of methane from landfills was regarded as unavoidable and a significant contribution to global warming. Climate change levy, etc. are going to figure increasingly in strategic considerations. Technologies for recovering energy from biosolids will continue to develop, but from the point of view of sustainability phosphorus should also be recovered, the warning signs are there that this could become a legal obligation.

Use of biosolids on land will continue to be a major route. Stakeholder concerns have shaken biosolids producers out of their old practices, it may not have been what they wanted, but the result is probably what they needed. Use of biosolids on land is now more sustainable but there is no time for complacency because competition is going to increase rapidly.

REFERENCES

1.   ASM (2000) *Copper pipes kill E. coli in drinking water.* American Society for Microbiology May 22, 2000

2.   HALL, J. E. (2000) *Sludge management in developing countries.* Proceedings of the 5th European Biosolids and Organic Residuals Conference. CIWEM / Aqua-Enviro, 2000.

3.   Codex (1997) *Basic Texts On Food Hygiene* Codex Alimentarius, June 1997

4.   ADAS (1999) *The safe sludge matrix – guidelines for the application of sewage sludge to agricultural land.* BRC, Water UK, ADAS

5.   Environment Agency UK (1999). *UK Sewage Sludge Survey.* R&D Technical Report P165. EA R&D Dissemination Centre, WRc, Swindon, UK.

6.   BROWN, S. AND SALE, R. (2000) *Operating the high rate digester.* Proceedings of the 5th European Biosolids and Organic Residuals Conference. CIWEM / Aqua-Enviro, 2000.

7.   HORAN, N. LOWE, P. GODFREE, AND A. CLARK, P. (2000) *The survival of pathogens in sewage sludge; a comparison of the behaviour of indigenous E. coli and verotoxigenic and non-toxigenic E. coli.* Proceedings of the 5th European Biosolids and Organic Residuals Conference. CIWEM / Aqua-Enviro, 2000.

8.   DAVIS, W. AND MESSERLI, P. (2000) *Pre-pasteurisation and operating cost savings using thermophilic aerobic digestion retrofit to conventional esophilic anaerobic digestion.* Proceedings of the 5th European Biosolids and Organic Residuals Conference. CIWEM / Aqua-Enviro, 2000.

9.   BRENTON, M.; THOMASON, M. (2000) *Thermal hydrolysis of sludge – operating experiences and cost of ownership.* Proceedings of the 5th European Biosolids and Organic Residuals Conference. CIWEM / Aqua-Enviro, 2000.

10.   EVANS, T.D. (2000) *Developments in regulation, controls and laibilities for the use of biosolids and other organic residuals on land.* Proceedings of the 5th European Biosolids and Organic Residuals Conference. CIWEM / Aqua-Enviro, 2000.

11.   CLARK, P. (2000) *Update on trials with a novel full-scale ultrasonic sludge processor for enhanced anaerobic digestion.* Proceedings of the 5th European Biosolids and Organic Residuals Conference. CIWEM / Aqua-Enviro, 2000.

12.   CHRISTY, P. (2000) *Alkaline stabilisation of biosolids, sludge lime mixing experiences within the United States.* Proceedings of the 5th European Biosolids and Organic Residuals Conference. CIWEM / Aqua-Enviro, 2000.

13.   CLARK, P. AND PEEBLES, J. (1999) *Advances in the development of an automated liquid* sludge *vermistabilisation syste for the treastment of sewage sludges.* Proceedings of the 4th European Biosolids and Organic Residuals Conference. CIWEM / Aqua-Enviro, 1999.

14.   LOTZOF, M. AND TRAFFORD, C. (2000) *Advances in vermiculture a new technique for biosolids management.* Proceedings of the 5th European Biosolids and Organic Residuals Conference. CIWEM / Aqua-Enviro, 2000.

15.   HENRIKSSON, H. AND SANDS, S. (2000) *Sludge drying using reed bed systems.* Sewage Sludge Treatment & Use. IQPC 6-7 July, 2000, Birmingham.

16.   EVANS, T.D. (2000) *Biosolids and residuals – innovations.* Water & Environmer Manager 5(5) 18-19

17.   BRIDLE, T. (2000) *Assessment of the ENERSLUDGE process for the management of biosolids in the European Community.* Proceedings of the 5th European Biosolids and Organic Residuals Conference. CIWEM / Aqua-Enviro, 2000.

18.   SCHWAGER, J. AND HEERMAN, C. (2000) *Gasification – a better management option for biosolids?* CIWEM / Aqua-Enviro, 2000.

19.   EVANS, T.D. (1998) *The roles of standards and biosolids in land reclamation.* in "Land reclamation: achieving sustainable benefits" Fox, Moore, McIntosh (eds) Balkema, Rotterdam

20.   EVANS, T. AND RAINBOW, A. (1998). *Wastewater biosolids to garden centre products via composting.* Acta Horticulturae no 469, 157-168.

PART ONE:

GENERATION, HANDLING AND TREATMENT OF SEWAGE SLUDGE

SEWAGE SLUDGE DISPOSAL: A LOGISTICAL ANALYSIS

E Cartmell   **C Diaper**

S J Judd   **P Kilgallon**

J Oakey

Cranfield University

United Kingdom

ABSTRACT. The key disposal options in the UK currently followed for sewage sludge comprise application to agricultural land (48%), incineration (17%) and landfill (11%). Continuing pressure from environmental legislation and consumer groups is limiting the long-term sustainable option to destruction and containment or reuse. However, for this the most established technology (incineration) incurs a high cost and invokes widespread public aversion. Forthcoming legislation is to compel the power uitilities to provide 10% of their generated power from renewable sources by 2010 (Climate Change Policy, DETR, 2000). This adds another dimension to the sludge destruction debate, since dewatered sludge has a normal calorific value (NCV) of between 3.5 and 6 MJ kg^{-1} (Wiess *et al*, 1998) and can therefore be regarded as a fuel for any thermochemical process (incineration, pyrolysis, gasification, etc). On the other hand, it is produced in relatively small quantities from geographically disparate sources and contains contaminants that can be onerous to some of these thermochemical processes.

The paper presents an outline logistical parametric analysis of biosolids disposal options pertaining to their treatment (biological and physicochemical), handling and transport, and ultimate thermolytic destruction. Impacts of such key parameters as sludge composition, biological and thermochemical treatment, plant type and operation, tankering costs and logistics, and sustainability are considered in turn and scenarios under which thermolytic treatment for power generation/heating may be viable identified.

Keywords: Logistical analysis, Sludge characteristics, Sludge CV, Thermal technology, Policy

Dr Cartmell, is a Lecturer in Water Sciences, whose areas of expertise include bioremediation and microbial modelling, as well as sludge management.

Dr Diaper, is a Research Officer in Water Sciences, investigating water reuse and recycling options in the urban environment and treatment options in the textile industry.

Dr Judd, is a Reader in Water Sciences who has conducted research into a wide range of chemical and, principally, membrane processes as applied to water and wastewater treatment.

Dr Paul Kilgallon, is a Research Officer in the Power Generation Technology Centre.

Mr John Oakey, is manager of Cranfield University's Power Generation Technology Centre, and has many years experience in combustion technology development acquired at former British Coal research centre.

INTRODUCTION

A logistical analysis implies the assessment of ensuring that the right goods are conveyed safely to the correct place at the right time at the lowest possible cost. For sludge treatment this appears to be an onerous exercise as there are many factors influencing the selection of the best sludge management and disposal route (Figure 1).

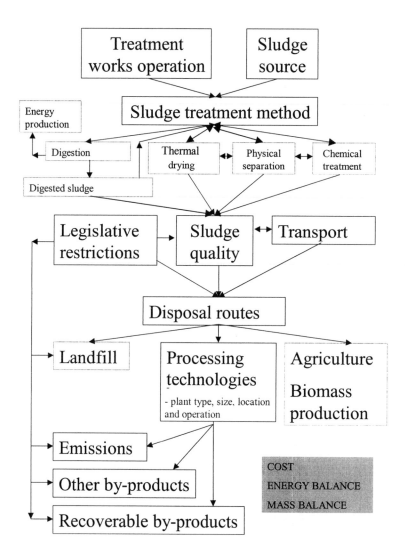

Figure 1 Factors affecting disposal/treatment routes for sewage sludge

RAW SLUDGE PROPERTIES AND WWTP OPERATION

Properties of raw sludge will vary according not only to location but also with sludge source within the specific wastewater treatment train. Sludge from primary settlement will have different characteristics from that produced during an activated sludge process. Both physical and chemical parameters will vary as will the calorific value of the sludge (Table 1). In most treatment plants the sludge collected from the different process stages will be combined prior to further treatment, such that the characteristics specific to the unit operation from which the sludge is generated will be lost. It is also the case that, since sludge is generally viewed as a waste material, treatment processes are operated so as to minimise sludge production, despite its prospective end use as a fuel.

Table 1 Sludge characteristics from different WwTP processes [1]

PARAMETER	UNTREATED PRIMARY SLUDGE	DIGESTED PRIMARY SLUDGE	ACTIVATED SLUDGE
Basic description	Settled solids. Grey colour, slimy with offensive odour	Biological solids. Dark brown colour, inoffensive odour	Biological solids. Brownish, flocculant appearance, 'earthy' odour
Total dry solids (TS) %	2.0 – 8.0	6.0 – 12.0	0.83 – 1.16
Nitrogen % of TS	1.5 – 4.0	1.6 – 6.0	2.4 – 5.0
Phosphorous % of TS	0.8 – 2.8	1.5 – 4.0	2.8 – 11.0
Potash % of TS	0 – 1	2.8 – 11.0	0.5 – 0.7
Silica % of TS	15.0 – 20.0	10.0 – 20.0	-
Energy content MJ/kg	23 - 29	9 - 14	19 - 23

However, viewing sludge as a marketable product would imply that sludge production should be optimised, rather than specifically minimised, according to the whole process cycle. The production rate will thus depend upon the processing operation utilised, and sludge properties could be manipulated to provide sludge with maximum calorific value.

SLUDGE TREATMENT METHOD

There are many methods for treating sewage sludge to reduce the overall volume, but nearly all are devoted either to reducing the carbon content or the water content (or possibly both). Processes ostensibly reducing carbon content proceed either through biological (aerobic or anaerobic digestion), or (thermo)chemical (e.g. wet air oxidation) treatment. Processes devoted to removing water (thickening, dewatering or drying) range from simple sedimentation, which can increase the solids content to around 5% by volume, to thermal drying, which increases the solids content to up to 95%. Conventionally, chemcial conditioning of the sludge – pre-dosing with chemical precipitants, coagulants and flocculants, is carried out to increase its dewaterability. Thus, a complete treatment train, designed according to the source and the end disposal route, may contain a number of unit operations which then have a profound effect on the quality of the sludge product.

Anaerobic digestion may reduce the calorific value of the sludge by up to 40%. The total volume of the sludge is also reduced and the dewaterability increased. Methane (65%) and carbon dioxide (35%) are produced and the methane can be used as an energy source. The heating value of the digester gas is approximately 22,400 kJ/m^3 and this can be used to fire boilers, diesel engines and gas turbines and produce electricity and/or heat. Digester gas will, however, contain contaminants such as hydrogen sulphide, particulates and water vapour and so requires some cleaning prior to use as an energy source. Aerobic digestion provides similar volatile solids reduction compared to anaerobic digestion but there are additional operating costs due to aeration and no useful combustible by-product, such as methane, generated. However, the end product is odourless and has an improved fertiliser value compared to anaerobically digested sludge.

Chemical treatment is used either to create an environment in the sludge that is not conducive to the survival of micro-organisms, although heat treatment is more usually employed for this specific goal, or to improve the dewatering characteristics of the sludge – i.e. to condition it. The process can increase the final product solids content by more than an order of magnitude in some cases, and chemicals used include ferric chloride, alum, organic polymers and lime. Organic polymers have been shown to promote the pyrolysis rate in dried sludge solids [2] but dosing with inorganic chemical coagulants or precipitants is likely to reduce the calorific value of the sludge.

Physical treatment, employed downstream of a conditioning operation, increases the solids concentration of the sludge. Thickening methods are used to produce a sludge of up to 10% solids whilst dewatering processes, most typically belt or filter pressing, following conditioning can produce a solids content of up to 35%. The nature of the processes implies that the total organic carbon content is unchanged, such that the calorific value of the sludge is increased by processing in accordance with the amount of water removed.

Heat treatment is most commonly used as a pasteurisation process but can also be used for conditioning. However, the high capital costs mean this method is most applicable to otherwise difficult-to-treat sludges on a large scale. The combustibility of the treated sludge is high at approximately 28–30 MJ/kg and the final solids content range from 30–50%. Thermal drying is a minimisation process that provides a product suitable for various reuse options, including agricultural recycling or as a fuel. Processing of sludge by thermal drying increases the dry solids content to around 95%. The calorific value of thermally dried products, based on bomb calorimetry, can be in the region 20 MJ kg^{-1}. However, this can be reduced (to 15 MJ kg^{-1}) if the source sludge material is digested and organic matter is lost in the digestion process. One of the noted problems in drying sewage sludge, however, is the formation of a very "sticky" and difficult-to-handle matrix at around 50-60% solids concentration [3]. Lower cost processes such as air drying using thin drying beds require a large land area but can produce solids concentrations up to 70%.

A further processing stage to consider is that of disinfection as requirements for the inactivation of pathogens in sludge for application to land are becoming more stringent. This can be achieved by pasteurisation, some stabilisation processes, long-term storage or composting. Composting alone can be utilised as a treatment option that reduces sludge volume and produces a stable, possibly marketable end product.

Thermal reduction is normally regarded as an final disposal route for the sludge although, like all other disposal options, this route results in a number of end products requiring further management. Thermal reduction processes are discussed in more detail subsequently.

FINAL SLUDGE PROPERTIES AND APPLICATION REQUIREMENTS

The final properties of treated sludge vary enormously and, when considering thermolytic destruction methods as a final process stage, the sludge solids content and heating value (Table 2) are of key importance [3].

Table 2 Solids content and heating value of selected processed sludge types*

TYPE OF SLUDGE	APPROXIMATE SOLIDS CONTENT, %	RANGE OF HEATING VALUE, MJ/kg
Raw sludge (all process stages)	2 - 8	19 - 29
Anaerobically digested primary sludge	5 - 10	9 – 14
Anaerobically digested primary + activated sludge	2.5 – 7.0	
- gas produced from anaerobic digestion	-	22 MJ/m^3
Aerobically digested primary sludge	2.5 - 7.0	
Aerobically digested activated + primary sludge	1.5 – 4.0	
Chemically precipitated primary sludge	10 – 35	14 – 19
Mechanically dewatered sludge	10-50	Same as previous process stage
Heat conditioned combined sludge	30-50	28 – 30
Thermal dried undigested sludge	up to 95	20
Thermal dried digested sludge	up to 95	15

Different disposal options will demand specific sludge properties (Table 3) and treatment processes can be selected to provide sludge with such required properties. Currently around 48% of the 949,000 tonnes of sewage sludge [4] produced in the UK is applied to agricultural land, 17% is incinerated mainly in single feed form and 11% is sent to landfill. For all disposal options there is a requirement for low heavy metal concentration. However, for land application and thermal technologies there is the possibility of heavy metal recovery.

In addition to the characteristics of the sludge required for different disposal routes the overall balance of energy, carbon and pollutants in the process should be considered. For example, for low solids concentration applications less energy is required for processing the sludge but transportation costs will be higher if the location of the application site is distant from the production site. Some techniques will produce useful by-products, in some cases fuels with a substantial calorific value. However, contamination of by-product streams by unwanted pollutants may increase treatment costs or limit the application as a useful resource. The point source of such pollutants should therefore be considered when assessing disposal options. Changes in wastewater treatment works (WwTW) operation and sludge processing or monitoring of feed streams to the WwTW should be considered as viable alternatives to post treatment options. For example mechanically dewatered sludge has a higher nitrogen content than pre-dried sludge and thus NO_x and N_2O emissions may be reduced during combustion by using the latter.

Table 3 Sludge requirements for different final disposal options

APPLICATION	SLUDGE REQUIREMENT
Land application (agriculture, forests)	2 – 99% dry solids Nitrogen, phosphorous and potassium (Ideal ratio 1:2:2) Pathogen reduction Trace metals and organic concentrations Low heavy metals Low organic micropollutants
Landfill	Pathogen reduction Volatile solids Low heavy metals
Thermal Technologies Mono combustion	
Fluidised bed	40 – 65% dry solids, supplementary fuel required at low solids
Multiple hearth	10 – 50% Supplementary fuel often required
Co-combustion	
In coal fired plants	With bituminous coal 90% dry solids With brown coal 50-60% dry solids
In municipal solid waste plants	55-65% dry solids
Wet oxidation	5% dry solids (homogenised). Pure oxygen requirement
Pyrolysis	20% minimum. Gas, oil and char produced
Gasification	90%. Hydrogen, carbon monoxide, carbon dioxide and methane plus other gas mix produced

NB All applications demand low heavy metals and organic micropollutants emissions; some incorporate gas cleaning as integral part of process.

TRANSPORTATION COSTS AND LOGISTICS

Following processing, sludge is transported for final disposal either directly or through a centralised facility. The cost of transportation is often a large proportion of processing costs and the location of the WwTW in respect to the final disposal facility should be considered when selecting the optimum disposal route. The rheological properties of the sludge are also important in selecting the best equipment to be used for transport.

Sludge can be transported by pipeline, barge, rail or truck, and despite contributing the highest environmental pollution load, the latter option is often used due to the flexibility of operation. For pumping sludge over long distances solids concentration must be below 6-10%; it is otherwise necessary to use higher specification pumping operations. For the other modes of transport there are no limitations on sludge solids concentrations.

LEGISLATIVE RESTRICTIONS AND POLICY DRIVERS

There are many legislative restrictions in the UK pertinent to the final disposal of treated sludge. When considering application to land the Agriculture Directive 86/278/EEC [5] on the protection of soil when sewage sludge is used in agriculture defines quality standards for sewage sludge. The directive includes limiting values for potentially toxic elements in the soil to which sludge is applied, and maximum annual quantities of contaminants which may be applied to the soil. The UK has implemented this directive by the Sludge (Use in Agriculture) Regulations 1989 (SI 1989), as amended 1990. These regulations are supported by a Code of Practice for Agricultural Use of Sewage Sludge (DoE 1996) and Ministry of Agriculture, Food and Fishery (MAFF) Protection of Soil (1999) and Water (1998) codes. Currently in consultation with the British Retail Consortium (BRC) a 'Safe Sludge Matrix' has now been introduced with a commitment to phase out the application of untreated sludges by 2001. The presence of heavy metals in sewage sludge i.e. cadmium, copper, nickel, lead, zinc, mercury and chromium will limit the application frequency to land.

The landfill disposal route for sludge is not restricted under the Landfill Directive (Landfill Directive 1999/31/EC) but there are requirements for the characteristics of the material to be land-filled. The Directive states that waste must be treated so to reduce its volume and its hazardous nature, or else facilitate its handling or enhance its recovery. There are also restrictions on fly ashes containing a high content of lime, since this can be corrosive. This may disallow the disposal of incinerated chemically-conditioned sludges to landfill. In addition to the restrictions on sludge characteristics, landfill is considered to be the least sustainable sludge disposal option. Also this option is likely to become more costly as landfill tax increases.

Policy is also providing drivers for selection of sludge disposal options. The Climate Change Policy [6] compels power utilities to provide 10% of generated power from renewable resources by 2010 (current figure is around 3%). In addition capital grants for energy crops are also to be announced and this may provide an alternative disposal route for sewage sludge. There is also a target of 10000 MWe of combined heat and power sources by the year 2010, part of the Government Climate Change Programme. A final general influence on the selection of sludge disposal route is the increase in public and political awareness of environmental and sustainability issues.

THERMAL TECHNOLOGY OPTIONS

For optimisation of sludge combustion processes the key characteristics of the sludge are the solids content, calorific value, water content, handleability, carbon content, ash content etc. The emission of polluting gases and the handling of solid by-products are also key factors in determining the feasibility. In comparison to alternative biofuels the combustion of sewage sludge may produce higher N_2O, NO_x and SO_2 emissions [7] and the ash produced may contain a higher concentration of heavy metals. Sub-micron particle size metal emissions from sludge incineration plants are reported to pose the greatest threat and account for almost all the potential cancer risks [8]. The high ash content of sludge could possibly intensify this problem, leading to high particulate concentrations in the flue gas which would then demand more rigorous gas cleaning.

The limits on gaseous emissions for different thermal processes also needs to be considered in the assessment of suitable disposal options as this will have a direct impact on the size and operating costs of the flue gas treatment plant. For example the emission of some gaseous species produced from some gasification processes can be an order of magnitude less than mono- and co-combustion processes [3].

SCENARIOS

In order to demonstrate the logistical analysis of biosolids disposal, three thermal technology scenarios are considered and the upstream process requirements are investigated. In addition, economic and environmental advantages and disadvantages and legislative restrictions are discussed for each scenario. (It is hoped that full case study information will be available for presentation at the conference in March)

Scenario 1. Co-firing sludge with coal.

For co-firing of sludge with coal the minimum dry solids requirement for the sludge is 50%. However, as co-firing is likely to be carried out at existing coal burning sites, the cost of transport may advocate drying of sludge to a higher % dry solids in order to reduce haulage costs. Chemical conditioning has to be restricted to organic polymer dosing, since inorganic coagulants (ferric and alum) reduce the calorific value of the sludge and increase ash production. Additionally, mechanically dewatered sludge should be avoided for some processes in order to help reduce possible NO_x and N_2O emissions. Alternative methods of transport should also be investigated and the feasibility of sludge drying facilities at the coal burning site.

The capacity of coal-fired furnaces in the UK is high and so this scenario will require large quantities of sludge (dependant on mix) in order to be feasible. As the siting of the producing plant in relation to the power plant is important in terms of transport costs this scenario is likely to be feasible in large cities located near coal burning sites.

The electrical generation efficiency of old large-scale conventional PF coal burning plant is low at around 37% but modern designs and processes are 45% efficient and this figure is rising. In terms of the carbon balance this is not the most economic utilisation of sludge as a biofuel. However, there will be minimal capital cost for the combustor and for flue gas cleaning equipment as processes will already be in place, although there is stricter legislation for co-firing than mono-combustion processes.

Scenario 2. Biofuel generation

For land application legislation requires stabilisation of the sludge but dewatering is optional; avoiding dewatering means that the liquid sludge can be applied directly whereas dewatered sludge will reduce the transport costs. Information on sludge for biofuel production is limited and at present no data on carbon conversion is available. The process is ostensibly low-tech and energy requirements are minimal. If non-dewatered sludge is used the capital and energy costs of chemical or physical dewatering equipment are eliminated. The nutrient content of the sludge will be important and nutrient addition may be required dependent on the crop and soil type. An advantage of this scenario is that the nitrogen content of the biofuel will be less than that of the sludge and so NO_x and N_2O emissions from combustion processes will be reduced by the sewage biosolids → biofuel conversion.

There are many options for the final burning of the biofuel produced; mono-combustion, co-combustion with municipal waste or coal, gasification or pyrolysis. The selection of the most apppropriate technology will depend on the type of biofuel produced. Straw has been found to reduce the performance of coal co-combustion power generation systems (which were designed for coal) and increase the capital costs [9]. As biofuels such as wood and straw are considered as CO_2-neutral they effectively give a reduction in CO_2 emissions. Thus for a range of technologies CO_2 emissions and NO_x are reduced in comparison to mono-combustion of coal. Similar trials with co-combustion with wood have also demonstrated reduced efficiency and reduced CO_2 emissions but the increase in capital costs was found to be minimal due to easier preparation and feeding in comparison to straw.

Scenario 3. Sludge gasification

The gasification of sludge requires a high solids content sludge of 90% or more. However, as the process produces heat, this can be used to thermally dry the sludge on site. A combination of gasification and anaerobic digestion processes may allow optimisation of the gas cleaning processes. Feed sludge for gasification should not be chemically dewatered using inorganic conditioners since, as already stated, these chemicals contaminate the ash and reduce the calorific value of the sludge.

Gasification can be used for smaller scale applications and the emissions may be an order of magnitude less than traditional mono- and co-combustion processes. Gasification also provides a more efficient energy generation option, and may provide heat and power to the locality. Additional transport costs for this mode of operation will be low if the gasifier is sited at a large WwTW with existing anaerobic digestion facilities. Sludge from smaller works could still be transported to this centralised facility.

CONCLUSIONS

With current policy and legislative drivers the use of sewage sludge as a biofuel appears to be the best disposal option. The combustion disposal route selected will depend on many factors and will be site specific. However, using a logistical analysis the best available technology option can be assessed.

REFERENCES

1.   METCALF AND EDDY (1991) Wastewater engineering treatment, disposal, and reuse. 3rd edition New York: McGraw Hill, 1990

2.   CHU C.P., LEE D.J. AND CHANG C.Y. (2001) Thermal pyrolysis of polymer flocculated waste activated sludge. *Wat. Res* 35(1) 49-56

3.   WERTHER J. AND OGADA T (1999). Sewage sludge combustion. *Prog. En. Comb. Sci.* 25 55-116

4.   Waterfacts (1998) OFWAT 1998-1999 Report on Levels of service for the water industry in England and Wales

5.   The Sewage Sludge Directive, Council Directive 86/278/EEC on the protection of the environment and in particular of the soil, when sewage sludge is used in agriculture

6.   Climate Change Policy, Department of Environment Transport and the Regions (2000)

7.   SPLEITHOFF H., SCHEURER W. AND HEIN K.R.G. (2000). Effect of co-combustion of sewage sludge and biomass on emissions and heavy metals behaviour. Trans. IChemE 78(B) 33-39

8.   LEE K.J. AND CHUN S.A. (1993). Two stage swirl flow fluidised bed incineration of sewage sludge. In: Rubow L.N. (ed). Proceedings of the 12th International Conference on Fluidised Bed Combustion, San Diego, CA 1181-1188

9.   MCILVEEN-WRIGHT D.R., MCMULLAN J.T. AND WILLIAMS B.C. (2000) Contribution of the Energy Research Centre of Ulster to; Joule Thermie Programme: Operational Problems, Trace Emissions And By-Product Management

HEAVY METALS REMOVAL FROM SEWAGE SLUDGE COMPOST USING NATURAL ZEOLITE – A FUNCTION OF TEMPERATURE AND CONTACT TIME

A Zorpas

National Technical University of Athens

Greece

ABSTRACT. The composting of sewage sludge is well recognized. However, the presence of toxic heavy metal such as, Cd, Cu, Cr, Ni, Pb and Zn give a serious disadvantage to the final product, (compost). The application of natural bulking agent such as zeolite, clinoptilolite, has the ability with ion exchange to uptake (and remove by sieving the zeolite from the compost) those metals.. 25% w/w of natural clinoptilolite has the ability to uptake after from 150 days of maturity 100% of Cd, 36 % of Cu, 12 % of Cr, 40% of Fe, Pb and Zn, 50% of Ni. Also, the temperature and the contact time of the mineral during the composting process are determinative. Three experiments were carried out in different conditions in order to indicate how the temperature and the contact time of the clinoptilolite affect the uptake of the heavy metals. 1,2,3,4,5,6,7,10,20 and 30 days of contact time and the temperature was set at 20, 40, and 60 $^{\circ}$C. The selectivity series for the removal of heavy metals differ from temperature to temperature and from day to day. The best result was carried out in 30 days and for 60 $^{\circ}$C. In those conditions 70% of Cd, 60% of Cr, 27% of Cu, 36% of Fe and 40% of Ni, Pb and Zn were taken up from clinoptilolite.

Key Words: Composting, Metal Uptake, Natural Zeolite, Clinoptilolite.

Dr. Antonis A. Zorpas, is a Chemical Engineer - Research / Scientific Cooperator in the National Technical University in Athens (Chemical Engineering Department). His research interest includes the use of zeolite in co-composting materials (sewage sludge, solid wooden residue, waste paper, saw dust, organic fraction of municipal waste etc) and in the design - application of new methods for the treatment of industrial wastes such as olive oil wastewater=s, textiles, pharmacy etc.

INTRODUCTION

The mineralization of biogenic substances is a part of the natural recycling processes, which occurs at any place where organic material is synthesized by plants and degraded by animals and microflora. Environmental problems associated with sewage sludge disposal have prompted legislative actions. At the same time, the upgrading and expansion of wastewater treatment plants have greatly increased the volume of sludge generated.

In the greater region of Athens, with almost 4,500,000 inhabitants, the main wastewater treatment plant operating is at the rock-island of Psittalia. At Psittalia, approximately 750,000 m^3/day consisting mainly of municipal wastewater and some industrial wastes, are subjected to primary treatment, producing approximately 250 t/day of dewatered anaerobically stabilized primary sewage sludge (DASPSS) [1]. Until now, landfilling was the main disposal route for sewage sludge in Athens, generating potential environmental hazards which included the production of odour, methane gas, and leachates [2].

Composting is under consideration in many municipalities throughout the world because it has several advantages over current disposal strategies. Firstly, composting can reduce the waste volume by 40-50% and thus require less landfill space for disposal [3]. Secondly, pathogens can be killed by the heat generated during the thermophilic phase [3, 4, 5]. Finally, composting has been well established and currently it is used to provide a final product which can act as a soil conditioner or fertilizer. Compost contains major plant nutrients such as N, P and K, micro nutrients such as Cu, Fe and Zn and humic substances which improve the physical properties of soils such as aeration and saturation capacity [3,6]. The heavy metal content of wastewater treatment sludge limits the possibilities for using and even disposing this waste. Application to soils for increasing their organic matter is restricted by metal content because it may indirectly be incorporated into the food chain or transported to aquifers. Natural zeolite, clinoptilolite, has the ability to uptake heavy metals. Zeolites have become known world-wide in the last decade because of their cation exchange and molecular sieving properties. Natural zeolites are used in soil benefication, water treatment and wastewater treatment [7,8,9].

The aim of this work is to examine the function of temperature and contact time when natural zeolite is used in the composting process in order to uptake the toxic heavy metals.

MATERIALS AND METHODS

The dewatered anaerobically stabilized primary sewage sludge (DASPSS) samples were collected from the Psittalia wastewater treatment plant. The samples were air dried at 25 - 35 °C, homogenized and stored.

The samples were dried at 105 °C and used to determine the heavy metals content (Cd, Cr, Cu, Fe, Ni, Zn and Pb). For the total metal concentration, a known quantity (1g) of sample was digested with 10 ml of c. HNO_3 according to Zorpas et al. [1]. After the completion of the digestion the samples were vacuum filtered and the filtrate was used for the determination of heavy metal concentration by flame atomic absorption spectroscopy, using a Perkin Elmer 2380 spectrophotometer.

The composting process was carried out in the laboratory with an In-Vessel reactor (1 m³ of active volume) according to the Rutgers Strategy. The thermophilic phase of composting lasted for 15 days. The temperature was approximately 60-65 °C the center of the reactor and the moisture ranged between 40 and 50 %. After the thermophilic period, the organic material was biodegraded and the compost was piled in an enclosed package where it remained for 4 months to mature. Table 1 presents a summary of the compost samples used in this study.

Table 1 Prepared samples for composting

So	-	100 % w/w sewage sludge
S1	5 % w/w clinoptilolite	95 % w/w sewage sludge
S2	10 % w/w clinoptilolite	90 % w/w sewage sludge
S3	20 % w/w clinoptilolite	80 % w/w sewage sludge
S4	25 % w/w clinoptilolite	75 % w/w sewage sludge

In order to observe how the temperature and the contact time of the mineral with the sewage sludge affected the uptake of the heavy metals the following three experiments were carried out. The temperature was set at 20, 40, and 60 °C and for 1,2,3,4,5,6,7,10,20 and 30 days of contact time respectively. Those experiments were carried out using the S4 sample (25% w/w clinoptilolite and 75% w/w sewage sludge).

RESULTS AND DISCUSSIONS

Table 2 presents the metal content in dewatered anaerobically stabilized primary sewage sludge (DASPSS) and in the final compost products. When comparing the metal content of the So, sewage sludge compost with no zeolite and DASPSS sample, it may be observed that the concentration of chromium, nickel, lead and zinc appeared increased while that of copper and iron decreased.

Composting can concentrate or dilute the heavy metals present in sewage sludge. This change in metal concentration depends on the metal loss through leaching and on the overall concentration of metals due to organic matter destruction [10]. As it is observed, in Table 2, natural clinoptilolite has the ability to exchange sodium and potassium.

It is also clearly seen that with the increasing amount of zeolite the concentrations of all heavy metals content in the compost samples decreases while the concentration of sodium and potassium increases. It is seen that in samples S4 containing 25% w/w of Clinoptilolite maximum metal uptaken and specifically 100% of Cd, 36 % of Cu, 12 % of Cr, 40% of Fe, Pb and Zn, 50% of Ni. Tables 3, 4 and 5 present the heavy metals content in deferent temperature and contact time.

As it is observed from Tables 3, 4, 5 the temperature and the contact time affect the amount of heavy metals which are taken up from clinoptilolite.

Table 2   Metals content in DASPSS and cured compost (after from 150 days of maturity).

METALS*	DASPSS	COMPOST - FINAL PRODUCT AFTER 150 DAYS						
		So	S1	S2	S3	S5	EEC Limits	EPA Limits
Cd	0.002	0.002	nd	nd	nd	nd	0.005	0.085
Cr	0.552	0.578	0.552	0.550	0.501	0.488	0.15 - 0.2	3
Cu	0.258	0.205	0.265	0.184	0.172	0.163	0.3 - 0.5	4.3
Fe	5.098	4.118	3.963	3.838	3.191	2.999		
Ni	0.041	0.045	0.040	0.038	0.034	0.019	0.05 - 0.1	0.42
Pb	0.326	0.335	0.199	0.187	0.177	0.157	0.75 - 1	0.84
Zn	1.739	1.801	1.400	1.216	1.083	1.027	1 - 1.5	7.5
K	0.723	0.772	0.772	0.902	1.121	1.215		
Na	0.724	0.732	0.783	0.796	0.901	1.011		

All value in dried matter, nd: not detected.; * : mg/g dry sludge ; significant diferent at $p < 0.05$

Table 3   Heavy metals uptake in %, at 20 °C and in respect
to the total amount of heavy metals in DASPSS

TIME, days	Cd	Cr	Cu	Fe	Ni	Pb	Zn
1	0	0	2.32	0.54	0	0	0
2	0	0	3.10	1.53	0	0	0.46
3	5	0.36	3.87	8.00	2.43	0.30	0.57
4	5	0.36	5.03	9.96	2.43	0.61	2.18
5	15	0.54	10.85	10.945	4.87	0.92	3.10
6	15	0.54	12.79	11.141	4.87	0.92	5.29
7	20	0.54	14.34	12.318	4.87	1.84	5.52
10	25	1.26	15.11	33.50	4.87	2.45	12.93
20	30	3.44	21.7	39.58	14.63	8.58	17.82
30	50	4.34	22.86	41.15	17.07	8.89	17.82
150	100	11.59	36.82	41.17	53.65	31.44	40.94

Table 4 Heavy metals uptake in %, at 40 $^{\circ}$C and in respect to the
total amount of heavy metals in DASPSS

TIME, days	Cd	Cr	Cu	Fe	Ni	Pb	Zn
1	0	0.72	3.48	0.74	0	17.17	2.35
2	5	3.07	3.87	1.72	2.43	18.71	3.39
3	5	5.79	5.03	3.49	2.43	20.24	3.68
4	10	13.04	6.97	3.68	4.87	20.55	5.11
5	15	17.39	12.28	4.27	4.87	20.85	5.34
6	25	27.53	14.34	6.63	4.87	21.77	5.98
7	30	29.71	15.50	8.59	7.31	23.312	6.55
10	30	42.93	21.70	29.18	12.19	24.23	16.10
20	55	43.84	22.48	37.03	24.39	26.99	18.63
30	60	45.10	24.80	38.21	31.70	38.34	18.63
150	100	11.59	36.82	41.17	53.65	31.44	40.94

Table 5 Heavy metals uptake in %, at 60 $^{\circ}$C and in respect to the
total amount of heavy metals in DASPSS

TIME, days	Cd	Cr	Cu	Fe	Ni	Pb	Zn
1	5	37.5	7.75	1.92	2.43	18.71	2.87
2	5	45.10	8.52	2.31	2.43	20.24	3.62
3	10	46.01	8.91	2.51	4.87	20.55	7.53
4	15	53.07	9.96	3.29	7.31	20.85	10.40
5	20	54.89	13.56	6.82	7.31	21.77	14.43
6	30	56.70	15.89	7.61	9.75	23.31	16.56
7	35	60.14	18.99	9.76	14.63	24.22	20.29
10	50	63.22	24.80	24.87	24.39	26.99	40.42
20	70	67.39	25.58	34.28	31.70	28.22	46.23
30	70	67.39	27.13	36.83	43.90	41.71	46.23
150	100	11.59	36.82	41.17	53.65	31.44	40.94

It is obvious that the selectivity series vary from day to day.

- The selectivity series at 20 oC

  in 5 days: Cd > Fe > Cu > Ni > Zn > Pb > Cr
  in 30 days: Cd > Fe > Cu > Zn > Ni > Pb > Cr
  in 150 days: Cd > Ni > Fe > Zn > Cu > Pb > Cr

- The selectivity series at 40 oC

  in 5 days :   Pb > Cr > Cd > Cu > Zn > Ni > Fe
  in 30 days: Cd > Cr > Pb > Fe > Ni > Cu > Zn
  in 150 days: Cd > Ni > Fe > Zn > Cu > Pb > Cr

- The selectivity series at 60 oC

  in 5 days :   Cr > Pb > Cd > Zn > Cu > Ni > Fe
  in 30 days: Cd > Cr > Zn > Ni > Pb > Fe > Cu
  in 150 days: Cd > Ni > Fe > Zn > Cu > Pb > Cr

The phenomenon of the deferent=s selectivity series may be the result of the follow:

- The clinoptilolite has the ability to uptake and extract selectively the heavy metals
- In constant temperature and for specific time the clinoptilolite has the ability to uptake certain metal in higher amount than in changeable conditions.
- The changeable conditions which affect the system are:
  - → the temperature,
  - → the pH,
  - → the concentration of ammonia which are absorb and disabsorp
  - → maybe the changes in microorganism
  - → acetic and stainless conditions due to the formation of the acetic acid (disruption of the organic matter from the *Bacilus Vacterium,,*) from the oxidation of lignin, [13] and ammonia (in the first step of the composting process).

CONCLUSIONS

The application of natural zeolite in the composting process seems to take up a significant ($p < 0.05$) amount of heavy metals. 25% w/w of natural clinoptilolite has the ability to uptake after from 150 days of maturity 100% of Cd, 36 % of Cu, 12 % of Cr, 40% of Fe, Pb and Zn, 50% of Ni..

Also, the temperature and the contact time seems to affect the ability of natural zeolite to uptake the heavy metals. As it is observed, in higher temperature the amount of Cr and Pb seems to be charged more than the other metals. Specifically, Cr seems to be bound from zeolite almost in 50 % at 60°C and in 5 days, while Pb seems to be bound almost in 20 % and 40 and 60 °C and in 5 days. Also, the amount of iron which is uptaken by the zeolite seems to be affected by the temperature and the conduct time. In 20°c and in any contact time the amount of iron which is taken up from clinoptilolite is higher than in 40 and 60 °C.

However, the application of 60 °C for a long period in any composting systems seems to be difficult to apply, due to high energy demand.

REFERENCES

1.   ZORPAS, A A, VLYSSIDES, A G AND LOIZIDOU, M. Physical and Chemical Characteristic of Anaerobically Stabilized Primary Sewage Sludge. Fresenious Environmental Bulletin, Vol. 7, 1998, pp. 502-508.

2.   ZORPAS, A A, KAPETANIOS, E, VLYSSIDES, A G AND LOIZIDOU, M. Technical Report in Communitie and Municipality in Attica Region 1997.

3.   WONG, J W C, LI, S W I AND WONG, M H. Coal Fly Ash as a Composting Material for Sewage: Effects on Microbial Activities. Environmental Technology, Vol. 16, 1995. pp 527-537.

4.   FURHACKER, M AND HABERL, R. Composting of Sewage Sludge in a Rotating Vessel. Water Science and Technology, Vol. 27, No 2, 1995. pp 121-125.

5.   FINSTEIN, M S, MILLER, F C, MACGREGOR, S T, AND PSARIANOS K M. The Rutgers Strategy for Composting: Process Desing and Control. International Symposium on Compost Recycling of Waste, Acta Horticulturae, Vol. 302, 1992 pp.75-86.

6.   EPSTEIN, E. The Science of Composting. Technomic Puplishing co. INC, Pennsylvania, U.S.A. 1997, p. 137-170.

7.   CONSTANTOPOULOU, C., M. LOIZIDOU, Z. LOIZOU, AND N. SPYRELLIS. Thorium Equilibria With the Sodium Form of Clinoptololite and Mordenite. Journal of Radioanalytical and Nuclear Chemistry. Vol. 178 (1), 1994. pp.143-151.

8.   KAPETAMIOS, E. AND LOIZIDOU, M. Heavy Metals Remoyval Using Zealites in Tomato Cultivation in Compost. Acta Horticulturae, ISHS, International Symposium on Compost Recycling of Wastes, Athens 4-7 October 1989, March, No. 302, 1992 pp 63-74.

9.   LOIZIDOU, M. Heavy Metals in the Effluents of the Metal Plating Industries and Their Removal by Zeolites. Heavy Metals in the Environment, 7th International Conference, Genova, 1989.

10. WAGNER, D.J., G.D. BACON, W.R. KNOCKE, AND M.S. SWITZENBAUM. Changes and variability in concentration of heavy metals in sewage sludge during composting. Environmental Technology. Vol 11. 1990. pp. 949-960.

11.   STENDIFORD, E.I. Recent Development in Composting. Commision of the European Communities, Compost Production Quality and Use, 1987 pp. 52-60.

12.   EPA. 1995. Decision-Maker's Guide To Solid Waste Management,.Second Edition, EPA, USA, August.

13.   LYNCH, J.M., Lignocellulolysis in Compost. Int. Sym. On Compost: Production Quality and Use. 1986 Udine.

LAND APPLICATION OF SEWAGE SLUDGE: THE TOLUENE ISSUE

K Devoldere   **B Laethem**   **D Huybrechts**

VITO

F Delaere   **F Roelandt**   **D De Vadder**   **P Ockier**   **M Peereman**

Aquafin AV

Belgium

ABSTRACT. In order to gain more insight into the origin of organic pollutants in sewage sludge a thorough characterisation of the major streams (influent, effluent, sewage sludge and intermediate streams) in two WWTP's; one with and one without sludge digestion; was conducted. The only pollutant that was found present in significant concentrations in the sewage sludge and in lower concentrations in some of the intermediate streams was toluene. Toluene levels depended highly on whether a sludge digestion was present or not. Literature data indicate the possibility of toluene formation through inhibited methanogenic fermentation, which was confirmed through lab-scale tests. Possible remedies to prevent the formation of toluene in sewage sludge are also discussed.

Keywords: Organic pollutants, Legislation, Toluene formation, Sludge digestion, Remedies.

Dr ir K Devoldere is Project Leader at the Process Technology Centre of Expertise of Vito, Belgium.

ir B Laethem is Account Manager Industry at Vito, Belgium.

Dr ir D Huybrechts is Project Leader at the Integral Environmental Studies Centre of Expertise of Vito, Belgium.

ir F Delaere is Head of the exploitation department of Aquafin NV, Belgium.

Dr F Roelandt is Head of the analysis department of Aquafin NV, Belgium.

ing D De Vadder is member of the technology department of Aquafin NV, Belgium.

ir P Ockier is Head of the technology department of Aquafin NV, Belgium.

ing M Peereman is responsible for instrumental analysis at Aquafin NV, Belgium.

INTRODUCTION

Recent legislation in Flanders imposes limit values on the concentration of a substantial number of organic pollutants in sewage sludge destined for direct land application [1]. In the course of 1999 press releases made the public opinion of Flanders aware of the presence of high levels (up to a few 100 ppm) of toluene in sewage sludge issued from both public and industrial WWTP's. These press releases triggered two independent studies on the origin of organic pollutants in sewage sludge. While the Federation of Food Industry (IVL) only considered toluene in its study [2]; Aquafin NV, operator of all public WWTP's in Flanders, took all organic pollutants into consideration [3]. Vito conducted the latter study in co-operation with and on behalf of Aquafin NV.

Literature data concerning toluene levels in sewage sludge are scarce, since legislation in most countries does not take toluene into consideration. Recent data from Germany indicate that toluene levels up to 140 ppm dm in sewage sludge are possible [4]. Toluene was found in concentrations higher than the limit of detection in 80-90% of the sludge samples investigated [5]. Toluene levels in sludge also seem to be higher during winter than in summertime [4]. Toluene was not added to the German list of priority pollutants in sewage sludge because of the following reasons [6]:

- The human, zoo- and exotoxicology of toluene is low.
- Toluene is quite soluble in water.
- Toluene persistence in soil is low. Most sources indicate a fast decrease of toluene levels in soil due to (mainly) evaporation and microbial degradation [7, 8]. Because of this fast decrease of toluene levels in soil, accumulation of toluene in plants has never been measured up till now [9].
- Toluene levels in sewage sludge are considered to be low.

LEGISLATION ON ORGANIC POLLUTANTS IN SEWAGE SLUDGE

The current European sewage sludge directive (86/278/EEC) does not take any organic pollutant into consideration. Five Member States have a stricter legislation than the sewage sludge directive and put limit values on some organic pollutants in sewage sludge for direct land application.

Table 1 gives an overview of the number of organic pollutants that are taken into consideration in these five Member States. From this Table it is immediately clear that Flanders imposes limit values on a very large number of organic pollutants, due to the fact that this list was taken identical to the list drawn up in the directive on soil protection [10] for reasons of transparency of legislation.

Besides for toluene, Flemish legislation imposes limit values on 4 more monocyclic aromatic hydrocarbons (benzene, ethylbenzene, styrene and xylenes), 10 polycyclic aromatic hydrocarbons and 13 organochlorine compounds and EOX. Swedish legislation only considers guide values for some organic pollutants but does not impose limit values for this class of compounds.

Table 1 Number of organic pollutants considered in the legislation of various Member States

POLLUTANT	DENMARK	GERMANY	FRANCE	FLANDERS	SWEDEN*
PCDD/PCDF		X			
PCB		X (6)	X (7)		X (7)
Monocyclic Aromatic Hydrocarbons				X (5)	X (1)
Polycyclic Aromatic Hydrocarbons	X (10)		X (3)	X (10)	X (3)
Surfactants	X (3)				X (1)
Organochlorine compounds				X (13)	
Other compounds				X (1)	
AOX		X			

X(#) *Pollutant considered (number of compounds taken into consideration)*
*   *Values are guide values not limit values*

EXPERIMENTAL

Description of Wastewater Treatment Plants

Various streams of two full scale wastewater treatment plants (WWTP's) were sampled and analysed for organic pollutants on a regular basis over a two month period.

WWTP 1 (Figure 1a) consists of a screen, two oxidation ditches with anoxic zones and three settling tanks. Part of the settled sludge is recirculated to the oxidation ditches and the rest is mechanically thickened and stored a buffer tanks. During the period of sampling, the mechanical stirrers of the buffer tanks were out of order so the sludge was not stirred regularly during storage. The following streams of WWTP 1 were sampled on a regular basis during the campaign :

- Influent (1_1)
- Effluent (1_2)
- Sludge stream from the settling tanks (1_3)
- Thickened sludge (1_4)
- Sludge from the buffer tanks (1_5)

WWTP 2 (Figure 1b) consists of a screen, a fat remover, two oxidation ditches and three settling tanks. Part of the settled sludge is recirculated to the oxidation ditches and the rest is prethickened and sent to an anaerobic digester. The digested sludge is thickened and sent to lagoons for storage. The following streams of WWTP 2 were sampled on a regular basis during the campaign :

- Influent (2_1)
- Effluent (2_2)
- Prethickened sludge before digestion (2_3)
- Thickened sludge after digestion (2_4)

Description of the Lab-Scale Tests

Four series of 2 sludge samples of WWTP 1 (1_3 and 1_4) and 4 series of 3 sludge samples from WWTP 2 (2_3 , 2_4 and recirculated sludge) were stored under anaerobic conditions at room temperature. Subsamples were analysed for toluene on a regular basis over a period of 14 days.

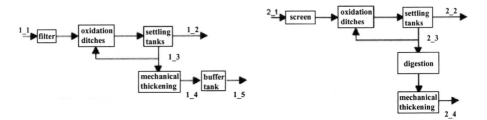

Figure 1 Layout of WWTP 1 (a) and WWTP 2 (b)

Analysis

All samples were analysed for their dry matter content (dm) by drying at 105°C until constant weight was obtained.

The analysis of the volatile organic substances and monocyclic aromatic hydrocarbons was performed by headspace GCMS. A capillary column with apolar chemically bonded phase with a length of 30 to 60 m, an internal diameter of 0.15 to 0.32 mm and a film thickness of 0.8 to 3 µm was used.

RESULTS

Results of the Campaign on the WWTP's

None of the organic pollutants, with the exception of toluene, was found in either of the sampled streams of both WWTP's in concentrations higher than the limit of detection. Toluene levels in influent and effluent were below the limit of detection. Intermediate sludge streams and the thickened sludges all contained toluene in measurable quantities (Figures 2 and 3).

Toluene levels in the sludge from the buffer tanks of WWTP 1 raise to values up to 500 ppm dm. The toluene content in all sludge streams (1_3, 1_4, 1_5, 2_3 and 2_4) exceed the limit value of 1.1 ppm dm which is imposed in Flanders on sludge destined for direct land application.

(Pre)thickened sludge in both WWTP's contains about the same amount of toluene (1_4 and 2_3). Toluene levels in sludge increase by about two orders of magnitude upon storage over a certain period of time under anaerobic conditions (1_5). Digestion of the sludge seems to be an effective means to keep the toluene concentration in sludge at an acceptable level.

The fact that, besides toluene, no other monocyclic aromatic hydrocarbon is found in neither of the streams and that the influent of both WWTP's is free of toluene allows the conclusion that toluene does not originate from an external source of pollution such as the illegal flushing of solvents down the drain.

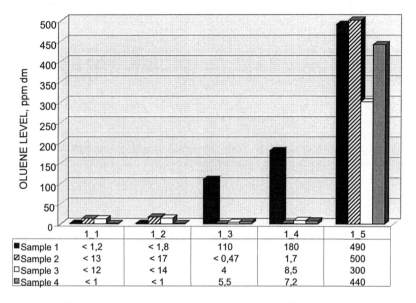

	1_1	1_2	1_3	1_4	1_5
■Sample 1	< 1,2	< 1,8	110	180	490
▨Sample 2	< 13	< 17	< 0,47	1,7	500
☐Sample 3	< 12	< 14	4	8,5	300
▦Sample 4	< 1	< 1	5,5	7,2	440

Figure 2 Toluene content of the various series in WWTP 1

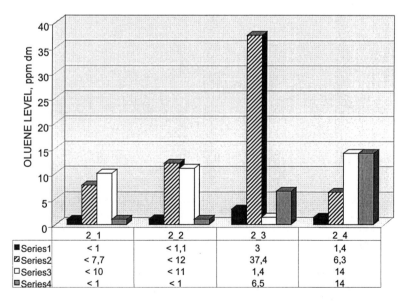

	2_1	2_2	2_3	2_4
■Series1	< 1	< 1,1	3	1,4
▨Series2	< 7,7	< 12	37,4	6,3
☐Series3	< 10	< 11	1,4	14
▦Series4	< 1	< 1	6,5	14

Figure 3 Toluene content of the various series in WWTP 2

Results of the Lab-Scale Tests

The evolution of the toluene content in the recirculated sludge and in the various thickened sludge streams of both WWTP's are given in Figures 4 and 5 respectively.

From these Figures, it is immediately clear that toluene levels rise very quickly in both recirculated and thickened undigested sludge upon storage under anaerobic conditions. Toluene levels easily reach those observed in the sludge from the buffer tanks of WWTP 1 (1_5). As toluene levels are initially very low in most sludge streams (except for thickened undigested stream of WWTP 2) tested in the lab-scale tests, the conclusion can be drawn that toluene is formed by natural processes and does not stand from an external source of pollution. Initial toluene levels in the thickened digested sludge are also in the same order of magnitude as those observed on WWTP 2 and are, as reported earlier, two orders of magnitude smaller than toluene levels in undigested sludge streams. Toluene levels in the digested sludge show a tendency to slowly decrease over time. Digesting the sludge thus seems an accurate measure to keep toluene levels low.

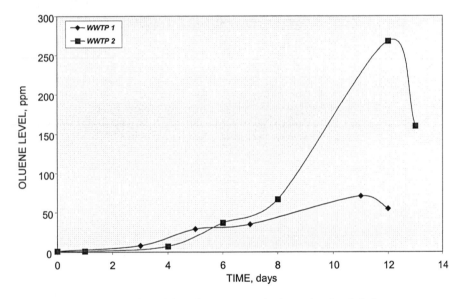

Figure 4   Evolution of the toluene content in the recirculated sludge
of WWTP 1 and WWTP 2 under anaerobic conditions

DISCUSSION

Toluene Formation in Sewage Sludge : Literature Data

The results of the lab-scale tests indicate clearly that toluene can be formed in sewage sludge under anaerobic conditions by some sort of natural process. Research on the formation of toluene under anaerobic conditions has been scarce. Only work by the group of Grbic-Galic at Stanford University [11, 12, 13] sheds some light on the possible mechanisms leading to the formation of toluene.

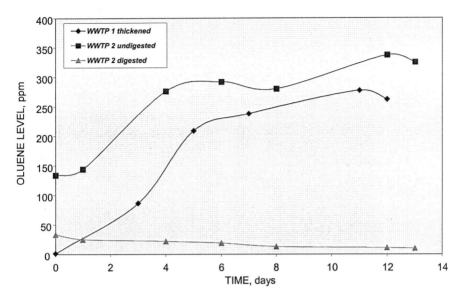

Figure 5 Evolution of the toluene content of thickened sludge streams
of WWTP 1 and WWTP 2 under anaerobic conditions

During methanogenic fermentation, complex organic compounds (cellulosis, proteins, fats) are converted to CO_2 en CH_4 by a consortium of bacteria. The process of methanogenic fermentation can be divided into three substeps [14]:

- Acid forming phase : complex organic matter is converted by fermenting, non-methanogenic bacteria to fatty acids, organic acids, alcohols, ammonia, sulphides, CO_2 and H_2.
- Acetogenic phase : conversion of the intermediate products of the acid forming phase by hydrogen producing acetogenic bacteria to acetate, CO_2 and H_2.
- Methanogenic phase : conversion of acetate, CO_2 and H_2 by hydrogen consuming methanogenic bacteria to CO_2 en CH_4.

These three substeps are strongly interconnected (syntropic association). One of these synergetic effects, which will be shown later to be responsible for the formation of toluene, is the consumption of the hydrogen produced in the acetogenic phase in the methanogenic phase. A schematic overview of the process of methanogenic fermentation is presented in Figure 6.

Due to the very high level of syntropic association in this system, any distortion can give rise to a completely different range of reaction products. In an attempt to elucidate the mechanism of methanogenic fermentation, the group of Grbic-Galic [11, 12, 13] inhibited the methanogenic phase by addition of BESA (2-bromoethane sulfonic acid), which has a structure identical to coenzyme M, being responsible for the methyltransfert in the methanogenic phase.

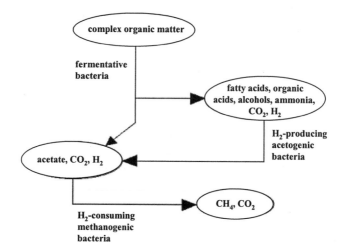

Figure 6 Schematic overview of methanogenic fermentation

Upon inhibition of the methanogenic phase a whole different range of compounds was formed : aromatics, cyclic ketones, naphtenes, substituted phenols and higher aromatic alcohols. The most plausible explanation for the formation of these products is that, in the absence of the hydrogen consuming methanogenesis reaction, hydrogen is disposed of through reduction of other compounds in the reaction mixture : decarboxylation of aromatic acids yielding aromatic compounds, hydrogenation of the aromatic ring yielding naphtenes and hydroxylation of the aromatic ring yielding alcohols. The formation of more reduced acids (butyrate, propionate, lactate, ...) has also been detected during methane suppressed fermentation by other authors [15].

A distortion of the methanogenic fermentation may be caused by a change in operating conditions (pH and/or temperature) or even a simple overload of the system because of a too high a concentration of degradable organic matter.

Toluene Formation in Sewage Sludge : Remedies

If the main reason for the formation of toluene during anaerobic storage of sewage sludge is indeed the inhibited methanogenic fermentation, three possible remedies exist for suppressing toluene formation, each having their own (dis)advantages :

- When sludge is digested previous to storage, the methanogenic fermentation takes place under controlled conditions. The low toluene levels observed in the digested sludge indicate that this method is very effective. The main drawback is the fact that sludge digestion is an expensive operation which is preferably centralised.

- Liming the sludge causes a pH-increase killing off all bacterial activity. Lab-scale experiments with limed sludges showed no formation of toluene in the sludge upon storage under anaerobic conditions. The main drawback of this remedy is the increase of the total amount of sludge that needs to be disposed off.

- Storage of the sludge under aerobic conditions might prevent the formation of toluene. Lab-scale experiments in which sludge was aerated showed a slight decrease of the toluene content.

CONCLUSIONS

- High levels of toluene may be formed in undigested sewage sludge stored under anaerobic conditions for longer periods. The cause of this toluene formation is presumably hindered methanogenic fermentation.

- Since toluene can be formed by natural processess in anaerobically stored sewage sludge, the question arises whether a stringent limit value (or any limit value at all) for this compound is appropriate.

- The main remedies to prevent the formation of toluene are : sludge digestion, sludge liming and storage under aerobic conditions.

REFERENCES

1.   OVAM, VLAREA (Flemish Regulation on Waste Prevention and Management), D/1998/5024/2, 1998.

2.   VANDERHAEGEN B, Onderzoek naar tolueen in bioslib van de voedingsindustrie. EPAS Seminar, d.d. 22/09/1999, 1999.

3.   DEVOLDERE K AND LAETHEM B, Controle van organische micropolluenten in slib, Vito Report 1999/GRO/R/047, 1999.

4.   LITZ N, Personal Communication, Fax, d.d. 18/05/1999, 1999.

5.   DRESCHER-KADEN U, MATTHIES M AND BRÜGGEMANN R, Organische Schadstoffe in Klärschlämmen, Wasser-Abwasser, 1989, 130(2), pp 613-620.

6.   LITZ N, BOJE-HADERER R, JUNG S, MERKEL D, OFFENBÄCHER G. AND SCHNAAK W, Konzept zur Ermittlung und Bewertung der Relevanz schädlicher organischer Inhaltstoffe im Klärschlamm, Korrespondenz Abwasser, 1998, 45(3), pp 492-498.

7.   JIN Y AND O'CONNOR G A, Behavior of toluene added to sludge-amended soils, J. Environ. Qual., 1990, 19, pp 573-579.

8.   ATLAS R M, Microbial degradation of petroleum hydrocarbons : an environmental perspective, Microbiol. Rev., 1981, 45(1), pp180-209.

9.   O'CONNOR G A, CHANEY R L AND RYAN J A, Bioavailability to plants of sludge-borne toxic organics, Rev. Env. Contam. Tox., 1991, 121, pp129-155.

10.   OVAM, VLAREBO (Flemish Regulation on Soil Sanitation), 1996.

11.   GRBIC-GALIC D AND YOUNG L Y, Methane fermentation of ferulate or
      benzoate : anaerobic degradation pathways, Appl. Environ. Microbiol., 1985, 50,
      pp 292-297.

12.   GRBIC-GALIC D, Anaerobic production and transformation of aromatic
      hydrocarbons and substituted phenols by ferulic acid-degrading BESA-inhibited
      methanogenic consortia, FEMS Microbiol. Ecol., 1986, 38, pp 161-169.

13.   VOGEL T M AND GRBIC-GALIC D, Incorporation of oxygen from water into
      toluene and benzene during anaerobic fermentative transformation, Appl. Environ.
      Microbiol., 1986, 52, pp 200-202.

14.   BRYANT M P, Microbial methane production – theoretical aspects, J. Anim. Sci.,
      1979, 48, pp193-201.

15.   SCHWITZGUEBEL J P, Metabolic interactions in mixed bacterial cultures,
      http://dgrwww.epfl.ch/GB/DP/JPS_3.html

ANAEROBIC BAFFLED REACTORS - MINIMISING SLUDGE PRODUCTION

P B Clark

W S Atkins Water

United Kingdom

ABSTRACT. In this paper results from an on-going 2-year programme of research into Anaerobic Baffled Reactors (ABRs) are presented. The Anaerobic Baffled Reactor is a novel compartmentalized reactor design which enables cell retention times (CRT) to be separated from the hydraulic retention times (HRT) thus making it possible to anaerobically treat wastewaters at short retention times (4 - 10 hours). ABRs can thus be viewed as an attractive alternative to aerobic treatment and/or primary settlement. It has been proposed that ABRs could be installed on a full-scale works with relative ease through the simple retrofitting of a conventional primary settlement tank.

Experimentation has been completed at both laboratory and pilot scale with a number of different pilot plant designs being operated at Ellesmere Port Wastewater Treatment works (owned by North West Water). In this paper results are presented from the pilot scale trials. The design of the ABR encourages the bacteria inherent within the wastewater to degrade the sludge *in situ,* thus significantly reducing the amount of primary sludge created. The performance of the ABR for reducing the COD and BOD load of the exit wastewater is also discussed.

Keywords: Anaerobic baffled reactor, ABR, Wastewater, Sludge reduction.

Dr Piers Clark is Head of Operations; Research and Technology Development for WS Atkins Water. He co-ordinates a team who undertake research projects across the whole water cycle: from potable through wastewater to solid waste management. He is the lead author of the Environment Agency's reference text on sludge treatment, recycling and disposal. He is also a Biowise Technical Advisor.

INTRODUCTION

In general, biological wastewater treatment, which involves the breakdown of contaminants in the wastewater by bacterial action, may be divided up into two major categories depending on whether oxygen is present (aerobic) or absent (anaerobic). Treatment times are rapid with aerobic systems since these systems provide more energy to the bacteria; subsequently bacterial doubling times may be as low as 0.5 hours. Unfortunately, this energy is also used to produce excess biomass, and sludge yields of 40 % (i.e. 0.4 kg biomass/kg COD consumed) are common. Aerobic systems are also expensive to maintain due to high aeration and nutrient costs.

In spite of these disadvantages, these systems were originally preferred to anaerobic techniques. This was due to the nature of anaerobic treatment, which involves the catabolism, fermentation and aerobic oxidation of the contaminants into a methane rich biogas via reduced intermediate products. Since the energy available to anaerobes is small, bacterial yields are typically only 3 % with anaerobic organisms. Consequentially, doubling times may be in the order of tens of days.

Originally, anaerobic treatment was confined to the Continuously Stirred Tank Reactor (CSTR). Since this reactor configuration could not differentiate between the time required for treatment – Hydraulic Retention Time (HRT) - and the time spent by the organisms within the reactor – Solids Retention Time (SRT), - treatment time was regulated by the slowly growing bacteria and was typically 20 – 30 days.

However, increasingly expensive sludge treatment/recycling costs, and the continuously high operating costs, have meant that anaerobic treatment has had to become more competitive. In recent years a number of novel reactor designs have been adapted and developed that separate the SRT from the HRT allowing a significantly higher rate of reaction per unit volume of reactor. The Anaerobic Baffled Reactor (ABR) is one such novel reactor

The ABR us a reactor design which uses a series of baffles to force a wastewater containing organic pollutants to flow under and over (or through) the baffles as it passes from the inlet to the outlet. Bacteria within the reactor gently rise and settle due to flow characteristics and gas production, but move down the reactor at a slow rate.

Although not commonly found on a large scale, the ABR has several advantages over other well-established systems and these are outlined below:

- No moving parts
- Relatively inexpensive to construct
- High void volume
- Low operating cost
- No requirement for biomass with unusual settling properties
- Low sludge generation
- High solids retention times
- Retention of biomass without fixed media or a solid-settling chamber

- No special gas or sludge separation required
- Low HRT
- Intermittent operation possible
- Extremely stable to hydraulic and organic shocks
- Protection from toxic materials in influent

Probably the most significant advantage of the ABR is its ability to separate acidogenesis and methanogenesis down the length of the reactor, allowing the reactor to behave as a two-phase system without the associated control problems and high costs. Two-phase operation can increase acidogenic and methanogenic activity by a factor of four as acidogenic bacteria accumulate within the first stage (front compartments of ABR), and different bacterial groups can develop under more favourable conditions.

PROJECT AIMS AND OBJECTIVES

The overall objective of the research presented here was *to investigate the ability of an ABR to treat low strength, low temperature wastewaters such as domestic sewage.*

One of the main novel aspects of the research is that it involves the treatment of relatively low strength, low temperature wastewaters in an ABR that could be retrofitted into an existing primary tank. This is in contrast to previous research work that has tended to concentrate on the application of anaerobic technology as an alternative process to conventional (aerobic) secondary treatment processes. There are a number of benefits associated with installing an ABR as a primary tank retrofit and these are detailed below. The overriding driver however must be recognised as the fact that, for the vast majority of sites, the secondary treatment plant is already constructed and thus the drivers for cost savings are focussed more on optimising existing capital assets rather than building new plant.

The expected benefits associated with retrofitting ABR technology into a primary tank include:

- Maximisation of existing capital assets
- Reduces load on downstream conventional secondary treatment plant
- Reduces sludge production (both primary and secondary)

The above objective is being met through a 2 year programme of research (June 1999 – June 2001) which involves the design, construction, commissioning, operation and optimisation of a pilot scale ABR plant. The pilot plant has been installed on at Ellesmere Port waste water treatment plant in North West Water

PLANT DESIGN AND ANALYSIS

Five separate reactors have been constructed (each simulating a baffled zone) with a header and exit tank at either end of the plant. The combined volume of the five tanks is approximately 25 - 30m^3 (depending on the levels in the tanks). Wastewater is passed from each tank/reactor to the next via a series of connecting pipes (simulating the ABR weir). Each reactor has viewing and sampling ports and a means for collecting gas composition and flow data. As the raw sewage flows across the tank, the solids settle to form a blanket, thus filtering the raw sewage. Connector pipes direct the sewage from the top of the first compartment, via another down-comer pipe, to the base of the second tank. All tanks are connected in a similar manner.

Samples of the effluent and the sludge blankets from each compartment are analysed on a regular basis. The treated effluent from the ABR is returned to the head of the works where it is mixed with the in-flowing raw sewage.

The reactor is monitored for the following :

- Temperature, flow, HRT, SRT
- Sludge: TS, VS, pH alkalinity, VFA, ammonia, sulphate, sulphide, pathogens, pH
- Effluents: BOD,COD, ammonia, SS, VSS, Sulphate, Sulphide, pH
- Gas: Volume and composition

RESULTS AND DISCUSSION

HRT and SRT

The HRT (Hydraulic Retention Time) for the whole reactor and the individual compartments is presented in Figure 1. Since day 50 (period of last modifications to reactor) the HRT for the whole reactor has been maintained at between 5 – 10 hours (target of 7 hours). This compares well to the operation of conventional primary tanks, which tend to have a design HRT of between 7 – 8 hours.

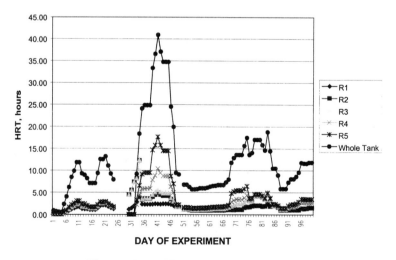

Figure 1 Mean HRT per compartment/tank

The SRT (Solids Retention Time) for the whole reactor and the individual compartments is presented in Figure 2.

By comparing Figure 1 with Figure 2 it can be seen that the reactor has been successful in separating the HRT and SRT (with the SRT being greater than 150 days on occasion, more typically between 40 – 50 days). This long retention time maximises the potential of the reactor for solids degradation since there is a greater period of time over which the bacteria in the reactor can degrade the organic matter in the sludge.

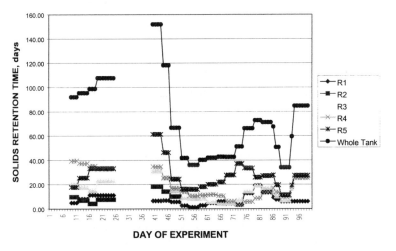

Figure 2 Mean solids retention time

Supernatant Analysis

In general the solids concentration of the influent has been between 400 – 600mg/l (volatiles between 200 – 600 mg/l) with a brief rise above 1000 mg/l around day 70. The influent and effluent supernatant samples were collected in automatic composite samplers.

The 'removal performance percentages' for the various analytical parameters for the whole reactor are presented in Figure 3. The percentage removals of solids (both volatiles and total) across the reactor are very good, generally being maintained above 80%.

The minor 'blip' around day 70 – 80 coincides with an unexplained increase in solids in the influents. The mean percentage removal for solids, COD and BOD respectively are 76% (+ 13), 49% (+ 12) and 50% (+ 14) respectively over the most recent 50 days of operation. The bracketed figures are the 95%ile confidence limits.

With regards the COD and BOD levels the percentage removals across the reactor during the first 50 days of operation were low – between 20 – 40%. This was because the reactors had only recently been commissioned and there was very little sludge blanket in any of the

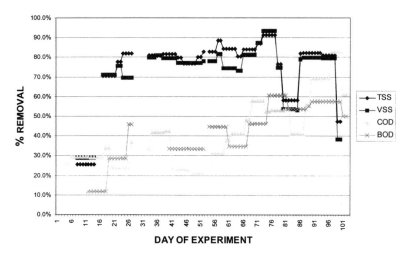

Figure 3 Percentage removals - whole tank

compartments. From day 50 (the period of last modification to the reactor) the COD and BOD removal efficiencies have steadily increased and are currently around 50 – 60% for both parameters.

The percentage removals for each of the individual compartments confirm what would be expected from an ABR: namely that the majority of treatment is being undertaken in the first two compartments. The percentage removals drop significantly across the compartments, with reactor 5 providing apparently little improvement in wastewater quality.

It should be noted however that the effluent entering this final compartment is considerably improved and that the prime purpose of the latter compartments is to provide a polishing/buffer zone.

Sludge Analysis

The sludge pHs in the different compartments are very variable, as presented in Figure 4. The pH in the first compartment is very low (around 5.5) rising to above neutral in the final compartment. This is very promising, indicating that bacterial segregation is occurring across the reactor with the acetogenic bacteria dominating in the first two compartments.

The mean VFA concentration in the different compartments is presented in Figure 5. As would be expected, very high VFA concentrations were observed in the initial compartment, dropping to very low in the final compartments. The VFA levels in compartment 5 were typically below 100 mg/l, the level widely recognised as indicative of a stable, well digested sludge.

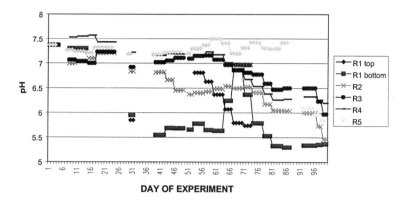

Figure 4 Mean Sludge pH

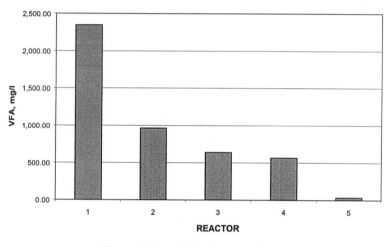

Figure 5 Mean VFA Concentration

With the increase in sludge stability across the reactor it is to be expected that the alkalinity of the sludges will also increase. The average sludge alkalinity rose from below 2000 mg/l in compartment 1 to over 5000 in the final compartment. Also as expected the ammonia concentration in the sludge increases across the reactors, rising from 200mg/l in reactor 1 to almost a 1000 mg/l in reactor 5.

The volatile solids (expressed as a percentage of the total solids) are presented in Figure 6. The volatile solids ratio decreases significantly across the ABR reducing from between 70 – 75% at the influent to around 50% in the final compartment. This reduction in the TS/VS ratio provides further evidence that the sludges are being biologically degraded in the ABR (the percentage VS of a conventional primary tank is approximately 70%).

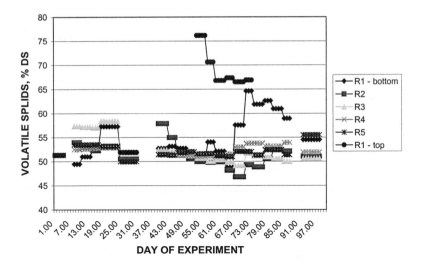

Figure 6 Mean volatile solids

Sludge Destruction

In Figure 7 the expected cumulative sludge volumes from the ABR are plotted for the period since day 50 (last major modifications to the reactor). As can be seen from this figure the expected cumulative sludge volume, assuming no sludge destruction in the ABR and that all sludge was removed from the final compartment, would exceed 60m^3 for the 50 day period presented. Even with a 20% sludge destruction figure the cumulative sludge volume is considerably greater than the actual volume removed (just over 5m3).

Interestingly, even if a worst case scenario is assumed in that the whole tank was empty at the start of the period of data presented in Figure 7 and that the reactor has simply filled up, then the actual sludge volume removed is significantly less than would be expected.

In reality the reactors were probably between 20 – 40% full of sludge at the start of the data period presented although the exact volume was not recorded.

The volume of the reactor is approximately 25m^3, thus the total volume of sludge (including that which has been removed to date) would only be about 30m^3 even with a worst case scenario. This is approximately half the volume expected.

CONCLUSIONS

The results presented here summarise the initial performance data from a large scale ABR plant operated on low temperature, low strength wastewaters. Initial results indicate that the ABR plants offer considerable potential for enhancing primary tank performance, in particular with regards minimising sludge production.

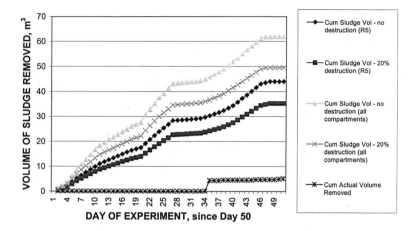

Figure 7 Expected Desludging Volumes

Performance of the plant has steadily improved in recent weeks (i.e. since the changes in design and operation were adopted) as the plant stabilises. High solids capture (>80%) rates have been consistently observed, with BOD and COD removal rates also gradually increasing as the sludge blankets grow and become established.

The plant is still going through a commissioning/stabilisation phase. However, despite this, the solids destruction capability of the plant appears to be very good, with sludge production rates currently 50% below that which would be expected from a conventional system.

ACKNOWLEDGEMENTS

This research is part of an on-going 2-year project financially supported by North West Water, Thames Water, Wessex Water, South West Water, Water Services NI and Orange County Sanitation Department. The research team includes personnel from WS Atkins Water (who are responsible for co-ordinating the whole research programme) and Imperial College. The author gratefully acknowledges the support of the above organizations.

BEST AVAILABLE TECHNIQUES FOR THE TREATMENT AND DISPOSAL OF SEWAGE SLUDGE IN FLANDERS

D Huybrechts

VITO

Belgium

ABSTRACT. While the amount of sewage sludge in Flanders is increasing, the use of sewage sludge as a fertiliser or soil conditioner as well as sludge disposal by landfill have become subject to more stringent environmental legislation. As a result, alternative systems for the treatment and disposal of sewage sludge have to be taken into use. In order to support and guide the introduction of these new systems, the Flemish authorities asked the Flemish Institute for Technological Research (Vito) to select the BAT (Best Available Techniques) for treatment and disposal of sewage sludge. The BAT selection was based on expert judgement of technical feasibility, environmental benefit and economical feasibility. In this paper, some results of the BAT evaluation are presented.

Keywords: Best available techniques, BAT, Sludge treatment, Sludge disposal.

Dr ir D Huybrechts is a staff member of the Centre for Best Available Techniques (BAT Centre) at the Flemish Institute for Technological Research (Vito). She was responsible for drawing up the Flemish BAT-report on the treatment of sludge from waste water treatment plants. She was assisted in this task by a steering committee consisting of representatives of the Flemish authorities, Aquafin (operator of all public WWTP's in Flanders) and the Federation of Food Industry.

INTRODUCTION

Due to the expansion of waste water treatment infrastructure, the production of sewage sludge in Flanders has increased from 48,000 TDS in 1995 to 83,000 TDS in 1999. In the year 2005, the sludge production is expected to amount to 115,000 TDS. While the amount of sewage sludge is increasing, disposal of sewage sludge has become subject to more stringent environmental legislation [1]. Landfill disposal of combustible waste is forbidden in Flanders since July 2000, although exceptions are still allowed in individual cases. High environmental taxes discourage sludge producers to make use of this disposal route. Less than 10 % of the Flemish sewage sludge meets the high quality standards that are imposed on sewage sludge that is destined for agricultural use. As a result, alternative systems for the treatment and disposal of sewage sludge have to be taken into use.

In order to support and guide the introduction of these new treatment and disposal systems, the Flemish authorities asked the Flemish Institute for Technological Research (Vito) to select the BAT (Best Available Techniques) for treatment and disposal of sewage sludge. The BAT selection was based on expert judgement of technical feasibility, environmental benefit and economical feasibility. All possible processing and treatment systems in operation or in design in Flanders, as well as some specific processes that are used in other European countries, were considered and evaluated. A steering committee consisting of representatives of the Flemish authorities, Aquafin (operator of all public WWTP's in Flanders) and the Federation of Food Industry assisted in the evaluation. The final aim of selecting the best options for the treatment of sludge is to provide the Flemish authorities with a basis for environmental permit legislation and environmental investment support.

The Flemish BAT-report on treatment of sludge from WWTP's will be published in 2001 and deals with sludge from industrial as well as from public WWTP's. In this paper, some selected aspects relevant to sludge from public WWTP's will be discussed.

BEST AVAILABLE TECHNIQUES (BAT)

Environmental permits often contain technology-based requirements, and BAT are usually taken as a reference point. In the European directive 96/61/EC [2], better known as the IPPC-directive (Directive on Integrated Pollution Prevention and Control), member states are asked to use BAT and environmental quality objectives as benchmarks to establish environmental permit conditions for certain industrial installations. In the term BAT, the words "techniques", "available" and "best" have the following meaning:

- "techniques" include both the technology used and the way in which the installation is designed, built, maintained, operated and decommissioned,

- "available" techniques mean those developed on a scale which allows implementation in the relevant industrial sector, under economically and technically viable conditions, taking into consideration the costs and advantages, whether or not the techniques are used or produced inside the Member State in question, as long as they are reasonably accessible to the operator,

- "best" means most effective in achieving a high general level of protection of the environment as a whole.

BAT thus correspond to technologies and organisational measures with a minimum environmental impact and acceptable cost.

TREATMENT AND DISPOSAL SYSTEMS FOR SEWAGE SLUDGE

Figure 1 gives an overview of possible treatment and disposal systems for sewage sludge. Raw sludge generally needs to undergo one or more (pre)treatment processes (e.g. thickening, stabilisation, dewatering, drying, etc.) before it can be finally disposed of, e.g. by use in agriculture, landfill disposal, incineration, co-incineration, wet oxidation, etc. A complete treatment and disposal system is therefore always a combination of different processes.

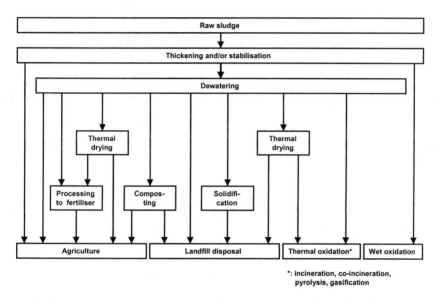

Figure 1 Overview of possible treatment and disposal systems for sewage sludge

Thickening and/or Stabilisation

Raw sewage sludge is usually (but not necessarily) thickened before it is further treated. Thickening can be done by gravity methods, but better thickening results are obtained with mechanical thickeners.

Sludge stabilisation is only required in Flanders when the sludge is used for agricultural purposes. Possible stabilisation processes are:

- aerobic stabilisation (e.g. simultaneous aerobic stabilisation, aeration, thermophilic aerobic stabilisation)
- anaerobic stabilisation (e.g. mesophilic or thermophilic digestion)
- chemical stabilisation (e.g. conditioning with lime).

Simultaneous aerobic stabilisation of sewage sludge is performed in all Flemish WWTP's that have been designed by Aquafin. Furthermore, about 25 % of the Flemish sewage sludge (21,7760 TDS) was digested in 1999. Aquafin plans to increase its digestion capacity to 60,000 TDS in 2005. Sludge digestion does not only offer the possibility to recover energy from the sludge through the production of biogas, but also reduces the amount of sludge that needs to be further treated and disposed of. Digested sludge can also be better dewatered.

Dewatering

Liquid sewage sludge can only be disposed of by using it directly in agriculture or by wet oxidation. For all other disposal routes, the sludge needs to be dewatered before it can be further treated. Dewatering can be done by gravity methods, but better results are obtained with mechanical dewatering.

Thermal Drying

Thermal drying involves evaporation of the majority of the water that is contained in dewatered sludge. When sludge is dried from 30 % DS to 90 % DS, the amount of sludge that needs to be disposed of is reduced by at a factor 3. Dried sludge is almost odourless, and more easy to handle, store and transport than dewatered sludge. Furthermore, it allows different disposal processes (see Figure 1).

However, drying of sludge requires high amounts of energy. The theoretical energy requirements for sludge drying, taking into account 10 % heat losses, are given in Table 1. The table shows that the energy requirement is very much dependent on the initial water content of the dewatered sludge, and, to a far lesser extent, on the final water content of the dried sludge. In order to reduce the energy use for drying, the sludge should therefore be dewatered as far as possible. The actual energy requirement of a sludge drying plant may be 25 % higher than the theoretical values. Direct sludge dryers, in which the sludge is dried by direct contact with the heating medium (e.g. air), usually have a higher specific energy use than indirect sludge dryers, in which the heat is transferred from the heat medium (e.g. steam, oil) to the sludge via a heat conducting interface. The heat that is needed in a sludge dryer can be obtained from different energy sources

- fossil energy sources (usually natural gas)
- biogas produced by sludge digestion
- waste energy (e.g. from a nearby waste incinerator).

In Flanders, Aquafin operates a sludge drying plant at the sewage treatment plant in Deurne (Antwerp). The plant has a drying capacity of 10,000 TDS/a and uses biogas from the nearby digester as energy source. Aquafin plans to take three additional drying plants in operation by 2002, each with a capacity of 10,000 TDS/a. Two of the three new drying plants will use biogas from a nearby digester as energy source, the third one will use waste energy from a nearby waste incinerator.

Table 1 Theoretical energy requirements for thermal sludge drying [3]

% DS in the dewatered sludge	40 %	40 %	25 %	25 %	20 %	20 %
% DS in the dried sludge	90 %	80 %	90 %	80 %	90 %	80 %
Energy requirement (MJ/TDS)	4,363	3,928	8,965	8,513	12,034	11,567

Processing to Fertiliser

Although stabilised sludge, possibly thickened, dewatered or dried, can be used directly as a fertiliser or a soil conditioner, the sludge may also be mixed with other compounds (e.g. lime) in order to increase the agricultural value or to achieve a further stabilisation. An example of such treatment that is applied in Flanders by the company Silt is the N-Viro process. This involves mixing dewatered sludge with alkaline reagents (e.g. dust from cement or lime kilns, certain fly ashes) and then subjecting the mixture to a controlled period of storage, mechanical turning and accelerated drying. The N-Viro process stabilises and pasteurises the sludge, reduces odour, and generates N-Viro Soil^{TM}, a product that can be used in agriculture.

Composting

Composting is an aerobic process in which biodegradable organic material is converted into mainly CO_2 and water. Due to the temperature increase that is caused by the biological proces, water evaporates from the composted material. The end-product is a stable material with typically 60 % DS and can be used a soil conditioner. Flanders has more than 20 plants in which kitchen and garden waste and landscape refuse are composted. None of these plants accepts sewage sludge. Sludge composting is practised in other European countries (e.g. the Netherlands). The composted sludge can not always be used as a soil conditioner and is then usually disposed by landfill.

Solidification

Sludge is only accepted at Flemish landfill sites if its shear strength is at least 10 kN/m5. In many cases, mechanically dewatered sludge cannot reach this shear strength and solidification becomes necessary. Solidification involves addition of quicklime to the sludge and results in an increase of the amount of sludge that has to disposed of.

Use in or as a Fertiliser or Soil Conditioner

Agricultural use of sewage sludge is subjected to stringent legal conditions in Flanders. The maximum concentrations of heavy metals and organic pollutants that may be present in the sludge are consistently lower than those that are given in the European Working Document on Sludge [4], and are exceeded in more than 90 % of the Flemish sewage sludge. Parameters that pose most problems are Zn, Cu, Ni and Pb, as is shown in Table 2. Some sludges have also a problem with toluene concentrations [5]. Furthermore, Flemish environmental legislation [1] ordains that it is forbidden to use sewage sludge as a fertiliser or soil conditioner in Flanders, unless the sludge has been pre-treated in such a way that the water soluble forms of phosphorous and nitrogen have been reduced by at least 85 %. The only treatment process that claims to reach such reductions is the N-Viro process (see higher). The prohibition, which applies only to municipal sewage sludge and not to sludge from industrial waste water treatment plants, is in force since December 1st 1999. It is expected to be withdrawn in 2002, when a revised version of the Flemish waste legislation will come into force. Withdrawal of the prohibition will eliminate the discrimination between sludge from industrial and municipal waste water treatment plants.

Table 2 Heavy metal concentrations and concentration limits in sewage sludge (mg/kg DS)

HEAVY METAL	LIMIT CONCENTRATIONS FOR AGRICULTURAL USE IN FLANDERS [1]	LIMIT CONCENTRATIONS IN THE EUROPEAN WORKING DOCUMENT ON SLUDGE [4]	TYPICAL CONCENTRATION IN FLEMISH SEWAGE SLUDGE*
Cd	6	10	0.37
Cr	250	1,000	52.5
Cu	375	1,000	278
Hg	5	10	1.0
Pb	300	750	165
Ni	50	300	31.0
Zn	900	2,500	1,067

*: median values of metal concentrations in 1,064 samples of sewage sludge taken from 156 WWTP's from January 1998 until September 1999 (data supplied by Aquafin)

The amount of Flemish sewage sludge that was used as a fertiliser in 1999 was 6,953 TDS, which corresponds to less than 10 % of the total amount that was disposed of.

Landfill Disposal

Landfill disposal of combustible waste is forbidden in Flanders since July 2000, although exceptions are still allowed in individual cases. High environmental taxes discourage sludge producers to make use of this disposal route. The amount of Flemish sewage sludge that was disposed of by landfill was 25,427 TDS in 1999, which is 34 % of the total amount disposed. This percentage is expected to decrease significantly in the next couple of years.

Incineration

Incineration of dried sewage sludge is possible, but usually dewatered sludge is incinerated. The sludge can either be incinerated separately in a sludge incinerator, or together with other waste fractions in a mixed waste incinerator.

A fluidised bed incinerator for sewage sludge has been in operation at the sewage treatment plant in Brugge since 1987. The plant has a capacity of 14,000 TDS/a and aims for auto-thermal incineration by double energy recovery from the flue gases. On the one hand, the air used in the incineration process is preheated. On the other hand, a part of the sewage sludge is thermally pre-dried to 90 % DS in a tray dryer. Due to technical and capacity problems with the dryer, auto-thermal incineration is currently not achieved and anthracite is supplemented as a fuel. A technical revision of the plant is planned in the near future and is expected to allow auto-thermal incineration conditions and to increase capacity up to 20,000 TDS/a.

Occasionaly, dewatered or dried sewage sludge is incinerated in the Flemish grate incinerators for non-hazardous and municipal waste. These incinerators are equipped with energy recuperation systems, and have an overall electricity yield of 20 %. However these incinerators were not designed to process sludge, and problems with incomplete combustion have been observed. A new fluidised bed incinerator is plant that would process dewatered sewage sludge together with waste streams with a higher calorific value.

Co-incineration

Dried sludge has a relatively high energy content and can therefore be used a fuel, e.g. in the cement industry or in coal-fired power stations. Brown coal-fired power stations also allow co-incineration of dewatered sludge. In 1999, 19,618 TDS of Flemish sludge was co-incinerated, which corresponds to 26 % of the total amount that was disposed of.

Co-incineration of dried sludge in coal-fired power stations has been applied in Flanders since 1995 in the power stations of Mol en Rodenhuize. The amount of sludge that may be co-incinerated in these plants is limited to 5 % on a DS basis. The co-incineration has no significant effect on the quality of the ashes, so the usual applications for these materials remain available. On condition that the sludge has a minimum calorific value of 10 MJ/kg and meets certain limit concentrations of metals, S, F, and Cl-compounds, current Flemish waste legislation [4] does not consider co-incineration of sewage sludge in a coal-fired power station as waste incineration. The co-incineration has therefore no effect on the emission limits that are imposed on the power station. This is expected to change in the future, when a revised version of the Flemish waste legislation will come into force, and co-incineration of sludge will, in line with the European directive on waste incineration [6], be considered as waste incineration.

Cement kilns are not present in Flanders, but dried Flemish sewage sludge is co-incinerated in the Walloon cement kilns. When dried sludge is co-incinerated in the cement industry, the calorific value of the sludge is used as a fuel and its mineral content is used as a raw material. Part of the Flemish sewage sludge is also dewatered and exported to Germany to be co-incinerated in the brown coal-fired power stations.

Pyrolysis or Gasification

Pyrolysis and gasification are thermal oxidation processes, respectively in the absence and in the limited presence of oxygen, that generate compounds that can be used as feedstock for the petrochemical sector and/or as energy sources. In a recent world-wide review of pyrolysis and gasification processes [7], 7 gasification and 2 pyrolysis technologies were identified that aim specifically (but not necessarily exclusively) at processing sewage sludge. However none of these 9 processes has reached a fully commercial status according to the review.

Wet Oxidation

Wet oxidation of aqueous waste streams involves oxidation of dissolved or suspended solids at high temperature (180 B 374 °C) and pressure (40 B 250 bar) by molecular oxygen. Organic material is oxidised to CO_2, water, and simple organic compounds, such as acetic acid. Organic nitrogen compounds are converted to ammonia. The effluent of the wet oxidation process contains ashes that are separated from the liquid, dewatered and disposed of by landfill. The liquid effluent, which is loaded with acetic acid, ammonia and other compounds, needs to be purified.

Wet oxidation is not applied in Flanders. A commercial wet oxidation plant is operated in the Netherlands by Vartech. The plant annually processes 15,000 TDS Dutch sewage sludge with 4.5 % DS in an underground reactor. During recent years, the plant had to be shut down several times due to obstructions in the reactor.

ECONOMIC EVALUATION

A first criterion that is used to determine whether a technique can possibly be considered as BAT, is its cost. Techniques that can not be afforded by the relevant sector or techniques whose costs are out of proportion to the environmental benefits, can not considered as BAT.

The total cost for treatment and disposal of sewage sludge in Flanders amounts typically to 500 EURO/TDS. Differences between disposal systems do exist (e.g. landfilling is more expensive than other disposal routes), but are not considered to be large enough to be used as a criterion for BAT selection. Therefore, none of the considered sludge treatment and disposal systems is excluded from possible BAT selection on the basis of its cost.

TECHNICAL EVALUATION

A second criterion that is used to evaluate whether a technique can possibly be considered as BAT, is its technical availability. According to the definition of BAT, techniques that are not developed on a scale which allows implementation in the relevant industrial sector, under economically and technically viable conditions, can not be considered as BAT. The technical availability of the following techniques is considered to be insufficient:

- pyrolysis and gasification: these techniques have not reached a fully commercial status in the sector of sludge treatment [7]

- wet oxidation: a commercial plant for sludge treatment exists, but has to deal with important technical problems.

ENVIRONMENTAL EVALUATION

In the environmental evaluation, the effects of the treatment and disposal routes on the environment as a whole are assessed. The different aspects that are taken into account are: emissions to air, water and soil, solid waste, energy use and recovery and material re-use.

Use of Sludge in or as a Fertiliser or Soil Conditioner

The use of sewage sludge in agriculture, whether in liquid form, or after dewatering, thermal drying, composting or processing to a fertiliser, allows the re-use of the organic material in the sludge and contributes to a closing of the carbon cycle. However, agricultural use of sewage sludge creates a potential risks of biological or chemical soil pollution. This risk is small and considered acceptable when the sludge has been properly stabilised, when it is applied in line with the legally specified conditions, and when the concentrations of chemical pollutants do not exceed the legally specified maximum values [1]. The use of sewage sludge as a fertiliser or soil conditioner requires relatively little energy, unless the sludge is thermally dried before being used as a fertiliser. From an energetic standpoint, drying of sludge with biogas (from sludge digestion) or waste heat is preferred over drying with fossil fuels.

Landfill Disposal of Sludge

In the Flemish environmental policy, great importance is attached to avoiding waste, more specifically combustible waste, to be disposed of by landfill. An indication of the amount of sludge that remains to be disposed of after different treatment processes, is given in Figure 2.

Composting or drying of sludge results in a significant decrease in the amount of sludge that remains to be disposed of. However, landfill disposal of composted or dried sludge is not considered as BAT, since the amount that remains to be disposed is still at least twice as high as in the case of incineration, and since better disposal options are available for composted or dried sludge. Landfill disposal of sludge is therefore never considered as BAT, irrespective of how the sludge has been pre-treated. Only the inorganic fraction of the sludge (incineration residue) may be disposed of by landfill in a BAT process.

Incineration and Co-incineration of Sludge

Incineration and co-incineration processes each have their advantages and disadvantages. From an energetic standpoint, co-incineration is generally considered to be more attractive than incineration, since the efficiency of energy recovery is higher. In the case of sewage sludge, the energy balance varies depending on whether or not the sludge has been digested prior to the incineration or co-incineration, and which energy source has been used for drying the co-incinerated sludge.

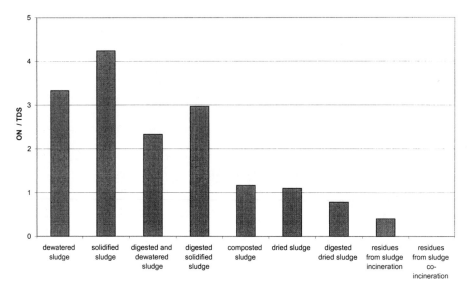

Figure 2 Amount of sludge to be disposed of after different treatments

The overall energy balances (energy production B energy use) of some incineration and co-incineration scenario's are shown in Figure 3. The presented energy data are the result of model calculations and include energy requirements for thickening, dewatering, digestion, drying and incineration or co-incineration.

Figure 3 shows that co-incineration of dried sludge has a significant energetic advantage over incineration of dewatered sludge on condition that the co-incinerated sludge has been dried with waste heat or biogas. When the co-incinerated sludge has however been dried with fossil fuels, the positive energetic effect of the co-incineration is largely undone by the large energy use for drying. It is further seen that digestion of sludge has a negative effect on the overall energy balance of co-incineration. This is due to the fact that the energy that is recovered by digestion can not anymore be recovered in the co-incineration process, where it would have been used with a higher efficiency. Co-incineration of digested sludge is only energetically attractive if the biogas is used as an energy source for the drying process.

Incineration and co-incineration processes also cause different levels of air emissions. A detailed LCA (Life Cycle Assessment) assessment of sludge incineration and co-incineration systems [8] has shown that incineration of sludge generally causes less emissions than co-incineration, thanks to the fact that incineration plants have more stringent emission limits and thus better emission control. The advantage of incineration is however at least partially undone by the fact that co-incineration generates more energy, and thus 'avoids' emissions caused by energy generation.

Finally, when sludge is co-incinerated, the inorganic material content ends up in a product (cement) or a residue (ashes) that is used as a building material. When sludge is incinerated, the ashes need to be disposed of by landfill (see Figure 2), unless an opportunity for recycling can be found.

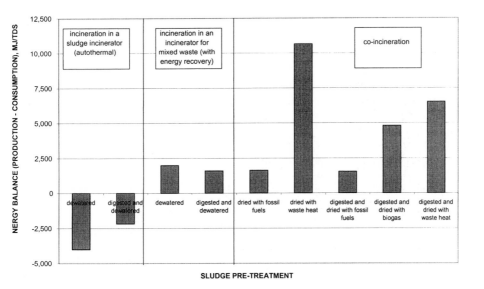

Figure 3   Energy balance for incineration and co-incineration systems

BAT SELECTION

Based on the above-mentioned considerations the BAT for treatment and disposal of sewage sludge were selected, and conditions on which they are considered as BAT were specified. The definite results of the BAT selection were not yet available at the time this paper was written, but will be presented at the symposium.

REFERENCES

1.   OVAM, VLAREA (Flemish Regulation on Waste Prevention and Management), D/1998/5024/2, 1998.

2.   EUROPEAN COMMISSION, Council directive 96/61/EC of 24 September 1996 concerning integrated pollution prevention and control, European Commission Publication Paper L257/26.

3.   TIZE R, Energie en besparende maatregelen op waterzuiveringsstations, Gevorderde cursus waterzuivering, KVIV, 1996.

4.   EUROPEAN COMMISSION ENVIRONMENT DIRECTORATE, Sludge Directive Working Document, 3rd draft, April 2000.

5. DEVOLDERE K, LAETHEM B, HUYBRECHTS D, DELAERE F, ROELANDT F, DE VADDER D, OCKIER P AND PEEREMAN M., Land application of sewage sludge: the toluene issue, Proceedings of the International Symposium: Recycling and Reuse of Sewage Sludge, Dundee, 2000.

6. Common position (EC) No 7/2000 adopted by the Council on 25 November 1999 with a view to adopting Directive 2000/ /EC of the European parliament and of the Council of on the incineration of waste, Official Journal of the European Communities, 2000.

7. JUNIPER CONSULTANCY SERVICES LTD, Pyrolysis & gasification of waste: a worldwide technology & business review, Volume 2: Technologies & Processes, 2000.

8. TORFS R AND DEVOLDERE K, Vergelijkende studie van slibverwerkingsopties, studie uitgevoerd in opdracht van Aquafin, Vito, 1999.

TECHNOLOGY AND REUSE FOR BIOSOLIDS, BIODEGRADABLE MSW, GREEN WASTE CONVERGE

K Panter

Ebcor Ltd

United Kingdom

ABSTRACT. This paper describes the drivers behind sludge and Biodegradable Municipal Waste (BMW) recycling. There is a convergence of legislation taking place in Europe between the landfill directive and the sludge directive, especially with the preparation of the Biodegradable Waste Management Directive by the Waste Management Unit of the Environment Directive in Brussels. Traditionally composting has been seen as the technology of choice for solid organic waste but this has suffered with problems of odour, inconsistent product safety and poor product quality. This paper discusses technologies that are being used to treat sludge and BMW giving some data on existing projects. These include combined thermal hydrolysis, anaerobic digestion and composting; lime pasteurisation combined with green waste composting; and gasification.

Keywords: Biosolids, Composting, Anaerobic digestion, Thermal hydrolysis, Alkaline pasteurisation, Green waste, Biodegradable municipal waste.

Keith Panter, is Managing Director of Ebcor Ltd. He has been involved in the recycling of biosolids and waste for over twenty years. He helped set up land application programmes for Thames Water. He was General Manager of Brophy Organic Products, a division of Thames Waste Management involved in the recycling of biosolids and waste and the development of a range of landscaping products and services. He was Sludge Product Manager for Thames Water International, responsible for a wide range of sludge technology in the US and Europe. Later he was a Business Development Manager for Swiss Combi Technology's thermal dryer. He set up Ebcor three years ago to develop biosolids projects world-wide and has successfully introduced technologies in Europe and the US.

INTRODUCTION

The Municipal Waste Directive requires biodegradable fraction of MSW to be reduced to 35% of 1995 levels by 2020. At current levels there will be 10 million tonnes to divert by this time. There are milestones along the way: 75% by 2010 and 50% by 2013. Furthermore the DETR has set non mandatory targets for recovery from waste of 40% by 2005, 45% by 2010 and 67% by 2015. Current and planned incineration will divert about 15% of MSW and about a further 15% can be sensibly diverted by separate collection of dry recyclables including paper, metals and glass. So to achieve a diversion above 30% at a National level will entail the introduction of new technology to deal with fractions of waste that are more difficult. In addition the Waste Management Unit at Brussels is promoting the a BMW directive which will ban the use of sink garbage grinders and make separate collection of BMW mandatory. This ruling has developed from the compost directive but now encompasses AD. Tough new standards for pathogen control are being promoted including the use of Clostridium as an indicator – Clostridium is a heat resistant spore forming organism that is very difficult to kill in conventional composting.

Table 1 Analysis of household dustbin waste

MATERIAL	PERCENTAGE BY WEIGHT IN DUSTBIN	PERCENTAGE RECYCLABLE
Paper and Board	33	16
Plastic film	11	2
Glass	10	9
Metal	7	5
Textiles	2	0
Organic	20	20
Others	17	0
TOTAL	**100**	**52**

An analysis of the contents of our dustbins suggests that the 50% diversion target can be met (just) without incineration but that to achieve the ultimate target some form of combustion technology is required.

Historically people have turned to composting to enable recovery of waste up to the 50% level. However results have been mixed. Authorities who start with composting green waste do not realise the BMW is an entirely different material. Green waste from Gardens has a very high C:N ratio and generally gives an open structured compost pile. It has low putrescibility and compost slowly. BMW is wet composts rapidly leading to anaerobic conditions. In the early nineties three major US projects in Portland OR, Miami Dade and

Fort Lauderdale FLA were shut down because of operational problems, especially odour causing about $100 million write off of assets.

The DETR has promoted incineration with energy production as a recovery technology, but public perception and acceptance of incinerators is very poor and it is unlikely that sufficient projects will be developed in time for the diversion targets to be met.

Two scenarios present themselves: one in which organic recycling is maximised and one in which incineration is maximised.

Annual fees for new capacity / £ millions - Incineration maximised

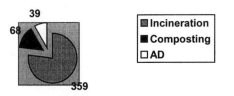

Annual fees for new capacity / £ millions - Organics maximised

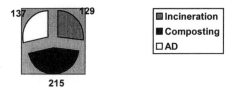

Figure 1 Comparison of processing revenues

Figure 1 is from an earlier study showing the extreme ends of the processing revenues. Either way there will be a large diversion from landfill with a rapid growth in recovery business. In the organic maximised version the quantities of recyclate will outstrip the quantities of biosolids being recycled leading to increased competition for land.

Different routes lead to different quantities. If all BMW is composted there would be about 10 million tonnes of compost to be recycled. Where would it all go? Obviously there is only one answer – agriculture. Scotland has been in the forefront of promoting the beneficial use of pathogen free biosolids. Concerns about BSE, E Coli 0157 and other known pathogens, has led to a very high standard specification for Scottish biosolids. It stands to reason that any BMW derived product has to meet the same standard if it is to be sustainable. Any compost process using BMW must be able to demonstrate time/temperature regimes to demonstrate pathogen kill and meet HACCP requirements. Only in-vessel systems can demonstrate time/temperature – open systems will not be able to demonstrate time/temperature for every particle and also run the risk of severe odour problems.

Figure 2 shows the effect of different processes on different volumes. Anaerobic digestion coupled with composting has the virtue of reducing sludge quantities and if the output from the anaerobic digestion (AD) can be pr-pasteurised the compost can be made with an open windrow system as AD reduces putrescibility. AD sludge mixed with green waste has a good overall CN ratio, composts well and can give a safe product if the AD sludge used is safe to start with.

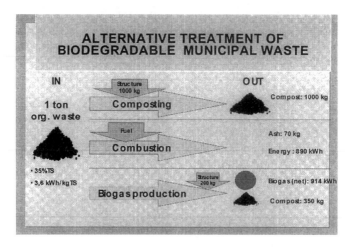

Figure 2 Relative volumes following alternative treatment of waste

THE GLOR PROJECT

GLOR is an inter-municipal co-operation centred around Lillehamar in central Norway. Household waste is source separated over the entire region. Since 1998 BMW has been restricted from landfill, composting has been tried but was too difficult to control in open windrows and considered too expensive in Vessel composting.

A biowaste plant is in comissioning now for the treatment of the BMW. The process train is shown in Figure 3.   Some 14000 tonnes will be processed per year to produce a pathogen free compost. A CHP unit is included and the plant can also make carbon source for the waste water plant denitrification plant.

One aspect of the plant is that the separation of plastic and glass is done in the wet phase. This is much more effective than separating dry materials from compost. Previous plants in the UK have demonstrated this. Trials carried out by Thames Waste Management at their West Hyde plant showed that wet separation was very effective and that the CN ratio of the combined BMW and sludge gave excellent digestion and dewatering. This is the basis of a long term contract being carried out by TWM at Oxford STW using BMW from the Hereford and Worcester waste contract.

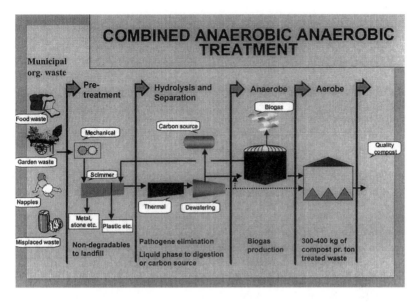

Figure 3 Process of combined anaerobic treatment

The advantage of the GLOR approach is that the pre-treatment with thermal hydrolysis give an absolute guarantee of pathogen kill and increases the dewaterability and digestibility of the final AD product. It also allows the inclusion of sludge. Adding this process to an existing anaerobic digester as advantages in that the overall solids loading can be increased as the viscosity of the sludge/BMW is low and existing capacity can be roughly doubled. Solids in excess of 10% DS can be fed to the digester. The time for complete stabilisation using composting is reduced because of the very low putrescibility of the AD product, see Figure 4.

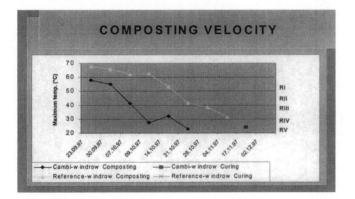

Figure 4 Temperature variation with time for different processing

This process will set the standard for new AD/composting projects. However it probably represents the smallest end of the capacity at which this type of technology is affordable – stated at about £35/tonne amortised. See cambi.com

NATURES BLEND, WARREN OHIO

In smaller projects it is difficult to see how BMW can be treated cost effectively unless considerable haulage is involved. In Scotland there has been a major investment in facilities to treat biosolids. There has been a rapid growth in the use of lime and other alkaline admixture to give a pasteurised product. See Figure 5. The two main technologies are lime only pasteurisation which use a high lime dose for exothermic heat and the RDP En-Vessel system which uses a lower lime dose combined with electrical heat to give pasteurisation. The latter technology can use other admixtures such as Pulverised Fuel Ash/ Quicklime blend (commonly used as cement replacement).

In the US there are about 50 RDP installations, many of them in quite small communities. Warren Ohio is a mid size facility designed for 20 dry tonnes of sludge per day at about 22% DS. The product is about 35% DS and because of the nature of the process is guaranteed class A product that in the UK meets HACCP requirements for demonstrating a pathogen free product. The product is further air dried and mixed with a variety of other materials to make products marketed as Natures Blend. These range from a soil blending material to a bagged potting soil that sells in branches of K Mart.

The potential in the UK is to use the product to accelerate green waste composting to make a pathogen free compost in windrows. This is probably as far as most small communities can go in integrating biosolids and waste.

For more information see rdptech.com

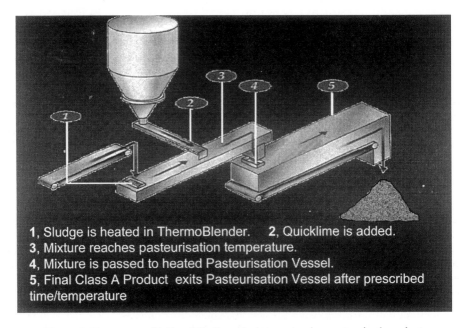

1, Sludge is heated in ThermoBlender.   2, Quicklime is added.
3, Mixture reaches pasteurisation temperature.
4, Mixture is passed to heated Pasteurisation Vessel.
5, Final Class A Product exits Pasteurisation Vessel after prescribed time/temperature

Figure 5   Treatment with lime/alkaline admixtures to give pasteurised product

COLGNA, ITALY

Cologna Italy is a 6 MW gasification plant based on MSW and other industrial wastes. There is potential to add a drier to this set up, in fact another project is being considered for such an arrangement in Italy. The idea is not new - Anglian Water has been carrying out trials with combining gasification and drying- what is new is a generation of low volume gasifiers that can operate in circumstances where conventional incineration cannot be installed economically. Generally a band dryer fits best as it can take low temperature air generated from low pressure steam. Such an arrangement is shown below: in Figure 6

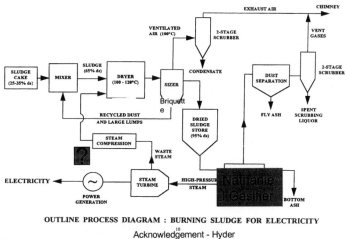

OUTLINE PROCESS DIAGRAM : BURNING SLUDGE FOR ELECTRICITY
Acknowledgement - Hyder [10]
Consulting

Figure 6 Updated steam loop idea

This type of arrangement may be useful in communities where it is difficult to collect BMW separately. In this case the gasifier can be used to generate energy from combined MSW and sludge instead of an incinerator. Even so it is unlikely to be cost effective in population centres much below 50,000.

CONCLUSIONS

There are a range of technologies that can be employed to meet the Landfill Directive targets. For larger projects these can be directed to BMW and be combined with biosolids. It is difficult to recycle BMW in small isolated communities, although gasification shows promise, albeit at a high cost and complexity. The alternative is long distance trucking to central facilities. There is considerable potential to use existing digestion capacity for treating BMW. Lime pasteurised products can be used to make good compost products with green waste.

There is going to be considerable competition for land. Only good quality pathogen free products are likely to be used in the long run.

PART TWO:

MAIN DISPOSAL ROUTES AND ENVIRONMENT IMPACT

RECENT DEVELOPMENTS IN THE ULTRASONIC PROCESSING OF SEWAGE SLUDGES FOR ENHANCED ANAEROBIC DIGESTION

P B Clark

WS Atkins

United Kingdom

ABSTRACT. 'Ultrasound' is the term used to describe sound energy at frequencies above 20kHz. This paper reviews the data collected to date from a 3 year ongoing research programme (funded by 7 water companies/agencies) to develop a large scale ultrasonic processor for the pre-treatment of sewage sludges prior to anaerobic digestion.

Results from a number of experiments are presented, including those undertaken at laboratory and pilot scales. The implications of sludge type on the performance of the sonication plant is discussed. Results indicate that the sonication of secondary and digested sludges can produce significant increases in gas production (ranging between 20 – 40%) with commensurate increases in solids destruction. Based on the results produced to date, a large-scale prototype ultrasonic processor is being constructed for installation and testing on a full-scale anaerobic digester in California.

Keywords: Ultrasonic processor, Pre-treatment of sewage sludge, Anaerobic digestion, Sonication plant.

P B Clark, is Head of Operations; Research and Technology Development for WS Atkins Water. He co-ordinates a team who undertake research projects across the whole water cycle: from potable through wastewater to solid waste management. He is the lead author of the Environment Agency's reference text on sludge treatment, recycling and disposal. He is also a Biowise Technical Advisor.

INTRODUCTION: ULTRASOUND AND SLUDGE TREATMENT

Sound energy above 20kHz (above the audible range to humans) is referred to as ultrasound. In recent years a number of ultrasonic devices have been developed for the water industry ranging from simple flow and level measurement apparatus to large-scale, high power applications for enhanced wastewater treatment.

Sludge processing applications in which the use of high power ultrasound has been considered include: sludge thickening/dewatering, disinfection, foam removal, degassing, improvement of filtration techniques and the enhancement of biological processes (such as anaerobic digestion).

Typically ultrasound is generated by a transducer (which converts mechanical or electrical energy into high frequency vibrations) and is delivered into a fluid by a horn or probe. In recent years there have been considerable advances in the design of ultrasonic horns. The research presented here has included the testing of a new patented horn design that provides a highly intense and focussed application of ultrasonic energy, overcoming the problems of energy dissipation and attenuation.

MATERIALS AND METHODS

A series of laboratory scale chemostats were operated over a 300 day period as Mesophilic Anaerobic Digesters (MADs). The chemostats were 10 litre glass vessels, stirred constantly at a rate of approximately 100 r.p.m., and maintained at 35 °C via a water bath. The biogas produced from the digesters was collected via the water displacement method. The digesters were fed once a day (six times per week) in accordance with their operating hydraulic retention time. Mean values calculated over the final full retention period of operation are quoted in this paper.

In addition to the chemostat experimentation two pilot scale anaerobic digesters were also operated, each with a working volume of 500lt. These digesters were continuously stirrer and maintained at 35 °C via an internal heating loop. Gas production was determined via rate measurements undertaken over the working day.

A 3kW ultrasonic processor was used to sonicated the sludges, operated as a continuous flow system. A variety of detailed experiments was undertaken to investigate the use of different sludge types and thicknesses, horn geometries, construction materials, sonication times and amplitude settings. Due to confidentiality restrictions the sonication plant and its mode of operation will not be discussed in detail here.

RESULTS AND DISCUSSION

Sonication of Feed Sludges

Three experimental runs have been completed (each run lasting approximately 3 HRTs) considering the effects of sonication on primary and secondary (SAS) sludges.

In the first experimental run, primary sludges alone were considered. A control sample (s0, unsonicated) was compared with 3 sonicated samples, each sonicated in a flow cell with slightly different sonication horn configurations. The pump speed in the sonication plant was 1 lt/ and the level of sonication for all samples was s1 (i.e. once past the ultrasound horn).

For these primary sludge experiments no statistically significant increase in gas rate or solids destruction (remaining between 40 – 45% in all samples) was noted. Similar results with primary sludges have been noted by other workers.[2,3] Primary sludges contain low levels of cellular material and high proportions of readily available /degradable organic matter and thus the beneficial effects of the ultrasonic cavitation activity are limited.

The second phase of experimentation with the chemostats considered the effect of sonication on SAS sludges alone (with two additional chemostats operated on a co settled sludge comprising 50% SAS and 50% primary).

Following sonication improvements in the gas production rate were noted (s0 = 2.37 lt/day versus s2 of 2.77lt/day for the SAS sludges, 1.35 for s0 vs 1.52 for s2 for the co-settled sludges). However, because of the difficulty in securing both a SAS and a primary sludge supply which had a consistent solids concentration the gas production tended to vary widely and thus the improvements in gas production are not statistically significant. In particular it should be noted that the gas production from the co-settled sludges were lower than those from the SAS sludges alone. This was due to their being only very thin primary sludges available on two occasions during the experiment run.

However, improvements in the solids destruction rates were noted following sonication in both the SAS and the co-settled sludges (see Table 1).

The third phase of experimentation with the chemostats investigated the effect of sonication on SAS sludges at levels of sonication ranging between s0 (unsonicated) to s12 (twelve passes by the horn). The sludge flow in all experiments was 1 lt/s.

Table 1 Solids Destruction for SAS sludges

REACTOR	CHEMOSTAT A CONTROL , SAS	CHEMOSTAT B S1, SAS	CHEMOSTAT C S2, SAS	CHEMOSTAT D S4, SAS	CHEMOSTAT E CONTROL, CO	CHEMOSTAT F S2, CO
% Solids Destruction ($\pm$ 95% CI)	36.7 (2.87)	47.9 (2.48)	42.7 (4.69)	47.5 (3.64)	56.4 3.72	61.0 (4.07)

Table 2 Gas Production Rates for SAS Sludges

REACTOR	CHEMOSTAT A CONTROL	CHEMOSTAT B S4	CHEMOSTAT C S8	CHEMOSTAT D S12
Gas Production Rate ($\pm$ 95% CI)	1.91 (0.12)	1.83 (0.11)	2.67 (0.24)	2.23 (0.29)

As noted in Table 2 the gas production was noted to increase for s8 and s12. This supports the theory that maximizing the total amount of sonication the sludge receives, be that by slowing the flow or increasing the number of passes by the horn) will maximize the beneficial effects.

With regards the solids destruction rates no statistically significant differences were noted. This was because the 95% confidence intervals tended to be 10 – 15% of the actual value. For example, s0 was 30.0% destruction $\pm$ 5% whereas s8 was 37.6% destruction $\pm$ 4%.

It should be noted that, in general, throughout all of the chemostat experimentation the biogas composition was slightly higher following sonication. The levels of improvement ranged between 1 – 2% methane and were often statistically insignificant at a 95% confidence interval. However, the general trend was one of slightly improved methane yields.

One of the main conclusions that can be drawn from the above chemostat work is that, whilst sonication of the feed sludges to a digester does offer improvements in digestibility, these levels of improvements are limited to particular sludge types. More importantly perhaps it is clear that the level of improvement is dependent upon the total sHRT that the sludge received. Whilst at small scale it is relatively simple to either construct a flow cell that has a slow flow (and thus a single pass by the horn has a long sHRT) or devise a re-circulation configuration (multiple passes by the horn with short individual sHRTs) this is not an appropriate design for larger scale systems. Other workers have also noted this problem[1-3]

Noting the above challenges, experiments have also been undertaken on digested (as opposed to feed) sludges. One of the main advantages of sonication digested sludges are that, if the sonication plant is installed on a digester re-circulation line, it is much easier to design a full scale system in which the sludge receive multiple passes of the sonication kit. This is because the typical turnover times in a recycle line (such as a heating loop) would be the digester contents once every 2 – 4 days.

The problem with undertaking sonication experiments on live digester systems is that, in order to overcome the difficulties of maintaining an anaerobic environment the experiments must be undertaken at a larger-than-chemostat scale. The following experiments were therefore been undertaken using two 500 litre pilot digesters.

Sonication of Digester Contents

Two pilot scale digesters have been operated over a 10 month period. Both digesters were operated identically, with design HRTs of 16 days (fed in batches on a bi-hourly basis). All sonication was undertaken on Digester 2. As indicated in Figure 1 there was some variability in the feed sludge characteristics but the digesters have remained stable as noted by the pH and methane composition data (Figures 2 and 3).

At the start of the experimental period there was a stabilization period in which no sonication was undertaken on either digester. The gas production from both digesters was statistically identical (Figure 4). The confidence intervals on this (and all subsequent figures) are 95%.

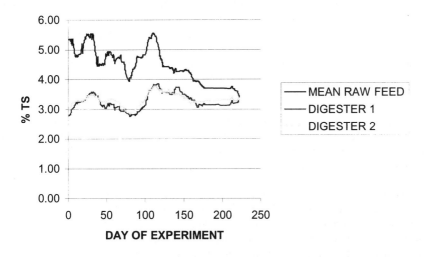

Figure 1 Feed and Exit Sludge Solids

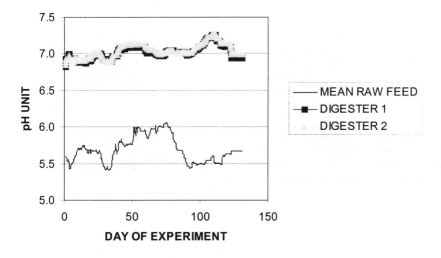

Figure 2 pH in Feed and Exit Sludge

Following the above stabilization period, sonication was undertaken on Digester 2. An aluminum horn was installed with an amplitude setting of 65% (power drawn of 1.65kW). The horn was operated for 3 x 15 minute periods throughout the working day. This equates to approximately the whole digester contents passing the horn once every day. This operational regime for the sonics was applied in all subsequent sonication experiments.

As can be seen from Figure 5 there was a significant increase in gas production of approximately 25% following sonication.

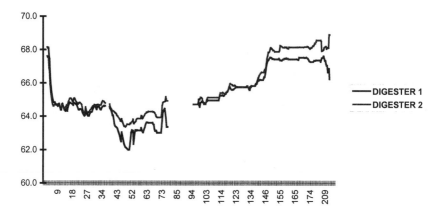

Figure 3 Methane Composition Data for Test and Control Digester

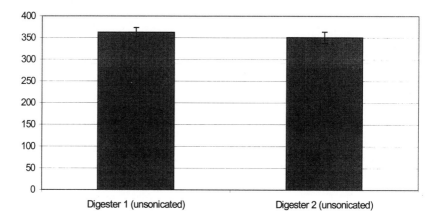

Figure 4 Mean Gas Production from Test and Control Digester during Stabilization Period

Following a period of sonication the horn on Digester 2 was switched off. As would be expected the gas production in Digester 2 dropped relative to the control i.e. the gas production became similar to the control. This is illustrated in Figure 6.

After a 2 week period of no-sonication the ultrasound plant was restarted (Al horn at 67% amplitude, 1.8kW power draw) and gas production was noted to rise again respective to the control (Figure 7). The level of improvement in gas production in digester 2 during this second period of sonics was over 40%.

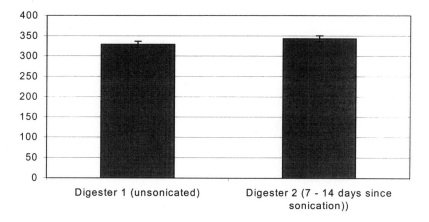

Figure 5 Mean Gas Production Increase Following Sonication 1

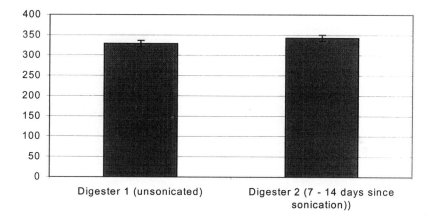

Figure 6 Mean Gas Production in the Test and Control Digester
2 weeks after Cessation of Sonics

After a second period of operation the sonics were again stopped. As noted before the gas production in the test digester (Digester 2) became similar to that of the control (Figure 8). Note that the error bars overlap indicating that, statistically, the performance of both digesters was identical.

A third and final period of sonics was undertaken with a titanium horn. The horn amplitude was set at 50% (1.7kW drawn). Unfortunately due to time constraints it was for this experimentation period to be extensive, lasting only a few days.

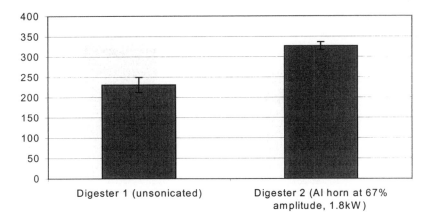

Figure 7 Mean Gas Production during Second Period of Sonication

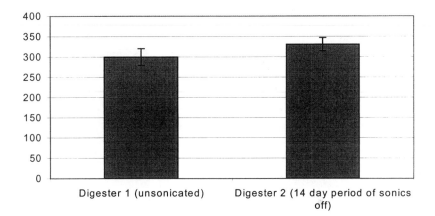

Figure 8 Mean Gas Production During 2 weeks of Non-Sonication Following
Second Sonication Period

However, as noted in Figure 9, the mean gas production increased significantly. The rise in gas production was approximately 25%.

From these results it can be concluded that, with sonication on a digester re-circulation line, improvements in gas production of between 20 – 40% can potentially be realized. It should be noted however that the sonications undertaken for the above experiments were not continuous but instead were achieved in three 15 minute sessions over the working day. The effect of this was to produce an increase in gas production profile that tended to exhibit variations over the working day that can be correlated to the time of sonication.

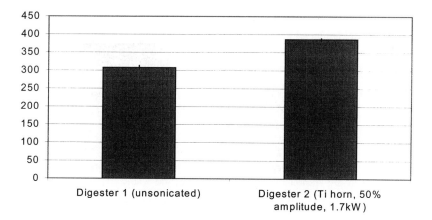

Figure 9 Mean Gas Production during Third Period of Sonication

In Figure 10 the daily gas production profile for a single day on which sonication was undertaken are presented. The times of sonication can be clearly identified (at around 9.30,am, 12 noon and between 2 – 3pm). Similar patterns in gas production were noted throughout the sonication period. This finding suggests that, with a more continuous sonication regime larger increases in gas production may be possible.

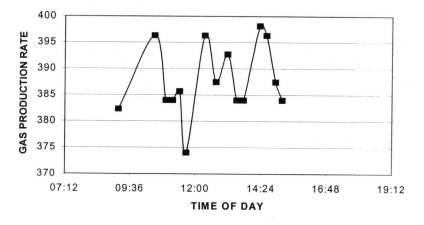

Figure 10 Variation in Gas Production Rate on the Sonicated Digester

CONCLUSIONS

From the work described it can be concluded that sonication of both the feed (secondary) and recycled sludges in an anaerobic sludge digester may produce significant increases in gas production and solids destruction. Increases in gas production of between 20- - 40% have been noted.

Based on the results produced to date a large scale prototype sonication facility is currently being constructed for installation on a full scale digester in Southern California. It is anticipated that the plant will be commissioned in April 2000.

ACKNOWLEDGEMENTS

This research is part of an on-going 3-year project financially supported by North West Water, Yorkshire Water, Severn Trent Water, Anglian Water, Thames Water, Wessex Water and Orange County Sanitation Department. The research team includes personnel from WS Atkins Water (who are responsible for co-ordinating the whole research programme), the National Physical Laboratory and FFR Ultrasonics. The author gratefully acknowledges the support of the above organizations.

REFERENCES

1. CHIU Y.C., CHANG C.N., LIN J.G., HUANG S.J., (1997) Alkaline and ultrasonic pre-treatment of sludge before anaerobic digestion. Water Science and Technology 1997 36 (11) pp 155 0 162

2. CLARK, P.B. AND NUJJOO, I. Ultrasonic sludge pre-treatment for enhanced sludge digestion. JCIWEM expected publication date January 2000

3. TIEHM A., NICKEL K., NEIS U. The use of ultrasound to accelerate the anaerobic digestion of sewage sludge. 1997 Water Science and Technology 36 (11) pp121 - 128

A LONG-TERM STUDY OF THE EFFECTS OF HEAVY METALS IN SEWAGE SLUDGE ON SOIL FERTILITY AND SOIL MICROBIAL ACTIVITY

J R Bacon   **C D Campbell**   **M C Coull**

Macaulay Land Use Research Institute

B J Chambers   **P A Gibbs**   **A Chaudri**   **S P McGrath**

ADAS Gleadthorpe Research Centre   The Institute of Arable Crops Research

C Carlton-Smith   **M Aitken**

WRc plc   Scottish Agricultural College

United Kingdom

ABSTRACT. The amendment of agricultural soils is generally considered to be the best practical environmental option for utilising the nutrient and organic matter content of sewage sludge, yet there is concern that heavy metals present could build up in the soil and have a long-term negative effect on soil fertility. In 1994 a long-term study was started at nine sites throughout Britain to evaluate the effects of heavy metals, added as a result of sludge application, on soil microbial activity and soil fertility. The sites were chosen to cover a range of soil properties, in particular pH and clay and organic matter contents, and different land uses (arable and grassland). Selected metal-rich sludge cakes were applied over a four year period (1994-97) to establish zinc (Zn), copper (Cu) and cadmium (Cd) metal dose-response curves in excess of current total soil limit values. The effects of Zn, Cu and Cd on soil microbial processes and soil chemical properties are being examined, with particular reference to nitrogen-fixing rhizobia, soil microbial respiration and biomass carbon, and soil extractable metal concentrations.

Ammonium nitrate extractable soil metal concentrations on the individual metal-rich sludge treatments were up to 53 mg Zn kg^{-1}, 3.8 mg Cu kg^{-1} and 0.18 mg Cd kg^{-1}, respectively, at the end of the four year sludge application cycle. Soil microbial biomass carbon contents and respiration rates increased on most of the sludge treatments compared with the untreated control. *Rhizobia* presence was confirmed at all sites after the four years of sludge cake application. *Rhizobium* most probable number (MPN) counts showed no treatment differences at seven of the nine sites, although at two of the sites they were lower (P <0.05) on the elevated Zn treatments than on the untreated control.

Keywords: Sewage sludge, Soil fertility, Heavy metals, Soil microbiology

Dr J Bacon, leads the chemical project area, **Dr C Campbell** leads the biochemical project area and **Mr M Coull** works within the Soil Quality and Protection Programme, at MLURI.

Dr B Chambers, is a Principal Research Scientist and **Dr P Gibbs,** is a Research Scientist at the ADAS Gleadthorpe Research Centre.

Dr A Chaudri, is a Postdoctoral Scientist and **Professor S McGrath,** is Programme Leader in the Soil Protection and Remediation Programme at Rothamsted.

Dr C Carlton-Smith is a senior research scientist at WRc Medmenham with responsibility within the project for the acquisition and distribution of sewage sludges and for data handling.

Dr M Aitken is a Senior Consultant (Soil and Waste Management) at SAC where he has worked for 8 years as a consultant and researcher. His main research interest is agricultural pollution prevention from organic manures and fertilizers.

INTRODUCTION

In 1996/7 the total UK sewage sludge production was approximately 1.1×10^6 tonnes dry solids per year (tds/yr) and was expected to rise to 1.5×10^6 tds/yr by 2006 [1]. Recycling of sludge to agricultural land is generally considered the best practical environmental option (BPEO) for utilising the nitrogen, phosphorus and organic matter present in sludges and is predicted to remain the principal outlet for sewage sludge. However, the heavy metal content of sludges is generally higher than that of soil so that the application of sludges to agricultural land may result in an accumulation of heavy metals in the topsoil. For this reason, legislation, based on the best scientific evidence available, is required to protect soils from excessive accumulation of heavy metals.

The long term effects of heavy metal accumulations on soil fertility are not well understood, although a number of studies have indicated changes in the soil microbial population and effectiveness. McGrath *et al.* [2] reviewed the evidence for impacts of metals on soil microbial activity and soil fertility, and found that adverse effects could occur at surprisingly modest concentrations of metals in soil. Giller *et al.* [3] considered the effect of gradually increasing soil metal concentrations on microorganisms and discussed the definition of "safe" or "critical" soil metal loadings in the context of soil protection. The extractability and bioavailability of Cd and Zn were found not only to be higher in a soil amended over about 20 years with sewage sludge than in soils amended with farmyard manure or fertiliser, but also not to decrease for at least 23 years after the last addition of sludge [4]. It follows that the prevention of adverse effects on soil microbial processes and, ultimately, soil fertility should be a factor which influences soil protection legislation.

The permitted metal concentrations in soils to be amended with sewage sludge, as laid down in a European Directive [5], have been implemented in England, Scotland and Wales by The Sludge (Use in Agriculture) Regulations [6,7]. A Code of Practice for Agricultural Use of Sewage Sludge contains additional advice on soil limits for metals not subject to the legislation, as well as guidance on sludge treatment and application practices. The second edition of the Code of Practice [8] introduced reduced limits for Cd and Zn as a result of recommendations made by the Independent Scientific Committee Reviewing the Soil Fertility Aspects of Sludge Applications to Agricultural Land [9].

The development of policies on soil protection requires a sound scientific base. There is a recognised need to improve the robustness of scientific information for setting soil metal limits to ensure that the nation's soils are not subject to long-term irreversible degradation. As part of the on-going review of the effects of heavy metals on soil fertility, a long-term study on the effects of sewage sludge applications on soil microbial activity was started in 1994. The project is being undertaken by ADAS, The Institute of Arable Crops Research (IACR-Rothamsted) and WRc in England and Wales, and by the Macaulay Land Use Research Institute (MLURI) and SAC Auchincruive in Scotland.

The main objectives of the study have been:-

- To establish dose-response curves for Cd, Cu and Zn on a range of soil types through the selection and addition of suitable metal-rich sludges or sludges spiked with metal salts.
- To examine the effect of Cd, Cu and Zn, added in the metal-rich sludges, on soil microbial processes, in particular soil organic matter turnover, nitrogen fixation by rhizobia, soil microbial respiration and microbial biomass turnover.

- To examine the effect of Cd, Cu and Zn, added in the metal-rich sludges, on selected soil chemical properties and the speciation of these metals in soil solution.

- To evaluate the results in terms of the different soil chemical and physical properties at the nine sites.

This paper describes the experimental design of the study and results obtained in Phase I of the project (1994-1998), the principle objective of which was to set up the dose-response curves at the sites. It should be stressed that this is an on-going project and that the intention is to monitor long-term effects resulting from the sludge applications. In the current Phase II (1998-2002), soil microbial and chemical parameters are being monitored to assess the effect of the heavy metal additions on soil fertility. Metals have been introduced into the soil through application of either sludge cake containing high levels of a particular heavy metal (Cd, Cu or Zn) or liquid sludges which had been equilibrated with metal salts. The use of liquid sludges could be regarded as a worst case scenario in that the metals were likely to be in a more available chemical form than in the sludge cake experiments. In both cases the sludges were incorporated into the soil by cultivation. The first method was used at all nine sites, whereas the second was only used at three sites, none of which were in Scotland. This paper describes only the sludge cake experiments, with particular reference to the Hartwood site.

EXPERIMENTAL DETAILS

Sites

Nine sites were selected to represent a range of soil physical and chemical properties, in particular clay and organic matter contents of the topsoil (Table 1 and Figure 1).

Table 1 Clay and organic carbon contents of the selected sites

SITE	LOCATION	% CLAY CONTENT	% ORGANIC CARBON
Gleadthorpe	Nottinghamshire	7	1.2
Woburn	Bedfordshire	8	1.3
Watlington	Oxfordshire	16	1.3
Pwllpeiran	Dyfed	23	3.3
Rosemaund	Herefordshire	25	1.7
Bridgets	Hampshire	30	1.5
Hartwood	North Lanarkshire	21	4.7
Auchincruive	Ayrshire	20	2.6
Shirburn	Oxfordshire	20	3.0

Sewage Sludges

Metal-rich sludge cakes were specifically selected to contain target concentrations of individual metals yet relatively low levels of other heavy metals (Table 2). The intention was to increase soil concentrations of single metals and thereby associate any observed effects with those individual metals. This was achieved very effectively, for the cadmium and copper sludges.

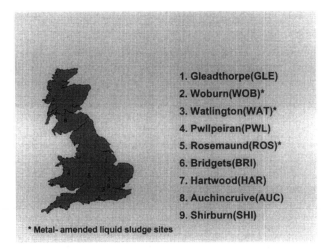

1. Gleadthorpe(GLE)
2. Woburn(WOB)*
3. Watlington(WAT)*
4. Pwllpeiran(PWL)
5. Rosemaund(ROS)*
6. Bridgets(BRI)
7. Hartwood(HAR)
8. Auchincruive(AUC)
9. Shirburn(SHI)

* Metal- amended liquid sludge sites

Figure 1 Location of sites

The zinc sludge, however, contained above background levels of the other two metals as well as a high zinc concentration. As it was necessary to use both digested and undigested metal-rich sludges to achieve the target concentrations, both digested and undigested 'control' sludges with low metal concentrations were also selected. The undigested control is used for comparison with the undigested copper sludge treatments.

Table 2 Metal concentrations in the selected sludge cakes

SLUDGE	TYPE	ORIGIN	TARGET, mg/kg	ACTUAL CONCENTRATIONS, mg/kg dry solids		
				Cd	Cu	Zn
cadmium	digested	Perry Oaks	30 (Cd)	**44**	550	1100
copper	undigested	Selkirk	3500 (Cu)	0.7	**5050**	550
zinc	digested	Coleshill	5000 (Zn)	11	1400	**6000**
control	digested	Banbury		1.8	600	550
control	undigested	Carterton		1.7	450	500

The concentrations were a typical of those found in sludges applied to agricultural land.

Experimental Design

Common protocols were followed at each site in order to limit variables to only inter-site differences. Twenty treatments were replicated in three fully randomised blocks of 23 plots (8 x 6 m), each with permanent grass strips (minimum width 1 m) between each plot in order to prevent soil movement during cultivation. Sludges were applied in four annual applications so that the target metal concentrations would be achieved at the end of the four-year period.

For each of the metals, there were four treatments with target soil metal concentrations (Table 3) chosen to establish metal dose-response curves of concentrations up to and in excess of current total soil limit values [5]. Appropriate amounts of the control sludges were also applied to the plots in order to equalise the amount of added organic matter added. In addition to the metal treatment plots, there were control plots receiving either no sludge at all or only the control sludges.

The annual application rates required to achieve the target concentrations within four years were above the maximum rates permissible under the legislation. Therefore, another set of plots is receiving the metal rich sludges at only the maximum permissible annual application rate of 0.15, 7.5 and 15 kg/ha for Cd, Cu and Zn, respectively. These will reach the soil limit values after some time and will be used later for comparative purposes.

Table 3 Target soil total metal concentrations (mg/kg in air dry soil)

TREATMENT	ZINC	COPPER	CADMIUM
Background	60	15	0.3
Rate 1	150 (200[I])	50	1.0 (1.5[II])
Rate 2	250	100	2.0
Rate 3	350	150	3.0
Rate 4	450	200	4.0
Current UK legal limits[III]	200-300	80-135	3.0

[I]   Pwllpeiran (taking into account the background concentration 140 mg/kg)
[II] Bridgets (taking into account the background concentration 0.95 mg/kg)
[III] dependent on pH in the range 5.0-7.0

After each application of sludge, the plots were cultivated (spaded and rotavated) to a depth of 20-25 cm using mechanised small plot equipment. The plots were subsequently re-seeded with Italian ryegrass and managed according to good practice. Soil pH at the English and Welsh sites was maintained at 6.5. At the Scottish sites of Auchincruive and Hartwood, pH was maintained at 6.0 and 5.8, respectively, which represent the values recommended for the l and uses of the individual sites.

Soil Sampling and Analysis

Soil samples were taken from all the plots both before the application of sludge in 1994 and following the final application of sludge in 1997. In addition, samples were taken from the rate 3 treatments and all controls after each annual addition of sludge. Samples were taken to a depth of 20 cm using soil corers, a minimum of 20 cores taken from random locations being bulked to form a composite sample for each plot. Particular attention was paid to cleaning and sterilising the sampling equipment between the sampling of individual plots. Samples for microbial analyses were maintained in field moist condition, whereas those for physical and chemical analysis were air dried at 30 °C prior to storage.

Selected physical, chemical and microbial properties were measured in the soil samples.
• Physical properties: Dry bulk density [10] and particle size distribution [11].

- Chemical properties: Soil pH; conductivity; cation exchange capacity; organic carbon; mineral nitrogen; total nitrogen; extractable P, K and Mg; total iron, aluminium and manganese oxides were determined by standard methods [11]. Total concentrations of Cd, Cr, Cu, Ni, Pb and Zn were determined following aqua regia extraction [12]. A measure of the labile concentrations of Cd, Cu and Zn was given by the determination of ammonium nitrate extractable concentrations [13].
- Microbial properties: Soil microbial biomass carbon [14], *Rhizobium* most probable number (MPN) [15] and soil microbial respiration [16].

The concentration of elements in the aqua regia and ammonium nitrate extracts was determined in the participant's laboratories either by Inductively Coupled Plasma Atomic Emission Spectrometry (ICP-AES) or Electrothermal Atomic Absorption Spectrometry (ETAAS) depending on the element and concentrations. At MLURI, where the Hartwood samples were analysed, ETAAS was used to determine Cd and Cu in ammonium nitrate extracts and Cd and Pb in aqua regia extracts.

Quality Control

As each of the participating laboratories carried out their own analysis, it was necessary to have strict quality control procedures in place so that data were comparable. Each year a proficiency testing exercise was performed by distributing a set of samples for analysis together with the collected samples. The distributed samples were extra samples taken from some of the sites and the analysis of these samples had the additional benefit of confirming the results found for each of the sites.

METAL DOSE-RESPONSE CURVES

The soil total metal dose-response curves were established at the nine sites, although at three of the sites the full range of metal values was not achieved for all the metal-rich sludge cakes. The metal dose response curves for the plots at Hartwood are shown in Figures 2-4 for Cd, Cu and Zn, respectively. For all three metals the dose response curves cover the range from background to beyond the current soil concentration limit.

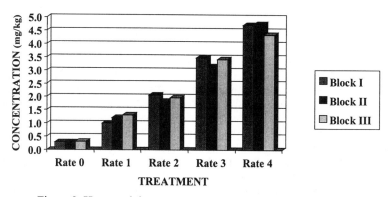

Figure 2 Hartwood dose-response curve for cadmium

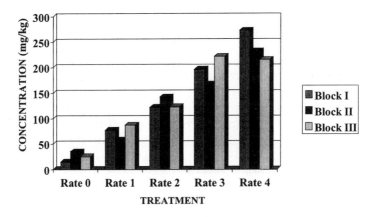

Figure 3 Hartwood dose-response curve for copper

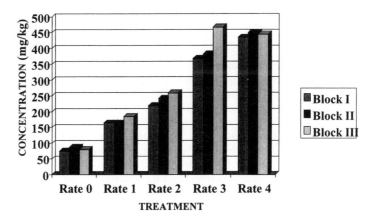

Figure 4 Hartwood dose-response curve for zinc

AMMONIUM NITRATE EXTRACTABLE METAL CONCENTRATIONS

At the end of the four year sludge application period, the ammonium nitrate extractable concentrations on the metal-rich treatments ranged between 0.03 and 0.18, 1 and 4 and <1 and 53 mg/kg for Cd, Cu and Zn, respectively. The highest levels were found at the Hartwood site (Figure 5) where the percentage of the total metal content that was extractable with ammonium nitrate was considerably higher for all the metals than at the other sites. The percentage of extractable copper in the treated plots at Hartwood was twice that of the controls, although there appeared to be little increase with higher total concentrations. The percentage of extractable zinc, on the other hand, increased with higher total concentrations.

The percentage of extractable cadmium varied across the sites and showed no discernible trends. This could be partly attributable to the analytical difficulty of determining the low concentrations of extractable cadmium.

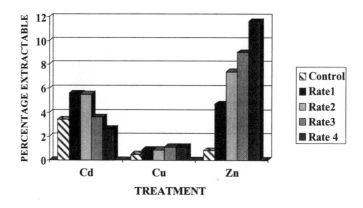

Figure 5 Percentage of total metal concentration extractable
with ammonium nitrate at Hartwood

MICROBIAL PARAMETERS

At all the sites, soil microbial biomass carbon contents were unchanged or increased on treatments that had received sludge cakes compared with the untreated control. At Hartwood, only small increases were measured (Table 4). No significant (p>0.05) increase in soil respiration was observed at Hartwood except for the plots that received copper sludge (Table 4). At the other sites, some increases in soil respiration were observed on some treatments but no overall consistent trends could be identified. *Rhizobia* presence was confirmed at all sites after the four years of sludge cake application. *Rhizobium* most probable number (MPN) counts showed no treatment differences at seven of the nine sites, but at Watlington (4x 10^3 and 45 x 10^3 cells/g soil, respectively) and Rosemaund (7x 10^3 and 35 x 10^3 cells/g soil, respectively)

Table 4 Soil respiration (mg CO_2 C/kg soil) and soil microbial
biomass carbon (mg C/kg soil) at Hartwood

TREATMENT	SOIL RESPIRATION		SOIL MICROBIAL BIOMASS CARBON	
	before sludge application	after sludge application	before sludge application	after sludge application
no sludge	1.43±0.14	1.00±0.16	710±36	642±56
digested control	2.17±0.10	1.48±0.04	730±63	775±49
undigested control	3.38±0.22	3.46±0.36	763±122	1153±135
cadmium rate 3	1.93±0.04	1.68±0.32	705±71	763±14
copper rate 3	2.50±0.25	5.10±0.94	767±52	1094±98
zinc rate 3	2.29±0.21	2.55±0.13	763±67	813±88

CONCLUDING COMMENTS

Experimental field sites have been successfully set up at nine locations in Great Britain to study the effects of sewage sludge applications on soil fertility. At each site, plots with a range of metal loadings up to and beyond current limits have been established. In this way it should be possible to identify the threshold concentrations for the onset of a measurable response. The setting up of this long-term experiment represents the first part of the study. The collection and assessment of chemical and microbial data are currently under way in Phase II of the experiment, and will provide a useful scientific information for the continued development of policies on soil protection when sludges are applied to agricultural land. Such policies will ensure that the recycling of sludge to land does not cause harmful effects on the environment in general and on soil quality in particular.

ACKNOWLEDGEMENTS

This work is jointly funded by the Ministry of Agriculture, Fisheries and Food (MAFF), the Department of the Environment, Transport and the Regions (DETR), the Scottish Executive, Rural Affairs Department (SERAD), the National Assembly for Wales Environment Division (NAWED), the Environment Agency (EA) and UK Water Industry Research Limited (UKWIR).

REFERENCES

1. GENDEBIEN, A., CARLTON-SMITH, C., IZZO, M., AND HALL, J.E. UK Sludge Survey - National Presentation, Environment Agency Final Technical Report, 1998, p165.

2. MCGRATH, S.P., CHAUDRI, A.M., AND GILLER, K.E. Long-term effects of metals in sewage-sludge on soils, microorganisms and plants. Journal of Industrial Microbiology, 1995, 14(2), 94-104.

3. GILLER, K.E., WITTER, E., AND MCGRATH, S.P. Toxicity of heavy metals to microorganisms and microbial processes in agricultural soils: A review. Soil Biology & Biochemistry,1998, 30(10-11), 1389-1414.

4. MCGRATH, S.P., ZHAO, F.J., DUNHAM, S.J., CROSLAND, A.R., AND COLEMAN, K. Long-term changes in the extractability and bioavailability of zinc and cadmium after sludge application. Journal of Environmental Quality, 2000, 29(3), 875-883.

5. COMMISSION OF THE EUROPEAN COMMUNITIES. Council Directive 12 June 1986 on the protection of the environment, and in particular the soil, when sewage sludge is used in agriculture. Official Journal of the European Communities, No L.181 (86/278/EEC), Commission of the European Communities, Strasbourg, 1986, pp 6-12.

6. STATUTORY INSTRUMENT. The Sludge (Use in Agriculture) Regulations, United Kingdom Statutory Instrument No 1263, HMSO, London, 1989.

7. STATUTORY INSTRUMENT. The Sludge (Use in Agriculture) (Amendment) Regulations, United Kingdom Statutory Instrument No 880, HMSO, London, 1990

8.   DEPARTMENT OF THE ENVIRONMENT. Code of Practice for the Agricultural Use of Sewage Sludge, Second Edition. HMSO, London, 1996.

9.   MINISTRY OF AGRICULTURE, FISHERIES AND FOOD AND DEPARTMENT OF THE ENVIRONMENT. Review of the rules for sludge application to agricultural land : Soil fertility aspects of potentially toxic elements: Report of the Independent Scientific Committee. MAFF/DOE, London, 1993.

10. MINISTRY OF AGRICULTURE, FISHERIES AND FOOD. Techniques for Measuring Soil Physical Properties. Reference Book 441 (Second Edition), HMSO, London, 1982.

11. MINISTRY OF AGRICULTURE, FISHERIES AND FOOD. Analysis of Agricultural Materials. Reference Book 427 (Third Edition), HMSO, London, 1986.

12. MCGRATH, S.P., AND CUNLIFFE, C.H. A simplified method for the extraction of the metals Fe, Zn, Cu, Ni, Cd, Pb, Cr, Co and Mn from soils and sewage sludges. Journal of the Science of Food and Agriculture, 1985, 36(9), 794-798.

13. DEUTSCHES INSTITUT FÜR NORMUNG. Extraction von Spurenelementen mit Ammoniumnitratlösung. Deutsche Norm DIN 19730, DIN, Berlin, 1997.

14. VANCE, E.D., BROOKES, P.C., AND JENKINSON, D.S. An extraction method for measuring soil microbial biomass-C. Soil Biology & Biochemistry, 1987, 19(6), 703-707.

15. VINCENT, J.M. A Manual for the Practical Study of Root-Nodules Bacteria. IBP Handbook No. 15. Blackwell, Oxford, 1970.

16. SMITH, S.R., AND HADLEY, P. Carbon and nitrogen mineralization characteristics of organic nitrogen fertilizers in a soil-less incubation system. Fertilizer Research, 1990, 23(2), 97-103.

SLUDGE AND HEAVY METALS: THE CONSUMER'S PERCEPTION

A Stenger
INRA

A Rozan   F Spitzenstetter
Universite Louis Pasteur (ULP)
France

ABSTRACT. The objective of the paper is to estimate consumer behaviour when informed of sewage sludge spreading. To use sewage sludge as a valuable resource in agriculture, policy makers are sometimes confronted by farmer opposition for reasons of potential consumer rejection of sewage sludge spreading. Consumer behaviour was therefore studied in a collaborative investigation between economists and psychologists with main objective to estimate consumer willingness to pay in the case of hypothetical control of heavy metals in agricultural food and to understand the underlying reasons for the response. In this way, an understanding of the consumer's implicit perception of sewage sludge in agriculture: (normally introduced as a source of heavy metals as well as pesticides) can be gained.

Keywords: Consumer, Sludge context, Risk perception, Qualitative interview, Verbal protocol, France.

Dr A Rozan, is Assistant Professor in the Faculty of Economics Science, University Louis Pasteur, in Strasbourg, France. She carries out her research at the B.E.T.A. (Bureau d'Economie théorique et Appliquée). She completed her PhD thesis in 1999 on health cost valuation due to air pollution. Her research interests are principally in the environmental economics fields and particularly on health valuation. The principal tools used are the contingent valuation method, econometrics, and benefit transfer method.

Dr F Spitzenstetter, is a teacher of social psychology at the faculty of psychology, University Louis Pasteur of Strasbourg. Her research interests, in the Social Psychology Research Group are risk perception and risk taking, especially in health related problems and the origin of optimistic bias. She has also worked on the impact of on risky decision-making using the experimental method.

Dr A Stenger, is a Researcher in the environmental economics fields at INRA, in the department of Rural Economics and Sociology, at Nancy. She has particularly worked on natural assets evaluation (groundwater quality, agricultural landscapes...) specific areas include externalities management, non market values, food security and waste recycling, with Technical issues of econometrics, statistics, contingent valuation, experimental economics considered. She has studied forest and agricultural economics since 1999.

INTRODUCTION

The purpose of this study is to define the theoretical means by which a consumer would perceive sludge through their consumption of food products. It is applied on a food safety valuation relative to heavy metals linked to some agricultural practices like sewage sludge disposal. One of the issues is how information about this practice can modify consumer behaviour in valuing food products. In our experiments, sludge was considered first alone, then in a group of heavy metal content inputs in agriculture. Risk perception, which is relevant, both for economists and psychologists is treated according to a joint collaboration between these two disciplines.

Recycling urban waste and especially sewage sludge on agricultural soils achieves at least two essential functions: it is a mode of production that improves fertilisation and that gives the farmer a new image as an agent in the elimination of urban waste. However, the recycling of urban waste on agricultural soils is regulated since it is necessary to preserve the quality of the soils and ensure the safety of farm products. Among urban forms of waste, sewage sludge constitutes a serious problem for everyone involved in the disposal system, from the producers of sludge to the consumers of agricultural products. This concern relates to the qualitative and quantitative aspects of sludge. If the present trend continues, more than 60% of the sludge will be recycled on agricultural soils in France in the future. At the same time, the quantity of sludge will increase since all landfills in France are to be closed by the year 2002. Sludge composition is also a matter of concern. Though sludge can serve as a fertiliser, it also generally contains various micro pollutants, including heavy metals, which tend to accumulate irreversibly in soils. This could modify the consumer's perceived safety concerning the agricultural products grown on these soils. In fact, the consequences of the agricultural use of sewage sludge on food contamination and health are not totally known. There still are many uncertainties and unknown elements.

The first part of this study focuses on the practical problems raised by increasing quantities of sludge in France, principally sludge management and public reactions. The second part presents some theoretical aspects implied by sewage sludge disposal in agriculture: the theoretical risk for health due to heavy metals in sludge and the theoretical risk perception in economics and in psychology. The third and last part introduces some methodological points to understand consumer's behaviour. The objective of this part is to give the tools of the two disciplines to understand the consumer's behaviour. This last section presents some results based on experimental results, qualitative interviews and verbal protocols that are the first step of a future contingent valuation. Sludge was explicitly taken into account in our first experiments but has been included in a group of heavy metals pollutants in agriculture afterwards. This revision is linked to the fact that the relationship between heavy metals in sludge and the potential effects on morbidity are not so easy to quantify. This sludge integration was based as well on our first results obtained by experimental economics and qualitative interviews.

SEWAGE SLUDGE IN FRENCH AGRICULTURE: SOME PRACTICAL ASPECTS

Sludge Management

Urban wastes come from households' activities as well as from some industrial activities. They consist of household wastes (20 MT), sewage sludge (0.9 MT), green wastes (gardens and green spaces, 4.9 MT), medical care wastes (0.7 MT), toxic household wastes, bulky wastes (electric and electronic equipment, 3 MT) and banal industrial wastes (5 MT). These urban wastes are recycled, incinerated or disposed of in landfills. Incineration and recycling generate new activities and new soil occupations. Another one, recycling in compost represents an activity which combines these, in general on agricultural soils. Except green wastes, the most important part of urban wastes recycled in agriculture is due to sewage sludge.

Agriculture contributes to the elimination of agricultural waste, essentially animal farming effluents (265 MT of animal waste/year in France), but also to non-agricultural waste of urban and agro-industrial origin. Agro-industrial waste is mainly sludge: the agribusiness produces 45 million tonnes of sludge each year, 9% of which is recycled in agriculture. Land disposal of non-agricultural waste, specifically sewage sludge, might cause harm to the environment and to public health. Unlike agro-industrial sludge that is essentially composed of organic matter, sewage sludge does not have a uniform composition, which introduces the problem of monitoring micropollutants in soils (heavy metals, organic and pathogenic pollutants). Approximately, 60% of total sludge production in France is used for land disposal, 15% is incinerated and 25% is placed in landfills. The agricultural use of sewage sludge in France will be a critical consideration in the future owing to two legal requirements. The first stipulates that after the year 2002 no waste can be disposed of in landfills (law of 13 July 1992), and the second that towns with more than 2,000 inhabitants must set up a sewage collection and processing system before the year 2006 (European directive 91/271). The resulting development of sewage plants will oblige public decision-makers to choose a distribution between agricultural uses and incineration for the increasing quantities of sludge. The situation is critical since sewage sludge increased by 55% between 1986 and 1996, is estimated today at 900,000 tons, and is predicted to reach 1.2 or 1.3 million tons by 2005 in France. These predictions take into account the expected qualitative and quantitative improvements in sewage processing.

Quantitative improvement is measured by the rate of connection to the sewage system. Only about 9% of the French population are still not connected [1]. Qualitative improvement of the treatment process is measured by the depollution rate, i.e. the portion of eliminated pollution in gross pollution. The objective of the National Plan for the Environment is to achieve a depollution rate of at least 65% by the year 2000. Consequently, an increased rate of depollution means improved performance of the processing system but also the creation of more polluted sludge.

Some Reactions

The agricultural use of sewage sludge appears to be an increasingly controversial solution for farmers and consumers alike since local complaints and decrees against land disposal of sludge tend to be more numerous. Those who oppose this technique cite risks for human health and nuisances such as foul odours for inhabitants living near farmland on which sludge has been spread. The "NIMBY" (not in my backyard) syndrome, which developed during the setting up of nuclear plants or facilities for the processing of industrial waste, seems to have extended to the domain of sludge disposal.

Farmers would therefore need to find a long-term advantage in this practice and at the same time satisfy consumer demands for quality and food safety. Thus, the problems of long-term soil fertility and protection of the food chain are raised simultaneously. Though the solution of land disposal of waste is more economic for society, there is certainly a plant toxicity threshold beyond which sludge disposal can lead to a more or less immediate increase in costs for society and the farmer. Thus, even if urban waste recycling has some benefits for fertilisation, it is more and more difficult to convince farmers to spread sludge, even though the operation is free of charge for them. Sludge spreading has certain limitations since it cannot be performed for all cultures or year-round. The disadvantages could even be greater for sales of the farmers' products because of the presence of heavy metals. Some manufacturers now refuse to can products, which have been cultivated with sludge. The farmer has to compare the advantages and disadvantages of sludge spreading relative to other fertilisers. A farmer's reluctance to use sludge can also be explained by an anticipation of the consumer's attitude in showing increasing concern about qualitative food safety.

Obviously, the consumer can only express a need for food safety if he is informed of all the potential risks involved. However, risk quantification due to the presence of heavy metals in plants is complex for at least three reasons. First, the influence of heavy metals in soils and cultures and their possible effects on humans are not totally known. Secondly, humans take in heavy metals from different origins (e.g. other food products or the atmosphere), so that the risk cannot be attributed only to sludge. Finally, apart from the heavy metals naturally present in the earth, agricultural soils concentrate other sources from household garbage, animal waste, crop residues, industrial waste, and organic or chemical fertilisers. Thus, a request for analysis of a product cultivated with sludge, with respect to food safety, has to be made in a complex informational context that needs to be known specifically.

Health risks are indirect, resulting from the consumption of agricultural products, animals raised on these soils, or polluted water. These risks have been reduced by regulations concerning maximum levels of heavy metals and organic matter and by assessment of the quality of sludge and its disposal. Trace elements or heavy metals should not exceed limit levels, as determined in France by AFNOR U 44.041 standards[1]. A recent decree (8 January 1998) has in fact reduced these limit levels by 50%. These standards have been set for heavy metals both in sludge and soils. The decree considers that the composition of sludge qualifies it as "waste" and not "fertilising material". Though its benefits as a fertiliser are still recognised, the need to reduce its nuisance value and health risks is stressed through the establishment of stricter standards and user practices. Yet, in spite of these regulations, the consumer may be sceptical about the reliability of standards, which are frequently revised. He may be uncertain about the degree of food contamination due to heavy metals as well as the degree of food toxicity involved.

Even though sludge is responsible for 70% to 90% of the heavy metals in sewage, it is not the only source. Soils naturally contain trace elements, depending on their nature. Heavy metals in soils also come from atmospheric inputs from industrial and urban activities as well as from other fertilisers (than sludge) and pesticides. Food contamination by heavy metals depends both on their mobility in the soil and on their bioavailability. The mobility and bioavailability of heavy metals depend on various factors related to soil (pH, temperature, etc.) or plant characteristics. Although these factors are generally easy to measure, determination of the risk of food pollution is limited by a lack of knowledge concerning the

---

[1] AFNOR, Association française de normalisation

processes for reducing the transfer of heavy metals to plants and thus by a lack of data and measurements of bioavalability [2].

SEWAGE SLUDGE IN AGRICULTURE: SOME THEORETICAL ASPECTS

Land Disposal of Sludge: What are the Theoretical Risks for Humans?

The increasing demand of consumers for food quality and safety is subsequent to events in which health issues have been associated with the consumption of agricultural products. The use of pesticides, nitrates, hormones and drugs and the introduction of genetically modified plants have been denounced as potentially injurious to human health. The interest in food safety is apparent in the consumer demand for organic (natural) products not treated with chemicals (these products now represent 10% of food expenditures in Northern Europe, but only 0.3% in France).

Sludge contains heavy metals that would not otherwise invade agricultural soils and that may cause soil pollution and eventual effects on human health via the food chain. This contamination is practically irreversible since it is impossible to eliminate the heavy metal surplus in soils. Moreover, heavy metals are not the only contaminants in sludge, which contains other bioaccumulative toxic substances (e.g. dioxin and furan) and pathogenic microorganisms. However, the risk is related more to heavy metals which, unlike the other toxic substances, accumulate in the edible parts of plants [3].

If only the heavy metals are taken into account, their ingestion via food can induce long-term effects through their bioaccumulation in certain organs. The consequences are not to be measured in terms of mortality but of morbidity, which means that life expectancy would be shorter. The toxicity of metals results from their accumulation, which occurs progressively. This problem concerns the entire population through the consumption of vegetables, beverages and meat. Animal production would be affected mainly through the use of contaminated pastureland and the feeding of fodder.

The determination of sludge-related food risk requires an understanding of how heavy metals can contaminate humans via the food chain. However, the risk of contamination from foods is not always easy to estimate because of a lack of knowledge of the bioavailability process. The risk depends on the mobility and bioavailability of a given heavy metal and on the nature of the soils and plants involved. Some metals are more or less mobile in soils and may or may not reach the upper parts of the plant. Moreover, it is impossible to establish a "dose-response" function because of a lack of experiments on humans. Animal experiments provide estimations of the carcinogenic effects of some heavy metals (e.g. cadmium, beryllium or lead), but epidemiological studies cannot confirm these hypotheses, except in the case of certain metals such as nickel for which "dose-response" functions have been found in the industrial sector [4] [2]. Moreover, some metallic micropollutants (e.g. iron or copper) are in fact essential to life and only become toxic for humans beyond a certain point. Finally, humans are also exposed to the effects of heavy metals through the consumption of meat and fish and the drinking of water as well as the ingestion and inhalation of dusts. For example,

---

[2] or in the case where some high contaminations occured in some populations (i.e., cadmium and mercury in Japan, satunirsm and lead on young children...).

mercury and its derivatives present in industrial areas produce atmospheric fallout. This is true as well for lead in the atmosphere, which also enters the organism by the respiratory tract. The food risk with sludge is relative to that of absorbing heavy metals through other food products or the respiratory tract. Finally, the risk is certainly different for consumers depending on their age, weight, height, etc. However, it is noteworthy that the dangers of certain trace elements for human health have been identified by investigations concerning the main sources of contamination. Thus, nearly half of the mean ingestion of lead, cadmium and mercury in foods is due to trace elements of plant origin (fruits, vegetables and cereals). Moreover, some population groups seem to be more exposed than others because of the frequency with which they absorb "tolerable daily doses", which is the case for vegetarians [5]. So we retain that the food contamination is the most important one for heavy metals. Moreover, the vegetables have a large part in this contamination.

Human exposure to heavy metals through consumption of vegetables depends on several types of factors which can be grouped in three categories: First, there are intrinsic factors such as pH, soil structure and types of cultures more or less favourable to the transmission of metals. Secondly, the risk of human contamination is naturally dependent on the nature and the quantity of toxic components in sludge and in the soil. The methods used in the processing and the land disposal of sludge have an influence on their concentrations of toxic components. Thirdly, the risk of contamination is related to the food consumption habits of the individual (type of purchase, eating food raised in his garden, etc.).

As epidemiological data are lacking for some heavy metals, it would seem advisable to rely on the notion of food risk as perceived by the consumer. However, a risk is perceived differently depending on the individual's knowledge, the information he possesses the way this information is communicated and the message received. Risk perception is based on the individual's confidence in the transmitted information, which is difficult to predict [6]. Concerning heavy metals, the questions of perception and risk evaluation imply a consideration of the relevance of standards and daily acceptable doses since the origins of heavy metals are various and the "dose-response" functions difficult to establish because of an inadequate number of cases and the long delay before symptoms become apparent.

Risk Perception in Psychology and Economics

A risky situation is related to the possibility of quantifying the probability of a given consequence. In the opposite case, the situation is considered uncertain. Pondering the distinction between established risk and perceived risk involves a consideration of the possibilities of estimating a particular risk and of the difference between the estimations of experts and the perception of individuals. This established or the consumer can deform objective probability, either because of a lack of understanding of the problem posed or because of individual beliefs[3]. The transformation (or deviation) of the objective probabilities gives rise to distorted probabilities that vary according to the opinions, knowledge or information of each individual and to his confidence in the programme and the decision-maker. Information is important both to risk perception and in the evaluation of risk reduction [7]. Risk perception *a posteriori* can be understood as the weighted sum of the perceived risk *a priori* plus an information. A significant difference between the consumers' perceptions

---

[3] cf. "cognitive dissonance", [8].

cannot be entirely explained by the individuals' lack of information. With the same information, risk can be perceived differently by each of the parties. Recognition of this result is based on acceptance of the role of cognitive factors in the formation of individual probabilities [9, 10]. The transformation of an objective probability is not automatic. However, this behaviour may well be more common when the potential consequences concern the health of individuals. Risks which involve natural assets are probably more difficult to quantify than industrial risks in which all the parameters are established by humans[4]. With respect to the environment or health, uncertainty may be the most common situation. The alteration of an environmental asset can have consequences on health, for which the probabilities of exposure are not always easy to determine. In the case of a quantified risk, as in that of an uncertain situation, the notion of perceived risk tend to be used for the consumer.

Psychologists' questioning about risk-perception is situated essentially at the level of cognitive processes and factors influencing this perception. They focused on, the perceptive bias, the complexity of risk perception and the link between perception and actual behaviour.

Risk perception depends on the way we code information about risks and dangers and filter these data through our individual experiences, believes, values and personality. So, the first contribution of social psychologists in the study of risk perception was to show that the individual is not a rational computer. For example, to present a situation with the probability of success or with the probability of failure will already modify the perceptive process. Moreover, the notion of extremely small probability, such a chance on a million, is difficult to understand and to imagine [11]. From a cognitive viewpoint, this type of information (and consequently risk-perception) is subjected to distortions because of individuals' cognitive limitation. This limitation has for consequence the application of some heuristics rules to simplify the treatment of information but can lead sometimes to errors of appreciation. These biases indicate existing distances between the judgements that can be done and judgements corresponding to normative models as the logical or statistical rules. Tversky and Kahneman [12, 13] put for example in evidence that the availability bias brings the individual to estimate the frequency of an event by the way of which this one appears spontaneously or consciously. It supposes that people privilege the search of easily recoverable or available examples in memory to judge the probability of an event. So the more the event is easy to imagine or to remember, the more it is frequent. The representativeness bias consists in the tendency of subjects to take into account data that they consider as being representative of a situation rather than objective elements. In food safety it implies that the individuals estimate differently a risk for which they have information than a risk that is not absolutely familiar to them. An important question is to know people levels of information about the practice of the sewage sludge. Secondly we shall investigate the impact of information. The lot of problems connected to the food evoked recently in France can bring the individuals to minimise their own risk because of tiredness and/or defence mechanism in front of too much danger (unrealistic optimism). This profusion of information may also provoke an overestimation of risks because the individuals are made extremely sensitive to them, the problem is considered as very probable (availability bias).

---

[4] The calculation of the probability of an engine breakdown implies a complete knowledge of all its components, which is more precise than that of all living elements in an ecosystem.

The second major contribution of the psychologists in risk perception was first to consider this estimation process as being multideterminated, second to show that different social groups perceive risks differently. For example in a lot of fields (transport, domestic, pesticides, etc.) women perceive more risks than men do especially when a child is present at home [14]. These researches also put in evidence that to estimate risks, the various groups base their evaluation on different criteria. The expert establishes his appreciation, on the number of deaths pro year for example. The judgement of the individual lambda is more sensitive to others criteria as catastrophe or threat for the future generations [15]. It is also clearly established that the persons do not estimate risk concerning themselves in the same way as risk for others. They are more optimistic about their own future [16] and especially when they think that their behaviour can act on the occurrence of event [17]. For example, the consumers consider that they are able to prevent from those risks according to their criteria of produce choice. The psychologists draw finally our attention to the relation existing between risk-perception and the possible preventive behaviour. Even though a relatively linear relation (the more the situation is perceived as risky, the more people are careful) may appear in many cases, it is far from being systematic. The predictive character of risk evaluation seems reserved to risks that recover only from the individual [18, 19] and not when the situation also implies others as potential risk factors [20]. So, within the framework of food context, risk should be perceived differently depending on the responsibility of the person for the choice of produces.

The problem of the heavy metals has not this day been the object of information campaign in France. Moreover, if it exists, this risk represents only a long-term danger, credibly not implying catastrophic dimension. Many problems in health present this gap among t1 (time of the actual behaviour) and t2 (time of consequences) with for corollary the decline of danger perception [21]. Thus, it is likely that risks associated to the consumption of fruits and vegetables are difficult to estimate. We shall attempt consequently to place heavy metals risk with regard to the other food risks.

TOWARDS AN UNDERSTANDING OF CONSUMER'S BEHAVIOUR: METHODOLOGY AND SOME RESULTS

Contrary to the economists, psychologists do not place maximum earning as the first motivation of the individual. Thus, willingness to pay can not be used as the only indication of risk perception. So, if one can admit that willingness to pay is an indicator of risk-perception, nothing allows us to assert that these two elements are proportional. Nothing allows us to assert it.

We could proceed to a direct qualitative evaluation of risks (I find this to "not risky at all" to "extremely risky"). Subject has simply to estimate the risk related to different situations or products. Another way of measuring risk-perception has been used by [22]. They describe the risk as a subjective evaluation of people susceptibility to be confronted with a risk. In that case, subject has to estimate if he has more or less chance than the others to be a victim. This second method is an interesting track in the study of risk perception, but it also has its limits. Indeed, the researchers using this method collided in a cognitive bias, subjects perceiving themselves as less susceptible to be confronted with the risk than the others (optimistic bias). The risk perception can also be estimated in an indirect way. The obtained measures are not a direct perception of the risk, but a variable influenced by this latter. For example, in multidimensions studies, subjects have to pronounce on their desire for regulation of such or such danger. Subject does not directly pronounce on its risk perception but his answer is indirectly influenced by its evaluation.

A combination of several methods of evaluation should allow us to make a fine measure of risk perception related to sewage sludge by taking into account possible contradictions inherent to the consumers. Experimental economics, qualitative interviews, protocol verbal and contingent valuation will be the principal tools used to understand consumer's behaviour in the case of sewage sludge spreading on agricultural soils.

Experimental Results

The purpose of one past exploratory study was to give some preliminary experimental results about a food safety valuation of sewage sludge disposal on agricultural soil [23]. An estimation of the perceived food safety has been obtained by consulting a student sample (64 students) was asked to respond on a computer on their added willingness to pay for products grown without sludge. Food safety was linked to a variation of one heavy metal content (cadmium) of the vegetables grown with and without sludge. Experiments were developed in two different contexts: the risky context where the risk to come closer to the "tolerable weekly dose" is estimated by a fictitious probability; the uncertain context where the risk is unknown. The mean willingness to pay represented a significant increase in the two cases, compared to the current expense per week, 14 per cent in the risky situation and 18 per cent in the uncertain one. The willingness to pay has approximately the same distribution in the two cases. The reasons for a null increase are the following: "the risk is not really established"; "the regulation must be stricter"; "I consume organic products". In the two contexts, the participants gave a reason grounded on a scientific uncertainty in which it has not been proved that there were some effects on health. Paradoxically, it is in the uncertain version that respondents mentioned more the risk notion: "the risk seems so weak" or "there is a heavy metal risk elsewhere than in sludge".

Qualitative Interviews

Semi-directive interviews are a first qualitative approach of people knowledge levels about sewage sludge and risk perception associated to this method of recycling. Two main subjects were approached. The first one is the fruit and vegetables' consumption to appreciate how persons are susceptible to feel with the sludge. The question of the criteria of choice allows also investigating the consumers 's requirement. We can emit the hypothesis that the more criteria people use, the more they will be sensitive to the problem of sewage sludge and will have an increased risk perception. The second topic in our interviews is the level of knowledge and the risk perception associated to the consumption of fruits and vegetables before and after information about sludge.

We led 29 discussions with 12 men and 17 women, 19 of these persons lived with a companion and 12 of them also with child (ren). These persons are all concerned with the purchase of foodstuffs exclusively (14 persons) or in cooperation with the other member of the pair (15 persons). In the interview we first approached the question of consumer habits in fruits and vegetables and then interrogated our subjects about possible risks associated with this consumption. We evoked then the sewage sludge problem. Whether the persons have or not this knowledge, we explained the positive and negative aspects of this practice to stimulate their reactions and comments. Finally we proposed them to express a willingness to pay for three different products: potatoes, leeks, and apples. We wanted to introduce basic produce (apple) and less common produce (leek) as well as a fruit, more remote from the ground. All the subjects buy and consume more or less regularly various fruits and vegetables. These fresh produces seem to have a particular place in the food. For example, they evoke the super market as the place for their general food shopping but the small shops and markets as the place for their fruits and vegetables purchase. The representation of fruits and vegetables covers the notions of coolness, vitamin and food balance. Qualitative criterion is evoked spontaneously by 25 persons and appears as the main criterion of choice. The quality notion means coolness, appearance, smell and/or taste. The second criterion of choice is the price; some people (13) evoke it spontaneously as the more important information or secondary after the quality (7). Inversely the produce process and geographic origin are quoted respectively only by one and two persons spontaneously. Subjects seem to trust particularly their senses to choice fruits and vegetables.

Only 4 persons evoke the possibility that the consumption of fruits and vegetables can contain risks like presence of pesticides and could be controlled by "an extensive wash and/or the cooking of produces". In any case these produces are not associated to severe risks. On the contrary, 6 persons said that it's the fact of not consuming fruits and vegetables that represents a risk. It creates a deficiency notably in vitamins. So globally we noted a weak perceived risk. Even if our region is particularly concerned by the practice of spreading sludge we notice that the level of knowledge of these inhabitants is weak: only 5 persons were able to evoke elements corresponding effectively to this practice (" residual sludge, water-treatment", " use of sludge in agriculture "). 13 persons did never hear about it and 11 knew the expression " sewage sludge ". As we gave information we noticed different reactions. 13 persons showed a positive or neutral reaction towards sludge. In this context three major arguments should be held: -the benefit of recycling; -the ancestral and traditional character of the use of waste as fertilising; economic character (it costs less than incineration).

One notices also that for some people this practice does not seem more dangerous than other food risks. To perceive a risk associated to the sewage sludge would be to admit the existence of a new group of dangerous products. At the same time, 16 persons revealed some surprise and anxiety. They evoke with disgust the link between sludge residues and food. These two notions are paradoxical. It seems that the notion of spreading comes above all for several subjects to disrupt the positive representation of fruits and vegetables, symbols of proper natural produces. The majority of the persons declare themselves effectively ready to pay more to have the level of heavy metals limited and controlled. For potatoes for example subjects are ready to go to an average increase of 68 % with however a big within subjects variability. Those who are opposed to pay (4 persons) defend the idea that they should not have to pay more because safety must be an obvious thing. All sold food should be safe.

Verbal Protocol

Verbal protocol is a good approach in order to test a contingent questionnaire before the survey. Cognitive psychologists first implemented this technique. The aim is to understand the respondents' mental accounting. Indeed, they are asked to read and to think the questionnaire. Schkade & Payne [24] recommend this method in the field of contingent valuation. In a contingent valuation, it is very important that the respondent correctly understands the scenario and the good he has to value; if not there is a risk of reliability of the obtained willingness to pay (WTP) given by the respondent.

In this way 11 interviews were implemented, 2 men and 9 women. For the contingent survey, it is very important that the respondent goes shopping, instead of he will not be able to answer correctly to the questions. Qualitative interviews highlight this fact. These respondents have various professional activities: 1 researcher, 3 secretaries, 1 accountant, 1 nurse, 1 housewife, 1 pensioner, and 1 student. The ages of the respondent are uniformly distributed, between 20 and 60 years old. Within the 11 household, 6 of them have children living in the same house. 2 household have a vegetable garden and eat their own product that is "free". It could be interesting to take into account the type of the house as a quota for the sample. Only one household consumes biological products.

First of all, the verbal protocols highlight that our first contingent questionnaire draft is too long. The disadvantage of a questionnaire, which lasts 30 mn, is the risk of tiredness and lassitude. Moreover, the verbal protocols show that the questionnaire must be improved in order to give more precise information, particularly in the scenario. Indeed the problem of heavy metal in sludge and then in fruits and vegetables and their health effects is not well known in the population. Respondents have to give the frequency of their fruits and vegetables consumption. This question is difficult to answer because there is a season effect, particularly for specific fruit or vegetable (apple, potatoes...). Another difficulty concerns the price of the good the respondent is willing to pay. Indeed, due to some packaging, the respondent is not always aware of the price of one kilogram.

Because of the different food safety problems (BSE, GMO, listeria...), people are aware that food could have some dangerous effects on their health state. On the other hand, every respondent thinks that eating fruits and vegetables are healthy. This particular problem of heavy metal in fruits and vegetables is not well known by the respondent, but we observe that their confidence is limited. Concerning the risk valuation, a risk scale is a better indicator than some space of probability. In the contingent scenario, all fruits and vegetables will be controlled. That means that the fruit or the vegetable will not be sold if the concentration of the heavy metal is too high. Every respondent is willing to pay more if this control will be implemented. But, every respondent is aware also that paying more than 2 francs for every kilo induce bigger expenses.

Contingent Valuation

A consumer would be willing to pay for food safety if he perceived a risk to his health. Food safety could thus be considered as a reduction in morbidity, measured by a decrease in the perceived or real probability of experiencing illness, for which the consumer is willing to pay an additional cost. Different techniques have been applied to estimate this value, including the contingent valuation method, which is often used to estimate food safety. Contingent valuation is the most direct method: it is based on the own consumer's perception of welfare and is synthesised in his willingness to pay indicator. The difficulty linked to a food security valuation is to give a risk reduction, i.e. probabilities. When these probabilities are not available it is the subjective probability which can be employed.

The consumption of certified sludge-free products is presented as a possibility of reducing the probability of being in poor health: *"Would you be willing to spend X francs in addition to the current price in order to consume heavy-metal-free products?"* To reply to this question, the consumer compares the level of expected utility relative to the consumption of certified metal-free products with that of non-certified products. Once informed, this consumer will also be led to associate his state of health with the positive and negative aspects of consumption.

CONCLUSIONS

The first objective was to evaluate consumer risk perception of the agricultural use of sludge. The first experiments showed that this use was not known. So sludge was more widely considered by taking into account all heavy metals sources in agriculture. The experiments were based on a joint collaboration between psychology and economics to detect the consumer behaviour through fruits, vegetables and cereals consumption. The results showed that food consumption and food safety linked to heavy metals was difficult to detect for the following reasons: there is a bad view of food safety in general but at the same time consumers are not informed of the heavy metals problem in food, neither of the agricultural use of sludge. The collaboration between psychology and economics allowed the development of risk perception scales on which a low risk perception was measured and how it is perceived. However with this very low risk, we have to be very cautious with the potential use of the results.

REFERENCES

1.   IFEN, Indicateurs de performance environnementale de la France, Lavoisier, Tec & Doc. 1996

2.   JUSTE C., CHASSIN P., GOMEZ A., LINÈRES M. AND MOCQUOT B. Les micro-polluants métalliques dans les boues résiduaires des stations d'épuration urbaines, INRA Centre de recherches de Bordeaux. Connaître pour Agir, Guides et cahiers techniques. Ademe (ed). 1995.

3.   DUCROT C AND MEFFRE C. et les membres du Comité de rédaction d'info Santé-Déchets. Risque sanitaire toxicologiques lié à l'épandage agricole des boues des stations d'épuration - Synthèse bibliographique. Revue de Médecine Vétérinaire. 1996. 147(6), pp. 439-44.

4.   MAXIMILIEN R. AND MASSE R. Evolution du risque toxicologiques des métaux non ferreux. Réalités Industrielles. février1994, pp. 56-60.

5.   DECLOÎTRE F. La part des différents aliments dans l'exposition au plomb, au cadmium, et au mercure en France. Cahiers de Nutrition et Diététique. 33(3). 1998. Pp 167-175.

6.   FREWER L J, HOWARD C, HEDDERLEY D AND SHEPERD R. What determines trust in information about food-related risks? Underlying psychological constructs. Risk analysis.1996.16, pp. 473-486.

7. POE L P AND BISHOP R C. Information, Risk perceptions, and Contingent Values for groundwater Protection. Center for Integrated Agricultural Systems, University of Wisconsin-Madison; Cornell University10. 1993.

8. AKERLOF G A AND DICKENS W T., The economic consequences of cognitive dissonance. The American Economic Review. 1982. 72, 3, pp 307-19.

9. ARROW K J., Risk perception in psychology and economics. Economic Inquiry. 1982. XX. Pp 1-9.

10. SMITH V K. AND DESVOUGES W H. Subjective versus technical risk estimates: do risk communication policies increase consistency? Economic Letters. 31. 1989. Pp 287-91.

11. COVELLO V.T., WINTERFELDT D. AND SLOVIC P. Risk communication: A review of the literature. Risk abstracts. 3, 1986, pp 171-182.

12. TVERSKY A AND KAHNEMAN D. Availability: A heuristic for judging frequency and probability. Cognitive Psychology. 5, 1973. pp 207-232.

13. TVERSKY A. AND KAHNEMAN D. Judgement under uncertainty: heuristic and biases. Science. 185, 1974. pp 1124-1130.

14. KARPOWICZ C. AND MULLET E. Societal risk as seen by French public. Risk analysis. 13, 3, 1993. pp 253-258.

15. SLOVIC P., FISCHHOFF B. AND LICHTENSTEIN S. Behavioural decision theory perspectives on risk and safety. Acta Psychologica. 56, 1984. pp 183-203.

16. WEINSTEIN N.D. Accuracy of smokers' risk perceptions. Annals of behavioral medicine. 20, 2, 1998. pp 135-140.

17. Mc KENNA F P. It won't happen to me: unrealistic optimism or illusion of control? British journal of psychology. 84, 1993. pp 39-50.

18. BLESCH K.S. Health beliefs about testicular cancer and self-examination among professional men. Oncology nursing forum. 13, 1986. pp 29-33.

19. FALCK R S, SIEGEL H.A., WANG J. AND CARLSON R.G. Usefulness of the health belief model in predicting HIV needle risk practices among injection drug users. Aids education and prevention. 7, 1995. pp 523-533.

20. GERRARD M., GIBBONS F.X. AND BUSHMAN B.J. The relation between perceived vulnerability to HIV and precautionary sexual behavior. Psychological bulletin. 119, 1996. pp 390-409.

21. GREGORY R. AND MENDELSOHN R. Perceived risk, dread, and benefits. Risk analysis.13, 1993. pp 259-264.

22. KOWALEWSKI M.R., HENSON H D AND LONGHORE D. Rethinking perceived risk and health behavior: a critical review of HIV prevention research. Health, education and behavior. 24, 3, 1997. pp 313-325.

23. STENGER A. Experimental valuation of food safety – Application to sewage sludge. Food Policy 25. 2000. Pp 211-218.

24. SCHKADE D A., PAYNE J W. Contingent Valuation: A critical assessment. J.A. Hausman editor. 1993. Where do the numbers come from? How people respond to contingent valuation. pp 271-304.

THE INFLUENCE OF COMPOSTING ON HEAVY METAL EXTRACTABILITY FROM TWO SEWAGE SLUDGES

A Stringfellow   **C J Banks**

University of Southampton

P F Hillman

Gifford and Partners

United Kingdom

ABSTRACT. Two sewage sludges, one anaerobically digested, one undigested, were composted under controlled conditions to assess the influence of composting on heavy metal extractability. Cd, Cu, Ni, Pb and Zn concentrations in the sludges and composts were analysed to assess changes in (1) total metal content, (2) plant-available and exchangeable metals, and (3) metal fractions, during composting and maturation.

The total metal content of the initial compost mixture was decreased relative to the parent sludges by dilution with a clean straw bulking agent. As composting progressed the total metal content increased as organic matter was decomposed. Both plant-available and exchangeable metals tended to increase during the active phase of composting, and decrease during maturation. It is suggested that active aeration leads to increase in metal mobility and that this is followed by binding into more stable forms as humification increases during maturation. Overall, the findings suggest that while the total heavy metal concentration can increase during composting, the process can also lead to a decrease in the extractability of some heavy metals if the compost is fully matured.

Keywords: Composting, Heavy metals, Sewage sludge.

Dr A Stringfellow, is a Research Fellow in the Dept. of Civil and Environmental Engineering at the University of Southampton. She is the research co-ordinator of the University's Environmental Body SUnRISE, which carries out research in sustainable waste management funded through the Landfill Tax Credit Scheme.

Dr C J Banks, is a Reader in Environmental Engineering and Director of Research in the Dept. of Civil and Environmental Engineering at the University of Southampton. His research interests are in the area of innovative technology for environmental protection, including: biological treatment of liquid industrial effluents; controlled anaerobic biodegradation of high cellulosic solid wastes; the removal of trace organic materials and heavy metals from water; and computer based management tools for effluent treatment plant operation and design.

Mr P F Hillman, is a senior consultant at Gifford and Partners Consulting Engineers and a former senior lecturer in the Dept. of Civil and Environmental Engineering at the University of Southampton.

INTRODUCTION

Sewage sludge production in the European Union is predicted to double in the next decade [1] because of more stringent treatment requirements set out in the EC UWWT Directive [2]. The Directive encourages the recycling of sewage sludge and a UK Royal Commission report [3] supports agricultural spreading of treated sludge as it is a beneficial soil conditioner and land is available in the UK. However, food retailers, farmers and the public have expressed concerns about the use of sewage sludge in agriculture, principally because it contains human pathogens and potentially toxic heavy metals.

Composting is a relatively inexpensive method of treating sewage sludge, rendering it fit for land application providing it meets EU standards. While composting is able to reduce pathogen levels [4], the problem of toxic heavy metals in sludge compost remains. Indeed composting may even be detrimental since heavy metals in the sludge may be concentrated by the loss of organic matter during decomposition [5]. Thus, total metal concentrations in composted sludge may be higher than those in the parent sludge unless it is mixed with uncontaminated bulking agents during composting [5, 6].

Total heavy metal content is an important determining factor in the calculation of sludge application rates to agricultural land [7]. However, the total metal concentration is not a good indicator of the metal toxicity of the sludge. A better indicator is the metal's form or "species", which determines the mobility and bioavailability of metals: for example, ionic, adsorbed, precipitated and organically-bound forms show decreasing metal mobility. While there has been much research on metal availability in sewage sludges and sludge-amended soils (for example, [8-10]), there have been relatively few studies on metal form in composted sludge. There is some evidence that the physical changes that occur during composting (such as pH, oxidation, and humification) can effect changes in metal speciation. Garcia *et al* [11] showed that concentrations of exchangeable and plant-available metals decreased when an aerobic sludge was composted. The decrease in metal mobility was attributed to oxidation processes and formation of organic-metal complexes. Henry and Harrison [12] showed the opposite; they found that the proportion of exchangeable metals *increased* during composting. The sewage sludge used in their study was anaerobically digested. The difference in results between these studies may be due to the different sludges, composting processes, sampling methods or analytical techniques used in each case.

The object of this research was to observe the influence of composting on heavy metal extractability from two different sludges, one digested and the other undigested, composted under the same conditions and analysed using the same techniques. Samples of compost were taken during the active (heating) and maturation phases of composting. The samples were analysed for total metal content and metal form. Changes in metal extractability were related to the changes in pH, redox potential, moisture content and humification which occurred during composting.

EXPERIMENTAL DETAILS

Two dewatered sewage sludges, one anaerobically digested (AD1) from a rural treatment works, and one undigested (UD1 & UD2) from an industrial catchment, were composted with chopped wheat straw; mixtures as given in Table 1. Both the sludges originated from a mixture of 1° and 2° sludges. The sludge samples were taken fresh after dewatering by a belt press; the samples were stored at 4°C until required. A high-energy amendment (vegetable margarine) was added to promote thermophilic composting in the digested sludge/straw mixture. Previous experiments (not described) had shown that the energy content and degradability of this sludge was too low to sustain thermophilic temperatures. Additional straw was mixed with the undigested sludge UD2 after the initial mixture ratio (10:1 by mass) of the sludge/straw mixture UD1 was found to be too dense for effective composting.

To ensure consistent conditions, composting was carried out in laboratory composters, Figure 1. Forced aeration, operating under a computer-controlled temperature-feedback regime, was used to limit the maximum compost temperature to 55°C. The stainless steel vessels (12L) were covered with heating mats, which were controlled to minimise conductive heat losses from the compost. This was achieved by maintaining a 0.5°C difference between the centre of the composting mixture and an air gap between the compost container and the outer vessel wall. After the active phase of composting the mixture was matured in polypropylene containers placed in a water bath at 30°C, and moist, aerobic conditions were maintained for two months.

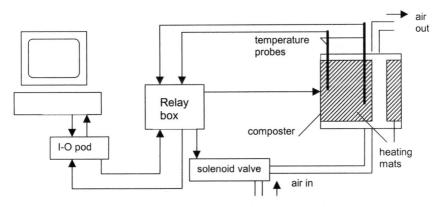

Figure 1 Schematic diagram of the laboratory composter used for the active phase of composting sewage sludge and straw mixtures. Maturation apparatus is not shown

Table 1 Mass of materials and initial conditions in the composts AD1, UD1 and UD2

	AD1	UD1	UD2
Sludge (kg)	1	1	1
Straw (kg)	0.1	0.1	0.33
Amendment (kg)	0.1		
Initial moisture %	68	67	65
Initial pH	7	7.7	8.4
Initial redox (mV)	-89	-144	-160

Temperatures within the composting mixture were recorded during the active phase which lasted approximately 20 days, Figure 2. The composts heated rapidly, but the use of forced aeration to limit the maximum temperature promoted excessive drying. Moisture limitation caused composting to decline after five days; this proved to be a problem using both the digested and undigested sludges. Re-mixing the composts with water enabled composting to restart and to continue at thermophilic temperatures until microbial activity declined as the easily degradable material was used up.

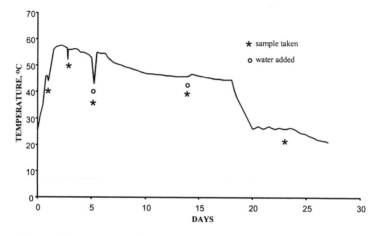

Figure 2 Temperature/time graph for composting of digested sludge AD1

Samples of compost were taken at approximately five-day intervals during the active phase of composting, and then after one week, two weeks, four weeks and eight weeks maturation. The compost samples were subjected to the following analysis: pH [13]; total solids (TS%) [14]; degree of humification, DH% [15]. A water extract (1:10, dry mass-volume) of each sample was measured with a Radiometer Combined Pt electrode to obtain a qualitative indication of the mixed redox potential.

The total metal content of the sludge and straw was determined after digestion of dried ground samples in HNO_3:HCl (1:3) [14]. Plant-available metals were extracted using DTPA, (diethylene-triamine-penta-acetic acid, 0.005M), 0.1 M $CaCl_2$, 0.1M triethanolamine (TEA) buffered to pH 7.3, [16]. Undried samples were mixed with DTPA at a solid-extractant ratio of 1:10 (dry mass:volume), and shaken for 2 hours. Exchangeable metals were determined using 0.5M $CaCl_2$ [17], shaking for 16 hours at ambient temperature at a ratio of 1:10 (dry mass:volume).

Sequential step extraction to determine metal form was also performed on fresh samples of sludge and compost employing the following series of reagents: 0.5M KNO_3, 16 hours; 0.5M KF, 2 hours; 0.1M $Na_4P_2O_7$, 4 hours; 0.1M EDTA, 8 hours; 1M HNO_3, 4 hours (adapted from [18]). These reagents extract metal fractions corresponding to exchangeable, adsorbed, organically-bound, carbonate and sulphide forms. Approximately 1g (dry weight) of sample was mixed with 30 ml of extractant. The suspensions from the digestion, batch and sequential extractions were centrifuged and filtered (Whatman 41) and metals in the filtrates (Cd, Cu, Ni, Pb and Zn) were analysed by AAS (Varian SpectrAA 200).

The extraction procedures were carried out on undried samples immediately after collection; this was done to avoid the effects of drying on metal speciation. Air-drying has been shown to release heavy metals to the exchangeable fraction [19]. Linear regression analysis was used to study the correlation between the extractability of metals and pH, redox potential, TS% and degree of humification.

RESULTS AND DISCUSSION

Figure 3 (a-d) shows the changes in pH, redox potential, degree of humification (DH%) and total solids during the three composting runs. In general, there was a decline in pH as composting progressed and ammonia was evolved. The redox potential rose rapidly during the active phase during which the compost was given maximum aeration, and then increased more slowly during maturation. However, the final redox potential values in AD1 and UD2 were higher than in UD1 because the density of this mixture prevented effective aeration during the active phase of composting. The degree of humification increased with composting time in both the digested and undigested sludges. The total solids content increased as composting progressed since aeration encourages loss of moisture by evaporation

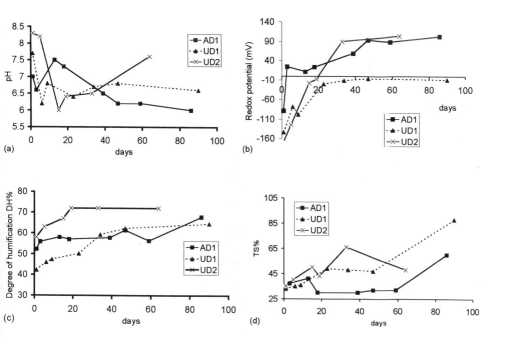

Figure 3: Changing physical parameters during composting of composts AD1, UD1 and UD2; (a) pH, (b) redox potential mV, (c) degree of humification DH%, and (d) TS%

Table 2 Concentration of total metals in initial and final composts, and straw (mg/kg)

	Cd initial	Cd final	Cu initial	Cu final	Ni initial	Ni final	Pb initial	Pb final	Zn Initial	Zn final
AD1	1.7	2.7	428	683			68.9	113	561	808
UD1	1.8	2.5	374	505	20.5	29.1	43.3	71	300	395
UD2	2.5	3.6	188	270	23.6	46.4	34.0	52	248	395
straw	0.1		9.8		1.9		7		8.5	

Total Metal Concentration

The total metal content of the initial sludge compost mixture was decreased compared to the parent sludge by dilution with relatively clean straw. During composting the total metal content of both types of sludge increased as volatile solids were lost. Wagner et al (1990) [5], and Qiao and Ho [20] reported similar increases in total metal concentration during composting. The increase in total metals is this study was not equal for all the metals, on average, increasing by 20 to 40%, Table 2. This variation indicates that the increase in total metal concentration does not depend solely on volatile solids reduction, but that there are losses of some heavy metals relative to others. Wagner suggested that leaching was a possible reason for differential losses, finding that total Cr, Pb and Zn increased relative to Cu and Ni.

In the current study, digested sludge Cd, Cu, and Pb were found to increase more than Zn. In the undigested sludge Cu showed less increase than the other metals; this might be due to leaching of Cu bound to soluble organics. Overall, the effect of dilution by straw and increase in heavy metal concentration by loss of volatile solids was such that the total metal concentrations of Cu, Pb and Zn in the final compost were not significantly higher than the parent sludges, except in the undigested sludge, in which total Cu decreased slightly.

Exchangeable Metals

Exchangeable metals (extracted by $CaCl_2$) formed only a small fraction of the total metal content of the sludges and composts; Pb was below detection limits. When the sludges were initially mixed with the straw bulking agent it was generally found that the proportion of exchangeable metals increased relative to that found in the parent sludge. It is suggested that this increase was caused by oxidation of metals during mixing in an aerobic environment. The oxidation overcame the dilution effect expected from the addition of the clean bulking agent. Additional straw was mixed with UD1 on day 9 of composting to improve aeration, and again this led to increases in the proportion of exchangeable metals.

In the digested sludge, the proportion of exchangeable Cu increased during the first few days of the active phase of composting and then decreased towards the end of this phase; the proportion of exchangeable Cd and Zn tended to decrease as composting progressed, figure 4a. By the end of maturation the proportion of exchangeable Cd, Cu and Zn extracted from the matured compost was less than that of the initial composting mixture.

In the undigested sludges (figures 4b and 4c) the proportion of all exchangeable metals increased during the active phase then decreased significantly during the maturation phase in UD1. In contrast, in UD2, exchangeable Cu and Zn did not decrease after the active phase. This may be because of a shorter maturation period in UD2 resulting in less organic binding of exchangeable metals.

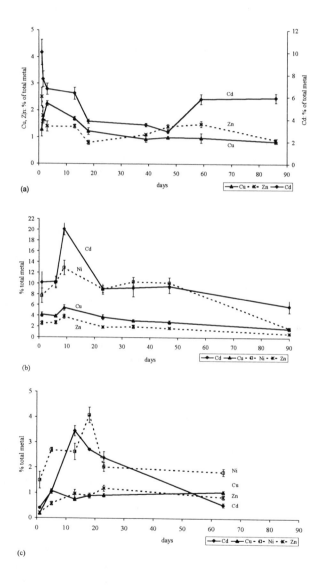

Figure 4 The proportion of $CaCl_2$-extracted Cd, Cu, Ni and Zn in samples taken from (a) AD1, (b) UD1 and (c) UD2 during composting and maturation

Plant-available Metals

In the digested sludge, plant-available Pb and Zn increased during the active phase of composting before decreasing in maturation, figure 5a. Overall, comparing the initial and final compost mixtures, there was no significant change in the proportion of extracted Zn, but Pb and Cd decreased. Plant-available Cu gradually increased throughout composting and maturation. Increases in plant-available Cu have also been demonstrated for digested sludge composted with sawdust [20].

In the undigested sludge UD1 the proportion of DTPA-extracted Cd, Ni and Pb increased during the active phase and decreased during maturation; Zn decreased throughout composting and maturation, figure 5b. Cu changed little during the active phase, and then decreased during maturation. During the active phase of UD2 there were larger increases in the proportion of plant-available Cd and Zn compared to UD1, figure 5c. All plant-available metals decreased during the maturation phase in UD2.

In general, the results showed that the proportion of extracted metal in the final undigested sludge compost was less than that in the initial mixture. These results suggest that composting sewage sludge is beneficial since the availability of heavy metals to plants (except Cu in digested sludges) is reduced in the mature compost. As with the exchangeable metals maturation plays an important part in making the compost heavy metals less extractable.

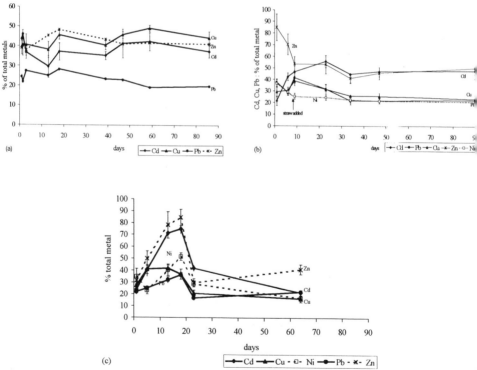

Figure 5 The proportion of DTPA-extracted Cd, Cu, Ni, Pb and Zn in samples taken from (a) AD1, (b) UD1 and (c) UD2 during composting and maturation

Neither DTPA nor CaCl$_2$-extractable metals showed any significant correlation with the change in total metal concentration. This indicates that changes in specific forms of heavy metals are related to chemical changes in the compost rather than the concentration effect of loss of volatile matter.

Sequential Extraction

The sequential extraction series can be used to examine the movement of metals between metal forms with composting time. During the active phase, the digested sludge compost (AD1) showed a decrease in exchangeable Zn, no significant change in Cu and Pb, and an increase in exchangeable Ni; all of these metals decreased in maturation, figure 6a. During the active phase the change in the proportion of exchangeable Cd was negligible, but there was a significant increase in extracted Cd during the maturation stage. Ni and Zn sulphide forms did not show significant changes, whereas for Cd, Cu and Pb there was a decrease in the proportion of metals in the sulphide form as composting and maturation progressed. This resulted in an increase in the adsorbed, organic and carbonate Cu forms in the final compost; Cd moved to the carbonate and exchangeable forms, while Pb moved to the adsorbed and organic forms.

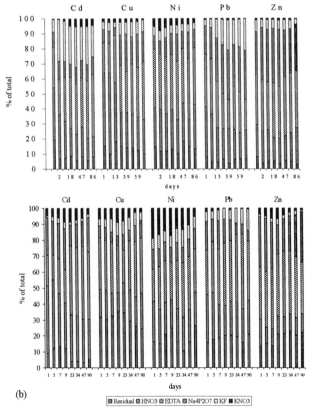

(b)

Figure 6 Sequential extraction of Cd, Cu, Ni, Pb and Zn from samples taken during composting and maturation of (a) AD1 and (b) UD1

The results for run UD1 are shown in figure 6b. There was an increase in the proportion of exchangeable Cd, Cu and Zn during the active phase, followed by a decrease in maturation; the proportion of exchangeable Pb and Ni decreased throughout the run. This also occurred in UD2 (not shown), although exchangeable Ni showed an increase during the active phase, resulting from the better aeration achieved in this composting run. This was also responsible for a greater decrease in the proportion of sulphide-bound metals in UD2 compared to UD1. UD2 showed similar changes in metals to those found in AD1; for example Cu moved from the sulphide to the adsorbed, carbonate and organic forms, Pb moved to the adsorbed form. Unlike AD1, Cd in the undigested sludge moved from the sulphide form to the organic form by the end of composting.

Regression Analysis

The exchangeable fraction was plotted against pH, redox potential, TS% and DH% to assess the influence of acidity, oxidation, drying and organic matter changes during composting. In the digested sludge, the proportion of exchangeable Cu was negatively correlated with increasing DH% ($r = 0.6$; significant at $P=0.05$); this correlation was also seen between Cu and DH% in the undigested sludge composts of UD1 ($r = 0.86$) and UD2 ($r = 0.81$). Exchangeable Cu also correlated with increasing redox potential in these sludges ($r = 0.65$). The change in exchangeable Cd in the digested sludge was significantly correlated with the increase in redox potential ($r = 0.55$). This relationship was not demonstrated in the undigested sludge composts. Ni demonstrated some correlation with redox potential, ($r = 0.6$), humification ($r = 0.58$), DH% ($r = 0.74$) and total solids ($r = 0.57$) in UD1 but there was no such correlation in AD1 or UD2. The lack of agreement between results for the undigested sludges with regard to exchangeable metals may be caused by the difference in aeration and humification in the composting runs.

The results from the sequential extraction experiments appear to show that when the composts were well aerated, metals associated with the sulphide fraction decreased. Changes in the sulphide fraction were more strongly correlated with the increase in redox potential in AD1 and UD2 ($r = 0.6$ to 0.9) than in UD1. This suggests that if the compost is well aerated, redox potential is the dominating factor in movement of metals from the sulphide fraction. Where aeration is less effective, other factors, such as pH, may play a more important part.

As composting progressed there was an increase in certain metals associated with the organic fraction. The change in proportion of organically-bound Cd, Cu, Ni, Pb and Zn was positively correlated ($r = 0.6$ to 0.8) with humification during composting in the undigested sludges; this relationship was not found in the digested sludges. Sequential extraction showed a greater increase in the proportion of organically-bound metals in the undigested sludges during composting and maturation. The association of Zn, Ni and Cd with DH% was not expected as Cu shows a strong affinity for humic substances whereas Zn, Ni and Cd tend to be more ionic in nature. The correlation between organically-bound Zn, Cd and DH% may result from the lack of selectivity in the extraction procedure as $Na_4P_2O_7$ has been shown to extract Zn, Pb and Cd carbonates [21]. Decreases in exchangeable Cu and increases in organically-bound Cu with increasing DH% in the undigested sludge may imply link between these processes: that is, exchangeable Cu becomes organically-bound as humification increases.

CONCLUSIONS

For both digested and undigested sludges, the change in total metal concentration depends on the amount of dilution (by mixing with uncontaminated bulking materials) and the loss of volatile solids which occurs during composting. With appropriate dilution it is possible that the total metal content in the compost at the end of maturation could be lower than an equivalent amount of the parent sludge. For both the digested and undigested sludges, the proportion of plant-available metals was lower (apart from Cu in AD1) at the end of maturation than it was in the initial composting mixture. The exchangeable metals, that is, those metals which are the most environmentally available, become more mobile during the active phase of composting but then bind in more stable forms during maturation.

Correlation between exchangeable metals and composting variables such as pH, redox potential, degree of humification and total solids varies with metal type. The efficiency of composting with respect to oxidation and humification appears to have a significant effect on the metal forms in the final compost. Exchangeable metals, extracted from samples during composting, show strong correlation with changes in oxidation and humification. The effects of pH and drying, which do not show good correlation with exchangeable metals, may be masked by changes in redox potential and DH%.

The periods of aeration and maturation have a considerable impact on the availability of heavy metals in sewage sludge composts. It appears to be important that sludge composts are given adequate maturation to reduce metal availability before the composts are applied to agricultural land to reduce the mobility of metals. If inadequately matured composts, or untreated sludges, are applied these may contain metal forms that are more mobile or bioavailable than present in fully matured composts. This research shows that, with appropriated dilution using clean bulking materials, the total metal concentration does not exceed that of the parent sludge, and that composting can decrease the proportion of available and exchangeable heavy metals in composted sewage sludge.

ACKNOWLEDGEMENTS

The authors would like to acknowledge the financial support of EPSRC and the University of Southampton.

REFERENCES

1.   GARNETT, P. AND MATTHEWS, P., (1996). European Union and UK present and future legislation on the management of sewage sludge. *Proc. Instn. Civil Engineers*, 115, pp 218-225.

2.   CEC (1991). Urban Waste Water Treatment Directive. *Official J. European Communities,* Directive 91/271/EEC, No. L 375/1-8.

3.   ROYAL COMMISSION OF ENVIRONMENTAL POLLUTION, (1996). *Sustainable use of soil.* 19th report. HMSO.

4. PEREIRA-NETO, J.T., STENTIFORD, E.I. AND MARA, D.D., (1986). Comparison of windrow and aerated static piles for refuse/sludge composting. *Int. Symp. Composting, Production, Quality and Use*, Udine, Italy, 1986.

5. WAGNER, D.J., BACON, G.D., KNOCKE, W.R. AND SWITZENBAUM, M. S., (1990). Changes and variability in concentration of heavy metals in sewage sludge during composting. *Environmental Technology*, 11, pp 949-960.

6. PARR, J.F., EPSTEIN, E. AND WILLSON, G.B., (1978). Composting sewage sludge for land application. *Agriculture and Environment*, 4, pp 123-137.

7. DoE (1989) *Code of practice for agricultural use of sewage sludge.* HMS

8. ALLOWAY, B.J. AND JACKSON, A.P., (1991). The behaviour of heavy metals in sewage sludge-amended soils. *Science of the Total Environment*, 100, pp 151-176.

9. HOODA, P.S., McNULTY, D, ALLOWAY, B.J. AND AITKEN, M.N., (1997). Plant availability of heavy metals in soils previously amended with heavy applications of sewage sludge. J. Sci. Agric., 73, pp 446-454.

10. LAKE, D.L., KIRK, P.W.W. AND LESTER, J.N., (1984). Fractionation, characterisation and speciation of heavy metals in sewage sludge and sludge-amended soils a review. *J. Environmental Quality*, 13 (2), pp 175-183.

11. GARCIA, C. HERNANDEZ, T. AND COSTA, F., (1990). The influence of composting and maturation processes on the heavy metal extractability from some organic wastes. *Biological Wastes*, 31, pp 291-301.

12. HENRY, C. AND HARRISON, R.B., (1992). Fate of trace metals in sewage sludge compost. In *Biogeochemistry of trace metals*, Ed: Adiano, D.C.

13. DoE. (1992). Standing Committee of Analysts. *Determination of the pH value of sludge, soil, mud and sediment.* HMSO, London.

14. DoE, (1986). Standing Committee of Analysts. *Methods for the determination of metals in soils, sediments, sewage sludge and plants by HCl/HNO₃ digestion, with a note on the determination of insoluble metal contents.* HMSO, London.

15. SEQUI, P., De NOBILI, M, LEITA, L AND CERCIGNANI, G., (1986). A new index of humification. *Agrochimica*, 30, pp 175.

16. LINDSAY, W.L. AND NORVELL, W.A., (1978). Development of a DTPA soil test for Zinc, Iron, Manganese and Copper. *Soil Science Society Am. J.* 42, pp 421-428.

17. GARCIA, C., MORENO, J.L., HERNANDEZ, T., AND COSTA, F., (1995). Effect of composting on sewage sludges contaminated with heavy metals. *Bioresource Technology*, 53, pp 13-19.

18.   STOVER, R.C., SOMMERS, L.E. AND SILVIERA, D.J., (1976). Evaluation of metals in wastewater sludge. *Journal of the Water Pollution Control Federation*, 48, (9), pp 2165-2175.

19.   QIAO, L., HOFSTEDE, H AND HO, G., (1993). The mobility of heavy metals in clay amended sewage sludge and municipal solid waste compost. In: Heavy metals in the Environment, Int. Conference. Toronto, CEP Consultants, Vol 2, 467-470.

20.   QIAO, L. AND HO, G., (1997). The effects of clay amendment and composting on metal speciation in digested sludge. *Water Research*, 31, (5), pp 951-964.

21.   RUDD, T., CAMPBELL, J.A., AND LESTER, J.N., (1988). The use of model compounds to elucidate metal forms in sewage sludge. *Environmental Pollution*, 50, pp 225-242.

PHOSPHORUS AND AGRICULTRAL RECYCLING
OF SEWAGE SLUDGE

N G Triner   **T Rudd**

Consultants in Environmental Sciences Ltd

S R Smith   **T Dearsley**

Imperial College, London   Thames Water Utilities Ltd

United Kingdom

ABSTRACT. Since the implementation of the Urban Waste Water Treatment Directive 91/271, an increasing number of waste water treatment works are using various nutrient removal techniques, in particular for phosphorus (P), which is subsequently transferred to the sludge. A laboratory incubation study was performed using two contrasting soil types to assess the orthophosphate content of sludge-soil systems by using P enriched and conventional sludges. The objective was to provide a basis for predicting the plant availability of P in soil amended with different types of conventional and advanced treated biosolids (thermal drying and thermal hydrolysis). The results indicate that sewage sludge can effectively supply phosphorus to soil in plant available forms. Phosphorus extractability was strongly influenced by both P removal and sludge treatment processes. The biological P removal sludge produced a greater percentage P extractability (41%) than the chemical P removal sludge (33%). Thermal drying markedly reduced (by 19-62%) the phosphate fertiliser value compared with matching samples of undried, dewatered digested sludge. For all biosolids types, phosphorus extractability was greatest with calcareous soil.

Keywords: Phosphorus removal, Agricultural recycling, Soil incubation, Phosphorus availability, Fertiliser value.

N G Triner, is an Environmental Scientist with Consultants in Environmental Sciences Ltd.

Dr S R Smith, is a Lecturer at the Department of Civil and Environmental Engineering, Imperial College, London.

Dr T Rudd, is a Director with Consultants in Environmental Sciences Ltd.

T Dearsley, is Environment Manager of Environment and Quality Group, Thames Water Utilities Ltd.

INTRODUCTION

The implementation of the Urban Waste Water Treatment Directive 91/271 [1] has led to increasing numbers of sewage treatment works in the UK employing phosphorus (P) removal.

Two principal methods of P removal in wastewater treatment are in current widespread use. These are enhanced biological phosphate removal (EBPR) and chemical precipitation. Iron (Fe) salts are most commonly used as precipitants, such as ferrous sulphate (Fe II) or ferric chloride (Fe III), although aluminium salts can also be used. Both approaches remove inorganic phosphate from solution and transfer P to the sewage sludge, markedly increasing the P content of the sludge.

In order to satisfy the EEC Directive (86/278/EEC) [2] on the use of sewage sludge on agricultural land, treatment must follow mandatory requirements transposed into UK legislation by Statutory Instrument No. 1263 (SI, 1989), The Sludge (Use in Agriculture) Regulations [3]. In addition there is further guidance on environmental practice provided by a voluntary code of practice [4].

There are several different options available in the treatment of sewage sludge (biosolids), but all have the same general objectives to stabilise the putrescible material and reduce pathogenicity. The treatment process is likely to influence the chemical composition of sludge, particularly in relation to components of agronomic significance, and is therefore likely to affect the agronomic value.

Phosphorus concentrations in sludge are typically in the range of 1-2% (ds) without P removal, but can increase to as much as 8% (ds) with nutrient removal [5]; on average 3-4% P (as ds) in nutrient removal sludges is more typical. The current application recommendations for P in conventional sludge products (raw and digested liquids and cakes) make the broad assumption that 50% of the P in all sludge types is available for crop uptake [6]. This is likely to be an inaccurate simplification of the actual P availabilities in sewage sludge. Furthermore, there are no data on P availabilities for biosolids in relation to the effects of advanced treatment (eg thermal drying and thermal hydrolysis) and P removal processes.

Information on these issues will be critical to the agricultural outlet in future, considering current developments in sludge treatment requirements and nutrient removal.

The nitrogen (N) content of sewage sludge governs its application rates to land in the UK. The current scientific consensus is that N and P uptake by plants is approximately in the ratio 1:0.1-0.25. Ratios of N:P in sludges are in the order of 1:0.5. Thus applying sludges on the basis of N requirements may result in an over application of P, in particular for dewatered cakes (from which water-soluble N compounds are removed, thereby reducing the ratio of N:P). Over-application can also be more significant where dried sludge products are used.

This means the P requirements could be satisfied from a single application of sludge for several cropping seasons, but in the longer term there is the possibility of soil enrichment. Once the P sorption capacity of the soil is exceeded, P will begin to be leached through the soil profile, in either water soluble or particulate fractions [7], with the subsequent risk of the eutrophication of surrounding natural water systems. The use of P enriched biosolids at conventional application rates may therefore exacerbate the extent of P inputs to soil in sludge.

This has important implications for sludge management on agricultural land because the MAFF Code of Good Agricultural Practice for the Protection of Water [8] requires that soil levels are not raised above those necessary for crop production, to avoid the potential leaching of P from soil and impacts on surface water courses. The Code recommends that, where organic manures, including sewage sludges, are applied on fields at ADAS soil P Index 3 or above, total P inputs exceeding the amount removed by crops in the rotation should be avoided.

In addition to reducing fertiliser costs to farmers, recycling P to soil in biosolids has a much wider global benefit by helping to conserve geological mineral P reserves, mined for phosphate fertiliser manufacture. These are dwindling in both quantity and quality, since much of the high grade volcanic deposits have been exhausted [9]. The use of low grade rock phosphate for fertiliser production may have long-term implications for soil fertility and human health due to the high cadmium (Cd) content. For example, Cd concentrations of up to 300 mg kg^{-1} have been reported in the USA [10].

EXPERIMENTAL

Two contrasting soil types were selected for the soil incubation study: a loamy sand (soil 1) and a calcareous clay (soil 2). The ADAS Index for P was 3 for the loamy sand and 1 for the calcareous clay. Selected physico-chemical properties of the soil are shown in Table 1.

The incubation trial examined 15 different biosolids (Table 2), 12 samples were from 7 different sewage treatment works (STW) operated by Thames Water Utilities and two were supplied by Wessex Water. All of the sludges were stabilised by mesophillic anaerobic digestion, except in the case of the hydrolysed liquid sludge sample.

Table 1 Selected physico-chemical properties of the soils

PARAMETER	LOAMY SAND, SOIL 1	CALCAREOUS CLAY, SOIL 2
% sand	82	24
% silt	12	35
% clay	6	41
pH	6.2	8.1
Available P (mg l^{-1}) [Index]	30.6 [3]	10.2 [1]
Available K (mg l^{-1}) [Index]	129 [2]	64 [1]
Available Mg (mg l^{-1}) [Index]	82 [2]	15 [0]
Exch. Ca (me 100 g^{-1})	5.0	10.2
CEC (me 100 g^{-1})	7.9	11.3
% Organic matter	3.8	5.9

In most cases, paired samples of the digested cakes (dc) and the corresponding digested thermally dried pellets were compared in the incubation study. The pelletised sludge samples were produced in sludge drying trials for Thames Water using a Kavaerna drier pilot plant. The Wessex Water product from Avonmouth STW was in the form of granules and is marketed under the brand name 'Biogran'. One of the two samples of Biogran tested in the trial was provided from material supplied by Thames Water. The other was collected directly from Avonmouth for the study, along with a corresponding sample of the undried digested cake. Three liquid sludges were also included, two of these were subjected to thermal hydrolysis treatment. Chemical properties of the biosolids are shown in Table 3.

Table 2 Biosolids descriptions

BIOSOLIDS TYPE	ABBREVIATION	
	Digested cake	Pellets
Fe precipitation P removal	MLC	MLP
High surplus activated sludge	SWC	SWP
	EHC	EHP
	POC	POP
Primary and secondary	WWC	WWB
Biological P removal	SLC	
Thames Water Biogran		TWB
Hydrolysed liquid	CHL	
Digested liquid	WDL	
Hydrolysed digested liquid	WHD	

The different biosolids were added to both soil types at a rate equivalent to 10 t ds ha^{-1}. The three liquid sludges were supplied at a rate of 40 ml kg^{-1} fresh soil, equivalent to a dressing in the field of 80 m^3 ha^{-1}. Control treatments were maintained in an unamended condition. A further control included the addition of single superphosphate fertiliser (SSP) (9% total P), at a recommended rate equivalent to a field application of 100 kg ha^{-1} as P_2O_5 [11]. The total P addition to the soils receiving the mineral fertiliser was 25 mg P kg^{-1} dry soil. The experimental treatments were replicated three times.

Soil samples were maintained at 25±0.2°C in the dark in a temperature controlled incubator for periods of 1, 3, 7, 14, 28, 42 and 56 days prior to chemical analysis. Samples were also retained for chemical analysis immediately after incorporation of the biosolids and fertiliser into the soils

Incubated soils were air-dried for 48 h at ambient room temperature. The extractable orthophosphate concentration was determined by shaking 5 g air dry soil with 100 ml of 0.5 M sodium bicarbonate solution at pH 8.5 for 0.5 h using a rotary shaker following standard procedures [12]. Soil extracts were filtered and the concentration of phosphate ions in the soil extracts was measured colorimetrically by a standard molybdate reaction technique.

Soluble phosphate concentrations in the soil extracts were converted to a mg PO_4-P kg^{-1} air dry soil basis. The concentration of PO_4 derived from the biosolids was calculated by subtracting the extractacted PO_4 of each treatment from the blank soil controls. The result was then converted to a percentage of the total P addition.

Table 3 Chemical properties of the biosolids

BIOSOLID	DRY SOLIDS, %	LOI[1], % ds	TOTAL Fe, % ds	TOTAL P, % ds	EXTRACTABLE P[2], mg/kg	P EXTRACTABLE, % Total P	P ADDITION TO SOIL, mg/kg ds
MLC	23.3	50.4	5.5	5.4	1164	2.1	255
SWC	18.6	50.2	6.0	3.8	1238	3.3	190
EHC	14.5	54.2	0.55	2.8	3724	13.3	140
POC	21.4	58.2	0.88	2.8	1346	4.8	140
WWC	26.7	nd	1.4	2.5	866	3.5	125
SLC	20.4	54.9	0.95	3.4	3436	10.1	170
MLP	90.3	45.0	6.4	4.8	226	0.5	240
SWP	89.1	46.8	6.7	3.5	293	0.8	175
EHP	89.3	50.6	0.76	2.6	711	2.7	130
POP	90.2	53.0	0.81	2.5	310	1.2	125
WWB	97.0	nd	1.3	2.2	321	1.5	110
TWB	96.1	43.1	1.4	1.8	451	2.0	90
CHL	5.8	74.4	nd	1.7	1735	10.2	39
WDL	2.6	55.3	nd	5.1	2311	4.5	52
WHD	3.8	11.8	nd	5.1	1318	2.6	77

nd: not determined.
[1]Loss on ignition at 550°C.
[2]Sodium bicarbonate extraction.
[3]On basis that 1 ha of soil weighs 2000 t (assuming 20 cm depth of soil and a soil density of 1).

RESULTS

Statistical analysis demonstrated that, besides soil, biosolids type and time being individually important, their combined effect also created significant differences in extractable P concentrations.

(a)

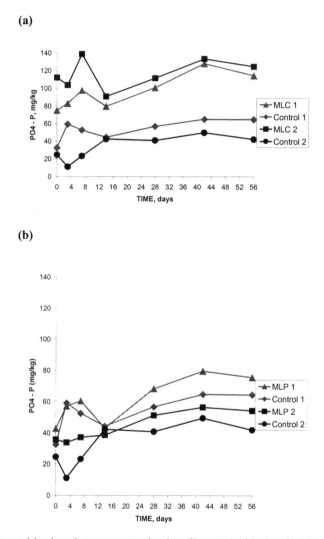

(b)

Figure 1   Extractable phosphate concentration in soil treated with chemical P removal sludge (Fe dosed) (a) cake and (b) pellets

The dewatered digested cakes gave the highest extractable P concentrations of the three different types of material tested (dewatered cakes, digested thermally dried pellets and liquid sludges). MLC (Fe dosed for P removal) exhibited the highest extractable P values of the dewatered cakes (96.8 mg kg^{-1} in soil 1 and 116.3 mg kg^{-1} in soil 2) (Figure 1). However, this sludge also had the largest overall P content and P addition (255 mg P kg^{-1} dry soil).

SLC (biological P removal) produced the second highest P extractability, despite a modest rate of P addition to the soil of 170 mg kg^{-1}) (Figure 2). The high surplus activated sludge from SWC (6.0% Fe, ds) had a slightly higher P addition (190 mg kg^{-1}) compared to the SLC (0.95% Fe, ds), but the extractable P content of soil was much smaller compared to SLC (Figure3).

Contrary to what might be expected, P activity with dewatered cakes, MLC, SLC and SWC was greater in the calacareous soil, which has a considerably lower native P status than the loamy sand (Soil 1) (Table 2).

The other cake products performed in a similar manner; producing equivalent increases in P extractability above the control soil, in relation to the amount of P added in the sludges for both soil types. These results suggest that P activity in soil amended with conventional dewatered digested biosolids may simply reflect the rate of total P addition in the product.

In contrast to the dewatered digested sludges, thermally dried biosolids have significantly smaller P extractabilities. For example, the extractable P content of soil amended with MLP was reduced by 37% in soil 1 and 62% in soil 2 (Table 4), compared with soil supplied with the equivalent dewatered cake from this STW. Phosphorus activity was not affected by the amount of P added in this case, since P enriched biosolids (MLP) did not perform better than dried products derived from conventional sludges. Compared to the digested cakes, the thermally dried products have exhibited a stronger time dependency. The results showed a statistically significant increase in the extractable P content of soil with time for all the thermally dried sludges in both soil types.

The hydrolysed liquid sludge (CHL) exhibited the lowest overall P extractability of all the materials tested (56.5 mg kg^{-1} and 41.0 mg kg^{-1} for soils 1 and 2 respectively) (not shown). The digested liquid (WDL) and hydrolysed/digested liquid (WHD) gave similar P activities (66.7 mg kg^{-1} and 67.3 mg kg^{-1} respectively for soil 1 and 53.9 mg kg^{-1} and 61.0 mg kg^{-1} respectively for soil 2) (not shown); at a level between the thermally dried products and the dewatered cakes.

The P fertiliser replacement value of the biosolids was calculated by taking into consideration the actual P additions supplied to the soil. Performance was compared on the basis of mean values for all times of incubation (Figure 4). This was reasonable because despite the apparent significant relationship with time, the relative changes of extractable P at each sampling time were small.

Without exception, all the biosolids gave larger P extractabilities (as a percentage of total addition) in calcareous soil, compared with the sandy loam, when expressed on the basis of P input. By contrast, however, inorganic fertiliser gave the largest extractability in the sandy soil (Figure 4).

Thermal drying significantly reduced the percentage extractable P contents of soils amended with these biosolids and, as expected, thermally dried products exhibited the lowest % extractable P values compared with the other biosolids types examined (Figure 4).

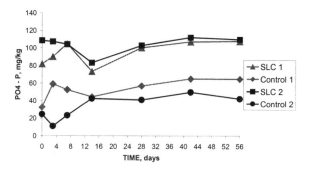

Figure 2 Extractable phosphate concentration in soil treated
with biological P removal sludge cake

(a)

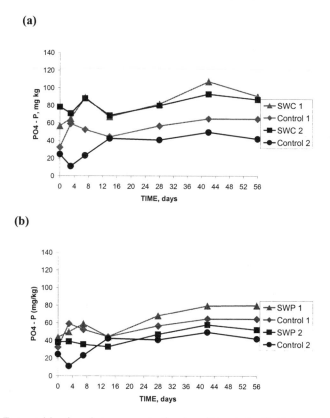

(b)

Figure 3 Extractable phosphate concentration in soil treated with high surplus activated
sludge (a) cake and (b) pellets

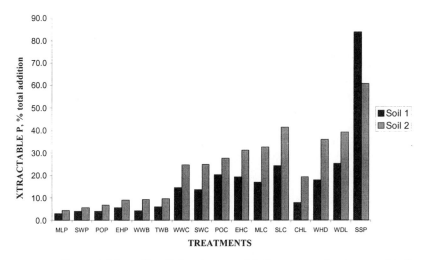

Figure 4 Mean (for all times) extractable P concentration in treated soil

MLP gave the lowest overall % extractable P in both soils (3.1%, soil 1 and 4.4%, soil 2). Large differences were apparent in P extractabilities between the thermally dried products and the corresponding cakes. For example, % extractable P from POP was only 4.1 % and 6.7% in soils 1 and 2, respectively, compared with 20.3% and 27.6% in these soils respectively, for the corresponding dewatered cake, POC.

Reductions in P extractability (expressed as %) of thermally dried products from their corresponding cakes are shown in Table 5. The largest difference in extractability of P for a thermally dried sludge and its equivalent cake was for MLP, which exhibited a 37% reduction in soil 1 and a 62% reduction in soil 2 relative to MLC.

Table 5 Reduction in P extractability of thermally dried biosolids relative to the corresponding dewatered cakes

DEWATERED CAKE	THERMALLY DRIED PELLETSS	REDUCTION IN P EXTRACTABILITY (%) FROM CORRESPONDING THERMALLY DRIED PELLETS	
		Soil 1 - loamy sand	Soil 2 - calcareous clay
MLC	MLP	37	62
SWC	SWP	24	46
EHC	EHP	25	42
POC	POP	28	35
WWC	WWB	19	32

The Fe contents of the thermally dried biosolids also influenced % P extractabilities in amended soil, with the % extractable P decreasing with increasing Fe concentration of thermally dried sludge. Thus, the thermally dried sludges with the highest Fe content (6.4% and 6.7% for MLP and SWP, respectively) gave the lowest overall % extractabilities. Linear regression analysis showed that this effect of Fe occurred in both soil types.

However, there was little evidence to suggest that the high Fe content dewatered cakes (MLC 5.5% Fe ds and SWC 6.0% Fe ds) reduced P extractability by the binding of P with Fe. For example, % P extractability of SWC was 13.7% and 24.9% in soils 1 and 2, respectively, and was comparable to low Fe sludges, such as WWC (1.4% Fe ds) which gave 14.5% and 24.7% P availability for soils 1 and 2, respectively. The biological P removal sludge from SLC exhibited the greatest % P extractability of the different biosolids types tested (24.3% and 41.4% available in soils 1 and 2 respectively), compared to 17% and 32.5% in soils 1 and 2, respectively for MLC (Fe dosed).

The hydrolysed liquid sludge (CHL) produced the lowest overall % P extractability of the liquid sludges (7.7%, soil 1 and 19.4%, soil 2), however, % extractabilities were larger than for the thermally dried products. In comparison with CHL and WDL, hydrolysed/digested liquid (WHD) gave the highest P extractabilities (67.3 mg kg^{-1} and 61.0 mg kg^{-1} for soils 1 and 2, respectively); but the digested liquid (WDL) produced the greatest % P extractabilities (25.2%, soil 1 and 39.2%, soil 2).

DISCUSSION

Thermal Drying

Thermal drying severely reduced P extractability in treated soil compared with corresponding digested cake products, the greatest reduction being 62% in soil 2 between MLP and MLC. A pot trial using digested, dried and pelleted sludge [13], produced availabilities of 9-12% compared to superphosphate fertiliser. This compares closely to the results obtained here for the thermally dried products, which produced % availabilities relative to superphosphate ranging from 3.7% for MLP in soil 1 to 15.8% for Biogran (TWB) in soil 2. Such large reductions in P extractability indicate that thermal treatment has major effects on the speciation and mineralogy of P in sludge, reducing its susceptibility to sodium bicarbonate extraction. It appears that heating has increased the rate of reaction of simple, readily dissolvable phosphate minerals to more complex, less soluble minerals.

Using ^{31}P nuclear magnetic resonance (NMR), Frossard et al [14] characterised P species in variously treated sewage sludges and found that sludge treatment significantly affected P speciation. They found that 50% of the P in raw sludge was organic. Anaerobically digested sludges contained more than 65% inorganic P, principally as dicalcium phosphates, but also Fe and Al precipitates. Anaerobically digested heat-treated sludge contained large proportions (84.4%) of Apatite P, compared to a value of 40.6% in an activated sludge. Sequential extraction of P from sludge [15] (extractions first carried out with deionised water, then 0.5M NaHCO$_3$, 0.1M NaOH and 1.0M HCl), showed that sludge type and treatment had major effects on the forms of P present in sludge. Thermally dried sludge showed a predominance of Apatite-P (extracted by HCl). Solubilities of Ca phosphates decrease in the order CaHPO$_4$·H$_2$O (brushite) > CaHPO$_4$ (monetite) > Ca$_8$H$_2$(PO$_4$)$_6$·5H$_2$O (octocalcium phosphate) > β-Ca$_3$(PO$_4$)$_2$ (β-calcium phosphate) > Ca$_5$OH(PO$_4$)$_3$ (hydroxyapatite) [16]. The solubility of hydroxyapatite is more than two orders of magnitude less than mono-calcium phosphate

$(Ca(H_2PO_4)_2)$, the major constituent of superphosphate fertiliser. For example, log K_s values for mono-calcium phosphate and hydroxyapatite are 113.7 and 1.1 respectively (K_s being the solubility product constant) [17]. Therefore, sludges with a large apatite P content will be relatively poor suppliers of plant available PO_4.

Iron Dosing

Phosphorus speciation in sludge ultimately determines availability to crops as a fertiliser nutrient, and is controlled to a large extent by the P removal process operated at the STW. Thus, Fe dosed sludges contain a large proportion of their P content as relatively insoluble pyrophosphates (eg ferrous pyrophosphate, $Fe_2P_2O_7$) [18]. From pot trials, Kyle and McClintock [19] found P availabilities decreased in the following order: fertiliser > raw sludge > biological P removal sludges > Al sludges> Fe sludges. Other reports also conclude that soil P availability is potentially reduced by the addition of Fe rich sludges [20,21]. In contrast to this published information, however, the results presented here provided no evidence of reduced P extractability in calcareous or sandy soils amended with Fe rich dewatered cakes, relative to conventional low Fe cakes.

The incubation trial has not assessed the potential long term effects of repeated applications of Fe enriched sludges. From the results presented here, there is no indication that the binding of P is a major obstacle to recycling high Fe sludges on agricultural land, even on soils with high P fixation capacities.

Thermal Hydrolysis

There was little difference in performance between the digested liquid (WDL) and the hydrolysed/digested liquid (WHD). Both these liquid sludges exhibited greater % extractabilities than the conventional dewatered digested cakes in both soils (except POP and EHC in soil 1), because dewatering has not removed the soluble P fractions. Results from sequential analysis of P, [22], corroborate this, since larger amounts of P were extracted by H_2O and $NaHCO_3$ from liquid sludges compared to solid sludges.

The hydrolysed only liquid (CHL), however, exhibited a % extractability of less than half of the values produced by the digested liquid and the hydrolysed/digested liquid. The thermal hydrolysis process has altered the P speciation of the sludge to less extractable forms. Anaerobically digesting the sludge following thermal hydrolysis has had the effect of reconverting the sludge P back into a form more amenable to sodium bicarbonate extraction when added to soil. The reasons for the low extractability from CHL are likely to be the high temperatures used in the hydrolysis treatment (165-180°C for 0.5 h), affecting P speciation in a similar way to the thermally dried biosolids. The low redox potential in the anaerobic digester may convert the less soluble Fe(III) phosphate complexes formed at the high temperatures to the more soluble Fe(II) forms [23].

Soil Type

The % extractable P values obtained from the incubation study are broadly similar to those obtained in other controlled experimental work.

All sludge types produced greater % P extractabilities in the calcareous clay (Figure 6), particularly the Fe enriched cakes which exhibited the largest proportional differences in % extractability between the two soil types.

Iron phosphates generally have higher availabilities in calcareous soils compared to low Ca soils due to the conversion of phosphates bound by Fe to Ca, allowing P release [24]. Furthermore, inorganic Fe is rapidly hydrolysed and precipitated under these conditions as insoluble Fe_2O_3, causing further P release. This mechanism offers a possible explanation for the high % P extractabilities obtained for the high Fe biosolids in the calcareous soil.

O'Connor and Knudtsen [25] also found sludge was better able to supply P than inorganic fertilisers in calcareous soils. They found the majority of sludge P was inorganic and comparisons between sterile and non-sterile soils, showed P supply to be controlled by abiotic processes. They concluded that sludge was more effective as a P source than mineral fertiliser due to a small reduction in pH value of sludge amended soil, causing increased P solubility and thus plant availability. The decline in pH value of sludge treated soil is a frequently reported phenomena that is caused by various factors. These include organic acid production, nitrification, sulphur transformations and increased partial pressure of CO_2 in the soil atmosphere due to the stimulated microbial biomass [26].

CONCLUSIONS

From the experimental results it can be concluded that sewage sludge can effectively supply phosphorus to soil in plant available forms. Moreover, sludge treatment and P removal processes strongly influence the P fertiliser replacement value of biosolids products.

The soil incubation study has shown:

- The biological P removal sludge produced a greater % P extractability (41%) than the Fe precipitated P removal sludge (33%).

- Thermal drying of sludge significantly reduced the concentration of extractable phosphate (by 19-62%) compared to the corresponding dewatered digested cakes. Thus, given the reduced extractability of P, the application of thermally dried biosolids to agricultural land at normal agricultural rates is unlikely to cause potential environmental problems from P loss.

- The trend of increased P extractability with time for the thermally dried biosolids suggests that these materials will act as slow release P fertilisers.

- Percentage P extractability from all biosolids types was greater when applied on calcareous soil, compared to a sandy loam, with the greatest differences exhibited from the Fe enriched dewatered digested cakes.

- Iron rich dewatered digested biosolids do not appear to reduce P extractability in soils and their performance is enhanced in calcareous soils (% extractable P was nearly doubled compared to the loamy sand). However, there is conflicting evidence in the literature on this subject and more research is needed to resolve this issue.

- Anaerobically digested liquid sludges exhibited greater extractable P (as a percentage of total P addition) compared to conventional dewatered digested cakes. The effect of thermal hydrolysis treatment, prior to anaerobic digestion, has little effect on P extractability from soil compared to anaerobic digestion only. The extractability of P in the thermal hydrolysis treatment alone was reduced to less than half in both soil types.

In order to give farmers more accurate guidance on the P fertiliser replacement value of both conventional sludges and new biosolids products, it is imperative that the dynamics of P in sludge-soil systems is better understood. Thus, further work is needed to accurately determine the complex issue of P speciation in sludge and how this is affected by sludge treatment and P removal processes.

ACKNOWLEDGEMENT

The research project described in this paper was funded by Thames Water Utilities Ltd.

REFERENCES

1. COUNCIL OF EUROPEAN COMMUNITIES Directive Concerning Urban Waste Water Treatment (91/271/EEC). *Official Journal L135/40*, May 1991.

2. COUNCIL OF EUROPEAN COMMUNITIES Directive on the protection of the environment, and in particular of the soil, when sewage sludge is used in agriculture (86/278/EEC). *Official Journal L187/6*, July 1986.

3. UK STATUTORY INSTRUMENT The Sludge (Use in Agriculture) Regulations 1989. *Statutory Instrument No. 1263*.1989. HMSO, London.

4. MINISTRY OF AGRICULTURE, FISHERIES AND FOOD (1998) *Code of Good Agricultural Practice for the   Protection of Water*, PB 0585, MAFF Publications, London.

5. COKER E.G. AND CARLTON-SMITH C.H. (1986) Phosphorus in Sewage Sludges as a Fertiliser. *Waste Management & Research*, **4**, 303-319.

6. MINISTRY OF AGRICULTURE, FISHERIES AND FOOD (1994) *Fertiliser Recommendations for Agricultural and Horticultural Crops*, MAFF Reference Book 209, HMSO, London.

7. SHARPLEY A.N. AND REKOLAINEN S. (1997) Phosphorus in Agriculture and its Environmental Implications. In: Tunney H. *et al* (eds.), *Phosphorus Loss from Soil to Water*. CAB International, Wallingford, pp. 1-53.

8. MINISTRY OF AGRICULTURE, FISHERIES AND FOOD (1998) *Code of Good Agricultural Practice for the   Protection of Water*, PB 0585, MAFF Publications, London.

9. STEEN I. AND AGRO K. (1998) Phosphorus availability in the 21st Century: Management of a Non-Renewable Resource. *Phosphorus and Potassium* **217**, pp. 25-31.

10. SOLER SOLER J. AND SOLER ROVIRA J. (1996). Cadmium in Inorganic Fertilisers. In: Rodriguez-Barrueco C. (ed.), *Fertilisers and Environment*. Kluwer Academic Publishers, Dordrecht, pp. 541-545.

11. MINISTRY OF AGRICULTURE, FISHERIES AND FOOD (1994) *FertiliserRecommendations for Agricultural and Horticultural Crops*, MAFF Reference Book 209, HMSO, London.

12. MINISTRY OF AGRICULTURE, FISHERIES AND FOOD (1987) *The Analysis of Agricultural Material*, MAFF Reference Book 427, 3rd ed. HMSO, London.

13. MARKS M.J. (1978) Evaluation of the Nitrogen and Phosphorus Content of Dried Pelleted Sewage Sludge. *Soil Science Annual Report*, Wye Sah Centre, Ministry of Agriculture, Fisheries and Food, HMSO, London.

14. FROSSARD E., TEKELY P. AND GRIMAL J.Y. (1994) Characterisation of Phosphate Species in Urban Sewage Sludges by High-Resolution Soild-State ^{31}P NMR. *European Journal of Science*, **45**, 403-408.

15. UK WATER INDUSTRY RESEARCH (UKWIR) (1997b) Form and Bioavailability of Phosphorus in sewage sludge (Experiment 1). Project **SL-02** *Impact of Phosphorus*, UKWIR, London

16. LINDSAY W.L. AND VLEK L.G. (1977) Phosphate Minerals. In: Dinaeur R.C. (ed.), *Minerals in Soil Environments*. Soil Science Society of America, Wisconsin, pp. 639-672.

17. HANSSON B. (1985) Practical Experiences and Official Tests with Chemically Precipitated Phosphate Sludges in Swedish Agriculture. In: Lester J.N. and Kirk P.W.W. (Eds), *Management Strategies for Phosphorus in the Environment*. Selper Publications, London.

18. FROSSARD E., TEKELY P. AND GRIMAL J.Y. (1994) Characterisation of Phosphate Species in Urban Sewage Sludges by High-Resolution Soild-State ^{31}P NMR. *European Journal of Science*, **45**, 403-408.

19. KYLE M.A. AND MCCLINTOCK S.A. (1995) The Availability of Phosphorus in Municipal Wastewater Sludge as a Function of the Phosphorus Removal Process and Sludge Treatment Method. *Water Environment Research*, **67 No. 3**, 282-289.

20. UK WATER INDUSTRY RESEARCH (UKWIR) (1997a) Literature Review WW-10: The Environmental Impact of Using Iron Salts in Sewage Treatment. Project **WW-10**: *The Environmental Impact of Using Iron Salts in Sewage Treatment*, UKWIR, London.

21. COKER E.G. AND CARLTON-SMITH C.H. (1986) Phosphorus in Sewage Sludges as a Fertiliser. *Waste Management & Research*, **4**, 303-319.

22. UK WATER INDUSTRY RESEARCH (UKWIR) (1997b) Form and Bioavailability of Phosphorus in sewage sludge (Experiment 1). Project **SL-02** *Impact of Phosphorus*, UKWIR, London

23. LINDSAY W.L. AND VLEK L.G. (1977) Phosphate Minerals. In: Dinaeur R.C. (ed.), *Minerals in Soil Environments*. Soil Science Society of America, Wisconsin, pp. 639-672.

24. HANSSON B. (1996) The Influence of Coagulants and Precipitants on the Behaviour of Sewage Sludge on Agricultural Land. *Vatten*, **52**, 31-38.

25. O'CONNOR G.A. AND KNUDTSEN K.L. (1985) Phosphorus Solubility in Sludge Amended Calcareous Soils. In: Lester J.N. and Kirk P.W.W. (Eds), *Management Strategies for Phosphorus in the Environment*. Selper Publications, London.

26. KIRCHMANN H., PICHLMAYER F. AND GERZABEK M.H. (1996) Sulfur Balances and Sulfur-34 Abundance in a Long-Term Fertilizer Experiment. *Soil Science Society of America Journal*, **59**, 174-178.

THE SCIENTIFIC BASIS TO RECYCLING SEWAGE SLUDGE IN AGRICULTURE

S R Smith

Imperial College, London

United Kingdom

ABSTRACT. The environmental effects of heavy metals in sewage sludge-treated agricultural soils are examined in this paper. The scientific evidence shows that the potential environmental risks from heavy metals applied to soil in sludge are small and that precautionary, technically based soil quality limits for metals can provide a pragmatic approach to facilitate recycling. Because they encourage recycling, they also provide an incentive to reduce metal discharges to sewers to enhance the environmental and operational sustainability of the agricultural outlet for sludge management. This is discussed within the context of current proposals to reduce the maximum permissible limit values for heavy metals in a revision of European Directive 86/278/EEC regulating the use of sludge in agriculture. The revised values are lower than precautionary, scientifically based soil limits. Copper is the most limiting element and the standard proposed for this metal would restrict the maximum number of applications of sludge to a particular field to 25, assuming an application rate of 5 t ds y^{-1}. Unless the European Commission can be persuaded to adopt a moderately more flexible approach to regulating PTEs in soil in the revised Directive, this short horizon may compromise the operational viability of sludge recycling operations under UK conditions.

Keywords: Agriculture, Biosolids, Dietary intake, Environmental effects, Heavy metals, Microbial biomass, Phytotoxicity, *Rhizobium*, Soil.

Dr S R Smith, is a Lecturer in Environmental Engineering and Director of the Centre for Environmental Control and Waste Management in the Department of Civil & Environmental Engineering, Imperial College, London. He has researched the agronomic value and environmental effects of sewage sludge re-use in agriculture for 18 years and has written more than 100 scientific papers and reports on the subject for Government and the Water Industry. He is also the author of a text book on the Agricultural Recycling of Sewage Sludge and the Environment.

INTRODUCTION

Sewage sludges always contain heavy metals, even if of entirely domestic origin. Domestic sources and surface run-off contribute to the background concentrations of heavy metals in sludge and represent the main diffuse inputs of metals to sewer. Heavy metals are ubiquitous and occur naturally in the environment so it is inevitable and normal to find them in sludge. Heavy metals are a normal constituent of all types of food stuffs and are present in human faeces. For example, human faecal matter is reported to contain: 250 mg Zn kg^{-1}, 68 mg Cu kg^{-1}, 4.7 mg Ni kg^{-1}, 2 mg Cd kg^{-1} and 11 mg Pb kg^{-1} (ADEME, 1995). Other important domestic inputs include leaching from plumbing systems and use in body care products. The other major source of heavy metals in sludge originates from direct discharges by industry connected to the sewer. The metal content of sludge is important in defining its quality and suitability for agricultural use and controls to restrict industrial discharges are a priority for the long-term sustainability and security of the outlet. Where trade effluent controls are rigorously enforced, metal concentrations in sludge have fallen markedly (Table 1 and Figure 1). This has been so effective at improving sludge quality that, in the EU and UK, the mean Cd content in sludge applied to farmland reflects the background content discharged to sewer in faeces. As industrial discharges decline, diffuse inputs of potentially toxic elements (PTEs) from domestic sources, small enterprises and institutions such as hospitals become more significant, but these are also more difficult to identify and control. Imperial College has recently prepared a report for the European Commission assessing the potential significance of these sources and identifying possible measures to minimise them (IC Consultants, 2001).

Table 1 Decline in heavy metal contents (works size weighted mean, mg kg^{-1} ds) in sewage sludge recycled to agricultural land in the UK as a result of industrial trade effluent control (Sleeman, 1984; DoE, 1993; EA, 1999)

PTE	1983	1990	1996	REDUCTION IN 1996 RELATIVE TO 1983 (%)
Zn	1319	922	792	40
Cu	703	574	568	19
Ni	107	65	57	47
Cd	14	5.0	3.3	76
Pb	462	201	221	52
Hg	5.0	3.5	2.4	52
Cr	312	208	157	50

A characteristic of heavy metals is that, once applied to the soil, they are effectively retained by the soil matrix indefinitely in the cultivated layers. Therefore, metals tend to accumulate when the concentration in a material that is applied to the soil is greater than in the soil itself. This has implications for the long-term quality of sludge-treated soil for crop production and controls are necessary to prevent excessive inputs to protect sensitive environmental end-points. The critical environmental end-points for setting limits for agricultural recycling sewage sludge vary according to the behaviour of particular elements and include:

- Phytotoxicity (Zn, Cu, Ni; Cr may also be listed here, but there is no evidence of crop damage due to Cr when sludge is used in agriculture);
- Human foodchain via crop uptake (Cd);
- Human foodchain via offal meat from animals ingesting sewage sludge or sludge-treated soil (Cd and Pb);
- Animal health (Cu, As, Se, Mo and F);
- Soil fertility (Zn).

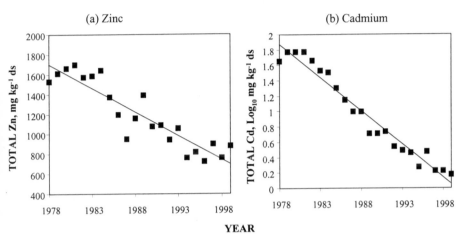

Figure 1 Reduction in (a) zinc and (b) cadmium concentrations (untransformed and $\log_{10}$ transformed data, respectively) in sewage sludge from Nottingham STW, UK during the period 1978 – 1999

Some PTEs are beneficial as trace elements such as Cu and Zn, whereas others have no known biological function. The environment can safely tolerate accumulations of PTEs up to certain limits before there is the potential to cause an adverse effect. The scientific approach to controlling PTEs in sludge-treated soil quantitatively defines the toxicological/ ecotoxicological dose-response relationship of the most sensitive environmental receptor to a particular element and establishes a limit value below the Lowest Observed Adverse Effect Concentration - LOAEC that allows for a further margin of safety (Figure 2).

The numerical standards for PTEs adopted in different countries vary considerably and reflect a political decision to adopt one of the following strategies, with increasingly limiting implications for land application of sludge:

- Risk/technical basis (US);
- Technically based, but precautionary (UK, Directive 86/278/EEC (CEC, 1986));
- No technical basis, highly precautionary (certain European countries, proposed revision of Directive 86/278/EEC (CEC, 2000)).

This paper examines the scientific and practical implications of these different approaches with particular reference to phytotoxicity, Cd accumulation in staple plant foods and soil fertility as critical environmental criteria for developing standards that protect the quality of soil when sewage sludge is recycled on farmland.

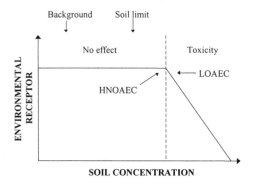

Figure 2 Defining concentration limits for PTEs in soil (HNOAEC = Highest No Observed Adverse Effect Concentration; LOAEC = Lowest Observed Adverse Effect Concentration)

ANIMAL INGESTION

Whilst a theoretical risk exists to livestock and offal meat consumed in the human diet from the surface application of sludge to grazing land, it is unlikely that animal health or the foodchain are affected by this practice because the exposure is short-term, absorption is suppressed by complex dietary antagonisms and there is no PTE accumulation in muscle tissue (Carrington et al., 1998). The amount of offal meat consumed in the diet is also very small and practically contributes a negligible input of PTEs to the diet. A reduction in the UK maximum permissible soil limit for Pb from 300 mg kg^{-1} to 200 mg kg^{-1} has been recommended, however, as a precautionary measure to avoid the risk of exceeding current and proposed food limit values for Pb in kidney and liver, under exceptional worse-case conditions of soil Pb accumulation and ingestion by sheep (Carrington et al., 1998; Stark et al., 1998). The intake of PTEs in sludge by grazing animals is avoided by injecting liquid biosolids into the soil or by applying dewatered product and the move towards enhanced treatment and thermal drying will also provide a barrier to the transfer of contaminants in sludge to grazing livestock.

PHYTOTOXICITY

The potential effects of heavy metals on crop yields are an important concern when sewage sludge is recycled on agricultural land and there is an extensive literature defining critical plant tissue and soil limit concentrations for the phytotoxic elements (Figure 3). The risk assessment models for Zn, Cu and Ni, that formed the basis of the standards for these elements in the US EPA Part 503 Rule (US EPA, 1993), included an assessment of 271 articles on crop phytotoxicity (Chang et al., 1992; US EPA, 1992). Relationships between metal concentrations in plant tissues and growth retardation, described as the phytotoxic threshold, were obtained from laboratory experiments, where plants were grown in media treated with single elements in salt form. Data from sludge-treated field trials were listed in a database and used to estimate appropriate soil metal loading rates corresponding to the phytotoxic threshold concentrations in plant tissues. The relationships between sludge, soil and crop concentrations of PTEs and yield were statistically evaluated and sludge quality limit values and loading rates for heavy metals to protect crop yields were calculated, assuming that sludge is spread annually for 100 years at a rate of 10 t ha^{-1} y^{-1} (1000 t ha^{-1} total sludge application).

The potentially phytotoxic effects of Zn, Cu and Ni have also been assessed in other independent field trials. For example, Smith (1997) estimated upper critical total soil concentrations of these elements for ryegrass in field trials on well equilibrated, historically sludge-treated field soils containing up to 2700 mg Zn kg^{-1}, 1350 mg Cu kg^{-1} and 540 mg Ni kg^{-1}. Historic site soils are usually situated on old sewage farms and have received long-term applications of sludge for periods of at least 10 years or often for >100 years. The pH value of the soils was in the range 4.5-8.0 with a mean value of pH 6.5. Despite these extreme conditions of soil contamination and low pH value, no reductions in crop yield were observed in practice in the field (Figure 4). This contrasts with conservative upper critical soil limits derived from pot experiments with sludge that form the basis of UK regulations for PTEs in sludge-treated agricultural land (Figure 3). Relationships between Zn, Cu and Ni in ryegrass and the total concentrations in long-term sludge-treated soil, as well as the influence of other important soil properties including pH value and organic matter content, were described by multiple regression models (Figure 5). The statistical analysis showed that:

- Metal concentrations in plant tissue were determined principally by total soil content;

- soil pH modulated crop uptake of Zn and Ni, but not Cu;

- soil organic matter had a relatively minor role in controlling crop uptake of metals in long-term and well equilibrated sludge-treated soils and could be removed from the regression models.

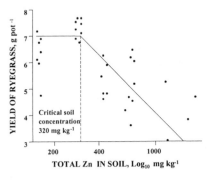

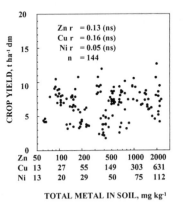

Figure 3 Yield of ryegrass in relation to soil Zn in a pot experiment (Davis and Carlton-Smith, 1984)

Figure 4 Yield of ryegrass in relation to the metal content of historically sludge-treated soils, n = 156 (Smith, 1997)

Total soil concentrations of metals that correspond to the Highest No Observed Adverse Effect Concentrations (HNOAECs) in plant tissues at pH 6.0 were derived from the regression models and are shown in Table 2. However, Cu and Ni concentrations in ryegrass were less than the HNOAEC for phytotoxicity despite the presence of significantly elevated concentrations of these elements in soil up to 1350 mg Cu kg^{-1} and 540 mg Ni kg^{-1}. Therefore it is unlikely that Cu and Ni would be phytotoxic in practice in long-term sludge-treated soil. By contrast, the HNOAEC for Zn of 200 mg kg^{-1} in plant leaves was exceeded for ryegrass and the maximum tissue concentration recorded for this element was 517 mg Zn kg^{-1}. The predicted soil Zn concentration at pH 6.0 corresponding to the HNOAEC in plant tissue, was 1290 mg Zn kg^{-1} (Table 2).

(a)   (b)   (c)

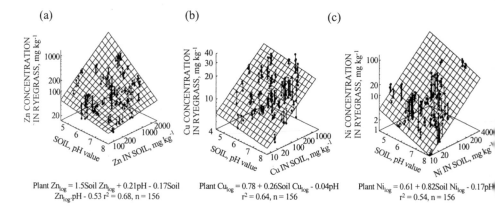

Plant Zn$_{log}$ = 1.5Soil Zn$_{log}$ + 0.21pH - 0.17Soil Zn$_{log}$·pH - 0.53 r^2 = 0.68, n = 156   Plant Cu$_{log}$ = 0.78 + 0.26Soil Cu$_{log}$ - 0.04pH r^2 = 0.64, n = 156   Plant Ni$_{log}$ = 0.61 + 0.82Soil Ni$_{log}$ - 0.17pH r^2 = 0.54, n = 156

Figure 5 Effect of soil total metal concentration and pH value on (a) Zn, (b) Cu and (c) Ni content in ryegrass (Smith, 1997)

In the limited number of cases where reported, phytotoxicity in sludge-treated soils is almost exclusively associated with elevated Zn concentrations. Only in exceptional circumstances is Ni phytotoxic and no reports of Cu toxicity have been found (Carrington et al., 1998). Indeed, the risk assessment by US EPA (1992) could provide no evidence of phytotoxicity due to Cu or Ni in sludge-treated soil at any of the loading rates of Cu and Ni or soil conditions tested in different field experiments. Furthermore, sewage sludge typically contains less Zn, Cu and Ni than the risk-based phytotoxic soil limits, the implication being that high quality sludges can be applied to soil indefinitely without danger of exceeding the critical phytotoxic concentrations of these elements in soil (Table 3). The data from long-term sludge-treated sites in the UK corroborate the US EPA risk assessment and limits to protect crop yields from the potentially phytotoxic effects of heavy metals when sewage sludge is used in agriculture (US EPA, 1992).

CADMIUM AND THE FOODCHAIN

Cadmium is the most labile of the potentially zootoxic elements present in sludge. In contrast to Pb and Hg, the other heavy metals of concern that are strongly adsorbed and immobile in sludge-treated soil, Cd traverses the soil-plant barrier and can potentially accumulate in staple

Table 2 Predicted soil concentrations of Zn, Cu and Ni at the HNOAEC in plant tissues for long-term sludge-treated soil (Smith, 1997)

PTE	PLANT TISSUE HNOAEC, mg kg^{-1}	MAX OVERALL RECORDED TISSUE CONTENT, mg kg^{-1}	MAX OVERALL RECORDED SOIL CONTENT, mg kg^{-1}	PREDICTED SOIL CONTENT, mg kg^{-1}[1]
Zn	200	517	2700	1290
Cu	40	35	1350	na[2]
Ni	90	72	540	na[2]

[1]Estimated from the multiple regression models in Figure 5 at pH 6.0
[2]not applicable since HNOAEC>maximum overall recorded tissue concentration

Table 3 Soil metal concentrations which protect against phytotoxicity compared with UK and US soil limits (mg kg^{-1})

PTE	PREDICTED[1] OR MAX[2] SOIL CONCENTRATIONS AT HISTORIC SITES	UK STATUTORY SOIL LIMITS, pH 6-7	SOIL CONTENT DERIVED FROM US EPA 503 CUMULATIVE APPLICATION[3]	TYPICAL CONCENTRATION IN SLUDGE, mg kg^{-1}
Zn	1290[1]	300	1500	800
Cu	850[2]	135	775	400
Ni	515[2]	75	230	50

[1]Based on Zn uptake model in Figure 5a
[2]Soil concentrations associated with the highest recorded plant tissue concentrations
[3]Cumulative Pollutant Loading Rate kg ha^{-1}/2.0 = mg kg^{-1} estimated concentration in soil

food crops and transfer to the human foodchain. Cadmium is not an acute toxin, but represents a potential chronic risk to health from life-time exposure. The WHO has set a Provisional Tolerable Weekly Intake (WHO/FAO, 1972), which is equivalent to 70 μg per day for a 70 kg person and this is used as the basis for assessing the toxicological risk of potential exposures to Cd from the agricultural use of sludge. The amount of Cd ingested in plant food depends on a number of factors including:

- Soil Cd content;
- Soil properties, particularly pH value;
- Species sensitivity to Cd accumulation;
- Edible crop component eg grain, root, tuber or leaf;
- The amounts of various crop types consumed in the diet;
- The proportion of food in the diet that is grown on sludge-treated soil.

Crops types vary in sensitivity to Cd accumulation (Figure 6). However, Cd uptake and concentrations in the staple food crops including, for example, potato tubers and cereal grain are much less than for certain leafy crop types, which usually represent a relatively small component of the total food intake.

Estimated intakes of Cd for typical UK diets are well within the WHO tolerable limit at the EU maximum permissible soil concentration for Cd of 3 mg kg^{-1} (Figure 7). These calculations conservatively assume that the vegetable portion of the diet is obtained entirely from sludge-treated soil. The proportion of cereal foods in the diet grown on soil receiving sludge is assumed to be 2 %, to reflect the relative area of sludge-treated arable land in the UK and the marketing and distribution of cereal crops. The Steering Group on Chemical Aspects of Food Surveillance (MAFF/DoE, 1993a) considered that the marginal erosion of the PTWI for Cd, compared with the background intake by the general population in the UK of 18.8 μg Cd d^{-1}, was inconsequential to human health.

Assumptions relating to the proportion of food in the diet that is obtained from sludge-treated soil are a major factor influencing the absolute values of risk-derived limits for Cd applied to farmland in sludge. Individuals consuming a large share of their total plant food intake from land receiving sewage sludge are potentially the most exposed group to Cd uptake by crops and this provides a conservative bias in estimating limit values that protect the human diet. For example, in Pathway 2 of US EPA's critical environmental pathway analysis for contaminants in sewage sludge-treated soil (US EPA, 1992), risk-derived limits were calculated on the basis that certain individuals producing a large proportion of their own food may consume up to 59 % of their fruit and vegetable intake and 37 % of their potato intake from soil containing the maximum allowable cumulative Cd addition. Linear soil-crop transfer factors for the major plant food groups were used to estimate the allowable intake based on the difference between the maximum average intake recommended by WHO of 70 μg Cd day^{-1} for a 70 kg person and the background ingestion level in the US of 16.14 μg Cd day^{-1}. This analysis showed that 120 kg Cd ha^{-1} could be safely applied to soil in sewage sludge without adverse effects. Ryan and Chaney (1994) argue that, from a technical perspective, no individual would be harmed even if sludge-amended soil reached a soil concentration of 60 mg Cd kg^{-1}. Stern (1993) reexamined this pathway using stochastic techniques, based on Monte Carlo probabilistic analysis of the exposure variables, to take account of the uncertainties and variability within the modelling process. This provided upper confidence limits to indicate the probability of exceeding the acceptable daily dietary exposure to Cd with increasing Cd cumulative application rate. The probabilistic analysis of the exposure variables was also restricted to Cd uptake slopes for soils with pH ≤6.5. The pH restriction had a moderate influence on the cumulative Cd loading compared with the complete EPA database (no pH restriction) Thus, without pH restriction, the 90th and 95th upper confidence limits for the acceptable cumulative loading rate for Cd were 30 and 17 kg ha^{-1}, respectively, and with pH restriction to ≤6.5, the 90th and 95th upper confidence limits were 23 and 13 kg ha^{-1}, respectively. In acid soils, the Cd loading rate at the 95th upper confidence limit equates to a total soil concentration of 4-6.5 mg Cd kg^{-1} (assuming conversion factors of 3.25 or 2, respectively; MAFF/DoE, 1993b).

In agricultural situations, the amount of food consumed from sludge-treated soil is significantly smaller than by individuals who grow most of their own plant produce. Indeed, the EPA (1992) estimated that 2.5 % of the diet in the general population may be affected by the agricultural use of sludge in the US. This further emphasises the extent of protection against potentially harmful accumulations of Cd in the human diet from the agricultural use of sludge. However, the criteria for assessing exposure to Cd in the human diet will change with the introduction of specific food quality limits on Cd in grains (CEC, 1997). These developments force a move away from a general dietary exposure assessment approach to setting soil limits for PTEs and targets specific soil concentration values to avoid the risk of exceeding the food quality standard. Using the relationships in Figure 6, it is possible to

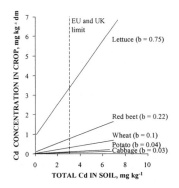

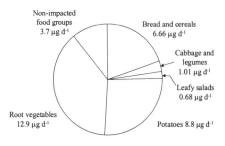

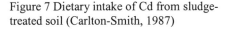

Figure 6 Cd uptake by different crops in relation to content in loamy sand soil (Carlton-Smith, 1987)

Figure 7 Dietary intake of Cd from sludge-treated soil (Carlton-Smith, 1987)

estimate the appropriate soil Cd limit concentration to avoid exceeding the proposed EU Cd limits in grain (0.1-0.2 mg Cd kg^{-1} in cereal grain, except wheat grain that has a limit of 0.2 mg Cd kg^{-1}; CEC, 1997). This analysis suggests that a reduction in the current maximum soil limit to 2 mg kg^{-1} would be necessary to comply with the grain quality standards for crops grown on potentially high risk soils.

Chang et al. (1995) have developed human-health related guidelines for the World Health Organization, Geneva for the application of sewage sludge in agriculture that may be generally applicable to different regions. Plant uptake was selected as the principal exposure route of concern and a 'global' representative diet was developed to provide the criteria for calculating technically-based standards. The model also conservatively assumed that 100 % of an individuals diet was obtained from a sludge-amended area and that acceptable exposure to a pollutant was limited to 50 % of the WHO maximum tolerable intake for an adult with a body weight of 60 kg. This analysis indicated that, as a general guide, a conservative soil limit value of 7 mg kg^{-1} was appropriate to protect the foodchain from Cd applied to soil in sewage sludge. The soil limit concentrations derived for the other potentially zootoxic elements were: 150 mg Pb kg^{-1}, 5 mg Hg kg^{-1}, 9 mg As kg^{-1}, 140 mg Se kg^{-1} and 2600 mg F kg^{-1}.

A comparison of different soil limits for Cd and of contents in sludge is presented in Table 4. This shows that, where effective controls are in place on industrial discharges of heavy metals to sewer, the Cd content of sludge is typically smaller than risk-derived limit values for Cd in soil. Under these circumstances, Cd cannot accumulate in soil to potentially harmful amounts. Therefore, whilst the potential risk to human health from Cd is a recognised concern associated with the land application of sewage sludge, it is a theoretical risk and not an actual risk. In the practical field situation, the agricultural re-use of sludge has minimal impact on Cd in the foodchain and environmental protection can be further assured by appropriate standards to control soil accumulations within well-defined toxicological thresholds.

Table 4 Cd content in sludge and soil limit values, mg kg^{-1}

TYPICAL SLUDGE CONTENT IN UK	CONTENT IN FAECES	EU CURRENT MAX. SOIL LIMIT	[1]GLOBAL DIETARY MODEL
3.3	2.0	3	7
	High intake consumer		[3]Agricultural use
[2]Stochastic model (95% CL)	[2]Stochastic model (90% CL)	[3]Single-point model	
4	7	60	305

[1]Chang *et al* (1995)
[2]Stern (1993); soil pH$\leq$6.5
[3]US EPA (1992); assuming a conversion factor of kg ha^{-1} to mg kg^{-1} = 2

SOIL FERTILITY

Early investigations of the possible effects of PTEs on C and N mineralisation and nitrification processes found no detrimental impacts of heavy metals on microbial activity in sludge-treated soil (Smith, 1996). However, later research on sludge-amended soil from the Woburn Market Garden Experiment, using more sensitive microbial assays including measurements of the total soil microbial biomass and symbiotic N$_2$-fixation, indicated detrimental effects of PTEs may be apparent close to the EU soil limits (Brookes and McGrath, 1984; McGrath *et al.*, 1988). These represent important indices of soil quality because the soil microbial biomass is a repository of labile nutrients and mediates biochemical transformations in soil, and the fixation of atmospheric N by leguminous crops is a significant source of N nutrition in agriculture and particularly for biological systems of crop production. An Independent Scientific Committee, convened by the UK Government to review the evidence on soil fertility aspects of PTEs in sludge-treated soil (MAFF/DoE, 1993b), concluded that Zn was the element potentially responsible for the observed effects of sludge on soil microbial processes. A decision to reduce the UK soil limit from 300 mg kg^{-1} (pH 6-7) to 200 mg kg^{-1} (pH 5-7) was taken on precautionary grounds largely based on results from a sludge-treated field trial at Braunschweig, Germany, which showed declining numbers of free-living *Rhizobium leguminosarum* biovar *trifolii* above a soil concentration of 200 mg Zn kg^{-1} (Figure 8). However, more recent research on a wide range of sludge-treated soils has found no adverse effect of Zn on the amount of microbial biomass in soil below a total concentration of 500-600 mg Zn kg^{-1} (Figure 9 and 10). Furthermore, no consistent effects of soil PTEs on the absence of *Rhizobium* are apparent in long-term, sludge-amended field soils and free-living bacteria may be routinely isolated from sites with significantly elevated PTE concentrations (Table 5). Many factors influence the presence/absence of *Rhizobium* sp in soil in the practical field situation; one of the most important being the period of time that has lapsed since the host crop was grown at a particular site. Indeed, rhizobia are always present in soil and fix N effectively when the host plant is established, irrespective of the soil metal content. Furthermore, other species of symbiotic N fixing bacteria have much lower sensitivities to metals compared with the white-clover bacteria isolated from Woburn soil. The extent to which indigenous strains are tolerant to metals may be highly site specific (El Aziz *et al.*, 1991; Angle *et al.*, 1993; Smith and Giller, 1992). The

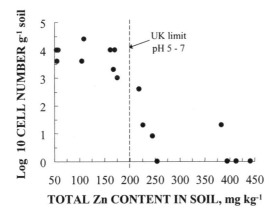

Figure 8 Rhizobial population in relation to Zn in a sludge-treated field trial, Braunschweig, Germany (Chaudri *et al.*, 1993)

potential significance and impacts of PTEs on the fertility of sludge-treated agricultural soil is a controversial area of ongoing research (McGrath and Chaudri, 1999; Smith, 2000). Some of the key issues to emerge are that:

- Zn is the only element of potential concern in the context of European legislation;
- Critical nutrient mineralisation and nitrification processes are not affected in soils with highly elevated PTE concentrations;
- The microbial biomass content of soil is not impacted by Zn in excess of the EU maximum limit value, but Zn is potentially toxic to the microbial biomass below the phytotoxic concentration of this element in soil;
- The variation and unique characteristics of particular species, groups or types of microorganism at specific sites mean that results from one field site or experiment may not be applicable for general extrapolation to other soils;
- There is no definitive assessment of the agronomic or ecological significance of microbial-PTE relations in sludge-treated soil.

Table 5 Mean metal concentrations in sludge-treated soils, according to the presence or absence of *Rhizobium* with no indigenous clover at the sampling sites

PTE	TOTAL SOIL CONCENTRATION, mg kg^{-1}	
	Rhizobia absent	Rhizobia present
Zinc	573	566
Copper	253	154
Cadmium	3.3	3.3

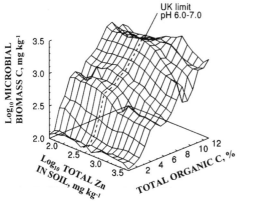

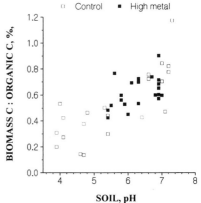

Figure 9 Microbial biomass in long-term sludge-treated field soils in relation to Zn and organic matter (Smith, 1998)

Figure 10 Microbial biomass in a long-term sludge-treated loamy sand soil; high metal = 450 mg Zn kg⁻¹; control = 45 mg Zn kg⁻¹ (Smith *et al.*, 1999)

LIMIT VALUES FOR HEAVY METALS IN SOIL

Limits for heavy metals in sludge-treated agricultural soil in some EU countries, the proposed EU limits for heavy metals in sludge-treated agricultural soil and the limit values estimated from the US EPA pollutant loading rates are presented in Table 6. Denmark, for example, has adopted a very stringent regime of soil limit values for heavy metals and this could not be transferred to UK conditions because many of the standards are less than the typical background concentrations in UK soils. These values also contrast markedly, by one to two orders of magnitude, with the technical risk-based limits estimated for sludge-treated soil from the pollutant loading rates in the US EPA 503 Final Rule for the Use or Disposal of Sewage Sludge (US EPA, 1993). Current proposals (CEC, 2000) for soil limits in the revision of EU Directive 86/278/EEC adopt the lower permissible limit from the Directive (CEC, 1986) for Zn, Cu and Cd, which, incidently, also fall half-way between the German and Danish limit values for these elements. The proposed limit for Ni is equivalent to the German value (50 mg kg⁻¹). The limits for Pb and Cr are also mid-way between the German and Danish standards and the Danish limit has been adopted for Hg (0.5 mg kg⁻¹). Simple metal addition calculations, that take account of the mass of biosolids added to soil and partial degradation of organic matter supplied in biosolids, show that Cu is most limiting PTE at typical sludge and soil concentrations for this element in the UK under the new proposed EU regime. If these limits were enforced, the number of applications to an area of land would be restricted to 25 (ie 25 years of annual dressings of 5 t ds ha⁻¹) to comply with the limit value for Cu in soil (50 mg Cu kg⁻¹). This is much shorter than the 50 years suggested by the WEF-EWPCA-IWA network for the minimum period required to maintain the operational viability of the land application route (Matthews, 1997). Under UK conditions, a soil limit for Cu of 80 mg kg⁻¹ would provide the flexibility for an operational time-frame of 50 years without placing the environment at risk. Zinc and Cd are not as restrictive as Cu and the limits for these elements would be approached after 40 and 47 applications of sludge, respectively. The

Table 6 Maximum permissible concentrations of heavy metals in sludge-treated soils (mg kg⁻¹ dry solids) in EC Member States and US

PTE	[1+2]SOIL (median)	EU (86/278/EEC)	UK pH 6 - 7	GERMANY	DENMARK	US[3]	EU (proposed) pH 6-7	[4]APPLICATIONS TO ATTAIN PROPOSED EU LIMITS
Zn	82.0	150-300	300	200	100	1500	150	41
Cu	18.1	50-140	135	60	40	775	50	25
Ni	22.6	30-75	75	50	15	230	50	241
Cd	0.7	1-3	3	1.5	0.5	20	1	47
Pb	40.0	50-300	300	100	40	190	70	70
Hg	0.1	1-1.5	1	1	0.5	9	0.5	79
Cr	39.3		400	100	30	1540	60	73

[1]Ure and Berrow (1982), [2]McGrath and Loveland (1992)
[3]Approximate values based on the cumulative pollutant loading rates in Part 503 Rule (US EPA, 1993)
[4]Number of applications estimated from the incremental change in soil concentration as follows:

Soil concentration (mg kg⁻¹) = (Soil PTE g + Σsludge PTE g)/(Soil mass t + Σsludge mass t)

The calculations assume a soil weight of 2000 t ha⁻¹ and that sludge is applied at a rate of 5 t ds y⁻¹ (this supplies 250 kg N ha⁻¹ at 5 % TN content). It is also assumed that 50 % of the applied organic matter degrades (the net contribution to the soil mass is therefore 3.5 t/y assuming sludge contains 60 % organic matter))

Smaller metal limit concentrations may be set for some elements at low soil pH value time-frame for Zn could be extended to 50 years, without impacting the environment, by increasing the soil limit for this element to 165 mg kg^{-1}. Sludge may be applied on 70 – 80 occasions before reaching the proposed limits for Pb, Hg and Cr and 240 applications of sludge to a field would be necessary for Ni to accumulate to its soil limit value. Following the WEF-EWPCA-IWA criteria and the simple metal loading calculations presented here, the proposed soil limits for these elements, whilst stringent and without scientific basis, are generally not restrictive of recycling sewage sludge to agricultural land under typical UK conditions.

CONCLUSIONS

The extensive scientific database on the environmental effects of heavy metals in sludge-treated soil shows that the risks are small and that precautionary, but pragmatic soil limit values can protect the environment, whilst at the same time, encourage agricultural recycling of sewage sludge by providing operational flexibility and security. Source controls may be more effective than stringent soil limits at improving the quality of sludge to increase the long-term environmental and operational sustainability of the agricultural outlet for sludge. Unless the European Commission can be persuaded to adopt a moderately more flexible approach to the limit values for certain PTEs in soil in the revision of the Directive controlling the agricultural use of sludge, and in particular for Cu and Zn, the operational viability of recycling sewage sludge to farmland in the UK could be potentially compromised without reasonable scientific justification. Tightening soil limits to the extent that discourages agricultural use would waste the valuable N and P resources contained in sludge and would remove a principal and practical incentive to reduce metal discharges to sewer.

REFERENCES

1. ADEME; Agence de l'Environnement et de la Maîtrise de l'Energie (1995) Les micropolluants métalliques dans les boues résiduaires des stations d'épuration urbaines, Pages 17-79, (2).

2. Angle, J.S., McGrath, S.P., Chaudri, A.M., Chaney, R.L. and Giller, K.E. (1993) Inoculation effects on legumes grown in soil previously treated with sewage sludge. *Soil Biology and Biochemistry* 25, 575-580.

3. Brookes, P.C. and McGrath, S.P. (1984) Effects of metal toxicity on the size of the soil microbial biomass. *Journal of Soil Science* 35, 341-346.

4. Carlton-Smith, C.H. (1987) *Effects of Metals in Sludge-treated Soils on Crops*. Technical report TR 251. WRc Medmenham, Marlow.

5. Carrington, E.G., Davis, R.D., Hall, J.E., Pike, E.B., Smith, S.R. and Unwin, R.J. (1998) Review of the Scientific Evidence Relating to the Controls on the Agricultural Use of Sewage Sludge: Part 2 - Evidence Since 1989 Relevant to Controls on the Agricultural Use of Sewage Sludge. Final Report to the DETR, DoH, MAFF and UKWIRL. WRc Report No. DETR 4454. WRc Medmenham, Marlow.

6. CEC; Commission of the European Communities (1997) Draft Commission Regulation setting maximum limits for certain contaminants in foodstuffs amending Commission Regulation (EC) 194/97 of 31 January 1997 setting maximum limits for certain contaminants in food. III/5125/95 Rev 3. CEC, Brussels.

7. CEC; Commission of the European Communities (2000) Working document on sludge: 3rd draft. ENV.E.3/LM. CEC, Brussels.

8. CEC; Council of the European Communities (1986) Council Directive of 12 June 1986 on the protection of the environment, and in particular the soil, when sewage sludge is used in agriculture (86/278/EEC). *Official Journal of the European Communities* No. L181/6-12.

9. Chang, A.C., Granato, T.C. and Page, A.L. (1992) A methodology for establishing phytotoxicity criteria for chromium, copper, nickel and zinc in agricultural application of municipal sewage sludges. *Journal of Environmental Quality* 21, 521-536.

10. Chang, A.C., Page, A.L. and Asano, T. (1995) *Developing Human Health-Related Chemical Guidelines for Reclaimed Wastewater and Sewage Sludge Applications in Agriculture.*WHO, Geneva.

11. Chaudri, A.M., McGrath, S.P., Giller, K.E., Rietz, M. and Sauerbeck, D.R. (1993) Enumeration of indigenous *Rhizobium leguminosarum* biovar *trifolii* in soils previously treated with metal-contaminated sewage sludge. *Soil Biology and Biochemistry* 25, 301-309.

12. Davis, R.D. and Carlton-Smith (1984) An investigation into the phytotoxicity of zinc, copper and nickel using sewage sludge of controlled metal content. *Environmental Pollution (Series B)* 8, 163-185.

13. DoE; Department of the Environment (1993) UK Sewage Sludge Survey. Final Report.CES, Gateshead.

14. EA; Environment Agency (1999) *UK Sewage Sludge Survey: National Presentation.* Technical Report P165.Environment Agency, Bristol.

15. El-Aziz, R., Angle, J.S. and Chaney, R.L. (1991) Metal tolerance of *Rhizobium meliloti* isolated from heavy-metal contaminated soils. *Soil Biology and Biochemistry* 23, 795-798.

16. IC Consultants Ltd (2001) Pollutants in Urban Waste Water and Sewage Sludge. Report for the European Commission Directorate-General Environment, Nuclear Safety and Civil Protection. IC Consultants Ltd, London.

17. MAFF/DoE; Ministry of Agriculture, Fisheries and Food (1993a) *Review of the Rules for Sewage Sludge Application to Agricultural Land: Food Safety and Relevant Animal health Aspects of Potentially Toxic Elements.* Report of the Steering Group on Chemical Aspects of Food Surveillance. PB 1562. MAFF Publications, London.

18. MAFF/DoE; Ministry of Agriculture, Fisheries and Food (1993b) *Review of the Rules for Sewage Sludge Application to Agricultural Land: Soil Fertility Aspects of Potentially Toxic Elements*. Report of the Independent Scientific Committee. PB 1561. MAFF Publications, London.

19. Matthews, P. (1996) Transatlantic comparison of biosolids practices. Presented at *Beneficial Reuse of Water and Solids*, organised by Water Environment Federation, 6 – 9 April, Marbella, Spain.

20. McGrath, S.P. and Chaudri, A.M. (1999) Long-term effects of metal contamination on *Rhizobium*. *Soil Biology and Biochemistry* 31, 1205-1207.

21. McGrath, S.P. and Loveland, P.J. (1992) *The Soil Geochemical Atlas of England and Wales*. Blackie Academic & Professional, London.

22. McGrath, S.P., Brookes, P.C. and Giller, K.E. (1988) Effects of potentially toxic metals in soil derived from past applications of sewage sludge on nitrogen fixation by *Trifolium repens* L. *Soil Biology and Biochemistry* 20, 415-424

23. Ryan, J.A. and Chaney, R.L. (1994) Development of limits for land application of sewage sludge: Risk assessment. In: *Proceedings of the 15th International Congress of Soil Science*, Acapulco, Mexico, 534-553.

24. Sleeman, P.J. (1984) Determination of Pollutants in Effluents (MPC 4332 C). Detailed Analysis of the Trace Element Contents of UK Sewage Sludges. WRc Report No. 280-S. WRc Medmenham, Marlow.

25. Smith, S.R. (1996) *Agricultural Recycling of Sewage Sludge*. CAB INTERNATIONAL, Wallingford.

26. Smith, S.R. (1997) Long-term effects of zinc, copper and nickel in sewage sludge-treated agricultural soil. Fourth International Conference on the Biogeochemistry of Trace Elements, 23-26 June, University of California, Berkeley.

27. Smith, S.R. (1998) Soil microbial biomass content of sewage sludge-treated agricultural land. In *Third International Conference on the Biogeochemistry of Trace Elements* (ed R. Prost). INRA Editions, Versailles.

28. Smith, S.R. (2000) *Rhizobium* in long-term metal contaminated soil. *Soil Biology and Biochemistry* 32, 729-731.

29. Smith, S.R. and Giller, K.E. (1992) Effective *Rhizobium leguminosarum* biovar *trifolii* present in five soils contaminated with heavy metals from long-term applications of sewage sludge or metal mine spoil. *Soil Biology and Biochemistry* 24, 781-788.

30. Smith, S.R., Alloway, B.J., and Nicholson, F.A. (1999) Effect of Zn on the microbial biomass content of sewage sludge-treated soil. Fifth Internationational Conference on the Biogeochemistry of Trace Elements, 11-15 July, Vienna.

31. Stark, B.A., Livesey, C.T., Smith, S.R., Suttle, N.F., Wilkinson, J.M. and Cripps, P.J. (1998) Implications of Research on the Uptake of PTEs from Sewage Sludge by Grazing Animals. Integration and review of the MAFF- and DETR-funded research programmes on the effects of sheep ingesting sewage sludge-amended soils. Report presented to the DETR and MAFF, Contract No. CWO 650.

32. Stern, A.H. (1993) Monte Carlo analysis of the U.S EPA model of human exposure to cadmium in sewage sludge through consumption of garden crops. *Journal of Exposure Analysis and Environmental Epidemiology* 3, 449-469.

33. Ure, A.M. and Berrow, M.L. (1982) The elemental constituents of soils. In: *Environmental Chemistry*, Volume 2. The Royal Society of Chemistry, London, 94-204.

34. US EPA; US Environmental Protection Agency (1992) *Technical Support Document for Land Application of Sewage Sludge, Volume I.* Eastern Research Group, Lexington.

35. US EPA; US Environmental Protection Agency (1993) Part 503-Standards for Use or Disposal of Sewage Sludge. *Federal Register* 58, 9387-9404.

36. WHO/FAO; World Health Organization/Food and Agriculture Organization (1972) *Evaluation of Certain Food Additives and the Contaminants Mercury, Lead and Cadmium.* WHO Technical Report Series No. 505. WHO, Geneva.

DEVELOPMENT OF AN AGRICULTURAL OUTLET FOR RECYCLING OF ENHANCED TREATED SEWAGE SLUDGE

A H Sinclair

Scottish Agricultural College

S Wright

North of Scotland Water Authority

United Kingdom

ABSTRACT. The paper describes the on-going development of an agricultural outlet for recycling of enhanced treated sewage sludge in NE Scotland. Classification of potentially suitable land is described, taking account of cropping restrictions and the impact of livestock manures. Responses of farmers to two questionnaires, regarding the important issues influencing their attitudes towards use of enhanced treated sludge on their farms, are presented. Results of field trials to test nutrient and lime values of thermally dried sewage sludge granules and lime-stabilised cake are shown in this paper.

Keywords: Agricultural outlet, Enhanced treated sewage sludge, Field trials.

Dr A H Sinclair, is a Soil and Fertiliser Specialist with SAC Aberdeen. He currently advises NoSWA on the rates and timing of their sewage sludge, which is applied to agricultural land. He was a member of MAFF/DOE Independent Scientific Committee on Soil Fertility Aspects of Sewage Sludge Use in Agriculture, 1993 and co-author of MAFF/DOE (1993) report "Review of the Rules for Sewage Sludge application to Agricultural Land. Soil Fertility Aspects of Potentially Toxic Elements." He is Team leader of various commercial projects aimed at the development, management and maintenance of an agricultural outlet for reuse of wastewater sludge and other industrial wastes.

Mrs S Wright, is part of the management team responsible for wastewater quality and regulation with North of Scotland Water Authority. She is the corporate Recycling Team Leader and provides scientific, technical and legal advice to operational managers. She is Representative for Scottish Water Authorities on various research steering groups focussed mainly on projects to demonstrate that land recycling of wastewater sludge is environmentally sustainable.

INTRODUCTION

Montgomery Watson Limited (formerly Watson Hawksley Limited) in association with Crouch Hogg Waterman and Environmental Management Limited were retained by the former Grampian Regional Council in November 1991 to undertake a sewage sludge strategy study (SSS Study) for the whole of the Grampian Region in NE Scotland. The recommendations of the SSS Study were that agricultural utilisation should continue to be the main route for sewage sludge disposal in the Region in the future and that forestry should be developed as a secondary outlet. The study investigated the capacity of agricultural land and concluded that there was, in theory, 63 times the required capacity in the Region as a whole, based on crop nitrogen requirements (SSS Study, 1992). However, the study did not quantify the need to protect water resources, field access difficulties, proximity of residences, field gradient, and most importantly farmer acceptance of sewage sludge.

This paper describes some aspects of the work undertaken by SAC in NE Scotland to develop an agricultural outlet for recycling enhanced treated sewage sludge, following the initial SSS Study (1992). The work was sponsored by the former Grampian Water Services, North of Scotland Water Authority, Montgomery Watson Limited, Hornblower House, Brown and Root Limited and Grampian Wastewater Services Limited.

EXPERIMENTAL DETAILS

Assessment of Area of Suitable Land in North East Scotland

Classification of land which is physically suitable for application of enhanced treated sewage sludge should take account of soil type, slope, topography and land cover. This approach to classification can be further refined by assuming that enhanced treated sewage sludge may be physically applied to the same land that receives either farmyard manure, livestock slurry or inorganic bagged fertiliser. Areas of crops and grass which are physically suitable for application of manures and fertilisers can be obtained from the Scottish Office Agriculture, Environment and Fisheries Department (SOAEFD) publication at regional level of the data collected in the Agricultural and Horticultural Census forms each June ("The June Census"). These data were used to assess areas of physically suitable land for application of sewage sludge in the North of Scotland Water Authority region (Towers et al, 1997).

Effect of Crops on Area of Suitable Land

The Sludge (Use in Agriculture) Regulations (HMSO, 1989) makes no reference to the prohibition of the use of sewage sludge on potatoes. However the Code of Practice (DOE, 1989, 1996), which complements these Regulations, excludes the use of sewage sludge on land used or to be used for a cropping rotation that includes seed potatoes. In the previous Grampian Region part of NoSWA, sewage sludge was not applied to land which was used in a rotation with seed potatoes or ware potatoes. This decision was based on previous advice from SAC that ware potatoes result in multiplication of potato cyst nematodes (PCN) in the soil and that some PCN may survive the sludge treatments used. We have, therefore, added land used in rotation with either seed or ware potatoes to the area of land unsuitable for sewage sludge. On some farms this will result in the whole farm being excluded from use of sewage sludge. However, currently in the NoSWA area, potato growing farms apply sewage sludge to fields that are never used for potatoes. Therefore, 7 times the total potato acreage is deducted, based on a 7 year interval between growing potatoes in any one field. We have also deducted the area of soft fruit and vegetables from the area of suitable land.

Impact of Livestock Manures on Suitable Land

Livestock farmers have their own supply of fertiliser in the form of animal manures, which further reduces the area of land available for sewage sludge. Outputs of excreta by livestock and quantities of total phosphate P_2O_5 produced by each livestock type during housing were based on Reference Book RB209 (MAFF, 1994).   The Sludge (Use in Agriculture) Regulations 1989 require that "sludge shall be used in such a way that account is taken of the nutrient needs of the plants and that the quality of the soil and the surface and ground water is not impaired". "The Review of the Rules for Sewage Sludge Application to Agricultural Land" (MAFF/DOE, 1993) recognised that phosphate requirements of crops puts a greater restriction than nitrogen requirements on the application rate of sewage sludge. In assessing the long term strategy for an agricultural outlet SAC adopted the more stringent restriction imposed by matching total phosphorus in sludge with phosphorus fertiliser recommendations.

Farmer Acceptance

SAC were contracted in 1993 to carry out research on the potential size of the market in the former Grampian Regional Council Area for treated sewage sludge. A postal questionnaire was sent to a random sample of 3,000 holdings greater than 20 ha, which comprised about 50% of the total greater than 20 ha. "A guide to using treated wastewater sludge for farmers and foresters" was enclosed with the questionnaire. Technical information for this document was provided principally by Montgomery Watson Limited.   Following return of the questionnaire, four farmer focus groups took place. Their purpose was to gain a more in-depth knowledge of attitudes and farming policies in the Aberdeen area.   Each group contained a selection of non-responders to the postal questionnaire, responders who gave negative response to their use of treated sludge, and those who replied positively.

A further questionnaire was sent in 1998 to 1000 farmers within 40km of the east coast from Fraserburgh in the north to the North Esk river in the south.

Market Testing of Dried Granules on Farms

SAC were contracted to carry out market research in 1995 into farmer acceptance of thermally dried sludge granules (Biogran) from Wessex Water with special reference to storage, handling and application of granules by farmers. Farmers who said in the initial, random survey questionnaire that they would be prepared to try wastewater sludge (Petchey and Sinclair, 1994) were contacted by telephone until a total of 30 farmers throughout Grampian Region were found who wished to participate in this market research. Farmers used their own machinery unless they wished, on their own initiative, to use a contractor.

Follow-up market research was conducted in 1996 on 13 of the original 30 farms, so that farmers responses could be compared with their initial reaction to using granules.

Field Trials to Test Lime and Nutrient Values

NoSWA have recently introduced lime-stabilised sludge cake to NE Scotland, as well as thermally dried sewage sludge granules. In order to provide specialised advice on the fertiliser value of thermally dried granules and lime-stabilised sludge cake, and on the liming value of the cake, three contrasting trials were started during 1998:

1.   Spring barley: sludge treatments applied in February or March.

2.   Winter barley: sludge treatments applied in August or September.

3.   Cut grass: sludge treatments applied in February or March.

Each trial was set up at 2 sites, one in the Aberdeen area and one in the Perth area. Each trial was proposed to run for 3 cropping/cutting seasons at the same site, and comprised of 5 main sludge treatments:

1.   Control - no sludge; plus ground mineral limestone

2.   Granules x 1 - thermally dried granules applied in each of the 3 years; plus ground mineral limestone.

3.   Granules x 3 - thermally dried granules applied at 3 times rate in (2) but applied in first year only; plus ground mineral limestone.

4.   Cake x 1 - lime-stabilised sludge cake applied in each of the 3 years.

5.   Cake x 3 - lime-stabilised sludge cake applied at 3 times rate (4) applied in first year only.

Each main treatment was divided into sub-plots: 3 nitrogen rates x 2 phosphorus rates with a guard plot at each end. The nitrogen rates were typical rates for the crop. The phosphorus rates were zero and a typical rate for the crop. Each main treatment was randomised in 3 replicated blocks. Sub-plots were randomised within each main treatment. Therefore, the total number of plots per trial was 90 plots, excluding guard plots i.e. 5 main sludge treatments x 6 sub-plots x 3 replicates.

Data were analysed by two factor analysis of variance (Genstat 5, Laws Agricultural Trust).

Advisory Service to Farmers

The former Grampian Water Services introduced Gemini in 1995, subsequently adopted and further developed by NoSWA. Gemini is a computer software programme designed to operate a fully computerised control system to monitor and record the transport and processing of wastewater sludge, Wright and Sinclair (2000). A pre-requisite when designing the system was the ability to monitor compliance with the DoE's Code of Practice on the use of sewage sludge to agricultural land (DOE, 1989, 1996). A module on the system incorporates the advisory service supplied to farmers by SAC on the fertiliser values of sludge products, application rates and fertiliser supplements in order to take account of the nutrient requirements of crops when sewage sludge is applied, as required in HMSO (1989).

RESULTS

Assessment of Area of Suitable Land in NE Scotland

Areas of crops and grass for NE Scotland (Table 1) are the Eastern Region data from SOAEFD (1997).   Numbers of livestock were also obtained from SOAEFD (1997). Estimates of production of total P_2O_5 in livestock manures produced during housing are given in Tables 2, based on MAFF (1994).   The areas of land unsuitable for enhanced treated sewage sludge due to the use of livestock manures, but not including 35% of the potato land which is assumed to receive livestock manures, are given in Table 3.

Rough grazing covers about 37% of the physically suitable land in Table 1.   Much of this land would be suitable for improvement through phosphate application to increase soil fertility. Therefore some farmers may be keen to use sludge as a phosphate source. However, rough grazing is also considered "semi-natural" and so there is a possibility of poor image associated with sludge application on such land.   On balance SAC recommend that sludge is not applied to rough grazing in NE Scotland, and therefore that the area of 233,109 ha are removed from the area of suitable land (Table 3).

The unsuitable areas due to potatoes, soft fruit, and vegetables are given in Table 3.   Fields within 50m of residences, industry and recreation areas, fields containing private wells, and buffer strips beside watercourses were estimated to be up to 20% of the total land remaining and were excluded (Table 3).

Table 1 Crops, grass and rough grazings in NE Scotland

	HECTARES
Wheat, barley and oats	142,533
Rape and linseed	18,425
Potatoes	6,554
Fodder crops	8,632
Fruit and vegetables	2,228
All other crops	930
Fallow	1,290
Set-aside	23,058
Grass for mowing	61,825
Grass for grazing	123,757
Rough grazings	233,109
Total	622,341

Table 2 Number of livestock and quantity of P_2O_5 produced in NE Scotland during housing

LIVESTOCK	NO.	P_2O_5(kg)
Dairy cows	31,300	657,300
Beef cows and bulls	128,495	2,055,920
1-2 yr. beef cattle	131,862	1,318,620
Sows / gilts / boars (75% indoors)	29,690	296,900
Fattening pigs	185,604	1,299,228
Fowls and broilers	1,588,037	834,163
Total		6,462,131

Table 3 Unsuitable areas due to livestock manures, rough grazing, crops, residences, wells and watercources.

UNSUITABLE DUE TO	HECTARES
Livestock manures	90,022
Rough grazings	239,109
Seed + ware potatoes x 7	45,878
Soft fruit + vegetables	2,228
Residences, wells, watercourses	50,221
Total unsuitable	421,458
Total suitable remaining	200,883

Farmer Acceptance

When farmers were asked in 1993 whether they would consider applying sewage sludge on their land, on the basis of their present knowledge of the product, 24% of holdings responded and over 70% of those that replied responded positively. When then asked to choose between dried granules and lime-stabilised solids the majority of farmers favoured the dried granules. Reasons for the greater preference for dried granules over lime-stabilised solids was not clear, although questions on acceptability of on farm storage indicated a much greater acceptance of dried granules compared with lime-stabilised solids; the margin was 4:1 (Petchey and Sinclair, 1994).

Over 75% of farmers preferring granules thought they would apply the granules themselves. However, these farmers had not handled granules themselves and were unaware of the difficulties in spreading granules (Robertson, 1995). When asked about their potential use of granules, a considerable number of farmers were only prepared to use treated sewage sludge after being given more information about the fertiliser value and its environmental effects. However ultimately there was only a small proportion of farmers who stated that they would never consider using treated sludge. When asked how much of their land farmers would be prepared to apply sludge products to, the average response was between 52-60%.

Farmers were asked about important issues influencing their attitudes towards sludge products. Factors such as NPK content, plant availability of NPK, benefits to soil structure, customer and public perception, avoidance of odour nuisance and compatibility with existing machinery were all considered important, with visual appearance not considered so important. Their responses were closely matched by answers to follow up questions on concerns about sludge products. Health issues (human or animal) and environmental concerns such as nitrate leaching and heavy metal all scored highly, as did concerns about variability of total and available NPK between deliveries, control of timing and quality of service provided by the contractor. The price of the product was also of major concern.

Health was also a very important issue brought up at the smaller Focus group meetings, which were held during 1994 with farmers, although at the time the discussions were mainly related to the possible use of raw sewage sludge. These concerns were related to both human and animal health, and in particular that the sewage sludge could contain waste from hospitals and abattoirs, potato washing plants and industrial sites. Other important concerns raised at these meetings included what the farmers had read about heavy metal contamination. Farmers were partially reassured to learn that there was strict monitoring, but would like this to be carried out by a neutral body and would also like to know where heavily contaminated sludge would be dumped - if not on farm land.

Thirty percent of farmers responded to the follow-up questionnaire in 1998. In the parishes within 40km of the wastewater treatment centre at Nigg, Aberdeen, 55% of respondents believed that they would use enhanced treated sewage sludge. The total area of land of those farms saying "yes" as a percentage of the total land area of all respondents was calculated. The suitable land then adjusted by this percentage, resulting in an area of about 58,000ha.

Market Testing of Dried Granules on Farms

All farmers, with one exception, said they could see themselves using granules again, and 50% of these farmers estimated that they would extend usage to 100% of their farm (Sinclair and Still, 1995).

Twenty-four percent of farmers had no reservations about using granules. Among the 76% who had reservations by far the most frequently expressed concern was that of heavy metals, followed by smell, dust and public perception. Sixty-nine percent of farmers said they would prefer granules to be spread by a contractor in future, and 38% said they would be prepared to pay a contractor to spread granules. This market research was repeated during 1996 using 13 farms which had previously received Biogran, so that farmers responses could be compared with their initial reaction to using granules. Sinclair and Still (1997) reported that all these farmers said they could see themselves using granules again. This was the same view as held by these farmers after the 1995 test, and was taken as an indication of the likely long-term acceptability of granules by these farmers.

Field Trials to Test Lime and Nutrient Values of Thermally Dried Granules and Lime-Stablised Cake

Data from the spring barley trial in the Perth area and grass trial in the Aberdeen area are reported in this paper. Dry matter and concentration of nutrients NPK and S were determined for granules and cake for each trial plus neutralising value for each lime-stabilised cake (Table 4). Rates of application of the four sludge treatments are shown in Table 5.

Yield of spring barley grain from the 1998 harvest is shown in Table 6. The overall mean yield was 6.63 t/ha. There were statistically significant responses in yield to N and P fertiliser, and to all sludge treatments. Yield increases in sludge treatments given 75 kg/ha N are equivalent to yield increases in the control with 22, 29, 28 and 40 kg/ha N for granules x 1, granules x 3, cake x 1 and cake x 3 respectively (Figures 1 and 2). There were statistically significant increases in % N in grain in the 1999 trial, due to both N fertiliser and sludge treatments (Table 7).

Table 4 Data for thermally dried granules and lime-stabilised cake applied to each trial.

PRODUCT	TRIAL	YEAR applied	DM %	N %	P_2O_5 %	K_2O %	S %	NV % CaO
Granules	SB	1998	98	4.0	3.3	0.22	0.73	
	SB	1999	89	4.3	3.2	0.20	0.78	
	SB	2000	87	4.7	3.8	0.22	0.75	
	Grass	1999	92	4.5	4.0	0.24	1.00	
Cake	SB	1998	47	0.77	0.55	0.05	0.12	12.4
	SB	1999	38	0.94	0.53	0.05	0.11	8.8
	SB	2000	43	0.60	0.48	0.03	0.12	15.3
	Grass	1999	44	0.80	0.54	0.05	0.095	15.5

SB – spring barley

Table 5 Rates of sludge for each treatment.

TYPE OF TRIAL	GRANULES x 1	GRANULES x 3 tonnes /ha	CAKE x 1	CAKE x 3
Spring barley	1.8	5.4	10	30
Grass	2.2	6.6	12	36

Table 6 Effect of granules, limed-cake and N fertiliser on yield (t/ha) of spring barley grain (85%DM) from Peel, Perth in 1998.

| SLUDGE TREATMENT | RATE OF N FERTILISER (kg/ha) | | | MEAN |
	75	100	125	
Control	5.90	6.40	6.81	6.37
Granules x 1	6.33	6.61	6.99	6.64
Granules x 3	6.46	6.46	6.98	6.63
Cake x 1	6.44	6.58	6.92	6.64
Cake x 3	6.64	6.86	7.02	6.84
Mean	6.35	6.58	6.94	6.63
SED N treatment				0.087 ***
sludge treatment				0.117 *
N x sludge				0.197 NS

NS not significant;   * $p<0.05$;   *** $p<0.001$

Mean grain yields over the 3-year period 1998 to 2000 at Peel are shown in Tables 8 and 9. The overall mean yield was 5.57 t/ha. There were statistically significant responses in yield to N and P fertiliser, and a significant interaction between sludge treatments and P fertiliser. Lowest mean yields were obtained in the cake x 3 treatment, applied prior to ploughing in 1998. In the other sludge treatments given 75 kg/ha, yield increases compared with the control were equivalent to yield increases with 31, 24 and 20 kg/ha N for granules x 1, granules x 3, and cake x 1 respectively (Figures 3 and 4). The effect of limed cake on soil pH was tested by determining soil pH after the 2000 harvest, 2.5 years after application of the first sludge treatment in February 1998. Lime was added to the control and granule treatments. Values of soil pH are shown in Table 10. Cake x 3 treatment produced the largest increase in soil pH. Soil pH of the trial site was 5.6 prior to application of sludge and lime treatments.

Table 7 Effect of granules, limed-cake and N fertiliser on % N in spring barley grain from Peel, Perth in 1998.

| SLUDGE TREATMENT | RATE OF N FERTILISER (kg/ha) | | | MEAN |
	75	100	125	
Control	1.27	1.28	1.39	1.31
Granules x 1	1.37	1.50	1.49	1.45
Granules x 3	1.40	1.42	1.48	1.43
Cake x 1	1.36	1.49	1.47	1.44
Cake x 3	1.42	1.51	1.63	1.52
Mean	1.36	1.44	1.49	1.43
SED N treatment				0.022 ***
sludge treatment				0.027 ***
N x sludge				0.048 NS

Table 8 Effect of granules, limed-cake and N fertiliser on mean yield (t/ha) of spring barley grain (85%DM) from Peel, Perth for 1998 to 2000 harvests.

SLUDGE TREATMENT	RATE OF N FERTILISER (kg/ha)			MEAN
	75	100	125	
Control	5.12	5.57	5.75	5.48
Granules x 1	5.61	5.72	5.98	5.77
Granules x 3	5.55	5.72	6.00	5.75
Cake x 1	5.48	5.64	5.78	5.64
Cake x 3	5.13	5.30	5.23	5.22
Mean	5.38	5.59	5.75	5.57
SED N treatment				0.051 ***
Sludge treatment				0.184 NS
N x sludge				0.206 NS

Table 9 Effect of granules, limed-cake and P fertiliser on mean yield (t/ha) of spring barley grain (85%DM) from Peel, Perth for 1998 to 2000 harvests.

SLUDGE TREATMENT	RATE OF P_2O_5 FERTILISER (kg/ha)		MEAN
	0	75	
Control	5.32	5.64	5.48
Granules x 1	5.80	5.74	5.77
Granules x 3	5.77	5.73	5.75
Cake x 1	5.57	5.70	5.64
Cake x 3	5.10	5.33	5.22
Mean	5.51	5.63	5.57
SED P treatment			0.037 *
sludge treatment			0.184 NS
P x sludge			0.193 *

Table 10 Effect of granules,limed cake and P fertiliser on pH of soil after 3 years trial of spring barley at Peel, Perth.

SLUDGE TREATMENT	RATE OF P_2O_5 FERTILISER (kg/ha)		MEAN
	0	75	
Control	6.07	6.07	6.07
Granules x 1	6.03	6.10	6.07
Granules x 3	5.97	6.07	6.02
Cake x 1	6.30	6.33	6.32
Cake x 3	6.57	6.53	6.55
Mean	6.19	6.22	6.20
SED P treatment			0.038 NS
sludge treatment			0.049 ***
P x sludge			0.078 NS

The cumulative yields from 4 cuts of grass at Aberdeen in 1999 are given in Tables 11. There was a statistically significant response in dry matter yield of grass to N fertiliser, but not to treatment with sludge, or P fertiliser (P data not shown). At the highest rate of 375 kg/ha N fertiliser dry matter production was very similar from all treatments being within $\pm$ 0.3 t/ha of the mean of 15.4 t/ha.   Yield increases in sludge treatments given 175 kg/ha N were equivalent to yield increases in the control with 43, 79, 43 and 100 kg/ha N for granules x 1, granules x 3, cake x 1 and cake x 3 respectively (Figures 5 and 6).

Table 11 Effect of granules, limed-cake and N fertiliser on yield (t/ha DM) of grass from Craibstone, Aberdeen in 1999.

SLUDGE TREATMENT	RATE OF N FERTILISER (kg/ha)			MEAN
	175	275	375	
Control	11.9	13.3	15.3	13.5
Granules x 1	12.5	14.1	15.3	14.0
Granules x 3	13.0	14.1	15.7	14.3
Cake x 1	12.5	14.3	15.2	14.0
Cake x 3	13.3	14.6	15.7	14.6
Mean	12.7	14.1	15.4	14.1
SED N treatment				0.156 ***
sludge treatment				0.351 NS
N x sludge				0.452 NS

DISCUSSION

The Integrated Communications and Marketing Strategy set up by the Water Services Department of the former Grampian Regional Council has led to raised awareness among farmers of recycling sewage sludge to agricultural land in NE Scotland. As well as the work described in the current paper, NoSWA published six Information Sheets under the banner "Recycling for a greater environment". These Sheets have been available to farmers at agricultural shows, evening meetings and handed to farmers currently using sewage sludge.

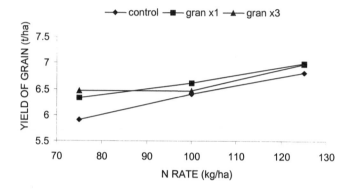

Figure 1 Effect of rate of granules on yield of spring barley at Perth, 1998

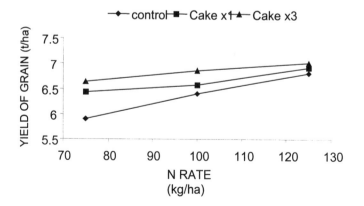

Figure 2 Effect of rate of cake on yield of spring barley at Perth, 1998

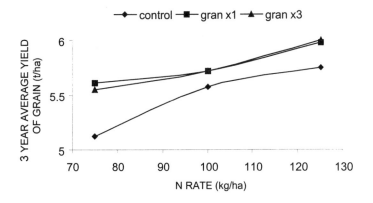

Figure 3 Effect of rate of granules on yield of spring barley at Perth, averaged over 3 years

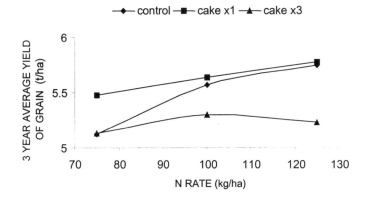

Figure 4 Effect of rate of cake on yield of spring barley at Perth, averaged over 3 years

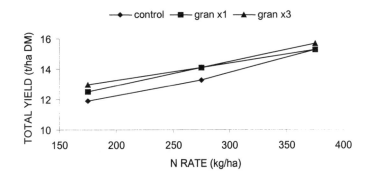

Figure 5 Effect of rate of granules on yield of grass at Aberdeen, 1999

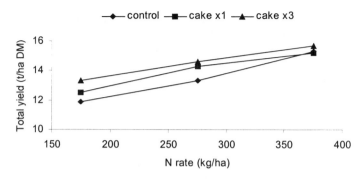

Figure 6   Effect of rate of cake on yield of grass at Aberdeen, 1999

Two news broadsheets, "Growing Benefits", were mailed in 1995 and 1996 to most of the 6000 farm holdings in the former Grampian Council region of NE Scotland.   "Growing Benefits" was compiled by Hornblower House, London.   The result of the increased awareness is that an area of about 58,000 ha are potentially available for recycling enhanced treated sewage sludge within a 40km radius of Aberdeen.

In assessing the long term strategy for an agricultural outlet, SAC Aberdeen have adopted the more stringent restriction imposed by matching total phosphorus in sludge with phosphorus fertiliser recommendations, rather than the limit of 250 kg/ha/year of 'total nitrogen' (MAFF, 1998).   Requirement for phosphorus depends on the crop or grass to be grown and the soil P status.   An average annual requirement of 70 kg/ha phosphate (P_2O_5) and a concentration of 35 kg P_2O_5 per tds sludge gives rise to an annual application rate of 2 tds/ha.   This requirement may be met in some cases by 4 tds/ha every second year, or 6 tds/ha every third year.   However, the important figure for calculation of total area of land required is 2 tds/ha. If 10,000 tds are produced from Aberdeen per year, then a minimum landbank of 5,000ha is required.   The potentially available 58,000ha gives rise to a safety factor of 11.6 for the potential market over the predicted production, or about 9% of the potentially available land is required.

The EU "Working document on sludge, 3rd draft", April 2000 proposed medium term (about 2015) limit values for amounts of heavy metals which may be added annually to soil, based on a ten year average.   The proposed limit values for copper and zinc are 2.4 and 6.0 kg/ha respectively.   At an average annual rate of 2tds/ha applied in NE Scotland, the copper and zinc limits would be added in a sludge containing copper and zinc concentrations of 1,200 and 3,000 mg/kg dry solids respectively.   The same EU working document proposed concentration limit values in sludge for copper and zinc of 1,000 and 2.500 mg/kg dry solids respectively.   Therefore, the sludge concentration limits pose a greater threat to a recycling strategy based on 2 tds/ha/annum than do the proposed limits on annual addition of copper and zinc.

Based on evidence from the market testing of dried granules on farms in NE Scotland, it might be possible to achieve near to 100 percent repeat uptake by those farmers who are prepared to try enhanced treated sewage sludge. This very high rate of uptake could only be maintained if the agreed tonnage was delivered on time, in good condition and there was subsequent evidence of increased profitability with minimal or no risk to the long-term viability of the farm. Any clients lost through poor service would probably be lost for a long time. However, there are considerable numbers of farmers only prepared to use treated sewage sludge after being given more information about the fertiliser value and its environmental effects. SAC studies have highlighted the wide range in solubilities of nitrogen and phosphorus in sludges produced by different thermally drying treatment processes (Sinclair et al., 1996).

Current field trials at Perth and Aberdeen have shown statistically significant responses in yield of spring barley to application rates of 1.8 and 5.4 t/ha of thermally dried granules. The 1.8 t/ha rate applied in 3 consecutive years produced very similar yield of spring barley compared with a single application of 5.4 t/ha (Figure 3). Nitrogen concentrations were higher in the grain in the season following application of both rates of granules (Table 7), but all values were below 1.8%N, the maximum concentration that has been accepted in contracts with the maltsters in the past.

It is particularly important in a sludge-to-land strategy in NE Scotland that malting-quality barley can be grown following sludge application, because between 80,000 and 90,000ha of malting varieties are sown annually. Responses in grass production following sludge treatments were not statistically significant in the first year, although there were consistent responses to sludge at the lower rate of N fertiliser at the Aberdeen site. Fertiliser N rates have been reduced for the second year of the grass trials.

Soil pH data in Table 10 show that the lime in the limed cake was effective in increasing soil pH. In fact, the single application of 30 t/ha increased soil pH to a level where manganese deficiency was induced in the barley crops and yield was reduced, compared with the annual applications of 10 t/ha limed cake. This highlights the importance of field trials with novel, enhanced treated sewage sludges, where there is currently a dearth of agronomic data. For example, there is a lack of information from field trials, which test sludges produced from thermal hydrolosis followed by conventional anaerobic mesophilic digestion.

A geographical information system (GIS) based program has been devised to facilitate quality control - in particular:

- the assessment of suitability of fields

- registering the fields with SEPA and local authority

- the allocation of sludge to field that meet the criteria of soil analysis and The Safe Sludge Matrix.

- Maintenance of statutory and management records

- Notification to farmers and spreading contractors is presented in map form with exclusion areas and buffer zones clearly marked.

Relevant data from this database is incorporated into a module on the Gemini system which provides an advisory service to farmers on the fertiliser values of sludge products, application rates and fertiliser supplements required for different crops (Wright and Sinclair, 2000).

ACKNOWLEDGEMENTS

The authors would like to acknowledge the help provided for this on-going project from staff of NoSWA, SAC, Montgomery Watson Limited, Hornblower House, Brown and Root Limited and Grampian Wastewater Services Limited.

REFERENCES

1. ADAS. The Safe Sludge Matrix, 2000. 4pp.

2. DoE. Code of Practice for Agriculture use of Sewage Sludge, 1989. 12pp.

3. DoE. Code of Practice for Agriculture use of Sewage Sludge, 1996. 12pp.

4. HMSO. The Sludge (Use in Agriculture) Regulations, SI No.1263, 1989. 8pp.

5. MAFF. Fertiliser recommendations, Reference Book RB209, 1994, p10-11.

6. MAFF. Code of Good Agricultural Practice for the Protection of Water, 1998. p43.

7. MAFF/DOE. Review of the Rules for Sewage Sludge Application to Agricultural Land. Soil Fertility Aspects of Potentially Toxic Elements, 1993. 91pp (Sinclair co-author).

8. PETCHEY A M AND SINCLAIR A H. Treated wastewater sludge products: A survey of farmers in Grampian Region. Report for NoSWA, 1994. 36pp.

9. ROBERTSON T. Spreading trials of dried sewage sludge granules. Report for NoSWA, 1995. 33pp.

10. SINCLAIR A H AND STILL E B. Spring Market Testing of Wessex Biogran granules on 30 farms in Grampian Region. Report for NoSWA, 1995. 38pp.

11. SINCLAIR A H AND STILL E B. Spring Market Testing of Wessex Biogran granules and N-Viro Soil using 14 farms in Aberdeenshire. Report for NoSWA, 1997. 19pp.

12. SINCLAIR A H, STEPHEN N H, PAULINE O, STILL E B, SHEPHERD M AND SIMPSON J. The short-term and longer-term water solubility of nitrogen and phosphorus in samples of sludge from different treatment works. Report for NoSWA, 1996. 29pp.

13. SOAEFD. Economic report on Scottish Agriculture, 1997.

14. SSS STUDY. Strategy for the treatment and disposal of sewage sludge. A report by Watson Hawksley, Crouch Hogg Waterman and Environmental Management Ltd for Grampian Water Services, 1992.

15. TOWERS W, SINCLAIR A H, HORNE P, AND STILL E B. Assessment of land availability for the recycling of digested sludge cake and digested dried granules within the North of Scotland Water Authority Area. Report for Halcrow Crouch Consultancy Engineers, 1997. 33pp (Part of NoSWA Sludge Strategy, 1998).

16. WRIGHT S, AND SINCLAIR A H. Management of a land bank for recycling sludge-derived fertiliser (SDF) using North of Scotland Water Authority Gemini Software (this conference proceedings), 2000.

REVIEW OF DANISH FIELD EXPERIMENTS WITH SEWAGE SLUDGE AND COMPOSTED HOUSEHOLD REFUSE AS A FERTILIZER SOURCE

J Petersen

Danish Institute of Agricultural Sciences

Denmark

ABSTRACT. The paper is concerned with the concentration and effect of nutrients and potential pollutants in municipal sewage sludge and composted household refuse in Denmark. The fertilizer value of these waste products corresponds approximately to the content of mineral nitrogen. Leaching of nitrate and increased phosphorus concentration in the soil were recorded at application rates of up to 21 t/ha/year organic matter of sewage sludge. The environmental effects were less at application rates not exceeding the current legal thresholds. These correspond to less than 1 t/ha/year organic matter. The concentration of heavy metals in the soil and the crop was increased by large application rates of highly loaded sewage sludge. Using lower application rates of sewage sludge with improved quality, the rate of heavy metal accumulation in the soil is reduced. In general, compost and animal manure contain less heavy metals than sewage sludge. Current application rates do not cause detectable increases in soil carbon content. Organic contaminants that originate primarily from household use appear to be degradable at treatment plants or in the soil, and there seems no risk for contamination of the grain of cereal crops.

Keywords: Nitrogen, Phosphorus, Potassium, Heavy metals, Soil concentration, Yield, Crop uptake, Fertilizer value.

J Petersen, is senior scientist at Dept. of Crop Physiology and Soil Science, Danish Institute of Agricultural Sciences. His research interest include agricultural use of organic manure, mainly animal manure, but also organic municipal waste such as sewage sludge and compost, with reference to utilisation of the nutrients in these products. During 1997-2000 he has been responsible for field experiments concerning utilization of nutrients in municipal wastes at Askov Experimental station. The experiments were conducted as a part of the co-ordinated interdisciplinary *Centre for Sustainable Land Use and Management of Contaminants, Carbon and Nitrogen* http://www.landuse.dk/uk/index.htm) financed by *The Danish Strategic Environmental Research Programme.*

INTRODUCTION

Municipal organic wastes such as sewage sludge and composted household refuse are not well defined products. The content of nutrients and heavy metals depends on the quality of the input material and the type and operation of the treatment plants. There are 1467 waste water treatment plants in Denmark. Due to the requirement for increased biological and chemical purification of the waste water [1], sewage sludge from 850 small plants is transported to about 230 modern treatment plants for final purification [2]. These are responsible for the major part of produced sewage sludge.

Statistical surveys from the 1990s indicate that 60-70% of the sewage sludge dry matter, equivalent to about 100.000 t DM/year, was applied to agricultural land [2]. Compared with these figures, composted household refuse is of minor importance. The number of composting plants is small, less than 20, and despite increased source sorting, the amount of composted household refuse applied to agricultural land was less than 2,000 t DM/year during the 1990s [3]. With reference to EEC [4] the Danish legislation [5] sets conditions for use, restrictions for application and options for crops in case of application of municipal waste to agricultural land. This is briefly outlined by Petersen [6]. The main substance is, with regard to handling in agricultural practice, that sewage sludge and household compost has to be incorporated into the soil before sowing of spring cereals.

The aim of this paper is to review the Danish experiences on the use of waste products as fertilizer for agricultural land. To a great extent this paper is based on field experiments at Askov Experimental Station [7-11], especially a long-term field experiment with application of sewage sludge [12] (See Appendix A). These experiments were part of a co-ordinated research programme during 1972-77 on sewage sludge with respect to agricultural use and problems relating to heavy metals and hygienic aspects. Also recent but more isolated results from Danish field experiments are considered. These report mainly the yield effect and have basically to be considered as single-year experiments.

Furthermore, preliminary results from the *Centre for Sustainable Land Use and Management of Contaminants, Carbon and Nitrogen* are included [13]. This research programme focusing on 1) the nutrient value of sewage sludge and compost applied at rates within the legal threshold and combined with an application of mineral fertilizer, 2) the fate and effects of organic contaminants in agricultural soils, and 3) the turnover of applied carbon. The field experiment at Askov Experimental Station has been carried out during 1998-2000.

Due to the isolated nature of the - in Danish only - published results of these experiments there is a need to compile these and to present some general conclusions on the nutrient value of waste products.

CONTENT OF NUTRIENTS AND HEAVY METALS

Efficiency purification for both nitrogen and phosphorus are required by the EEC for urban waste water treatment [1]. Biological purification removes more than 80% of the waste water nitrogen [14], but due to the nitrification-denitrification processes, nitrogen is lost from the sewage sludge. The remaining nitrogen content varies (Table 1), and of a mean content of 40 kg N/t DM about 20% is present as mineral nitrogen [12]. The mineral quota is about 30% in aerobic, compared with 10-15% in anaerobic digested sewage sludge.

In modern treatment plants with chemical purification, more than 90% of phosphorus in the waste water is precipitated [14], and therefore the P concentration in sewage sludge depends to a great extent on the quality of the waste water.

Table 1 Total-N and phosphorus content in waste products. Legislated thresholds for heavy metals and the heavy metal content in different types of waste products

TYPE [1] Ref.	L [2] [5]	S1 [12]	S2 [12]	S3 [15]	S4 [16]	S5 [2]	S6	S7	C	FYM [17,18]
kg/t DM										
Total-N		21	27	–	6	43 (26-60)	30	62	16	30-33
Total-P		10	23	–	3	31 (18-40)	30	39	3	7-12
mg/kg DM										
Cd	0.8	5	23	99	2.4	2.3 (0.8-7.4)	2.2	1.6	0.4	0.5 (0.3-0.7)
Hg	0.8	–	–	–	6.5	1.3 (0.3-3.1)	3.3	0.9	0.2	–
Pb	120	226	1350	874	304	79 (14-211)	132	81	28	3 (3-4)
Ni	30	31	265	187	12	24 (8-53)	23	20	8	8 (5-15)
Cr	100	111	831	919	60	38 (10-85)	31	21	10	6 (2-12)
Cu	1000	179	1120	1138	440	262 (84-464)	364	278	40	70-300
Zn	4000	1033	2282	2780	2080	748 (380-1204)	1287	691	120	175-750

– not analyzed

1) L=Legislation; S1 = Sewage sludge 'low' in heavy metals (Appendix A); S2 = Sewage sludge 'high' in heavy metals (Appendix A); S3 = London sewage sludge; S4 = Composted mixture of sewage sludge and organic household refuse; S5 =DK survey 1998; S6 = Anaerobic digested sewage sludge 'low' in organic contaminants; S7 = Aerobic sewage sludge 'high' in organic contaminants; C = Composted organic household refuse. S6, S7 and C had been used in field experiments 1998-99. FYM = Manure and slurries. These figures are included for comparison to a common used organic nutrient source.
2) As an alternative the thresholds could be relative to phosphorus. For Cd, Hg, Pb and Ni these thresholds are 100, 200, 10000 and 2500 mg/kg P, respectively.

The fertilizer value of sewage sludge is related to the content of nitrogen and phosphorus (S5, Table 1). The potassium content in sewage sludge is low, 1-7 kg K/t DM [2], whereas the content in compost is significantly higher at 8-13 kg/t DM. The nitrogen and phosphorus content in composted household waste also depends on the origin of the compost [19] presents values of 17-30 kg N/t DM and 3-6 kg P/t DM. The content of mineral nitrogen is less than 1 kg/t DM corresponding to less than 10% of total-N [19,20]. Unlike potassium the contents of mineral nitrogen as well as total phosphorus are lower in composted household waste compared with sewage sludge.

Furthermore, the nutrient content in sewage sludge is influenced by the dewatering method. Compared to de-watering by centrifuges, sand-bed de-watering (settling pond) 'dilutes' the sludge as even the sand is taken away when the sand-bed is emptied [10]. However, the use of settling ponds has been reduced, and in 1998 the sewage sludge was de-watered by centrifuge, strainer band press, filter press and settling pond with the quota of 41, 36, 14 and 1% respectively [2].

The potential use of waste products as fertilizer is reduced by the content of environmentally harmful compounds, such as heavy metals. The content of heavy metals in waste products applied to agricultural land is limited by legislation [5] (L in Table 1). The waste products have to respect either the thresholds in Table 1 or the thresholds, which relate the content of heavy metals (Cd, Hg, Pb and Ni) to the phosphorus content (Table 1, note 2). For Cd and Hg only 10-20% of sewage sludge DM was below the DM-related threshold, and for Pb and Ni the figure was 80% [2]. The thresholds for Cr, Cu and Zn were not surpassed [2]. More than 75% of the sewage sludge DM meets the P-related threshold.

The content of heavy metals in sludge S2 (Table 1) corresponds to values given by McGrath [15] for sewage sludge produced at a treatment plant near London during 1942-61 (S3 in Table1). During the 1980s the exclusion of metals at source had improved the quality of sewage sludge. Today, the content of heavy metals in sewage sludge has stabilized at a lower level (S5, Table 1). However, this level is in general higher compared with composted household refuse and farmyard manure (C and FYM in Table 1), but FYM could be a significant source of Cu and Zn.

The content of nutrients and heavy metals is usually presented on a dry matter basis (DM). Application rates in experiments are often presented as organic matter (OM), calculated as ash-free DM.

YIELD EFFECT

In most experiments the effect on yield (or nutrient uptake) is related to applied nitrogen. Only few experiments consider the effect of applied phosphorus.

To obtain high phosphorus precipitation rates at the wastewater treatment plants, different compounds are used. In a pot experiment the effect of phosphorus precipitated as Al-, Ca- or Fe-complexes were compared with mechanical precipitation as well as superphosphate fertilizer [11]. In this experiment the plant uptake and soil analyses were unaffected by the phosphorus source, despite the low initial P-concentration (about 90 μg P/g dry soil extracted by 0.2 N H_2SO_4) in the sandy soil.

The effect of phosphorus in sewage sludge could not be calculated in a short-term cereal experiment due to no effect of fertilizer phosphorus in the zero-nitrogen reference treatment [21].This may be due to the generally high level of available phosphorus in Dansih soils (40-50 μg P/g dry soil extracted by 0.5 N NaHCO$_3$) [22]. Furthermore, in long-term P-experiments, it was found that more than 15 years have to elapse before P-depletion causes a significant yield decrease [23]. Therefore, direct fertilizer effects of P-applications may not be expected, but application of wastes may contribute to the maintenance of the P-balance. Hence, for Danish conditions it seems reasonable to use nitrogen in the applied waste to explain the effect on the response variable.

In experiments from the 1970s and 1980s sewage sludge was applied at rates of up to 21 t OM/ha/year to fulfil the crop requirement for mineral nitrogen. These rates result in significant yield increases, often comparable with the mineral fertilizer treatment [12]. In experiments performed during the 1990s, the application rates were reduced and adjusted according to the legislation then in force.

Independent of application rate, the fertilizer value is defined as the amount in kg N/ha of mineral nitrogen fertilizer, which is able to replace 100 kg total-N/ha in the waste product to obtain the same response, often grain yield or nitrogen uptake. In this way a fertilizer value of total nitrogen in sewage sludge of 20-30 was obtained [12,21]. The highest values were obtained by spring application [21]. The fertilizer value of total nitrogen in household compost was 10-15 in the first growing season after application [20, 24 -26]. The obtained fertilizer values correspond approximately to the fraction of mineral nitrogen in the waste products. The nitrogen fertilizer value obtained in the first season after application is therefore ascribed to the content of mineral nitrogen in the applied waste product.

The applied organic nitrogen is mineralized during the following years. The residual effect depends on the level of supplemental mineral fertilizer [12]. In the unfertilized section there was a significant residual effect of applied sewage sludge, and for beets the yield was nearly the same as for mineral fertilizer (Table 2). The residual effect was caused by an application of 4.3-6.1 t N/ha during the experimental period 1974-79, but despite this huge application rate, the residual fertilizer value was only 1-3 kg N/ha for cereals and 4-6 kg N/ha for long season crops (beets and grass). Application of mineral fertilizer reduced the residual effect significantly, but crops with a long growing season still benefited from the applied sewage sludge during 1974-79 (fertilized section in Table 2). In fertilized cereals Knudsen [21] obtained a fertilizer value in the second year after application of sewage sludge corresponding to 5-7 kg N/ha when the calculations are based on the first year application. Damgaard-Larsen et al. [9] measured the residual effect of sewage sludge application in fertilized crops in the 2nd, 3rd and 4th experimental year. Compared with no sewage sludge application the yield increases in the 2nd and 3rd year were only 2 and 1% per 100 kg N/ha applied in sewage sludge in the 1st year, respectively. Thus, the residual effect is not that high.

Table2 Residual effect 1980-84 [hkg DM/ha] of 115 t OM/ha applied during 1974-79 [12]

	CROP	TREATMENT 1974-79				LSD.95
		Untreated	Type S1	Type S2	Fertilizer	
Without	Winter cereal	19	36	34	52 [1]	4
Supplemental	Spring barley	13	31	27	34 [1]	3
Fertilizer	Beet	45	83	81	88 [1]	11
1980-84	Grass	19	56	48	85 [1]	8
Supplemental	Winter cereal	48	49	51	48	3
Fertilizer	Spring barley	32	33	30	32	4
Applied	Beet	88	98	103	88	7
1980-84	Grass	72	95	94	80	5

1) Fertilizer application was continued in 1980-84.

Despite an application of 50 t DM/ha household compost, corresponding to 400 kg total-N/ha, it was concluded that the nitrogen value was diminutive and that application of compost always has to be combined with the application of a mineral nitrogen source [20].

The current Danish legislation [5] limits the application of waste products to a maximum of 210 kg total-N/ha/year, 30 kg total-P/ha/year as a mean of 3 years and 7 t DM/ha/years as a mean of 10 years. From August 2002 the legislation will reduce the maximum total-N application to 170 kg/ha/year, which correspond to the Nitrate Directive [27]. Application of sewage sludge is mainly limited by the P-threshold, whereas application of composted household refuse is often limited either by the DM-, N- or P-threshold.

Table 3 Expected average amounts of carbon and nutrients applied in sewage sludge and composted household-refuse not exceeding the current legal thresholds

WASTE PRODUCT	RATE [t DM/ha]	CARBON [kg/ha]	TOTAL-N [kg/ha]	MINERAL-N [kg/ha]	PHOSPHORUS [kg/ha]	POTASSIUM [kg/ha]
Sewage sludge	1 t each year	400	36	11	29	1
Sewage sludge	3 t every 3rd year	1200	107	32	86	4
Composted household refuse	7 t each year	2800	170	7-14	30	84

Due to the low application rate of mineral nitrogen (Table 3), it may be expected that all organic municipal waste products have to be combined with a source containing mineral nitrogen. Combined applications of waste and manure have to respect the threshold of 30 kg P/ha/year [5]. An application of 30 t/ha of animal slurry containing on average 1 kg P/t is common on livestock farms. This practice leaves no space for the application of imported municipal waste. Therefore the supplemental nitrogen source has to be mineral fertilizer, meaning that the composted household refuse and sewage sludge have to be applied on arable farms.

The results from the recent experiment at Askov Experimental Station concerning nutrient value support the impression from the reviewed reports (Table 3). Application of household compost had a very poor influence on the nitrogen uptake of a cereal crop, even at the high level. This agrees with the low content of mineral nitrogen, which is about 3% of the total nitrogen in the compost. The effect of the two types of sewage sludge is better, but there are differences. The effect of anaerobic digested sewage sludge (S6) is less than the 80 kg N/ha reference treatment. Also the effect per applied kg of nitrogen is less than for aerobically digested sewage sludge (S7). This may be explained by the differences in the quota of mineral nitrogen as mentioned above. Thus, the nitrogen fertilizer effect of sewage sludge may be related to the treatment procedure at the plants.

The effects of aerobic sewage sludge (S7) and farmyard manure were nearly comparable, but about 50% more nitrogen was applied using FYM (Table 4).

Therefore, the effect per applied kg nitrogen in FYM is more similar to anaerobically digested sewage sludge. The grain yield effect of waste was over-shadowed using supplemental mineral nitrogen (data not shown), but there was still an effect on total nitrogen uptake (Table 4).

Only one experiment has focused on the fertilizer value of potassium. A cabbage crop with a high potassium demand has been used for this purpose. In a three-year experiment the effect of 170 kg K/ha in composted household refuse corresponded to the effect of the same amount of potassium in animal slurry [28].

Table 4 Total nitrogen uptake [kg N/ha] in spring cereals
during 1998-2000 at Askov Experimental Station

	1× LEGAL THRESHOLD/year		3× LEGAL THRESHOLD/year	
	Applied total N in waste	Supplemental mineral nitrogen [kg/ha]	Applied total N in waste	Supplemental mineral nitrogen [kg/ha]
	[kg/ha]	0	80	[kg/ha]	0	80
Type S6 [1)	50	45	88	150	62	115
Type S7 [1)	71	58	102	213	94	130
Type C [1)	160	43	88	480	50	97
FYM	105	51	99	315	81	126
Reference treatments applied mineral nitrogen [kgN/ha]			0	40	80	120
Nitrogen uptake in reference treatments			35	74	90	121

1) Type compare with Table 1.

An attempt to increase the low potassium concentration in sewage sludge was made by the addition of incinerated straw from central heating installations. The ash contained 120-130 kg K/t DM, whereas the phosphorus content was low. The fertilizer effect of the mixture and the residual effect were investigated in spring barley and undersown grass, respectively, using soils low in phosphorus (13 μg P/g dry soil extracted by 0.5 N NaHCO$_3$) or potassium status (35 μg K/g dry soil extracted by ammonium acetate) [29]. The mixed products were fused together by heating and granulated to different degrees.

The effect of phosphorus and potassium was reduced by increased intensity of the treatment compared to the untreated mixture. The yield effect of citrate extractable phosphorus in the untreated waste product corresponded to the effect of an equivalent amount of phosphorus in mineral fertilizer. Citrate extractable phosphorus in the treated mixtures overestimated the crop response to applied phosphorus. A yield response to potassium was not observed even on the soil low in potassium. Application of the untreated mixture increased the phosphorus and potassium contents in the grass but not the yield. Thus, the results did not indicate any advantage in nutrient utilization, and therefore the method has not been adopted in Denmark.

ENVIRONMENTAL EFFECTS

In general, the environmental effects were obtained by using application rates exceeding the current legislation (Table 3).

Nitrate Leaching

An application rate of 200 kg total-N/ha/year (=1×SSR in Table 5) increased the leaching compared with mineral fertilizer [12]. The difference was more noticeable at higher application rates (Table 5). The sewage sludge was applied in November/December, four months before sowing of spring cereals. The leaching increased in this period for the application rates 2×SSR and 4×SSR compared with the background leaching of 0.8 g N/m²/year (Table 5). Irrespective of application rate, 2/3 of the total leaching occurs between harvest and the next application of sewage sludge.

Table 5 Leaching of nitrate-N [g/m²/year] in the lysimeter experiment (Appendix A). Figures in brackets are the leaching from the time of application in November/December until sowing of spring cereals in April. Sewage Sludge application Rate (SSR) = 400 g OM/m²/year [12]

	1× SSR		2× SSR		4× SSR	
Type S1	3.0	(1.0)	5.5	(1.7)	10.6	(2.9)
Type S2	2.4	(1.0)	3.5	(1.4)	5.7	(2.0)
Fertilizer [1]	1.7	(0.8)	2.0	(0.8)	3.3	(0.8)

1) The mineral nitrogen was applied at rates of 6, 12 and 24 g N/m².

Phosphorus Accumulation

The 1×SSR corresponds to an application of 100 kg P/ha/year, which is more than the crop requirement. Increasing the application rate 2×SSR or 4×SSR results in accumulation of phosphorus in the topsoil (Table 6). The accumulation was most pronounced for sewage sludge Type S2, due to its higher phosphorus content (Tables 1 and 6).

Table 6 Content of phosphorus [μg P/g dry soil extracted by 0.2 N H_2SO_4] in the topsoil layer of the lysimeter experiment (Appendix A). Sewage Sludge application Rate, 1×SSR = 400 g OM/m²/year. Calculated on basis of [12]

TREATMENT	YEAR	SANDY LOAM			COARSE SAND		
		1×SSR	2× SSR	4× SSR	1× SSR	2× SSR	4× SSR
Before start	1973	240	–	–	150	–	–
Type S1	1981	330	570	870	270	450	720
	1987	300	450	780	240	420	780
Type S2	1981	510	780	1590	450	720	1170
	1987	420	600	1290	390	630	1110
Fertilizer	1981	270	420	600	210	360	480
	1987	270	360	480	270	300	450

The phosphorus application rate at the 1×SSR in the lysimeter experiment was 3-4 times higher than the current legal threshold. Thus, sewage sludge application within the thresholds may be assumed to have insignificant effects on nitrogen leaching and phosphorus accumulation. Application of sewage sludge at rates of about 1 t DM/ha/y or 3 t DM/ha/3y appears to be an environmentally friendly way to utilize the nutrients.

Carbon Accumulation

Considerable change in the carbon content of the soil has been obtained at high application rates of organic matter and in long-term experiments only [30]. Due to the turnover of applied organic matter, only a proportion will accumulate and cause an increase of the soil carbon content [31]. The increases in the soil C content per t of organic matter added per hectare were in the order of 0.005-0.010 percentage point, depending on the duration of application [30,31].

Considering the restricted application rates (Table 3), an increase in the C content of the soil as a result of waste application may not be detectable in the short-term experiments reviewed. In addition, the C determination can be reproduced to within an accuracy of ± 6% relative, only. Thus, the significance of using sewage sludge or compost as source of organic matter is difficult to ascertain.

Heavy Metal Accumulation

The contents of Cu, Zn, Pb and Cd in the topsoil layer of the lysimeter experiment (Appendix A) increased during the experimental period. By an application of 2×SSR and 4×SSR, the legal thresholds of heavy metal content in the soil (Table 7) were exceeded in the topsoil layer [12]. Six years after the last application the contents were still high (Table 7), whereas the soil at 20-40 cm depth was only slightly affected [12]. Similar results were obtained in the field experiments (Appendix A). Also application of a composted mixture of organic household refuse and sewage sludge (S4 in Table 1) in rates of 100 and 200 t DM/ha affect the soil. Nine years after application an increased concentration of Cu, Zn, Cd and Pb was still measurable in the soil [16].

Table 7 Current thresholds and the content of heavy metals [mg/kg dry soil] in the Askov long-term experiment (Appendix A), the Market Garden Experiment at Woburn, and in 393 Danish soils

	CURRENT THRESHOLD S [5]	HIGHEST VALUES OF ASKOV LONG-TERM EXPERIMENT [12]	MARKET GARDEN EXPERIMENT [15]	MEDIAN OF DANISH SOILS [32]	95 PERCENTILE OF DANISH SOILS [32]
Cu	40	71	239	7	16
Zn	100	205	635	27	60
Pb	40	107	209	11	19
Cd	0.5	2	109	0.16	0.45

The apparently recovery of the applied Cr was 76% in the plough layer (0-25 cm) and 22% in the 25-50 cm layer [7]. The remaining 2% was recovered at 50-100 cm. Despite the tannery sludge being alkaline for precipitation of Cr as $Cr(OH)_3$, a considerable amount had moved below the plough layer presumably due to leaching. Similarly, the recovery was about 85% in the plough layer after 20 years of application of 15 or 30 t DM/ha/y in sewage sludge loaded with heavy metals (S3 in Table 1) [15]. In this experiment, the application of heavily loaded sewage sludge (S3) at a total rate of 546 t DM/ha results in an extremely high content of heavy metals in the soil (Table 7).

In the lysimeter experiment the percolating water was analyzed for heavy metals. None of the samples had a content above the detection limits (Cu, Mn, Ni < 10 ppm; Cr, Co < 5 ppm; Pb< 1 ppm; Cd < 0.1 ppm) [12].

In an accelerated leaching experiment 200 t DM/ha of sewage sludge were mixed into the top 4 cm soil layer which was then irrigated with a total of about 19 m of water during 24 months [33]. The heavy metals Zn, Cu, Pb, Cd, Ni and Co were nearly entirely retained within the 4-cm topsoil layer. Only the leaching of Pb and Co was slightly higher compared with the reference.

The contents of Cu, Zn, Pb and Cd in 393 Danish soil samples were analysed [32], and the concentrations are in general well below the thresholds (Table 7). Despite the reduced concentration of heavy metals in wastes, they are still undesirable due to their almost linear accumulation in the soil, but the time until they reach an unacceptably high level in the soil is prolonged.

Crop Uptake of Heavy Metals

High application rates of sewage sludge highly loaded with heavy metals (S2, Table 1) influence the plant uptake. The concentration of Cu, Zn, and Cd in the grains of barley and oats was increased by 50% compared with mineral fertilized plants, whereas the grain concentration of Cr, Co and Pb was not affected (Table 8). The concentrations of Zn and Cd in the straw of barley and oats were affected in the same way as the grain [12].

Table 8 Content of heavy metals [mg/kg in DM] in grains of spring barley 1974-79 [12]

METAL	CROP	UNTREATED	TYPE I	TYPE II	FERTILIZER	LSD.95
Cu	Barley	4.0	5.5	5.5	3.4	0.8
	Oats	3.6	4.4	4.1	3.2	0.7
Zn	Barley	28	58	39	31	10
	Oats	34	56	42	36	9
Cd	Barley	0.06	0.12	0.14	0.08	0.03
	Oats	0.15	0.38	0.36	0.22	0.10
Ni	Barley	0.5	0.5	0.7	0.5	0.1
	Oats	1.0	3.6	6.1	2.2	0.6

The crop uptake of Cr, Co and Pb was not affected by soil type, whereas the Zn, Ni and Cd uptake increased on the coarse sand soil [12]. The availability of Cd is linked to pH [34], which normally is lower on coarse sandy soils. Christensen & Tjell [35] suggest that inputs of Cd to agricultural soils should not be allowed to exceed the average Cd output of around 1 g/ha/y from soil through leaching.

Tannery sludge applied had a very high content of Cr [7]. During 1966-72 a total of 6 t Cr/ha was deposited to 5 ha of a sandy soil. In 1975 grain and straw of spring barley were sampled at harvest and analysed for content of Cr. The grain was unaffected, but the content in the straw had increased 5-15 times compared to samples from an adjacent field. Damgaard-Larsen & Larsen [7] supposed that this increase was due to soil contamination of the straw as a result of splash during heavy rain.

The fresh weight and heavy metal concentrations in lettuce, white cabbage, carrots, trimmed leek leaves and leek stems were not affected nine years after application of 100 and 200 t DM/ha of a composted mixture (S4 in Table 1) [16].

Organic Contaminants

During recent years organic contaminants (linear alcylbenzensulphonates (LAS), polycycle aromatic hydrocarbons (PAH), nonylphenolsethoxylates (NPE) and di(2-ethylhexyl)phthalate (DEHP)) have been brought into focus. The sources of these substances are diffuse. For example, LAS and NPE are ingredients in products used for household cleaning and washing. There are other risky substances, but the four included in the legislation have to be considered as indicator groups of substances. Legal threshold values for organic contaminants in waste products [5] may reduce the potential amount suitable for application on agricultural land. Without finishing treatment, 57% of the sewage sludge has values below the prescribed thresholds [2].

Preliminary results from the *Centre for Sustainable Land Use and Management of Contaminants, Carbon and Nitrogen* (http://www.landuse.dk/uk/index.htm) indicate that the organic contaminants may be decomposed by anaerobic and aerobic process at the treatment plants. Organic contaminants applied would be degraded in the soil and there seems no risk for uptake by cereal crops [13].

CONCLUSIONS

The first-year effect of mineral nitrogen and citrate extractable phosphorus contents in wastes corresponds to the effect of the nutrients in mineral fertilizer. Application of waste products at rates not exceeding the application thresholds does not supply sufficient nitrogen to the crop, and satisfactory yields cannot be obtained by application of waste products solely. Therefore supplementary mineral nitrogen has to be applied, but this reduces the nitrogen fertilizer effect of the applied waste.

The increase of soil carbon content is insignificant at the application rates within the thresholds. This may explain the small residual fertilizer effect of wastes. Application of huge amounts of sewage sludge with a high content of heavy metals increased the heavy metal contents in soils and crops. Restricted application rates and improved waste quality have reduced the accumulation rate of heavy metals in the soil.

ACKNOWLEDGEMENT

For their valuable comments the author would like to thank Margit Schacht, Danish Institute of Agricultural Sciences, and W. Towers, The Macaulay Land Use Research Institute, Scotland.

REFERENCES

Most references are in Danish, but references with an English summary are marked with an *.

1. EEC Council Directive 91/271/EEC of 21 May 1991 concerning urban waste-water treatment

2. MILJØSTYRELSEN. Spildevandsslam fra kommunale og private renseanlæg i 1998. Miljø- og Energiministeriet 2000, Miljøstyrelsen, Rapport, 55 pp.

3. DOMELA I. Personal communication.

4. EEC Council Directive 86/278/EEC of 12 June 1986 on the protection of the environment, and in particular of the soil, when sewage sludge is used in agriculture

5. MILJØ- OG ENERGIMINISTERIET. Bekendtgørselse om anvendelse af affalds-produkter til jordbrugsformål, January 2000, Nr. 49.

6. PETERSEN J. Legislation in Denmark and nutrient value of waste products. In: Petersen, J and Petersen, S O, *Use of municipal organic waste*. Proceedings of NJF seminar no. 292, November 23-25, 1998, Agricultural Research Centre, Jokioinen, Finland. Danish Institute of Agricultural Sciences, DIAS report, 1999, no. 13, pp 13-18.

7. DAMGAARD-LARSEN S AND LARSEN K E. Investigation on use of tannery sludge to agricultural land. Tidsskrift for Planteavl Beretning S1551, 1981. *

8. DAMGAARD-LARSEN S, LARSEN K E AND SØNDERGAARD KLAUSEN P. Yearly application of sewage sludge on agricultural land. Tidsskrift for Planteavl, 1979, vol. 83. pp 349-386. *

9. DAMGAARD-LARSEN S, SØNDERGAARD KLAUSEN P AND LARSEN K E. Once for all application of sewage sludge to agricultural land. Tidsskrift for Planteavl, 1979, vol. 83. pp 387-403. *

10. SØNDERGAARD KLAUSEN P. Sewage sludge dewatered on sandbed or by centrifugation. Tidsskrift for Planteavl, 1980, vol. 84, pp 331-334. *

11. LARSEN K E AND DAMGAARD-LARSEN S. Phosphorus effect of precipitated sewage sludge. Tidsskrift for Planteavl, 1981, vol. 85. pp 185-191. *

12. LARSEN K E AND PETERSEN J. Long-term field- and lysimeter experiments with large annual dressing of heavy metal loaded sewage sludge, SP-report 1993, no. 3, 69 pp.*

13. CENTER FOR BÆREDYGTIG AREALANVENDELSE OG FORVALTNING AF MILJØFREMMEDE STOFFER, KULSTOF OG KVÆLSTOF. Evalueringsrapport 2000, Aalborg Universitet, 2000, 112p.

14. MILJØSTYRELSEN. Vandmiljø-94. Redegørelse fra Miljøstyrelsen, 1994, nr. 2, 150 pp.

15. McGRATH S P. Metal concentration in sludges and soil from long-term field trial. Journal of Agricultural Science, Camb., 1984, vol. 103, pp 25-35.

16. SØRENSEN J N, HENRIKSEN K AND HANSEN H. 1997 Heavy metal contents of vegetable crops 1, 2 and 9 years after application of composted municipal waste and sewage sludge. Statens Planteavlsforsøg, SP-report, 1997, no. 12. 12 pp. *

17. DAM KOFOED A AND KJELLERUP V. The content of heavy metals in animal manure. Tidsskrift for Planteavl, 1984, vol. 88. pp 349-352. *

18. PETERSEN J. (ed.). Husdyrgødning og dens anvendelse. SP-rapport, 1996, no. 11, 160 pp. *

19. MILJØSTYRELSEN. Dyrkningsforsøg med kompost 1989-1993. Miljøprojekt nr. 258. Miljøministeriet 1994. *

20. SØNDERGAARD KLAUSEN P. Compost of houshold garbage. Tidsskrift for Planteavl, 1980, vol. 84, pp 209-214. *

21. KNUDSEN L. Gødskning og kalkning. In: C Å.Pedersen (ed.) Oversigt over Landsforsøgene 1994, 1995.

22. MUNKHOLM L AND SIBBESEN E. Tab af fosfor fra landbruget. Det strategiske miljøforskningsprogram, temanummer July 1997, 63 pp.

23. RUBÆK G H AND SIBBESEN E. Long-term phosphorus fertilisation – Effects on crop yield and soil phosphorus status. Danish Institute of Agricultural Sciences, DIAS report, July 2000, Plant Production no. 31, 43 pp.

24. KNUDSEN L. Gødskning og kalkning. In: C Å Pedersen (ed.) Oversigt over Landsforsøgene 1992, 1993.

25. KJELLERUP V. Evaluation of composted source-graded household refuse: Nitrogen effect. Tidsskrift for Planteavl Report S2254, 1993, 38 pp. *

26. ARENFALK O AND HAGELSKJÆR L. The use of different type of manure in organic vegetable growing. SP-report no. 6, 1995. 27 pp. *

27. EEC Council Directive 91/676/EEC of 12 December 1991 concerning the protection of waters against pollution caused by nitrates.

28. MIKKELSEN G. Stategier for anvendelse af komposteret husholdningsaffald ved økologisk grønsagsdyrkning. In: Henriksen, K. (ed.) Forskningsdag om grøntsager. SP-report 1994, no. 2.

29. HANSEN J F AND KJELLERUP V. The nutrition effect of phosphorus and sodium in sewage sludge and straw ash - Micro plot experiment. SP-report no. 14, 1994. 44 pp. *

30. CHRISTENSEN B T AND JOHNSTON A E. Soil organic matter and soil quality – Lessons learned from long-term experiments at Askov and Rothamsted. In: Gregorich, E G and Carter, M R (eds.) Soil quality for crop production and ecosystem health, 1997. pp 399-430.

31. JOHNSTON A E. The Woburn Market Garden Experiment, 1942-69 II. The Effects of the Treatments on Soil pH, Soil Carbon, Nitrogen, Phosphorus and Potassium. Report Rothamsted Experimental Station 1974, Part 2, pp. 102-131.

32. LARSEN M M, BAK J AND SCOTT-FORDSMAND J. Monitering af tungmetaller i danske dyrknings- og naturjorder. Prøvetagning i 1992/93. Faglig rapport fra DMU 1996, nr. 157, Miljø- og Energiministeriet. 77pp. *

33. WILLEMS M, PEDERSEN B AND STORGAARD JØRGENSEN S. Accelerated leaching of some commom and trace elements from soil mixed with sewage sludge or sludge ash. Acta Agriculturae Scandinavica, 1981, vol. 31, pp 323-342.

34. TJELL J C AND CHRISTENSEN T H. Sustainable management of Cadmium in Danish agriculture. In: Vernet, J-P. (Eds.) Impact of Heavy Metals on the Environment. Trace Metals in the Environment, 1992, vol. 2. Elsevier.

35. CHRISTENSEN T H AND TJELL J C. Cadmium in Danish agricultural soils. Folia Geographica Danica, Tom. XIX, 1991. Copenhagen.

APPENDIX A

Brief describtion of the long-term sewage sludge field and lysimeter experiments [8,12].

The field experiments were carried out at Askov (sandy loam), Lundgård (coarse sand) and Rønhave (sandy loam) Experimental Stations during 1974-79 and the residual nitrogen effect was investigated in 1980-84. Until 1997 the experimental field at Askov was maintained as permanent grass, but is today expropriated in favour of a kindergarten! In spring 1998 3-5 kg soil samples of each of the 28 plots were taken in layers of 0-15 cm and 25-35 cm depth and dried before storage.

Two types of sewage sludge with different loads of heavy metals (type S1 and S2, Table 1) were applied at two rates (7 and 21 t OM/ha/year) during 1974-79. The main crops were spring barley or oats, beet, grass, potatoes, carrots, and cabbage or kale grown in a 4-course rotation. During 1980-84 the residual effects were investigated in two sections: with and without applied mineral nitrogen. In this period the crop rotation was spring barley, grass, winter wheat/rye and beet. Corresponding rates and types of sewage sludge were used by Søndergaard Klausen [10].

Dry matter yields were measured, and the contents of N, P, Na, Ca, Mg, Cu, Mn, Zn, Ni, Cr, Co, Pb and Cd in the crops were analyzed in the untreated plots and the plots receiving the high rate of sewage sludge. Prior to and following application the soil was analyzed for Mn, Cu, Zn, Ni, Cr, Co, Pb and Cd. In addition, the Cd concentration in the soil was analyzed 11 years after the last application.

The lysimeter experiments were carried out at Askov Experimental Station in lysimeters (0.8 m², circular) filled with soil from Rønhave (sandy loam) and Lundgård (coarse sand). The two types of sewage sludge (S1 and S2, Table 1) were applied at three rates (400, 800 and 1600 g OM/m²/year) and the 4-course rotation was spring barley, beet, grass and oats, but only one crop was grown each year during 1974-81. The recording of yields and uptakes were similar to the field experiment, but in the lysimeter experiment the leaching was also determined.

Damgaard-Larsen *et al.* [8] present the results of the first three years of the field experiment, whereas Larsen & Petersen [12] present the results from the full experimental period, including the residual effects, as well as the results of the lysimeter experiment.

ENVIRONMENTAL CONSIDERATIONS ON THE FBC COMBUSTION OF DRY SEWAGE SLUDGE

M H Lopes   **P Abelha**

I Cabrita   **I Gulyurtlu**

INETI-DEECA

J S Oliveira

UNL – GDEH

Portugal

ABSTRACT. This paper presents results of on-going research on the incineration of pre-dried granular sewage sludges using a FBC system. Co-combustion is compared with mono-combustion, taking into account the gaseous pollutants and quality of the ashes. Special attention was given to the behaviour of heavy metals, and it was found that mono-combustion of the sludge leads to minor emissions and higher retention of Cd, Pb, Cu and Zn in the bottom ashes, when compared to co-combustion with coal. The leachability of the sludge is reduced through combustion, as none of the metals, Cd, Cr, Cu, Ni, Pb, Zn, Co and Mn were leached from the bottom ashes. These findings may contribute to an improvement in the incineration of sewage sludges and to the development of applications for the ashes in civil engineering activities.

Keywords: Sewage sludge, Combustion, FBC, Pollution, Heavy metals.

Eng. M.H Lopes, is a Research Assistant at INETI, with 12 years experience on the characterisation of wastes and environmental aspects of combustion. She is preparing a PhD on the subject of heavy metals in FBC combustion of sewage sludges.

Eng. P. Abelha, is a PhD student working at INETI. His thesis will be devoted to the formation of gaseous pollutants in FBC combustion.

Dr. I. Cabrita, is head of the Department of Energetic Engineering and Environmental Control, at INETI, and a Senior Researcher with interests in the environmental issues.

Dr. I. Gulyurtlu, is a Senior Researcher at INETI. He is the Portuguese expert on FBC systems and leader of many European and National projects.

Prof. J. S. Oliveira, is a Professor at UNL and head of the group of Hydrosphere Ecology. He has interests on the impact and recycling of ashes from incineration and is a leader of many National and European Projects.

INTRODUCTION

The management of sewage sludge represents an important environmental concern due to its potential toxicity and the amounts generated worldwide, which solely in Europe is estimated to be about 9-million t d.m. (dry matter) [1, 2]. This is a consequence of unbalanced contents, mainly of heavy metals, which may lead to restrictions in use as a fertilizer, due to possible contamination of edible crops. In reality, several crops have a very high capacity for accumulation of heavy metals in specific organs, leading to contamination of edible items. Nevertheless, its calorific value is highly attractive for energy recovery through combustion, which suggests there is scope for increased use of sludges for energy from the present 10% to about 40% by 2005, in Europe [1, 2].

Although heavy metal concentrations of the sewage may present values below the limits fixed for agriculture purposes as a fertilizer [3] (which prevent them being classified as a hazardous residue), environmental problems exist, whatever management option is assumed. Harmful effects may arise due to the leachability of trace metals (even in low concentrations), from the sewage sludge itself, when used directly in agricultural lands or landfills, or even from the ashes produced in combustion processes.

Therefore, other means for environmental dissemination of pollutants must be considered. As far as incineration is concerned, volatile compounds, containing chlorine, sulphur, nitrogen and phosphorus are released with the combustion gases. In addition, many trace heavy metals may be volatilized under combustion conditions, usually being enriched in the smaller particles and aerosols, as e.g. lead, cadmium, and many others, or even in the gaseous state, such as mercury and arsenic. The treatment of flue gases leads to new secondary streams that must be handled in accordance with environmental regulations to prevent the release of metals and possible dispersion of other contaminants to the environment. The re-utilization of any ashes resulting from combustion should receive the same kind of safety precautions, as when this is not carried out, requiring a detailed characterization in an environmental perspective.

COMBUSTION TESTS

The combustion tests were performed in a 90 kW atmospheric fluidized bed system (AFBC). The combustor, described previously [4] has a square cross section of 0.3x0.3 m, and is 5 m high. The system is insulated and refrigerated with water coils, in order to control temperature. It is provided with two serial cyclones for the removal of particles from the gas stream. Several sampling points are located along the reactor for the measurement of gaseous species. There is a sampling port in the stack duct for sampling dust carried with the flue gases. The combustion air was staged in order to control NO_x formation and to avoid major elutriation of particles from the bed. The cool primary air is supplied through the distributor plate, acting as the fluidizing fluid of the sand bed. The feeding of fuel is achieved with a screw feeder 50 cm above the distributor plate.

Three types of tests were performed: 100% coal, mixtures of coal and sewage sludge (65% to 35%) and mono-combustion of the sludge. Relevant combustion parameters are given in Table 1.

Table 2 presents the characterization of the coal and sludge that were used. The US coal is highly volatile and exhibits a high heating value, low ash, and significant sulfur contents. The sewage sludge utilized was received already thermally dried (DSS) in a granular and non-dusting form. The ash content is very high, and the fixed carbon much smaller than in coal, although the volatile matter (46.5%) is higher (37.2%).

The sludge has high phosphorous, but smaller sulfur contents and nitrogen levels twice those of coal. The heating value of the sludge is half of that of coal, but similar to other lower grade coals, which enable the sustained self-combustion of the dry sludges without auxiliary fuel. The main ash constituents are Ca, Al, Fe and Si. Significant concentrations of trace metals giving case for environmental concern were found in this sludge, which meant that special attention in its characterization, both in terms of ashes and flue gas emissions was required.

In order to capture the SO_2 formed, co-combustion tests were also performed with the addition of limestone, continuously mixed with the fuel feed. The mixtures of coal and DSS were used in proportions of 65% to 35% respectively and lasted for about 8 hours. The mono-combustion tests of DSS were shortened, because the accumulation of ashes disturbs fluidization, even if periodic bleeding of the bed material through the bottom is made.

Despite the lower density of the ashes, their size was large enough such that their terminal velocity outranges the fluidization conditions. This suggests that for the combustion of granular sludges it is preferable to have an alternative FBC operation, as for example a continuous ash extraction in other zones of the bed section, while the sand make up is required.

The most important pollutant gases generated, SO_2, NO_x, and CO, as well as O_2 and CO_2 were measured with continuous gas analyzers, along the reactor and in the stack gases. HCl was captured by a wet technique [5] and determined by capillary electrophoresis.

Table 1 Combustion Parameters

FUEL	SIZE mm	FUEL RATE (kg/h)	T BED (°C)	T FREEBOARD (°C)	STAGED AIR 2nd/1st	EXCESS AIR (%)
Coal(65%)	0.5–4	9.0–10.8	800 - 850	740 – 770	0.3	40–60
DSS(35%)	2-5					
DSS (100%)	2–5	12.5–14.5	750 - 830	710 - 770	0.3	55–60

GENERATION OF ASHES

The residual material obtained from combustion was collected in the bed, mixed with the sand material. The particulate material, separated by the cyclones, was collected in hoppers.

The ashes escaping the cyclones through the stack were sampled with an isokinetic probe and retained in glass fiber membranes for further analysis [5].

Table 2 Characterization of Coal and Sewage Sludge

PROPERTY		COAL C	DRY SEWAGE SLUDGE DSS
%	Moisture.	1.6	6.6
	Ash (750°C)	7.5	42.0
	Fixed Carbon	59.2	6.2
	C	77.7	28.8
	Ht	5.13	4.30
	N	1.77	3.50
	Cl	0.06	0.07
	S	2.12	0.90
	P	0.50	2.9
	Ca	0.20	5.0
	Fe	0.64	1.6
	Al	1.15	2.8
	K	0.04	0.6
	Na	0.03	0.2
	Mg	0.02	0.5
mg/kg	Mn	12.1	368
	Co	1.8	5.0
	Ni	5.0	40
	Cr	12.0	196
	Pb	<0.2	341
	Cu	4.9	352
	Cd	<0.2	9.4
	Zn	9.4	1057
	Hg	<0.5	3.4
	As	0.35	0.09
	HHV (MJ/kg)	33.4	12.4

The amounts and partition of the ashes produced differs considerably, depending on the composition of the fuel feed, as can be seen in Figure 1. For coal, the retention in the bed ashes is minimal, being the major proportion collected in the first cyclone. The material captured in the second cyclone was usually very scarce (below 10 g/kg of fuel) and the stack particulates represent usually less than 3.0 % of the total ashes produced.

For coal, the material of the first cyclone gives high levels of unburned carbon. In continuous operation this fraction should return to the reactor, increasing the combustion efficiency. These specific experiments required separate collection of the ashes in order to allow a better assessment of heavy metal behaviour.

For the runs with mixtures of coal with DSS, the retention of ashes in the bed is very high, although there is still a large quantity of material captured in the first cyclone. This fraction still presents an exaggerated amount of unburned carbon, although this is much lower than for runs with coal. For the DSS runs, the loss on ignition (LOI) problem is completely overcome, showing a high combustion efficiency of the sludges.

Another major finding of these tests is that more than 90% of the ashes from DSS are retained as bottom ashes in the bed zone, giving insignificant carbon content. It was also observed that these ashes keep their original shape, as inorganic light weight granulate, that could be sieved above 0.5mm.

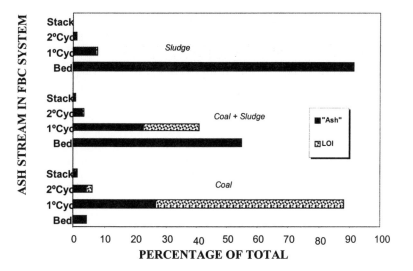

Figure 1 Distribution of Ashes in the FBC system

POLLUTANT EMISSIONS

The concentration of pollutants measured during the test runs may not be considered as absolute values, for comparison with regulations. Emission regulations are being revised which will overcome the problem of classification of residues, that dictate what limiting values have to be achieved [6].

The fact that the system is not provided with any further dedusting, or other air pollution devices, than cyclones and that it is not operated continuously, may lead to higher emission rates than in full industrial incinerators.

Figure 2 compares the gaseous emissions of specific typical runs performed. The most abundant pollutant is SO_2.

For coal, the conversion of S to gaseous SO_2 is almost complete. For the mixtures, the SO_2 emissions decrease, not only due to a lower S content of the sludge, but also because there is some degree of retention of S in the ashes formed. To minimize emissions to about 300mg/Nm3, (10% of the S entry), it was necessary to introduce limestone.

In mono-combustion, although the Ca content of the sludge accomplishes the useful Ca/S ratio of 2.5, the SO_2 reduction was only about 30% of the potential gas to be formed, reaching relatively high values of 800 mg/Nm^3 (11% O_2). Industrial incineration would require flue gas treatment. In the case of HCl emissions, they are below 100 mg/Nm^3 and do not vary much between tests. The Cl content was low for both fuels.

The NO_x formed is relatively low in all the runs (below 300mg/Nm^3), which is related to the low temperatures and the staged air conditions used in the FBC system [7]. Mono-combustion of the sludge gives the lower levels of NO_x, although its N content was higher than in coal. Considering the conversion ratio of N into NO_x, the sludge gives the lowest conversion (0.01), compared with the values observed for the mixture (0.03) or coal (0.03-0.07, depending on the excess air).

The levels of CO increased when the sludge was mixed with coal or when it is burned alone, showing that different combustion mechanisms are involved for those materials. Regulatory levels for CO emissions could however be more liberal for fluidized bed systems than for other incinerators [8].

The particulate matter escaping from the cyclones with the flue gases was also much lower for the single combustion of sludges than for coal and for mixtures. It attains about 2/2.7g/kg of the fuel feed for the runs of coal and mixtures, and less than 0.3g/kg for the sludge. This is consistent with the decreased quantities of ash found in the cyclones, observed for the sludge runs.

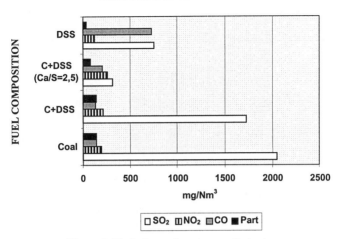

Figure 2 Emissions of gaseous pollutants

Considering the heavy metal emissions in the flue gases, the values are very low. Cd is always below 0.01 mg/Nm³, although there was an increase when the sludges were feed in co-combustion compared with the values obtained in mono-combustion. All of the other metals measured (Cu + Pb + Ni + Mn + Cr + Co) are below 0.5 mg/Nm³, in all experiments which is below the limits fixed for incineration of hazardous residues [6]. Zn, that is not restricted, gives the higher emission rates, although lying below 0.3 mg/Nm³.

In addition, to the extremely low values observed, it was possible to verify that there was a clear rise of the emissions of Pb, Cu, Cd, and Zn for the mixtures of sludge with coal, compared with the coal runs. In the mono-combustion of sludges the values for each of the metals were lower (below 0.03mg/Nm³) than in co-combustion.

In spite of the accomplishment of the regulatory levels for emissions, it is necessary to consider the specific emission rates (plotted in Figure 3). An emission of 1 mg of metal by 1kg of fuel mixture represents a release of about 3 t of that metal if 1 million t of sludge (d.m.) is co-combusted with coal. According to the results obtained, this seems to be less probable if sludges are burned alone at relatively low temperatures.

Other metals like As and Hg, which are more readily volatised, have also been evaluated. Computation of full emission of the Hg content found in the sludge showed that a maximum of 0.7 mg/Nm³ could be emitted.

Hence, the Hg emissions may exceed regulatory limits. The As may reach an emission of 0.05 mg/Nm³ in the coal runs. The partition of these metals will be further investigated in order to verify the retention of those metals in ashes.

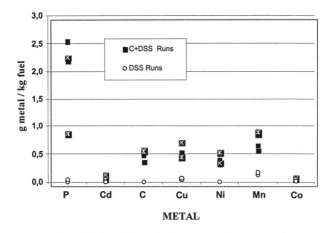

Figure 3 Specific emission rates of heavy metals

HEAVY METALS IN ASHES

The heavy metal concentration of the bottom ashes corresponding to the sludges is plotted in Figure 4. There is an enrichment of metals in the ash compared to the original sludge, due to the combustion of organic matter and to possible losses of inorganic volatile matter. However, when comparing with the theoretical levels that could be expected if the metals were completely retained in ashes (horizontal black line in the graphics) we may verify that there is clear evidence of losses especially for Cd, Pb, and Cu for the co-combustion runs. In mono-combustion, the experimental concentrations observed fit more closely with theoretical values. This is in agreement with the different gaseous emissions observed for those runs.

The influence of coal on the differences observed, taking into account that the two main dictating parameters, temperatures in the reactor and chlorine concentrations, were similar in the two types of tests performed, remaining to be explained.

EVALUATION OF THE LEACHABILITY OF HEAVY METALS

The ashes collected in the bottom of the reactor, for which management could be more troublesome due to the huge quantities produced, were investigated in order to evaluate the solubility of harmful metals. The potential release of those metals was also investigated in the sewage sludge. The leachability was accessed through prEN 12457-2 method [9]. In this methodology, the samples are subject to contact with water for 24 hours with continuous agitation and a liquid to solid ratio of 10.

Table 3 presents the concentrations found in the eluates that were obtained by filtration of the suspensions through 0.45-micron acetate cellulose membranes. For the ashes the leachability of Cd, Pb, Zn, Cu, Ni, Mn, Cr and Co was negligible. The sewage sludge released significant levels of metals which were greatest for Cu and Ni.

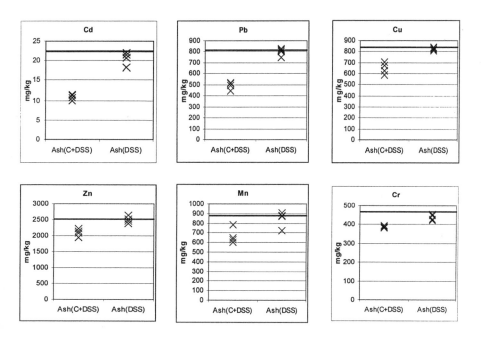

Figure 4 Concentration of heavy metals in ashes from co-combustion and from mono-combustion of the sewage sludge

In spite of the allowable use of these sludges as fertilizers, these results bring into our mind that if even only 10% of the actual European production of sludge are used this way, something like 0.5T of Pb, 4.5T of Zn, 27 T of Cu, 4.5 T of Ni, 0.1T of Cd, 0.7 T of Co and 0.8 T of Mn might be released to the soils and freatic water layers. These figures could be even worst considering the biodegradation of organic matter and the possible oxidation of mineral matter of the sludges that would enhance the release of metals to the environment over a long-term period.

Further investigation is proceeding to consider the other ash streams, although their impact will be probably less important due to the lower amounts generated.

Table 3 Leachability of sewage sludge and ashes (mg/l)

FUEL	Pb	Zn	Cu	Ni	Cd	Mn	Co	Cr (total)
DSS	0.05	0.40	2.73	0.44	0.01	0.08	0.07	<0.05
Ash (C+DSS)	≤0.02	<0.005	<0.005	<0.01	<0.005	<0.07	<0.01	<0.05
Ash (DSS)	<0.02	<0.005	<0.005	<0.01	<0.005	<0.07	<0.01	<0.05

CONCLUSIONS

The preliminary evaluation of results shows that, the combustion of thermally dried sewage sludge in FBC system seems to be successfully achieved in a fluidized bed system. The combustion efficiency is improved in mono-combustion when compared with co-combustion. In addition, the mono-combustion of the sludge leads to smaller heavy metal emissions than those of co-combustion, and to higher retention of heavy metals in the bottom ash.

Looking at the environmental performance, these ashes give a safer behaviour regarding leachability of heavy metals. The FBC Incineration seems to be a useful technology capable of diminishing the leachability of the sewage sludge, either in mono- or co-combustion. The full-scale incineration would however require highly efficient flue gas treatment.

An interesting environmental contribution of the combustion process is the generation of granulated bottom ashes with an insignificant LOI, low density and some degree of mechanical resistance, which may represent a valuable material for specific civil engineering processes, such as, e.g. fillers for lightweight aggregates.

AKNOWLEDGMENTS

The authors would like to acknowledge the European Community for financing this study.

REFERENCES

1. DAVIS, R.D.   Legislative Developments and Sewage Sludge Disposal Strategy in Europe. Proceedings of Sewage Sludge Disposal Symposium, Prague, 1995

2. WERTHER, J. AND OGADA, T.   Sewage sludge combustion. Progress in Energy and Combustion Science, Vol 25, 1999. pp 55-116

3. COMMISSION OF THE EUROPEAN COMMUNITIES Directive on the protection of the environment, and in particular of the soil, when sewage sludge is used in agriculture (86/278/EEC) Official Journal of the European Communities L181/6-12 June 1986

4. GULYURTLU, I., FRADE, E., LOPES, H., FIGUEIREDO, F., AND CABRITA, I. Combustion of various types of residues in a circulating fluidized bed combustor, Proceedings of the 14 th International Conference on Fluidized Bed Combustion, volume 1, 1997. pp 423-431

5. US ENVIRONMENTAL PROTECTION AGENCY Methods Manual for compliance with the BIF regulations, EPA/530-SW-91-010, US Department of Commerce, NTIS, Springfield, VA 22161, 1990

6. COMMISSION OF THE EUROPEAN COMMUNITIES Directive on the Incineration of hazardous residues (94/67/CE) Official Journal of the European Communities L365/34 31 de December de 1994

7. OGADA, T., and WERTHER, J. Combustion Characteristics of wet sludge in a fluidized bed. Fuel. 75, 1996, n°5, pp. 617-626

8. COMMISSION OF THE EUROPEAN COMMUNITIES Amended proposal for a European Parliament and Council Directive on the Incineration of waste, COM(1999)330 final, Brussels, 12.07.1999

9. EUROPEAN COMMITTEE FOR STANDARDIZATION, ed., Compliance test for leaching of granular waste materials and sludges: one stage batch test at L/S ratio 10, Draft prEN 12457-2, CEN/TC 292/WG2, Doc.109-2, Brussels, 1998), 12.

THE REUSE OF INDUSTRIAL SLUDGES FOR THE CONSTRUCTION OF RESERVOIR DAMS

J Tennekoon   **D Van Gemert**   **J Maertens**

Katholieke Universiteit Leuven

J Houtmeyers   **J Erven**

Tessenderlo Chemie n.v.   Constructor n.v.

Belgium

ABSTRACT. Proper disposal of large quantities of industrial sludges is at present a critical problem. Certain industrial sludges may be suitable for use in the construction industry such as for embankments. However, the behaviour of these materials is highly specific and the geotechnical and engineering properties need to be comprehensively and as accurately as possible assessed. This paper deals with such a study on a sludge material that is to be used to construct an embankment founded on previously disposed sludge. The preliminary testing programme includes both laboratory and in-situ analysis of the sludge material as well as the construction and monitoring of a full-scale test embankment. The behaviour of the test embankment was monitored over a period of two years with measurements of settlements and pore water pressures made at regular intervals in both the embankment itself and in the supporting sludge. Conclusions regarding the general behaviour of the sludge, its suitability for the construction of the embankment and its ability to support the embankment have been attempted from the data gathered during the preliminary testing programme.

Keywords: Industrial sludge, Geotechnical characterisation, Embankments, Computer simulation, Full-scale test embankment.

Ir J Tennekoon, is a doctoral student in the Department of Civil Engineering, Katholieke Universiteit Leuven, Leuven, Belgium.

Professor Dr Ir D Van Gemert, is a professor at the Department of Civil Engineering, Katholieke Universiteit Leuven, Leuven, Belgium.

Professor Ir Jan Maertens, is a visiting professor at the Department of Civil Engineering, Katholieke Universiteit Leuven, Leuven, Belgium.

Dr Ir J Houtmeyers, is a director of Tessenderlo Chemie n.v., Tessenderlo, Belgium.

Ir J Erven, is a director of Constructor n.v., Antwerpen, Belgium.

INTRODUCTION

At present large quantities of different industrial sludges are produced while the extent of lands available for their safe disposal is limited. Governments have also brought in legislation that strictly enforces environmental safety. As sites presently being used for industrial sludge disposal are being rapidly filled up, these industries face stiff financial and environmental pressures in order to identify suitable alternate means of disposal or locations.

Certain industrial wastes containing a high percentage of sand are suitable for construction purposes such as the construction of embankments. However, before this can be done, it is important that the geotechnical and engineering properties of such material is comprehensively and as accurately as possible determined. Several studies have been conducted to investigate several sludges of different origins such as flue gas desulpherisation sludges, papermill sludges, domestic and municipal waste sludges and sludges from steel manufacturing activities [1]. Due to the specific behaviour of sludges of different origins it is not possible to apply the findings of one type in entirety to another.

This paper deals with a study of a sludge material in order to use it for the construction of an embankment with a view of increasing the storage capacity of an existing disposal site. As such, the embankment will not only be constructed with the sludge but will also be founded on sludge already disposed in the basin. At Tessenderlo Chemie in Tessenderlo, Belgium, the production of mainly phosphates as well as other chemical products results in the generation of large quantities of a sand rich sludge. This sludge containing a high percentage of water is pumped into a large basin and allowed to de-water. In order to enhance the dry material content and thus the storage capacity of the basin, the sludge is dredged out of the basin, de-watered by means of a chamber filter press and then returned to the basin. This final sludge has a water content of about 70 to 80%. The water collected in the basin is pumped back to the plant and re-used in the production process.

A test programme is being carried out to search for the optimum dumping, drying and compacting methods of the sludge, to enable the safe construction of the planned embankment. This paper focuses on the monitoring and analysis of a test embankment built at the disposal site in conditions similar to the planned embankment.

SLUDGE DISPOSAL BASIN

The sludge disposal basin is located at Tessenderlo, Belgium encompassing a total area of about 273,000 m^2. An outline of the entire basin is shown in Figure 1 and the cross-sections of the existing and proposed dikes are shown in Figure 2.

The main products of the company include different sulphur derivatives, inorganic feed phosphates and fertilizers such as sulphate of potash. The production processes and products used are numerous but the main raw materials used at the Tessenderlo plant are materials such as sulphur, rock phosphate, potassium chloride and sodium chloride. The main constituent of the sludge deposited is SiO_2-bonded calcium fluoride sludge (CaF_2) [4].

An impermeable geomembrane has been provided at the bottom of the basin. This is to prevent the contamination of the groundwater and the nearby canal by the leachate from the sludge reservoir. At the onset of the planning, the height of the dike proposed was to be 9 m.

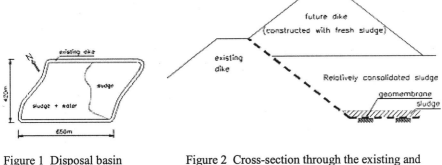

Figure 1 Disposal basin

Figure 2 Cross-section through the existing and
proposed dikes

However, the dike is to be constructed on a layer of relatively compact and drained sludge of about 6m thickness. The exact degree of compaction is unknown and there is a possibility that the sludge just above the geomembrane is more wetter and less compacted than the overlying sludge. Hence, the exact behaviour of the sludge under loading and therefore its ability to support a dike of 9 m are questionable. These are the main questions that have to be answered during the testing programme.

GEOTECHNICAL CHARACTERISATION

Laboratory Testing

Various standard laboratory tests have being carried out on both disturbed and undisturbed samples to ascertain some of the important mechanical properties of the sludge. The tests executed include moisture content determination, areometer, x-ray diffraction, liquid and plasticity limits, permeability, consolidation, optimum water content and density, vane shear and direct shear. The mechanical properties of the sludge determined from some of the above tests are given in Table 1.

Table 1 Basic geotechnical properties [6]

W_L	w_P	Ip	C_u^*	ϕ_u^*	K	w_{opt}	$\gamma_{wet,opt}$	$\gamma_{dry,opt}$
85%	48%	37%	3 kPa	33°	$1x10^{-9}$ to	38%	18,8 kN/m^3	13.6 kN/m^3
			5 kPa	39°	$5x10^{-10}$ m/s			

*The two sets of values were obtained from a tri-axial test and from a direct shear test.

Figure 3 gives the particle size distribution obtained from laser diffraction analysis. A general conclusion that can be made from the results of table 1 and figure 3 is that the basic physical and mechanical characteristics of the sludge is typical of fine grained soils. However, the optimum water content at 38% is high even for clayey soils. This high value is confirmed by the fact that the lowest value for the water content obtained during analysis of several samples has been 42%. A reason for this is that the sludge particles have a high affinity to water molecules. Therefore, the dewatered sludge in the basin in the long run can be expected to have a water content of not less than about 40%.

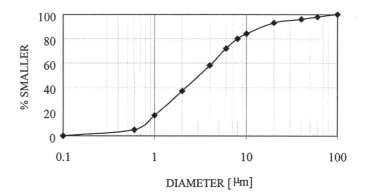

Figure 3 Particle size distribution from laser diffraction analysis [4]

In addition to the above, permeability and consolidation characteristics under different vertical stresses were also investigated. These results are summarised in table 2.

Table 2 Permeability and consolidation characteristics

STRESS (kPa)	K (m/s)	CONSOLIDATION COEFFICIENT(m^2/year)	COEFFICIENT OF VOLUME COMPRESSIBILITY (m^2/MN)
12.75	5.10E-10	2.02	2.83
25.5	5.06E-10	0.02	2.05
51	4.76E-10	0.06	1.67
102	3.34E-10	0.61	1.12
204	2.63E-10	1.43	0.82
408	2.39E-10	1.67	0.62

As expected there is a general decrease in permeabilities with increasing stresses due to the reduction of pore water spaces. The consolidation and volume compressibility coefficients are typical of clay soils indicating high compressibility but very low rates of primary consolidation [5]. The relatively high value at low stresses is possibly due to the sludge being normally consolidated at this load.

An analysis of the sludge under the electron microscope clearly showed the sludge particles having a strong tendency to flocculate [4]. This will have an effect on both the grain size distribution and on the density. The possible reason for this is the presence of salts and chlorine which enhances the interaction between the clay particles.

FIELD TESTS

The in-situ tests carried out on the sludge are density measurement, permeability measurement, vane shear tests and cone penetration tests. The results of he first two are shown in table 3 and the other two are shown in Figures 4 and 5 respectively.

Table 3 Results of in-situ density and permeability measurements

k (m/s)	γ (kN/m^3)	w (%)
2 to 3 E-09	12 to 15	80 to 95

The in-situ permeability measurement leads to a somewhat higher value than in the laboratory analysis. This can be attributed to the presence of laminations and fissures in the sludge which enhance the flow of water. In practice, it is unlikely that the sludge will attain the optimum density of 18.8 kN/m^3 but will lie around 15 kN/m^3 and will vary on the degree of compaction (i.e. depth) and on the water content.

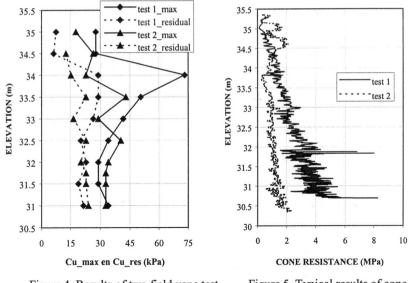

Figure 4 Results of two field vane test

Figure 5 Typical results of cone penetration tests

From the vane shear test, the undrained shear strength of the sludge lies between 20 kPa for uncompacted sludge to over 30 kPa for compacted sludge at the bottom of the sludge layer. The cone penetration tests also show a general increase in the cone resistance with depth. However, the rate of increase and the actual values show marked variations in the tests executed. This is possibly due to the non-uniformity in the degree of compaction between the locations tested and/or variations in the water contents.

Remarks

The conclusions that can be drawn from the various laboratory and in-situ tests is that the behaviour of the sludge is similar to that of clay with low shear strengths, permeabilities and consolidation coefficients [5]. However, the high water content, due to adhesion of water molecules to the sludge particles, and the presence of various ions cause a degree of uncertainty in the behaviour of the material especially in the long term. For this reason, it is not possible to apply all theories that are valid for clays to the sludge. Furthermore, the general macro-fabric of the sludge is not represented accurately in small specimens that are used for the laboratory tests. Hence, a certain degree of uncertainty exists in these measured values too. With the above remarks in mind it was decided to construct a full scale test embankment to observe the real behaviour of the sludge during and after construction.

TEST EMBANKMENT

Location

Figure 6 shows the situation of the 30 x 60 m test embankment and its cross-section. The test embankment is constructed on a layer of sludge of about 6m thickness. The construction of the embankment took place in stages with a period of about 10 months allowed for consolidation. The height of the embankment was limited to 6 m as above this its stability cannot be guaranteed. The height limitation is based on the following calculation based on the simplified solution to the bearing capacity under a strip footing under undrained conditions [3]:

$$q_f = (2 + \pi)\ c_u = 5.14\ c_u$$

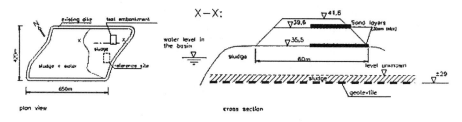

Figure 6 Situation of the test embankment

The shear stress of the sludge is approximately 25 kPa as given by the vane shear tests. The Bjerrum correction factor for a soil of plasticity index of 37% is 0.85 [3]. The corrected field shear strength becomes, c_u = 25 x 0.85 = 21.25 kPa, and q_f = 5.14 x 21.25 = 109.2 kPa. Applying a safety factor of 1.2 and taking the density of the sludge as 15 kN/m^3, the safe height of the embankment is: h = 109.2/(1.2 x 15) = 6.07 m. Hence, the height of the dike is actually limited to 6 m. In the first phase 4 m was constructed and in the second phase a further 2 m was added.

Measuring Equipment

Instruments were installed in the dike and the underlying sludge to monitor settlements (ZB) and pore water pressures (WSM and PB). Similar instruments were also installed at a site close to the test embankment which acts as a reference. On one half of the embankment two sand layers of 30 cm thickness were provided at the base of the dike and at the top of the firs raise, to enhance drainage. The different phases in the construction of the test dike are given in Table 4.

Table 4 Embankment construction phases

| DATE | | ACTIVITY |
From	To	
12/11/97	24/03/98	Installation of measuring instruments
07/04/98	29/04/98	4 m of the section of the dike without drainage sand is constructed
05/06/98	30/06/98	4 m of the section of the dike with drainage sand is constructed
04/05/99	08/06/98	2 m raising of the section of the dike without drainage sand
08/06/99	24/06/99	2 m raising of the dike with drainage sand

The location of the various measuring instruments installed at both the reference and test sites are shown in Figure 7. Some instruments were installed only before the second phase. Settlement plates were also installed adjacent to the dike before the second phase. These were to measure the degree of bulging of the sludge around the test embankment which were visible after the first raise too but not measured.

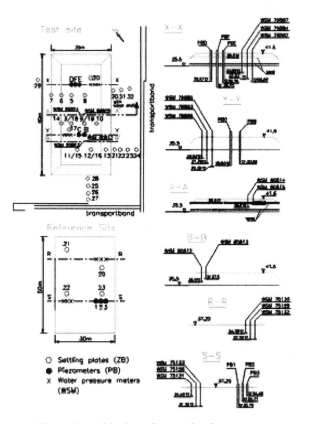

Figure 7 Positioning of measuring instruments

RESULTS

Measurements were made at regular intervals during and after the construction period and are still being made at present. The results of the water pressures for the reference site are shown in Figure 8. Figures 9 and 10 show the water pressures in the sections of the embankment with and without drainage sand respectively. The piezometric tube PB A is not used after 30 June 98 due to damage. The 4 water pressure meters, WSM 80812-5, were installed in May 1998 after the construction of the first phase.

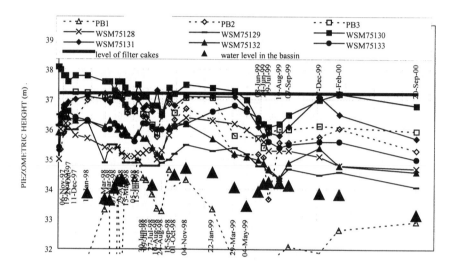

Figure 8 Piezometric heights for the reference site

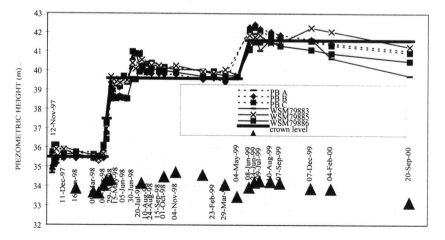

Figure 9 Piezometric heights for the section of the test
embankment without drainage sand

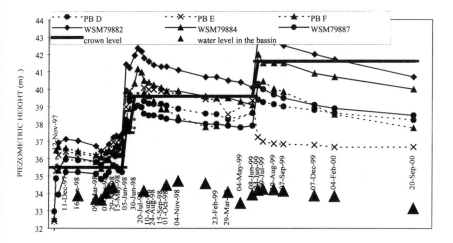

Figure 10 Piezometric heights for the section of the test embankment with drainage sand

It was noted that the piezometric tubes also settle with the sludge. The degree of setting has been measured and taken into account in the calculation of water levels. However, the results of the water pressure meters could not be adjusted as the degree of settlement is not known. Hence, this should be taken into consideration when interpreting the results of the water pressure meters.

Discussion

Initially, the piezometric heights are increasing due to the filling up of the instruments. Thereafter, the piezometric levels closely follow the construction of the dike. During construction of the dike the pore pressures increase followed by slow dissipation. The rate of dissipation is visibly faster in the section of the dike with drainage sand. In the reference site, the initial increase in piezometric heights is followed by a slow decrease due to the consolidation of the sludge in this area.

The settlements in the test embankment are shown in Figure 11. The settlements directly below the test embankment vary between 0.4 m to 1.6 m during the first raise and between 0.1 m to 0.5 m during the second raise. The actual total settlements during the two consolidation periods are only about 0.2 m at the most. Hence, of the total settlement, over 90% occur as immediate settlement during the raising of the embankment. This is most certainly due to the squeezing of the sludge under the embankment.

The settlement plates next to the test embankments showed lifting varying from about 0.1 m to about 0.6 m. This also occurred immediately during the raising of the embankment and thereafter the bulge decreased slowly. It can be concluded that the settlement under the dike is mostly plastic (squeezing of the sludge) and to a lesser extent elastic (causing bulging of the sludge around the embankment).

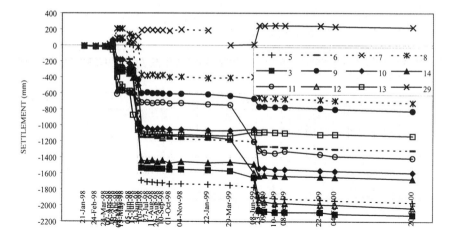

Figure 11 Settlement results in the test area

The bulging of the sludge around the dike and the large settlements noted readily confirm the fact that a dike of 6 m height is the limit. Any additional heights can lead to serious problems with greater bulging of the sludge around the embankment and settlements of the sludge below the embankment. This will not only cause problems for the equipment but can also lead to collapse of the dike.

PRELIMINARY COMPUTER SIMULATION

A computer simulation of the dike has been undertaken with two major aims:

- Firstly, to compare the actual behaviour of the dyke as obtained from monitoring measurements with that of a dyke composed of a typical soil using as far as possible the parameter values calculated during the various tests.

- Secondly, to use the model to identify critical areas where more attention may be required (e.g stability of slopes) or where the sensitivity of uncertain parameters is greatest and to predict the general behaviour of the dyke in the long term.

The model is constructed using the PLAXIS finite element programme for soil and rock analysis [2].

Model Geometry

The side slopes have been taken as 1:1.5 (33.7°). Due to symmetry, only half the embankment has been modeled. The underlying sludge has been divided into two layers to account for the expected differences in the degree of compaction of the sludge (high compaction and sludge of high water content) while the dike is constructed with sludge of low compaction. Two sand layers of thickness 30 cm have been incorporated on half of the Embankment section modeled.

The simulation is carried out in 8 phases of alternating loading and consolidation phases to account for the actual mode of dike construction. The height of the dike during the first raise is taken as 5m and that during the second phase is taken as 2.5m. This is due to the fact that each raise of the dike occurs over a period of 3 to 4 weeks. And during this process considerable immediate settlements occur and thus at the end of the raising period the exact height of the raise would have been more than the measured values.

Figure 12 shows the cross-section of the dike used in the model along with the finite element mesh. The boundary at the bottom of the model is fixed (no deformations are assumed to occur) and it is also considered as a flow and consolidation boundary.

Figure 12 Model geometry

Material Characteristics

The material behaviour is modeled as that of a soft soil. This model is ideal for situations where primary compression is of great importance as is the case here. Here, the failure is modeled according to the Mohr-coulomb criterion but in addition it takes into consideration stress dependant stiffness with primary compression playing an important role [2]. In order to take this into consideration it is necessary to input the compression index λ, of the material as accurately as possible. Furthermore, in this model the permeabilities have also been increased (from the measured values) to ensure a comparable rate of dissipation of excess pore pressures as noted during the measurements. The material characteristics used are shown in Table 5.

Table 5 Material characteristics used in the model

MATERIAL SET	HIGH COMPACTION	LOW COMPACTION	SLUDGE	SAND
Material model	Soft-soil	Soft-soil	Soft-soil	Mohr-coulomb
Material type	Undrained	Undrained	Undrained	Drained
γ_{dry} (kN/m^3)	9	9	8	12
γ_{wet} (kN/m^3)	15	12	12	16
k (m/s)	1.0E-08	1.0E-08	10E-07	1.0E-03
λ	1	1	1	E = 500 kN/m^2
κ	0.15	0.15	0.15	ν = 0.35
c (kN/m^2)	18	18	8	10
ϕ (°)	25	28	25	30
ψ (°)	0	0	0	0

The dilatancy angle, ψ for the sludge and the sand has been taken as zero. The values of the compression index have been obtained from the consolidation test results while the swelling index, κ has been estimated. It has been found that the behaviour of the model is highly sensitive to the value of these parameters. The strength parameters c, ϕ and ψ for the thin sand layers have been assumed.

Results

The model has been simulated for a period of 890 days (corresponding to the number of days from the date of construction of the dyke, 07/04/1998, to the date of last measurement, 20/09/2000). Eight separate phases have been modeled corresponding to the: (i) first 4 m raise of the section of the dike without sand drain; (ii) 4 m raise o the section of dike with sand drains; (iii) second raise (2 m) of the section of dike without sand drains; (iv) 2 m raise for the section of dike with sand drains. Each construction phase is followed by a consolidation phase. The results obtained are classified into settlements, water pressures and stability and are given below.

Settlements

The model was unable to reproduce the instantaneous large settlements that were noted during loading. The model results also showed higher consolidation on the side with the drainage sands and hence more settlement in this half. Figure 13 shows the comparison of settlements for plates 17 (no sand layers) and 5 (with sand layer) with the modeled values.

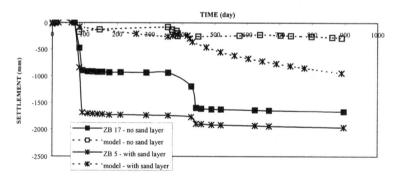

Figure 13 Comparison between modeled and measured settlements

Water pressures

In general the pore pressures calculated show better correlation with the measured values than the settlements. However, the rate of dissipation of excess pore pressures modeled is less than that in the field. Using higher permeabilities in the model can rectify this but will also result in much larger consolidations which are not apparent in the measurements.

The effect of the sand layer has been to reduce somewhat the excess pore pressures and increase in the rate of dissipation. However, both these have not been achieved in the model to the extent they are apparent in the field.

Figure 14 shows a comparison between measured and model pore water pressures for piezometers B and C (no sand layer) and D and E (with sand layer).

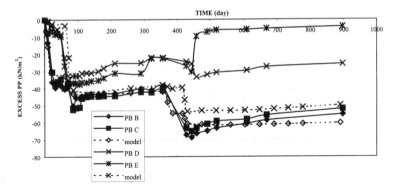

Figure 14 Comparison between modeled and measured pore water pressures

Stability

Figure 15 shows the final settlements of the dyke using the soft –soil material model. Though large settlements of over 2 m are prevalent the dyke does appear to be stable with no slope failures visible.

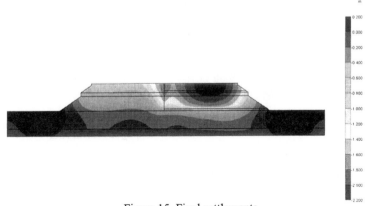

Figure 15 Final settlements

Comments

Use of the soft-soil model has not lead to the required immediate settlements. However, the total amount of settlement is large especially in the half of the dike with drainage sand. As seen from the comparisons, shortcomings exist in the ability of the model formulated to simulate the real behaviour of the sludge. The reason for this is not only the in-accuracy of some of the model parameters but mainly also due to the actual behaviour of the sludge. In order to obtain a satisfactory and more accurate model much greater emphasis is required in the future in identifying the sludge characteristics.

CONCLUSIONS

The analysis so far carried out is only a fraction of what is required to obtain a final and applicable model. The main problems encountered are:

- accurate identification of the exact behaviour of the sludge,

- identifying variations in its behaviour with time and incorporation of this phenomena in the model,

- identification of the various material characteristics of the sludge. It is important that these are known, as closely as possible, for the whole sludge mass and not just for a localised small sample.

It is proposed to undertake the following in order to improve the model.

- Application of other material behaviour models in which the squeezing effect of the sludge can be incorporated.

- Assess the presence and the possibility of taking into consideration fissures and laminations in the base sludge.

- Investigation of the effect of changing the model structure,

- Further monitoring of the behaviour of the existing test embankment as well as the construction and monitoring of a new proposed embankment. This will make available additional calibration data and also help to identify areas where errors in the measurements made in the test embankment may be present.

REFERENCES

1. ALVI P M AND LEWIS K H. Geotechnical Properties of Industrial Sludge. Proceedings of the International Symposium on Environmental Geotechnology Vol. 2 Edited by Fang H-Y, Envo Publishing Company, Inc., USA, 1987. pp 57-76.

2. BRINKGREVE R B J AND VERMEER P A. Finite Element Code for Soil and Rock Analysis – Version 7, PLAXIS Manual, A. A. Balkema, Rotterdam, Netherlands, 1998. 381 pages.

3. CRAIG R F. Soil Mechanics. Van Nostrand Reinhold (UK) Co. Ltd., England, 1987, 410 pages.

4. DELVEAUX T AND DE BROE E. Recyclage van Afval Slib voor Dijkbouw, Theses, Departement Burgelijke Bouwkunde, Faculteit Toegapaste Wetenschappen, Katholieke Universiteit Leuven, 1993, 133 pages.

5. HEAD K H. Manual of Soil Laboratory Testing – Volume 2: Permeability, Shear Strength and Compressibility Tests. Pentech Press, Great Britain, 1982, 747 pages.

6. MAERTENS J, VAN GEMERT D, WILLOCX R, HOUTMEYERS J AND D'HONDT M. Geotechnical characterisation of industrial sludges. Proceedings of 12th European Conference on Soil Mechanics and Geotechnical Engineering, Amsterdam, Netherlands, 1999.

IMPLICATIONS OF THE RECYCLING OF SEWAGE SLUDGE TO THE AGRO-ECOSYSTEM: ZINC TRANSFER IN THE SOIL-PLANT-ARTHROPOD SYSTEM

I D Green

M Tibbett

Bournemouth University

United Kingdom

ABSTRACT. This study examines the transfer of zinc from an agricultural soil amended with sewage sludge through the soil-wheat-aphid system. Total zinc concentrations of the amended soil were well within the recommended limit. The results indicate that there is variation in the accumulation of zinc in the shoots of winter and spring wheat cultivars, with spring wheat showing higher concentrations. The subsequent transfer of zinc from the wheat to a sap feeding herbivore (*Sitobean avenae*) resulted in the biomagnification of zinc by a factor of two. A high sewage sludge application rate was associated with a significant decrease in the biomass of aphids. These results are discussed in the context of sewage sludge recycling in the modern agro-ecosystem.

Keywords: Biomagnification, Sewage sludge, Zinc, Sitobean avenae, Triticum aestivum.

Mr I D Green, is a research student at Bournemouth University. He is currently completing his PhD on the subject of the transfer and fate of trace metals derived from sewage sludge amendment of agricultural soils in arthropod food chains.

Dr M Tibbett, is a Senior Lecturer in Soil Science at Bournemouth University. He has experience of heavy metal pollution in soils both inside and outside the water industry. Other research interests include soil microbiology, especially mycorrhizal symbiosis and plant nutrition.

INTRODUCTION

Heavy metals enter wastewater from a variety of industrial and domestic sources. The treatment of wastewater leads to concentration of these metals in sewage sludge, which must then be disposed of in a safe and economic manner. In the United Kingdom most sewage sludge production is disposed of by application to agricultural soils [1]. Sewage sludges can be beneficially recycled to agricultural due to the significant quantities of nitrogen and phosphorous contained within them [2]. However, sewage sludges also contain a wide range of potentially toxic elements (PTEs), including Zn [3].

Sewage sludges generally contain heavy metals at higher concentrations than are found in soils, therefore repeated applications of sewage sludge leads to the accumulation of heavy metals within the soil [4,5]. For example we have shown this in field plots amended with sewage sludge (three and four years prior to soil sampling), where the concentration of zinc in the Ap horizon was dependent on the rate of sludge application (Figure 1). The plant availability (phytoavailability) of heavy metals depends on the properties of the soil. These include the content of organic material, particle size distribution, solute behaviour, redox conditions, content of electrolytes, pH, and the composition of ions in the soil solution [6,7]. The organic and inorganic binding sites present in sewage sludges can also alter phytoavailability. Sewage sludge applied at rates greater than 50 t ha^{-1} have been shown to increase the affinity of amended soils for heavy metals [8]. However, typical agricultural applications rates of sewage sludge are now commonly less than 10 t ha^{-1}. Single applications of sludge below 20 t ha^{-1} have been found to have no effect on the binding capacity of the soil for cadmium and to decrease the binding capacity for zinc [9].

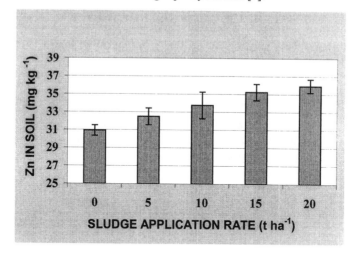

Figure 1 Concentration of zinc in an agricultural soil amended with varying rates of sewage sludge three and four years prior to sampling.

Natural processes take decades or longer to reduce heavy metal contamination in soil to background concentrations [10] and current interventionary techniques for the decontamination are still in their infancy [4]. It is therefore important to ensure that soil heavy metal levels do not reach a concentration were the health of humans, domesticated animals and the fertility of soil may be put at risk. In order to reduce this risk many developed countries have legislative frameworks and codes of practice to control the agricultural use of sewage sludge [3]. During the drafting of these controls, little consideration has been given to the accumulation of PTEs in the arthropod communities in agro-ecosystems. This is despite the fact that arthropods can play an important role in the transfer of trace metals through food webs [11,12]

Early studies produced conflicting results on the extent of heavy metal biomagnification in arthropod food chains [13]. Further developments have led to the general acceptance of the hypothesis that arthropod physiology, rather than trophic level, determines heavy metal body burden [12-15]. The physiological ability to excrete trace metals varies widely, even between closely related species [12,16]. In a food chain where the component species have a poor ability to regulate metal accumulation, a 'critical pathway' is established [17]. The consequent biomagnification of heavy metals may lead to toxic effects in higher consumers.

The potential biomagnification of zinc resulting from the recycling of sewage sludge to agricultural land has been investigated. The current paper reports the results of two glasshouse trials modelling the soil-wheat-aphid system.

METHODS AND MATERIALS

Pot Trial One

A bulk soil sample of a freely draining sandy loam of the Fyfield series [18] was taken from the Ap horizon of an agricultural soil near East Lulworth, Dorset, UK. Selected physio-chemical parameters of the soil and sewage sludge are given in Table 1. Soil was amended with a dried, anaerobically digested municipal sewage sludge at rates equivalent to 0, 10 or 30 t ha^{-1} (dry solids). Each amended soil and an unamended control were used to fill six replicate 7.5 litre pots.

Each pot was adjusted to field capacity and then seeded with spring wheat (*Triticum aestivum* L. cv. Alexander) at a rate equivalent to 400 kg ha^{-1}. The pots were then covered with netting and placed in a fully randomised block in a glasshouse. Plants were watered regularly with distilled water. At the emergence of the flag leaf (decimal growth stage between 37 and 51[19]) 200 mixed instar grain aphids (*Sitobean avenae*), taken from laboratory cultures uncontaminated with heavy metals, were added to each pot. Netting was replaced to prevent the transfer of aphids between treatments. Aphid cultures were then left to establish. After three weeks the wheat plants began to fail, presumably due to the stress of sap feeding, and aphids were harvested and frozen prior to analysis.

Pot Trial Two

This was set up in a similar way to trial one, but with the following differences. Soil was amended at rates equivalent to 0, 10 and 100 t ha^{-1}, the pots were seeded with winter wheat (cv Challenger), aphid cultures were established during tillering (decimal growth stages 14,20 to 17,23 [19]) and harvesting was conducted four weeks after cultures were established.

Table 1 Concentrations of zinc in sewage sludge and selected physiochemical
parameters of the unamended soil (mean value ± 1 SE)

	AGRICULTURAL SOIL	SEWAGE SLUDGE
pH	5.3	-
Bulk density	1.1	-
Organic C (%)	2.9	-
Sand (%)	61	-
Silt (%)	18	-
Clay(%)	21	-
'Total' Zn (mg kg^{-1})	40	725

Sample Analysis

Representative soil samples were collected from the top 15 cm of each pot, passed through a 2 mm sieve and refluxed in 70% nitric acid for 48 h [20]. Wheat plants were randomly sampled from each pot, washed once in 0.1% teepol solution and twice in distilled water before being dried to constant weight at 70 °C. Sub-samples of shoot material (0.20-0.25 g) were digested in a nitric acid for 8 h [21]. Aphids were washed and dried as described for the wheat. A 40 mg (dry weight) sub-sample of aphids was digested in 2 ml of 70% nitric acid in sealed glass vessels at a temperature of 80 °C. The clear residue was then diluted to volume (5 ml) using de-ionised water.

Analysis of samples for zinc content was conducted using flame atomic absorption spectroscopy (both with and without STAT trap), using deutritium background correction (ATI Unicam Solar 939). Relevant certified reference materials (CRM 143R & BCR 281) and reagent blanks were also digested and analysed with each batch of soil, wheat and aphids. Total nitrogen content of finely ground winter wheat plants was determined using a Carlo Erba EMASyst 1160 Elemental analyser using a certified rye grass standard (BCR 281). Subsequent statistical analysis was undertaken using SPSS.

RESULTS

As anticipated, sewage sludge amendment lead to an increased zinc concentration in the soil. Concentrations increased inline with sewage sludge application rate in both trials (Figures 2a and 2b). The Kruskal-Wallis (KW) test indicated that observed differences between treatments were significant (KW= 13.2, $P <0.01$ and KW= 15.16, $P<0.01$, for trial one and two respectively). Zinc in the soil was subsequently transferred to wheat in line with sewage sludge application rate in trial 1, while in trial 2 only the 100 t ha^{-1} amendment resulted in an elevated concentration in the wheat (Table 2a and b). Differences in the zinc concentrations between treatments were significant (KW= 13.0, $P<0.01$ and KW= 11.66, $P<0.01$, trials 1 and 2 respectively). Biomagnification factors (BFs) in the spring wheat were in the order of 2, in contrast the corresponding BFs for winter wheat were all below 1. The amendment of soil with sewage sludge did not significantly effect the dry matter yields of spring or winter wheat (Table2) (KW=0.10, $P>0.1$, Kw=5.1, $P>0.05$ for spring wheat and winter respectively). Total nitrogen levels in the winter wheat shoots increased with the rate of sludge amendment. There was no difference in nitrogen content of the control and 10 t ha[-1] amendment (Newman-Keuls procedure, $\alpha=0.05$, $R_j = 0.61$), but a significant difference existed between the control and the 100 t ha[-1] amendment ($\alpha=0.05$, $R_j = 0.74$).

Table 2 Dry matter yield (g plant[-1]) and fresh mass of aphids (g pot[-1]) harvested in trials one and two and total nitrogen (%) content of Wheat harvested in trial 2 (mean ± 1 SE)

RATE	TRIAL 1		TRIAL 2		
	Wheat	Aphids	Wheat	N	Aphids
0	0.20 ± 0.09	0.32 ± 0.06	0.18 ± 0.02	4.61 ± 0.15	1.08 ± 0.08
10	0.21 ± 0.02	0.25 ± 0.07	0.21 ± 0.01	5.02 ± 0.23	1.09 ± 0.07
30	0.27 ± 0.03	0.29 ± 0.06	-	-	-
100	-	-	0.18 ± 0.01	5.38 ± 0.22	0.56 ± 0.12

Table 3 Zinc biomagnification factors in wheat plants and aphids.

RATE	TRIAL 1		TRIAL 2	
	Wheat	Aphid	Wheat	Aphid
0	1.64	2.36	0.95	1.85
10	2.05	2.15	0.75	2.20
30	1.85	2.16	-	-
100	-	-	0.60	1.87

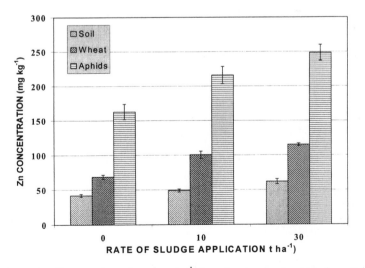

Figure 2a Zinc concentrations (mg kg[-1]) in soil, wheat and aphids from Trial 1 (mean ± 1 SE) at varying rates of sewage sludge application (t ha[-1])

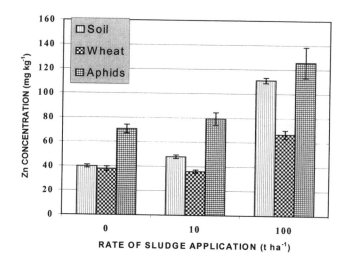

Figure 2b   Zinc concentrations (mg kg^{-1}) in soil, wheat and aphids from Trial 1
(mean ± 1 SE) at varying rates of sewage sludge application (t ha^{-1})

Concentration of zinc in aphids increased with sewage sludge amendment rate in both trials. Zinc levels were higher in trial one than in trial two, reflecting the higher levels of zinc in spring wheat. For both trials there were significant differences in aphid zinc concentration between the treatments (KW=11.1, $P<0.01$ and KW=8.92, $P<0.02$ for trials one and two respectively). The largest biomagnification factors were found for this trophic step, with all BFs in the order of 2 (Table 3). No significant differences were observed in the fresh weight of aphids harvested in trial 1 (KW = 0.67, $P >0.1$). In trial 2 the fresh weight of aphids harvested from the highest amendment rate was approximately half that of the control and the lowest amendment rate. This difference was significant (KW = 7.94, $P<0.02$).

DISCUSSION AND CONCLUSION

The additions of sewage sludge to soil resulted in an increase in soil zinc concentration. This fell within the recommended UK limit for sludge amended soils of 200 mg kg^{-1} for soils in the pH range 5.0–5.5 [1]. Elevated soil concentrations were reflected in higher zinc levels in wheat, but in all cases tissue concentrations were within the typical range for plants (27-150 mg kg^{-1} [22]). Concentrations in winter wheat were lower than those found in the spring wheat. This is presumably due to varietal differences [23]. Aphids biomagnified zinc in all treatments in both trials, leading to soil-aphid biomagnification factors of over 4. Concentrations in aphids reached a level of circa 250 mg kg^{-1}. Similar biomagnification of sludge derived zinc has been reported in the bird-cherry oat aphid feeding on winter wheat [21]. However, BFs of up to 8 have been found in *S. avenae* under field conditions using sludge amendments up to 20 t ha^{-1} [9].

Aphid population growth rates are known to increase with nitrogen levels in wheat leaves [24]. The nitrogen results from trial 2 would therefore suggest that the largest aphid biomass would be associated with the highest amendment rate. That the converse occurred leads us to hypothesise that some factor was placing the aphids under stress. There is little literature regarding zinc toxicity to terrestrial arthropods, but a body burden of 800 mg kg^{-1} proved lethal to the isopod *Porcelio scaber* [25]. In the current study body burdens are far below this level. It would therefore seem unlikely that zinc is causing direct toxicity to the aphids. Aphids form an obligate symbiotic relationship with bacteria of the genus *Buchnera* [26]. The bacteria synthesise essential amino acids that are lacking in the aphid's diet [27]. Without *Buchnera* aphids grow poorly and produce few offspring [26]. Soil dwelling microorganisms are sensitive to heavy metals in sludge amended soil [28], with particular concern expressed about zinc [1]. This leads to the possibility that PTEs from the sludge may be harming *Buchnera*. The malnutrition suffered by the aphids would then decrease the population growth rate and result in the reduced biomass observed in this study. Sewage sludges may contain many PTE's [2], of which several could be causing stress to aphids or *Buchnera*. It is therefore difficult to determine the component, or components, of sewage sludge responsible for the reduction in aphid biomass.

Sitobean avenae is a common pest in the agronomic production of wheat [29]. The economic damage threshold (EDT) of the species is five aphids per shoot at flowering, at which insecticide application is recommended [30]. If the reduced biomass observed in this study is repeated in the field, then the recycling of sewage sludge to agriculture may help to keep *S. avenae* populations below the EDT. The subsequent reduction in the use of insecticide may provide an economic gain. On the other hand, the results of this study suggest possible implications for integrated pest management (IPM). Such methods, as part of integrated crop management, are being increasingly promoted as the result of pressures such as public concern over the environment [31]. Natural predators of aphids can contribute to IPM by keeping population densities below the EDT [32,33]. However, the biomagnification of zinc by aphids suggests that they can form part of critical pathways. Little is known at present about the transfer of heavy metals from aphids to predators, though the existence of a pathway for zinc transfer to a carabid beetle has been established [34]. It is also not yet known if the heavy metal levels seen in aphids have adverse effects on their predators. Biomagnification in aphid predators may consequently have serious implications for the success of IPM techniques in controlling aphid populations.

The results of the trials presented in this paper demonstrate that sewage sludge derived zinc is highly labile in the soil-plant-arthropod system when total soil Zn concentrations are well within current UK limits. These findings question the efficacy of the current metal limits in protecting the wider agro-ecosystem from the adverse effects of PTEs in sewage sludge. However, there is little corroborating data to support this and further study is needed to establish the consequences of the food chain transfer of PTEs in the agro-ecosystem.

REFERENCES

1.   MAFF/DOE. Review of the rules for sewage sludge application to agricultural land; soil fertility aspects of potentially toxic elements. PB1561, HMSO, London, 1993.

2.   PIMENTAL, D AND WARNEKE, A. Ecological effects of manure, sewage sludge and other organic wastes on arthropod populations. Agricultural Zoology Reviews. Vol. 3, 1989. pp1-30.

3.   SMITH, S R. Agricultural recycling of sewage sludge and the environment. CAB International, Wallingford, 1996.

4.   HANI, H. Heavy metals in sewage sludge and town waste compost. In: Merian, E. (ed) Metals and Their Compounds in the Environment. VCH, Weinheim, 1991. pp 357-368.

5.   BENNINGER-TRAUX, M AND TAYLOR, D H. Municipal sludge metal contamination of old field ecosystems: do liming and tilling affect remediation. Environmental Toxicology and Chemistry. Vol. 12, 1993. pp1931-1943.

6.   PUNZ, W F. AND SIEGHARDT, H. The response of roots of herbaceous plant species to heavy metals. Environmental and Experimental Biology. Vol 33, 1993. pp 85-98.

7.   RIEUWERTS, J S, THORNTON, I, FARAGO, M E AND ASHMORE, M R. Factors influencing metal bioavailability in soils: preliminary investigations for the development of a critical loads approach for metals. Chemical Speciation and Bioavailability. Vol. 10(2), 1998. pp 61-75.

8.   HOODA, P S, ALLOWAY, B J. Sorption of Cd and Pb on selected temperature and semi-arid soils: effects of sludge application and ageing of sludged soils. Water Air Soil Pollution. Vol. 74, 1994. pp 235-250.

9.   MERRINGTON, G, WINDER, L, GREEN, I D. 1997. The bioavailability of Cd and Zn from soils amended with sewage sludge to winter wheat and subsequently to the grain aphid *Sitobion avenae*. Science of the Total Environment. Vol. 205, 1997. pp 245-254.

10.   ALLOWAY, B J, AYRES, D C. Chemical Principles of Environmental Pollution. Blackie Academic & Professional, Glasgow, 1993.

11.   ROBERTS, R D AND JOHNSON, M S. Dispersal of heavy metals from abandoned mine workings and their transference through terrestrial food chains. Environmental Pollution. Vol. 16, 1978. pp 293-310.

12.   JANSSEN, M P M, DE VRIES, T H AND VAN STRAALEN, N M. Comparison of Cd kinetics in four soil arthropod species. Archives of. Environment Contamination and Toxicology. Vol. 20, 1991. pp 305-312.

13.   STRAALEN VAN, N M AND VAN WENSEM, J. Heavy metal content of forest litter arthropods as related to body size and trophic level. Environmental Pollution. (Series A). Vol. 42, 1986. pp 209-221.

14.   JANSSEN, M P M. Species dependent cadmium accumulation by forest litter arthropods. Proceedings of the third international conference on environmental contamination, Venice, 1988. Pp 436-438.

15.   LASKOWSKI, R AND MARYANSK, I M. 1993. Heavy metals in epigeic fauna: Trophic-level and physiological hypotheses. Vol. 50, 1993. pp 232-240.

16. GLOWACKA, E, MIGULA, P, NUORTEVA, S-L, NUORTEVA, P AND TULISAL, O. 1997. Psyllids as a potential source of heavy metals for predators. Archives of Environmental Contamination and Toxicology. Vol. 32, 1997. pp 376-382.

17. STRAALEN VAN, N M AND ERNST, W H O. Metal biomagnification may endanger species in critical pathways. Okios. Vol. 62(2), 1992. pp 255-256.

18. RUDEFORTH, C C, HARTNUP, R, LEA, J W, THOMPSON, T R E, WRIGHT, P S. Soils and their uses in Wales. Soil Survey of England and Wales. Bulletin No. 11. Harpenden, Herts, 1984.

19. ZADOCKS, J C, CHANG, T T, KONZAK, C F. A decimal code for the growth stages of cereals. Eucarpia Bulletin. Vol 7, 1974.

20. TYLER, G. Leaching of metals from the A-Horizon of a spruce forest soil. Water Air Soil Pollution. Vol. 15, 1981. pp 353-369.

21. MERRINGTON, G, WINDER, L, GREEN, I D. The uptake of Cd and Zn by the bird cherry oat aphid *Rhopalosiphum padi* (Homoptera: Aphididae) feeding on wheat grown on sewage sludge amended agricultural soil. Environmental Pollution. Vol. 96, 1997. pp111-114.

22. KABATA-PENDIAS, A AND PENDIAS, H. Trace Elements in Soils and Plants. CRC Press, Boca Raton, 1992.

23. CIESLINSKI, G , VAN REES, K C J , HUANG, P M , KOZAK, L M , ROSTAD, H P W AND KNOTT, D R. Cadmium uptake and bioaccumulation in selected cultivars of durum wheat and flax as affected by soil type. Plant and Soil. Vol. 182, 1996. pp115-124.

24. HONEK, A. Factors determining the peak abundance of *Metopolophium dirhodum* (Homoptera, Aphididae) on cereals. Bulletin of entomolgical Research. Vol. 81(1), 1991. pp 57-64.

25. HOPKINS, S P AND HAMES, C A C. Zinc, among a 'cocktail' of metal polltants, is responsible for the absence of the terrestial isopod *Porcelio scaber* from the vicinity of a primary smelting works. Ecotoxiclogy. Vol. 2. 1994. pp 68-78.

26. DOUGLAS, A E. Nutritional interactions in insect-microbial symbioses: Aphids and their symbiotic bacteria *Buchnera*. Annual review of Entomology. Vol. 43, 1998. pp 17-37.

27. WILKINSON, T L AND ISHIKAWA H. Injection of essential amino acids substitiutes for the bacterial supply in aposymbiotic pea aphids (*Acyrthosiphon pisum*). Entomologia Experimentalis et Applicata. Vol. 94 (1), 2000. pp 85-91.

28. MCGRATH, S P, CHAUDRI, A M AND GILLER, K E. Long term effects of metals in sewage-sludge on soils, microorganisms and plants. Journal of Industrial Microbiology. Vol 14 (2), 1995. pp 94-104.

29. SOFFE, R J. The Agricultural Notebook. 19th ed. Blakewell Scientific. Oxford, 1997.

30. GEORGE, K S AND GAIR, R. Crop loss assessment on winter wheat attacked by the grain aphid *Sitobean avenae* (F.). Plant Pathology. Vol. 28, 1978. pp 143-149.

31. MAFF. Integrated farming: agricultural research into practice. PB3618, HMSO, London, 1998.

32. CHAMBERS, R J, SUNDERLAND, K D, STACY, D L AND WYATT I J. Control of cereal aphids in winter wheat by natural enemies: aphid specific predators, parasitoids and pathogenic fungi. Annals of Applied biology. Vol. 108, 1986. pp 219-231.

33. HOLOPAINEN, J K AND HELENIUS, J. Gut contents of ground beetles (Col., Carabidae), and activity of these and other epigeal predators during an outbreak of *Rhopalosiphum padi* (Hom., Aphididae). Acta Agriculturae Scandinavica –B. Vol.42 (1), 1992. pp 57-61.

34. WINDER, L, MERRINGTON, G AND GREEN, I D. The tri-trophic transfer of Zn from the agricultural use of sewage sludge. The Science of the Total Environment. Vol. 229, 1999. pp 73-81.

PART THREE:

MATERIAL RECOVERY AND REUSE IN VALUE ADDED APPLICATIONS

HYDRATION REACTION OF SEWAGE SLUDGE ASH FOR USE AS A CEMENT COMPONENT IN CONCRETE PRODUCTION

T D Dyer

J E Halliday

R K Dhir

University of Dundee

United Kingdom

ABSTRACT. Sewage sludge ash is largely recognised as being a pozzolanic or latent hydraulic material with potential for use in concrete and similar materials. However, the chemical composition of the material varies quite considerably from source to source, and its performance as a cement component is equally varied. This paper illustrates the importance of the chemical composition of the amorphous fraction of sewage sludge ash, and outlines some approximate relationships between composition and performance of the material. In general, the contribution of the material towards strength development is defined by the amorphous phase CaO / SiO_2 ratio, in a similar way to latent hydraulic slags. Similarly, the Al_2O_3 / SiO_2 ratio defines the extent to which C-S-H gel or calcium aluminate hydrates are formed. Whilst C-S-H gel formation should be generally favoured for most construction applications due to its significant contribution to compressive strength development, calcium aluminate hydrates are of value in some construction applications where resistance to chloride ingress is required. Since sewage sludge incinerator operations define the composition of the ash to some extent there is scope for tailoring ash performance through modification of these operations.

Keywords: Sewage sludge ash, Recycling, Cement component, Amorphous fraction, Chemical composition, Hydration.

Dr T D Dyer, is a Research Lecturer in the Concrete Technology Unit, University of Dundee. He is involved in a number of research projects examining issues related to sustainability and recycling in concrete construction, including a large-scale project examining recycling opportunities for incinerator ashes in the UK.

Miss J E Halliday, is a Research Assistant in the Concrete Technology Unit, University of Dundee. She is currently co-ordinating full-scale demonstration trials of incinerator ashes in concrete construction applications, as well as completing her PhD on the topic of incinerator fly ash recycling in concrete.

Professor R K Dhir, is Director of the Concrete Technology Unit, University of Dundee, Scotland UK. He specialises in binder technology, permeation, durability and protection of concrete. His interests also include the use of construction and industrial wastes in concrete to meet the challenges of sustainable construction. He has published and travelled widely and serves on many Technical Committees.

INTRODUCTION

The use of waste materials derived from industrial thermal processes as cement components is now a fairly established practice in concrete construction. Such materials undergo pozzolanic or latent hydraulic reactions whose products contribute to the strength development of concrete. In many cases the chemistry of the waste or by-product imparts additional properties to the cement matrix which are of benefit in special applications.

The terms 'pozzolanic reaction' and 'latent hydraulic reaction' broadly relate to a complex range of chemical reactions usually involving amorphous (glassy) phases and portlandite produced during the normal hydration reactions of Portland cement.

The most important products of pozzolanic and latent hydraulic reactions are calcium silicate hydrate (C-S-H) gels (which may also contain other cations) and calcium aluminate hydrates. The C-S-H gel makes the most significant contribution to strength development and is, therefore, largely viewed as being the most important pozzolanic reaction product. Whilst the formation of calcium aluminate hydrates makes a much less significant contribution to strength development, one group of these compounds, known as AFm phases, are of great benefit in enhancing the resistance of concrete to chloride-induced corrosion of steel reinforcement. When AFm phases come in contact with solutions containing chloride ions they are converted into another AFm phase known as Friedel's salt ($C_3A.CaCl_2.H_{10}$), thus removing a proportion of chloride ions from solution. Whilst this 'chloride binding' capacity is clearly finite, it can have a significant effect on the period of time required for reinforcement corrosion to initiate in a structure.

It has been demonstrated that sewage sludge ash (SSA, the product of the incineration of sewage sludge) is pozzolanic [1], and that the reaction contributes to strength development. The authors have recently been involved in research carried out on SSAs from around the UK as part of a larger project examining routes available for recycling incinerator ashes in concrete. It has been observed that the range of sewage sludge ash chemical compositions is relatively broad. Furthermore, the behaviour of each ash in combination with Portland cement varies considerably. This paper aims to demonstrate that the chemical composition (and more specifically the chemical composition of the amorphous fraction of the material) is an important determinant in the performance of a given sewage sludge ash.

MATERIALS AND EXPERIMENTAL METHODS

Four SSAs from incinerators around the UK are examined in this paper. Bulk oxide analyses carried out using x-ray fluorescence spectrometry are shown in Table 1. The mineralogies of the materials, estimated using Rietveld refinement methods applied to x-ray powder diffraction traces, are shown in Table 2. Further details of the Rietveld refinement procedure is provided in the subsequent text. The term 'Others' in the Table refers largely to amorphous material, but due to the complex nature of the ashes may also include small quantities of crystalline phases. Details of the Portland cement used during the studies are also provided in Tables 1 and 2.

Compressive Strength

Compressive strength measurements were taken at an age of 28 days on specimens prepared, cured and tested in accordance with BS 196 Part 2. Specimens were prepared containing sewage sludge ash at Portland cement replacements of 20, 35 and 50% by mass.

Table 1 Bulk Oxide Analyses of the Materials

	MATERIAL				
	SSA1	SSA2	SSA3	SSA4	PC
SiO_2	29.36	35.21	26.39	33.01	21.1
TiO_2	1.25	1.52	1.31	1.24	0.2
Al_2O_3	10.86	12.42	14.09	24.03	5.0
Fe_2O_3	13.00	7.27	11.34	6.67	2.7
MnO	0.23	0.60	0.32	0.19	0.1
MgO	1.36	2.24	1.38	1.02	1.6
P_2O_5					0.00
CaO	14.27	12.43	9.61	5.69	64.9
Na_2O	0.17	0.22	0.37	0.00	0.3
K_2O	1.19	1.77	1.63	1.29	0.6
SO_3--	1.27	0.48	0.61	0.18	3.3
Cl-	0.14	0.04	0.01	0.00	0.03

Isothermal Conduction Calorimetry

Isothermal conduction calorimetry measurements were carried out on pastes at 20°C. Again, sewage sludge ash was included in the pastes at Portland cement replacement levels of 20, 35 and 50% by mass. Measurements were conducted on samples comprising 30g of solid material and distilled water at a water / cement ratio of 0.5.

Cement Hydration

Cement pastes identical to those used for isothermal conduction calorimetry were prepared for analysis using powder x-ray diffraction and thermogravimetry. Hydration reactions were stopped at an age of 28 days by first grinding with acetone before being dried under vacuum at a temperature of 40°C.

Thermogravimetry was carried out with platinum crucibles containing 10mg samples in a nitrogen atmosphere. A temperature regime of ambient to 1000°C was used at a rate of 2°C/minute.

Powder x-ray diffraction was carried out using a Philips diffractometer with a Cu-kα radiation source and a single crystal graphite monochromator. An angular range of 3-90° 2θ in 0.05° 2θ increments was used throughout.

Table 2 Mineralogies Estimated Using Rietveld Refinement Techniques

	FORMULA	MATERIAL				
		SSA1	SSA2	SSA3	SSA4	PC
Calcite	$CaCO_3$	1.24	-	-	-	-
Anhydrite	$CaSO_4$	1.96	1.77	-	-	7.12
Quartz	SiO_2	6.49	9.49	11.86	18.30	-
Hematite	Fe_2O_3	2.25	2.11	2.05	1.34	-
Ettringite	$Ca_6Al_2(SO_4)_3(OH)_{12}.26H_2O$	5.35	-	-	-	-
Silicon carbide	SiC	2.19	2.33	2.01	1.65	-
Butlerite	$FeSO_4(OH).2H_2O$	0.71	-	-	-	-
Anorthite	$CaAl_2Si_2O_8$	2.61	3.31	3.02	2.14	-
Aphthitalite	$(K,Na)_3Na(SO_4)_2$	0.68	-	-	-	-
Iron sulfite	$FeSO_3$	1.45	2.14	1.84	1.49	-
Gehlenite	$Ca_2Al_2SiO_2$	1.24	1.88	6.30	3.37	-
Frederickssonite	$Mg_{1.93}Mn_{1.07}BO_5$	-	3.65	2.80	2.01	-
Cristobalite	SiO_2	-	2.59	1.09	3.16	-
Tridymite	SiO_2	-	2.12	-	3.05	-
Rutile	TiO_2	-	-	2.33	-	-
Muscovite	$K_2Al_4Si_6Al_2O_{20}(OH)_4$	-	-	2.35	4.29	-
Syngenite	$K_2Ca(SO_4)_2.H_2O$					2.31
Tricalcium Silicate	"C_3S"	-	-	-	-	48.55
Dicalcium Silcate	"C_2S"	-	-	-	-	24.29
Tricalcium Aluminate	"C_3A"	-	-	-	-	6.74
Tetracalcium Aluminoferrite	"C_4AF"	-	-	-	-	9.25
Portlandite	$Ca(OH)_2$					1.72
Others	-	73.8	61.5	60.0	66.0	-

Rietvelt refinement was conducted on the diffraction traces, enabling an estimate of the mineralogical composition of each blend to be obtained. The computer programs X-FIT and KOALARIET were used [2-7]. The non-crystalline materials in the hydrated pastes in the form of amorphous materials in both the PFA and SSAs, as well as calcium silicate hydrate (CSH) gel produced during reaction, could not be quantified using Rietveld refinement.

However, determining the quantity of Portlandite present from thermogravimetry measurements allowed this phase to be used as a 'pre-existing' internal standard, allowing quantification of the total amorphous content of each sample.

The hemicarbonate phase ($C_4AC_{0.5}H_{12}$) was identified in many cases. Whilst some researchers [8] have suggested that the structure suggested by Ahmed and Taylor [9] is appropriate for this phase, this has been queried more recently [10]. Nonetheless, this proposed structure was used for Rietveld refinement in this study.

Where Rietveld refinement was carried out on constituent materials, a 5% corundum internal standard was used.

RESULTS AND DISCUSSION

Chemical Composition of the Amorphous Fraction

The amorphous fraction of a pozzolanic material is usually regarded as the most important component in terms of defining the material's performance when used in combination with Portland cement [10]. For this reason, the composition of the amorphous portion of each of the SSAs was calculated by subtracting the composition of each of the crystalline phases (Table 2) from the overall composition of the material (Table 1). The results of these calculations are shown in Table 3, and the positions of each ash on the CaO - SiO_2 - Al_2O_3 ternary diagram are shown in Figure 1. Also shown in this diagram is the region defined by Smolczyk [11] as being inhabited by latent hydraulic materials such as ground granulated blastfurnace slag, defined by the relationships $0.5 <$ CaO/SiO_2 (C/S) < 2.0 and $0.1 <$ $Al2O_3/SiO_2$ (A/S) < 0.6. It is apparent that SSAs 1-3 lie very close to this region suggesting they undergo such reactions.

Compressive Strength and CSH Gel Formation

As previously discussed, C/S and A/S ratios have previously been used to determine a material's propensity to undergo latent hydraulic reactions. This paper concentrates on the C/S ratio since the 'spread ' of A/S values for the materials studied is not suitable for analysis.

Figure 2 shows the 28 day compressive strength values plotted against the C/S ratio of the amorphous components of each ash. These plots appear to indicate that, at least for cement combinations containing 35 or 50% SSA, the optimum C/S ratio lies around 0.3. However, this takes no account of the fact that each ash contains a different quantity of amorphous material. The amorphous content of each ash is plotted against the C/S ratio in Figure 3. There is certainly some correlation between features of this plot and those of Figure 2, which is probable, since the quantity of amorphous material present will clearly influence the material's role as a pozzolanic or latent hydraulic material. The results shown in Figure 2 were therefore corrected to compensate for the effect of differing amorphous phase contents using the equation:

$$\text{Corrected Strength} = \text{Strength} \times \frac{\text{Amorphous content of ash}}{\text{Lowest amorphous content value}}$$

Table 3 Estimated Chemical Compositions of the Amorphous Component
of the SSAs (quantities under 1% have been ignored)

	SSA1	SSA2	SSA3	SSA4
CaO	13.13	16.08	8.70	5.32
Al_2O_3	13.76	15.31	12.20	34.75
Si_{O2}	46.74	56.80	52.76	47.55
Fe_2O_3	19.58	4.51	23.99	9.72
MgO	2.29	-	-	-
TiO_2	2.10	3.33	-	2.67
K_2O	1.77	3.88	2.32	0
C/S	0.281	0.283	0.165	0.112
A/S	0.294	0.270	0.231	0.731

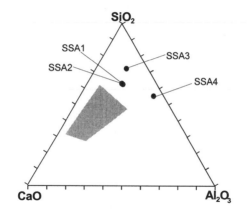

Figure 1   Positions on the $CaO-SiO_2-Al_2O_3$ ternary diagram
of the amorphous phases of the SSA ashes

Whilst this method of correction is clearly over-simplistic, the results imply that the contribution of the amorphous fraction of an SSA increases with the C/S ratio within the compositional range studied here (Figure 4). Thus, it would appear that the materials are undergoing a latent hydraulic reaction and that this reaction becomes more effective with respect to strength development as the composition of the amorphous phase approaches the region defined by Smolczyk. Materials in this region react in a manner that yields high quantities of C-S-H gel, which makes a significant contribution to compressive strength.

Whilst it is impossible to directly quantify C-S-H in a hydrated paste using x-ray diffraction and thermogravimetry alone, the quantity of gel-bound water can be estimated by measuring the total bound water in a sample from the thermogravimetry measurements and subtracting the quantity of water which is known to be present in the crystalline hydration products, quantified using Rietveld refinement. It should be noted that, since the quantity of water present in C-S-H gel will vary with its chemical composition, this measurement is only a rough indicator of how much of the substance is present.

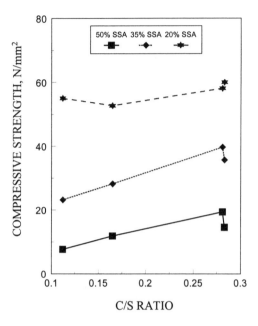

Figure 2   28 day compressive strength versus amorphous
phase C/S ratio for mortars containing SSAs

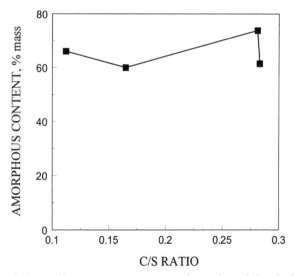

Figure 3   Amorphous content versus amorphous phase C/S ratio for the SSAs

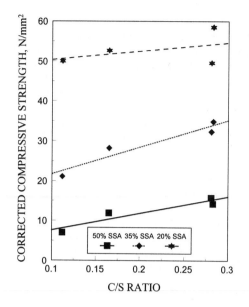

Figure 4 28 day compressive strength corrected for amorphous phase content versus amorphous phase C/S ratio for mortars containing SSAs

Figure 5 shows the results of the calculations (corrected in an identical manner as before) which indicate that quantities of C-S-H gel generally increase with C/S ratio within the compositional range studied here.

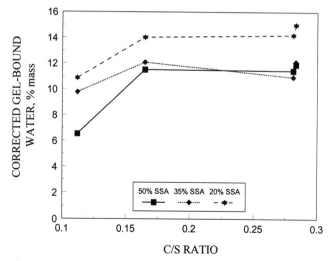

Figure 5 Gel-bound water at 28 days (corrected for variations in SSA amorphous content) versus C/S ratio

AFm Phase Formation

The initial formation of AFm phases is frequently identified using isothermal conduction calorimetry, as a small peak occurring shortly after the main heat evolution peak which corresponds to the formation of portlandite, ettringite and CSH gel [10]. However, it can be seen in Figure 6 that this peak is by no means small when SSAs are combined with Portland cement. With the exception of SSA2, the size of the AFm peak is roughly proportional to the Al_2O_3 content of the amorphous phase, although many factors including particle size and ash chemical composition will influence the peak's shape and size. It is also worth noting the presence of a third unidentified peak at around 68 hours evolved by the SSA4 / cement combination.

Isothermal conduction calorimeter peaks of this magnitude would suggest that large quantities of AFm phase are generated during the hydration of blends containing SSAs. Figure 7, which shows the quantities of crystalline hydration products present in each of the pastes investigated, confirms this. The AFm phases monosulfate ($C_4A\bar{S}H_{12}$), hemicarbonate ($C_4A\hat{C}_{0.5}H_{12}$) and monocarbonate ($C_4A\hat{C}H_{11}$) were present in nearly every blend containing SSA. The paste containing the largest quantities of SSA4 also contains large quantities of the mineral strätlingite (C_2ASH_8) which is also an AFm phase.

Since the hydration products of pozzolanic and latent hydraulic materials are divided between calcium aluminate hydrates and C-S-H gel, the A/S ratio of the amorphous phase will, in most cases, dictate the relative quantities of these two types of hydration products. This would appear to be the case for SSA, although the limited number of ashes under scrutiny means that it cannot be demonstrated conclusively in this paper. Figure 8 plots both gel-bound water and the total quantity of AFm phases at 28 days against A/S ratio. Due to the differing quantities of water associated with different AFm phases, the total quantity of AFm phases is expressed in terms of the anhydrous material. There appears to be an increase in AFm phase coupled with a decrease in gel-bound water as the A/S ratio increases, although there are insufficient data points to determine any clear relationship.

CONCLUSIONS

The performance of SSAs when used as cement components is determined by both the composition of the amorphous portion of the material and how much of this portion is present.

The contribution of the ash towards compressive strength development improves as the composition of the amorphous fraction approaches that identified previously as being optimal for latent hydraulic slags.

As far as can be determined from the limited amount of data available in this study, the A/S ratio of the amorphous fraction defines whether C-S-H gel or calcium aluminate hydrates are the dominant product from the reaction of a given SSA. Whilst the dominance of C-S-H gel should be favoured in most situations due to enhanced strength development, the generation of AFm calcium aluminate hydrates provides benefit in the form of enhanced chloride resistance which may be of great value in certain construction applications.

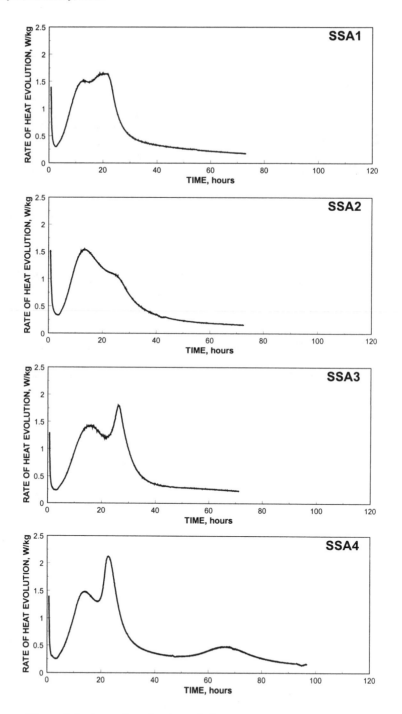

Figure 6   Isothermal conduction calorimeter plots obtained from 50%
Portland cement / 50% SSA combinations.

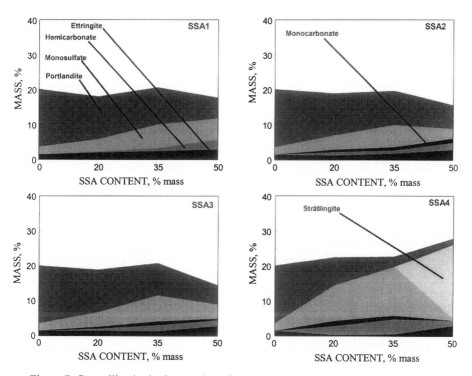

Figure 7 Crystalline hydration products in Portland cement / SSA pastes at 28 days.

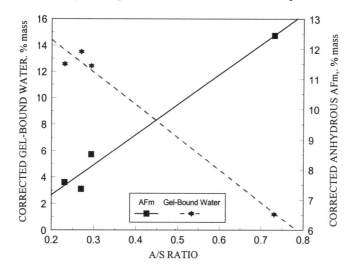

Figure 8 Corrected values of gel-bound water and total anhydrous
AFm phases in 28 day old pastes containing 50% SSA

The treatment of sewage sludge before and during incineration involves the addition of various inorganic chemicals. There is, therefore, some scope for controlling the composition of the final ash. Given the influence of ash composition on performance in cement combinations, there is some potential for tailoring incinerator operations to obtain better performance from a given ash, assuming economic and operational viability are not compromised.

REFERENCES

1. MONZO, J., PAYA, J., BORRACHERO, M.V., and CORCOLES, A., Use of sewage sludge ash (SSA) - cement admixtures in mortars, Cement and Concrete Research, Vol.26, 1996,   pp1389-1398

2. BERGER, H., Study of the k-alpha emission-spectrum of copper, X-ray Spectrometry, Vol.15, 1986, pp241-243

3. CHEARY, R.W., and COELHO, A.A., A fundamental parameters approach of x-ray line-profile fitting, Journal of Applied Crystallography, Vol.25, 1992, pp109-121

4. CHEARY, R.W., and COELHO, A.A., Synthesising and fitting linear position-sensitive detector step-scanned line profiles, Journal of Applied Crystallography, Vol.27, 1994, pp673-681

5. CHEARY, R.W., and COELHO, A.A., Theoretical model for axial divergence with primary and secondary Soller slits in x-ray line-profile analysis, 1996, in preparation

6. MARQUARDT, D.W., Journal of the Society for Industrial and Applied Mathematics, Vol.11, 1963, pp431-331

7. NASH, J.C., Compact Numerical Methods for Computers, Adam Hilger, Bristol and New York, 1990

8. FISCHER, R., and KUZEL, H.-J., Reinvestigation of the system $C_4A.nH_2O$ - $C_4A.CO_2.nH_2O$, Cement and Concrete Research, Vol.12, 1982, pp517-526

9. AHMED, S.J., and TAYLOR, H.F.W., Crystal structures of the lamellar calcium aluminate hydrates, Nature, Vol.215, 1967, pp622-623

10. TAYLOR, H.F.W., 'Cement Chemistry', Thomas Telford, London, 1997, pp159

11. SMOLCZYK, H.G., Structure et charactérisation des laitiers, 7th International Congress on the Chemistry of Cement, Paris, 1980, Vol.1 ppIII-1/3-1/17

STABILIZATION OF WET SEWAGE SLUDGE IN CIVIL ENGINEERING

S Valls   **E Vàzquez**

Universitat Politècnica de Catalunya- ETSECCPB

V Kuchinow

UBENA

Spain

ABSTRACT. One of the most serious problems faced at present is the volume of waste that is generated, including wastewater sewage sludge. The aim of this study is to show that not only can wet sewage sludge be stabilised and solidified, but it can also be applied in a number of very specific areas of civil engineering.

After various studies of the compatibility of wet sludge and binder (Portland cement) and its environmental impact (papers in *Waste Management* and *Cement and Concrete Research*, in press) we have carried out a feasibility study of the use of sludge as an additive in building materials, bulk concrete for filling, and as bases and sub-bases for roads. The study consists of physical (density, porosity), chemical (leaching tests according to Dutch standards) mechanical (compressive strength and elastic modulus) and durability testing of the system developed. The applications yielded satisfactory results.

Keywords: Sewage sludge, Portland cement, Stabilisation / Solidification, Civil engineering application.

Dr S Valls, is Assistant Professor of Construction Engineering in the Universitat Politècnica de Catalunya, ETSECCPB. Her research interests include durability concrete and environmental impact of sewage and its use of construction with news materials.

Dr E Vàzquez, is Director of the Building Materials Section and Professor of Construction Engineering in the Universitat Politècnica de Catalunya, ETSECCPB. He specialises in binder technology and durability concrete. His interests also include the use of wastes (slag, recycle Aggregate concrete, sludges ..) in concrete.

Mrs V Kuchinow, is Director of Research and Development of UBENA, BBS, S.L.

INTRODUCTION AND OBJECTIVES

There is a need for consistent measurements of the environmental impact of sewage sludge and other residues so that decisions can be made on the use, treatment or disposal. In Catalonian the sewage sludge production is very high, and immediate solutions are needed. The recovery of waste material has priority over disposal.

Wastewater sewage sludge is a waste product with toxic potential, therefore we have considered a stabilisation process of sewage sludge with Portland cement. Once checking the compatibility of both, Portland cement and sewage sludge, it is therefore necessary to make an environmental assessment of the material.

Assessment of the environmental quality of the final product and the consequent guarantee of its use in the building industry demand that it meets a number of requisites, one of which is that the effluents extracted by water action should be contamination-free, or at least that the concentration of contaminants should be below certain pre-set limits [1- 2].

WET SEWAGE SLUDGE CHARACTERISATION

The sewage sludge used is a wet biological sludge generated by the anaerobic digestion process occurring during treatment of the waste water generated in the area of Manresa, near Barcelona. The anaerobic digestion allows to diminish its bacteriological activity and fermentation. The principal characteristics of the sludge are reflected in Table 1, they have been obtained by elemental analyser [2]. One of the limitations, which can be encountered in the system of stabilisation/solidification of sludge with cement, is the nature and concentration of certain constituents in the sewage matrix, such as fats (3.07%), proteins (12.64%) and carbohydrates (33.87%), these directly affect the setting and hardening process [2-3].

Table 1 The main characteristics of the wet sewage sludge of Manresa.

Humidity	68 ± 2 %
Loss on ignition (Organic matter)	38 ± 4 %
pH	7.93 ± 0.36
Nitrogen	2.46 ± 0.003%
Carbon	22.27 ± 0.08 %
Hydrogen	3.46 ± 0.02 %
Sulphur	0.84 ± 0.02 %

The total heavy metal content of the sludge is shown in Table 2; the chemical analysis was carried out by plasma source atomic emission spectrometry (ICP).

However, the content of soluble heavy metals in the sewage sludge that is extractable by means of an acid medium is based on the ISO/CD 11466 standard [3]. In this type of acid attack (HNO_3 and HCl) the totality of heavy metals present is not necessarily extracted, because the matrix of silicates is not destroyed. The samples in solution were also analyzed by plasma source atomic emission spectrometry (ICP). The results are shown in Table 3.

Table 2 Heavy metal content of the Manresa Treatment Plant sludge, by total sample digestion. The results are expressed in mg of metal per kg sample of dry waste analyzed.

Cd	Cu	Mn	Ni	Pb	Cr	Zn	Ba
<0.58±0.05	157.43±14	391.65±2.7	60.61±5.75	116.18±3.0	202.11±6.4	4130±353	618.8±72.2

Table 3 Concentration of heavy metals extractable in sewage sludge by acid digestion according to ISO/CD 11466 standard. The results are expressed in mg of metal per kg sample of dry waste analyzed.

Cd	Cu	Mn	Ni	Pb	Cr	Zn	Ba
<0.6±0.0	152.3±1.6	331.62±3	46.13±4.5	101.71±3.8	197.1±2.2	3931±21.4	373.7±7.2

CIVIL ENGINEERING APPLICATION

Previous projects carried out by this research team evaluated the solidification/stabilisation mechanisms of treatment plant sludge in a Portland cement matrix. These projects showed that it is possible to apply the inerting system with this matrix, in which physical and chemical stabilisation [1-2, 4] is guaranteed. Once the inerting is shown, the objective is to explore the possibilities for attainment of materials applicable to construction with the inclusion of wastewater treatment plant sludge. To do so, the possibilities of two types of compound materials are explored:

- Mass concrete for pavements and/or non-structural applications.
- Treated gravel (gravel-cement) for road bases and sub-bases.

Each of the applications considered has an independent composition methodology and properties study.

Mass Concrete System

Of the entire set of test pieces elaborated, according to mixing criteria, groups of three were selected for each of the different types of tests and variables.

- Mechanical tests: compressive strength, elastic modulus and density.
- Durability test: wetting and drying cycle. Permeability.
- Environmental impact tests: Leaching process.

Mixing mass concrete

The concrete was mixed with crushed limestone sand and recycled aggregate from demolition. The recycled aggregate was used in gravel size (5/12 mm) and was constituted on average by 60% rock and old concrete elements and 40% ceramic elements.

The granulometric distribution was determined according to Füller's curve [5]. The percentage relationship was attained, 35% gravel and 65% sand. The value of D_{max} was 12.7 mm.

A total of six mixtures were tested with the same mineral framework, two percentages of sludge in the mix (25 and 35%), three sludge/cement ratios (S/C = 1, S/C = 1.5, and S/C = 2) and cured in a humidity chamber up to the performance of the tests (see table 4). The type of cement used is Portland I 45/A cement (medium-high strength cement) (European Standard 197-1:92) [6-7].

The sludge-concrete mixes complied with the results of another study on physical stabilisation/solidification in cement pastes containing sludge, in which 35% to 25% wet sludge in the mixture was found to be the maximum amount compatible with compressive strength [2, 4].

Table 4 Mixture of concrete test pieces

NOMENCLATURE	% SLUDGE IN CEMENT	SLUDGE/CEMENT
H25-1	25	1
H25-1.5	25	1.5
H25-2	25	2
H35-1	35	1
H35-1.5	35	1.5
H35-2	35	2

Each mixture was also tested with and without accelerant additive, $CaCl_2$, the ideal percentage of this additive being 3% of the weight of cement in a 33% solution [8]. When $CaCl_2$ was added to the concrete, the letter **C** was added to the foregoing nomenclatures. When this additive was not used, the letter **S** was added. Finally, an **N** is added to the nomenclature if it was subjected to normal curing in the humidity chamber until the pertinent test.

The total quantity of water present in the concrete is made up of that contained in the sludge and that added until the desired consistency is obtained. Following several experimental attempts, a total water/cement ratio of 0.8 was opted for, thus making for a dry, more or less constant consistency. The use of a water/cement ratio of 0.8 corresponds to the principle of obtaining a workable concrete with little added water. The compaction process was achieved using a vibration table for 2 or 3 minutes depending on the type of test piece. For cylindrical test pieces the time was 3 minutes and in prismatic test pieces it was 2 minutes.

Mechanical and Physical Properties of the Concrete With Sludge

The determination of the compressive strength is carried out according to UNE standard 83-304 [9] for 15x30 cm cylindrical test pieces. Three test pieces from each series were tested at 7, 28 and 60 days. The results are listed in table 5. The values obtained show the possibility for utilisation of the sludge as a component in mass concrete.

In the short term, at 7 days, the values were low, and in some cases, the test pieces could not be tested as they were not hardened sufficiently, due to a retardant effect of the setting and hardening by the heavy metals and the organic material in the sludge. The compressive strength results are similar to those attained in the solidification/stabilisation system of the sludge in the mortar system [1, 2].

Table 5 Compressive strengths of the cements in MPa

NOMENCLATURE	7 DAYS	28 DAYS	60 DAYS
H25-1CN	15.4	17.7	20.1
H25-1.5CN	7.1	9.9	10.4
H25-2CN	---	4.0	4.5
H35-1CN	12.1	14.1	14.3
H35-1.5CN	---	6.0	6.6
H35-2CN	---	3.8	4.6
H25-1SN	13,6	16.4	19.8
H25-1.5SN	---	8.4	7.6
H25-2SN	---	3.4	4.2
H35-1SN	7.0	13.7	13.8
H35-1.5SN	---	6.1	6.3
H35-2SN	---	3.3	4.2

The elastic modulus was determined using cylindrical test pieces measuring 15x30 cm elaborated according to UNE 83-301 [10] and kept in the humidity chamber for 60 days. The test procedure is performed as per UNE standard 83-316 [11]. For the calculation of the elastic modulus, we took the three series of stress and strain values registered in the second and third cycles of the ascendant phase of the load and the load process up to 75% of the breaking load.

The tests were carried out on five types of mix, one for reference and the remaining four with the inclusion of treatment plant sludge in proportions of 25% and 35% of the total mixture, ratios of sludge/cement of 1 and 1.5 and addition of $CaCl_2$. Considering the poor results of compressive strength for mixtures with a sludge/cement ratio of 2, determining the elastic modulus is discarded. The results are listed in table 6.

Another of the properties of the concrete studied is density according to ASTM standard C127 (1988) [12]. The results are expressed in Table 7; they confirm that the concrete in different mixtures is a lighter material than classical mass concrete.

Table 6 Results of the elastic modulus

REFERENCES OF THE SERIES	ELASTIC MODULUS
Reference concrete (without sludge)	30000 MPa
H25-1CN	11000 Mpa
H25-1.5CN	7000 Mpa
H35-1CN	10000 Mpa
H35-1.5CN	4400 Mpa

Table 7 Saturated density on dry surface of concretes

NOMENCLATURE	DENSITY, d_{sss}
H25-1CN	1.99±0
H25-1.5CN	1.99±0.004
H25-2CN	1.943±0.006
H35-1CN	1.788±0.003
H35-1.5CN	1.840±0.007
H35-2CN	1.82±0.01

DURABILITY

Wetting and Drying Cycles

To determine the stability of concrete with treatment plant sludge in environmental conditions, the wetting and drying test was performed over 22 days. The tested pieces were prismatic [13] and measured 7.6x7.6x25.4 cm. Three test pieces per series were tested. The test was performed after four months in the humidity chamber. It consisted of eleven cycles in which the test pieces were submerged in water for 24 hours at 20°C and exposed to air for 24 hours. Each cycle lasted two days. The lengths and weights of the test pieces were measured at 4, 8, 12, 18 and 22 days, and then after the test pieces had remained exposed to air for 24 hours. The lengths and weights were calculated using the values prior to the beginning of the cycles. The test pieces were tested for compressive strength (R_c) at the end of the test.

The results obtained at the end of the eleven cycles are included in table 8. It can be observed that the pieces tested dilated slightly, and that the dilatation was inversely proportional to the concentration of the treatment plant sludge in the test piece. The more sludge, the less dilatation. Further, an increase in the mass ratios was observed, but there is not a correlation between the percentage of sludge and the increase in the mass ratios. The compressive strengths continue to be high. The results produced by this durability test show that the elaborated mass concrete has satisfactory performance.

Table 8 Wetting and drying cycle results

SERIES	$\Delta l/l_o .10^6$	$\Delta l/l_o .100$	R_c (MPa)	$\Delta m/m_o .100$
H25-1CN	789	0.079	25.2	1.8
H25-1.5CN	500	0.050	12.9	2.5
H25-2CN	419	0.042	7.1	2.6
H35-1CN	693	0.069	18.6	3.1
H35-1.5CN	215	0.022	11.0	1.9
H35-2CN	36	0.004	7.1	2.0

Permeability

Permeability is an essential property of the material that governs the mechanisms of transport in concrete, and therefore its durability in the face of aggression, including leaching. It is indispensable to know this parameter for the material studied, to judge both its durability and its environmental impact.

The concretes with sludges tested had an age of 3 months. Basically, the process as described in NF standard (Pr P 18-155) [14] consists of submitting a face of the test piece to the action of a liquid under pressure, and measuring the filtered volume collected on the opposite face. If the water passes through the test piece, the permeability coefficient is determined using Darcy's equation [5]. The test pieces were first impermeabilized on their lateral surface, so that the injected fluid was unidirectional. The pressures applied were 2, 4, 6 and 8 Kp/cm² during 24 hours for each of the test pieces. To perform the test, the cylindrical test pieces measuring 15x30 cm were cut to attain discs with thicknesses of 5 cm.

The results by mixture are the following:

- **H25-1CN**: no water passed. The system had impermeable behaviour at each of the pressures tested.
- **H25-1.5CN**: 25 ml had passed through at the end of the 4 Kp/cm² period. At the end of the test, the volume collected was 96 ml.
- **H25-2CN**: 32 ml had passed through at the end of the 2 Kp/cm² period. At the end of the test, the volume collected was 120 ml.
- **H35-1CN**: no water passed. The system had impermeable behaviour at each of the pressures tested.
- **H35-1.5CN**: 12 ml had passed through at the end of the 4 Kp/cm² period. At the end of the test, the volume collected was 128 ml.
- **H35-2CN**: only 21 ml was collected in the last period of 8 Kp/cm².

From these values, it can be concluded that the system has impermeable behaviour in the mixtures with a sludge/cement ratio of 1 at a maximum pressure of 8 Kp/cm², and that beyond this pressure, the permeability increases proportionally with the percentage of sludge in the total mixture and the sludge/cement ratio. The ratios with sludge/cement ratios of 1.5 and 2 present permeability to water at low pressures.

Environmental Impact

The stabilisation/solidification efficacy as regards the environmental impact of the concrete is evaluated based on the leaching process for the most toxic pollutants, such as heavy metals. The method used is the Netherlands Tank Leaching Test (NTLT) NEN-7345 [15]. In this type of test, the accumulated leaching is measured for each pollutant, to later evaluate and classify the material into one of three possible categories. The eluates obtained were analysed by plasma source atomic emission spectrometry (ICP) (table 9).

In each extraction the pH was evaluated, with the objective of also determining the behaviour of the leaching liquid, acidified water, during the process of contact between this liquid and the solid material in monolithic state. The water can solubilize some material-forming chemical species and its pH can adjust to that of the material.

The results obtained in the leaching process are very satisfactory, as heavy metal concentrations were not detected in any mixture, as the levels are below the detection limits of the technique. Thus, the material, concrete, is within category 1 of the Netherlands Tank Leaching Test (NTLT) standard, which corresponds to an inert material due to its heavy metal concentration [15].

In all of the extractions from each test piece, the pH evaluation in the eluates obtained shows a highly alkaline system and a buffering capacity for the system of around pH 11, throughout the leaching test.

Table 9 Results of the heavy metals in the NEN-7345 leaching process

	HEAVY METALS (mg/m^2)						
	Cd	Mn	Zn	Cu	Pb	Cr	Ni
H25-1CN	<1.63±0	<1.63±0	<1.63±0	<1.63±0	<6.5±0	<3.25±0	<3.25±0
H25-1.5CN	<1.63±0	<1.63±0	<1.63±0	<1.63±0	<6.5±0	<3.25±0	<3.25±0
H25-2CN	<1.63±0	<1.63±0	<1.63±0	<1.63±0	<6.5±0	<3.25±0	<3.25±0
H35-1CN	<1.63±0	<1.63±0	<1.63±0	<1.63±0	<6.5±0	<3.25±0	<3.25±0
H35-1.5CN	<1.63±0	<1.63±0	<1.63±0	<1.63±0	<6.5±0	<3.25±0	<3.25±0
H35-2CN	<1.63±0	<1.63±0	<1.63±0	<1.63±0	<6.5±0	<3.25±0	<3.25±0

Mass Concrete System: Conclusions

The results obtained in the various tests on application of treatment plant sludge as fine aggregate in mass concrete allow us to conclude:

-       The possibility of including a maximum of 35% sludge in the mixture but with a maximum sludge/cement ratio of 1. In sludge/cement ratios of 1.5 and 2, the mechanical properties drop significantly.

- The elastic modulus of the system are much lower than those of normal concrete. Thus, the material presents lower rigidity than could be useful for certain civil engineering applications. The modulus oscillates between 4400 MPa for 35% sludge and sludge/cement ratio of 1.5 and 11000 MPa for the 25% sludge with sludge/cement relation equal to 1. There is a drop in the elastic modulus in the sludge/cement ratio of 1 at approximately 60% and in the ratio of 1.5 at a percentage of 77%.

- The density of the concrete is lower than that of a concrete without waste, oscillating between 1.9 and 1.8 g/cm^3. It is a light material that is very useful for covering various needs in the field of backfill materials and compacted surfaces.

- With a sludge/cement ratio of 1, the impermeability of the material is guaranteed at a maximum pressure of 8 Kp/cm^2, which generally prevents penetration of agents aggressive to concrete.

- In all processes, the mixtures tested by the leaching process released non-detectable quantities of heavy metals. Therefore, this application of mass concrete is characterised by high environmental stability, improving the results of the mortar system (work in press) [1].

- A system with a highly alkaline pH is created which guarantees microbiological and organic inerting, favouring the chemical retention of certain environmentally harmful ions.

- The presence of recycled aggregate does not alter the stability of the stabilisation/solidification system of the sludge in concrete. It only results in lower elastic modulus values [16].

- In all the mixtures tested this mass concrete presents sufficient compressive strength which allows its application as a controlled low-strength material [17], which must have a strength of 3 MPa in concretes. This material has several applications in the field of civil engineering, such as a backfill material with sufficient load-bearing capacity to support light vehicle traffic. Its low strength makes it compatible with the strength of flooring or surrounding areas, without creating excessively rigid zones.

Road Base and Sub-Base Gravel-Cement System

Another of the possible applications of wastewater treatment plant sludge in construction materials is its inclusion in a gravel-cement type material for road bases and sub-bases in flexible foundations. Up to the present time, it has been clearly observed that the mixture of sludge with a material with a hydraulic binder (Portland cement) gives rise to a lighter, less rigid material, as is shown by the values of the elastic modulus and the compressive strengths in the application of mass concrete, which make this material recommendable for road surfacing.

Mixture

The water content to add is based on reaching the minimum necessary workability to spread and compact the aggregate-sludge-cement system. Only two sludge/cement ratios were studied: S/C = 1 and S/C = 1.5. In all mixtures $CaCl_2$ was added in a proportion of 3% cement weight to 33% added solution. The mixture is shown in Table 10.

Three cylindrical test pieces were elaborated measuring 10x10 cm of each series with proctor compaction. The tests performed for this type of material were mechanical: compressive strength and elastic modulus.

Table 10 Gravel-cement mixtures for road bases and sub-bases with inclusion of sludge, according to workability of the compaction process

	SLUDGE/CEMENT	% SLUDGE	% CEMENT	% WATER ADDED[*]	ADDITIVE
S	1.0	7.5%	7.5%	4.9%	3% $CaCl_2$
A 2	1.0	7.5%	7.5%	5.2%	3% $CaCl_2$
S 2	1.5	7.5%	5.0%	4.9%	3% $CaCl_2$
B 2	1.5	7.5%	5.0%	5.1%	3% $CaCl_2$
C 2	1.0	5.0%	5.0%	3.4%	3% $CaCl_2$
R 1.1			7.5%	0.3%	3% $CaCl_2$
R 2.2			5.0%	0.2%	3% $CaCl_2$

(*) The addition of water is the percentage of water added over the total weight of the mixture, considering the wetness of the treatment plant sludge, which is approximately 70%, to obtain optimum workability with minimum addition.

RESULTS

The compressive strength of gravel-cement must be determined 7 days after its elaboration, according to the Particular Technical Specifications [18], and its value must not be lower than 3.5 MPa in base layers for heavy or medium traffic, or 3.0 MPa in other cases. For sub-base layers the compressive strength at 7 days must not be lower than 2 MPa. These strengths are applicable as long as Portland cement is used as binding. The results are shown in Table 11.

Table 11 Compressive breaking in MPa at 7, 14 and 28 days for gravel-cement, according to workability criteria

NOMENCLATURE	7 DAYS	14 DAYS	28 DAYS
S	4.7	5.3	6.5
A 2	5.4	6.6	5.8
S 2	1.7	3.5	3.2
B 2	3.3	4.2	5.0
C 2	3.0	3.9	--
R 1.1	12.8	13.5	--
R 2.1	6.4	6.4	--

As regards the elastic modulus of gravel-cement, the same procedure described for mass concrete was followed. The standard used is UNE 83-316 [11] at 28 days of its elaboration. The elastic modulus was only studied in those mixtures with best results in the compressive strength test, or mixtures with the following references: A 2, B 2 and C 2, which have greater additions of water in the mixture to attain the desired workability. The results are shown in Table 12.

Table 12 Elastic modulus of the gravel-cement application in MPa

NOMENCLATURE	ELASTIC MODULUS (MPa)	SLUDGE/CEMENT
A 2	9900	1.5
C 2	12000	1
B 2	9000	1.5
R 1.1	27400	No sludge
R 2.1	21600	No sludge

The mixtures with nomenclatures R 1.1 and R 2.1 are the reference values. This is why they have a higher modulus value.

Road Base and Sub-Base Gravel-Cement System: Conclusions

The results obtained in the tests for application of Manresa treatment plant sludge in gravel-cement allow us to reach the following conclusions:

- All of the mixtures with a sludge/cement ratio of 1 and a wetness of approximately 5% (workability criteria) are applicable as gravel-cement for road bases and sub-bases. And for a sludge/cement ratio of 1.5, with the mere addition of the water contained in the sludge, it is applicable in the sub-base gravel-cements.

- The results of the elastic modulus in the mixtures show low rigidity of the system, optimum for the application of road bases and sub-bases for flexible surfacing. The reduction of the elastic modulus, as regards the reference value (without sludge), is 44% in the mixture with a sludge/cement ratio of 1 and 63% in that of the sludge/cement ratio of 1.5.

DISCUSSION OF THE STUDY

It is possible to stabilize and solidify wastewater treatment plant sludges with a hydraulic binder such as Portland cement. Studies carried out by this research team [1-3] on the physical, chemical and environmental impact properties of the sludge-cement system show an inerting process by the cement on the waste product (Manresa sludge). We must bear in mind that waste products like treatment plant sludge, aside from being stabilised and inertized, and, if is possible as a sub-product of other industries. In this work, the possible applications in construction as aggregate in low-strength mass concrete and as additive in road bases and sub-bases are discussed. In no case is a material with outstanding properties being sought. It will be highly useful in those countries which require a great deal of backfill material for their infrastructures and access roadways (roads, highways, etc.).

These two applications which we contemplate here are possible because they meet the minimum requirements for mechanical strength without neglecting the fact that there is an inerting of the contaminant ionic substances and species in a system based on the setting and hardening of a cement matrix, in turn based on the ratio between the pollutants and binding components with the production of substances insoluble in water and other liquids, the incorporation of toxic elements (heavy metals ..) in the crystalline structure of some cement hydration products, the adsorption of hydrates formed from cement which have a high specific surface, and finally of the low transport velocity by capillarity and diffusion, in the material once properly hardened.

ACKNOWLEDGMENTS

The authors wish to thank the support of Junta de Sanejament of the Dpt.de Medi Ambient of the Generalitat de Catalunya and UBENA, BBS (Barcelona, Spain).

REFERENCES

1.   VALLS S AND VÁZQUEZ E. ARTICLE DE LIXIVIACIO , Leaching properties of stabilised/solidified cement-admixtures-sewage sludges systems. Waste Managament. (In press, accepted October 2000).

2.   VALLS S. Estabilización física y química de los lodos de depuradora de aguas residuales y de material de demolición para su utilización en ingeniería civil, Doctoral thesis, Barcelona July 1999.

3.   INTERNATIONAL STANDARD (ISO/CD 11466). Soil Quality – Extraction of Trace Metals Soluble in Aqua Regia. Doc, ISO/TC 190/SC 3 N112.

4.   VALLS S AND VÁZQUEZ E. Stabilization and solidification of sewage sludges with Portland cement. Cement and Concrete Research (In press, accepted June 2000).

5.   FERNANDEZ CANOVAS M. Hormigón. Colegio de Ingenieros de Caminos, Canales y Puertos. Tercera Edición, Madrid, 1993.

6.   ASOCIACIÓN ESPAÑOLA DE NORMALIZACIÓN Y CERTIFICACIÓN. Cementos. Especificaciones Químicas para sus constituyentes. UNE 80-302, Madrid, 1985.

7.   ASOCIACIÓN ESPAÑOLA DE NORMALIZACIÓN Y CERTIFICACIÓN. Métodos de Ensayo de Cementos. Determinación de la resistencia mecánica. UNE 80-101, Madrid, 1986.

8.   RAMACHANDRAN V S. Calcium Chloride in Concrete. Science and Technology. Applied Science Publishers LTD, London, 1976.

9.   ASOCIACION ESPAÑOLA DE NORMALIZACIÓN Y CERTIFICACION. Ensayos de hormigón. Rotura por compresión.. UNE 83-304, Madrid, 1991.

10. ASOCIACION ESPAÑOLA DE NORMALIZACIÓN Y CERTIFICACION. Ensayos de hormigón. Fabricación y conservación de probetas. UNE 83-301, Madrid, 1991.

11. ASOCIACIÓN ESPAÑOLA DE NORMALIZACIÓN Y CERTIFICACION. Ensayos de hormigón. Determinación del módulo de elasticidad en compresión. UNE 83-316, Madrid, 1998.

12. AMERICAN SOCIETY FOR TESTING AND MATERIALS. Specific Gravity and Absorption of Coarse Aggregate. ASTM C127, 1988.

13. AMERICAN SOCIETY FOR TESTING AND MATERIALS (ASTM C 192/C 192 M-95). Standard Practice for Making and Curing Concrete Test Specimens in the Laboratory. Volume 4.02. 1998.

14.   PROJET DE NORME FRANCAISE HOMOLOGUEE (AFNOR) Produits speciaux destines aux constructions en beton hydraulique. Produits ou systemes de produits destines aux applications superficielles sur beton durci. Essai de permeabilite aux liquides. NF Pr P 18-855. Abril de 1985.

15. NEN 7345. Determination of the release of inorganic constituents from construction materials and stabilized waste products. NNI, Delft (Netherlands). Formerly Draft NEN 5432. 1993.

16. BARRA M. Estudio de la durabilidad del hormigón de árido reciclado en su aplicación como hormigón armado. Doctoral thesis, Barcelona, December, 1996.

17. VICARIO F. Los materiales de baja resistencia controlada (MBRC). Hormigón preparado. Volumen XIII N° 39, pp: 39-42. Febrero de 1999.

18. DIRECCION GENERAL DE CARRETERAS Y CAMINOS VECINALES. MOP. Pliego de Prescripciones técnicas generales para obras de carreteras y puentes. PG 3. 1975.

STUDY OF THE HYDRATION OF CEMENT PASTES AND DRY SEWAGE SLUDGE

A Yagüe   **S Valls**   **E Vàzquez**

Universitat Politècnica de Catalunya

V Kuchinow

UBENA, BBS, S.L.

Spain

ABSTRACT. The great amount of dry sewage sludge that is generated and the need to stabilize, solidify and, whenever possible, reuse it has led us to attempt the application of new approaches to its treatment.

Portland cement paste of different strengths mixed with various proportions of dry sludge were studied to determine the compatibility of the binder with the waste, and also to evaluate the delay in the setting process of these mixes and the optimum percentage and type of Portland cement. For each mix, we tracked the process and the various hydration products of the pastes over time (on setting, and at 2, 14 and 28 days) using NMR and XDR techniques. Variations were seen in the evolution of the hydrated compounds as a function of the proportion of dry sludge used.

Keywords: Dry sewage sludge, Portland cement, Hydration products, NMR, Setting speed

Mr A Yagüe, is Assistant Professor of Construction Engineering in the Universitat Politècnica de Catalunya, ETSECCPB. He is preparing his Doctoral Thesis: "Inerting of dry sewage sludge and its use in civil engineering".

Dr S Valls, is Assistant Professor of Construction Engineering in the Universitat Politècnica de Catalunya, ETSECCPB. Her research interests include durability concrete and environmental impact of sewage and its use of construction with news materials.

Dr E Vàzquez, is Director of the Building Materials Section and Professor of Construction Engineering in the Universitat Politècnica de Catalunya, ETSECCPB. He specialises in binder technology and durability concrete. His interests also include the use of wastes (slag, recycle Aggregate concrete, sludges ..) in concrete.

Mrs V Kuchinow, is Director of Research and Development of UBENA, BBS, S.L.

INTRODUCTION AND OBJECTIVES

The Sabadell (Barcelona) treatment plant sludge which we will study is the result of a primary treatment followed by anaerobic digestion. The resulting sludge is subjected to a partial drying process to reduce the total volume of waste, facilitate its handling and achieve the elimination of any pathogenic micro-organisms which it may contain.

In the biochemical analysis of this sludge we detect large proportions, of the order of 65%, of carbohydrates which can delay the hydration of the Portland cement that we intend to use to stabilise and recycle this sludge, using it as an additive in the preparation of mortars and concretes.

In an initial phase of the investigation we seek to determine the alterations which the sludge can produce in the hydration mechanisms of the Portland cement, studying the delay which the addition of different proportions of sludge produces in the processes of beginning and end of setting, relating these variations to the changes in the appearance of the hydration products of the Portland cement, detected by means of the XRD and ^{29}Si NMR-MAS techniques.

DRY SLUDGE CHARACTERISATION

Prior to the studies of inerting of the waste with hydraulic binder, it is necessary to know the type of waste which we will be treating, and to do so we require a basic characterisation of it. Table 1 show the results of the chemical, organic and microbiological characterisation of the Sabadell dry sludge.

Table 1 Characterisation of dry sewage sludge

PROPERTY	LEVEL
Loss mass at 105 °C	19 %
Loss mass at 500 °C	47 %
pH	7.1
Proteins	0.41 %
Fats	0.33 %
Carbohydrates	65.47 %
Organic Nitrogen	0.09 %
Phosphorus	0.38 %
Ashes	31.79 %
Aerobics	26 ufc/g
Enterobacterium	< 10 ufc/g
E. Colli	< 3 mnp/g
Coliform	< 3 ufc/g
Mushroom	< 10 ufc/g
Clostridium	< 10 ufc/g

The sludge leaves the plant in the form of very soft approximately spherical particles, which, if introduced into a cement mixer, would crumble and alter the granulometry of the material. In order to avoid these drawbacks, the sludge is ground in order to transform it into sand, the granulometry of which is shown in Table 2

Table 2 Granulometry of dry sewage sludge

SIEVE, mm	% PAST THROUGH
4,76	100
2,38	99
2,00	96
1,19	91,4
0,59	74,9
0,42	63
0,29	44,4
0,149	14
0,063	4,2

In addition to the organic fraction of the sludge, there is an inorganic part determined by X-ray diffraction, and consisting of the following crystalline mineral phases: calcite, quartz and clays.

DRY SLUDGE - CEMENT PASTE SYSTEM

For the preparation of the pastes of normal consistency and the subsequent determination of the beginning and end of setting, we will use two types of Portland cement: one type CEM I/52.5 R and the other type CEM I /42.5 R, according to European Standard ENV 197-1:92 [1].

Sufficient water was added, it is the amount necessary to prepare the paste of normal consistency, according to standard EN 196-3: 96 [2]. We prepare mixes with a fixed amount of each of the cements, 500 g, to which we will add proportions of 1%, 2.5%, 5% and 10% sludge with regard to the weight of cement (see Tables 3 and 4). For each of the mixes, we will determine what amount of water is necessary to prepare the paste of normal consistency, and for these proportions we will determine the beginning and the end of setting according to standard EN 196-3: 96.

Table 3 Pastes with CEM I 42,5 R

% SLUDGE	0 %	1 %	2,5 %	5 %	10 %
Cement + Sludge, g	500 + 0	500 + 5	500 + 12,5	500 + 25	500 + 50
Water , g	128	131	133	137	149
% W/, C + S	25,6	25,9	25,4	26,1	27,1

Table 4 Pastes with CEM I 52,5 R

% SLUDGE	0 %	1 %	2,5 %	5 %	10 %
Cement + Sludge, g	500 + 0	500 + 5	500 + 12,5	500 + 25	500 + 50
Water, g	148	149	150	158	167
% W/, C + S	29,6	29,5	29,3	30,1	30,4

Having determined the beginning and end of setting, we will take samples of the pastes prepared at the moment when the end of setting occurs, and we will study the hydration products by the XRD and ^{29}Si NMR-MAS techniques. We will leave the remaining samples of the pastes in the humidity chamber, and at different times we will extract samples and also observe how the hydrated components of the Portland cement have evolved with time with the above-mentioned techniques.

For the discussion, we must point out that if we calculate the ratio water/(cement + sludge), the value will vary very little with the addition of sludge, which apparently acts as a fine which is equivalent to the cement, with a small increase in requirement of water when the proportions of sludge are high, but always in values of the same order of magnitude.

SETTING SPEED RESULTS

In this part of the study [3] we can determine the delaying effect of the dry sludge on the process of hydration of the cement pastes for each type of cement. This is shown in Tables 5 and 6.

Table 5 Beginning and End of Settting with CEM I 42,5 R

% SLUDGE	0 %	1 %	2,5 %	5 %	10 %
Beginning of Setting, min	135	145	175	285	335
End of Setting, min	200	210	255	386	1320

Table 6 Beginning and End of Setting with CEM I 52,5 R

% SLUDGE	0 %	1 %	2,5 %	5 %	10 %
Beginning of Setting, min	120	135	160	203	292
End of Setting, min	165	174	230	398	1265

From the tables, it is deduced that for both cements a delay occurs at the beginning and end of setting, which is greater for the pastes with greater addition of sludge. The delay is very large in the pastes with 10% sludge, with a beginning of setting time approximately 2.5 times greater than that the reference paste (without sludge), and which for the end of setting is of the order of 7 times greater than the reference paste. The end of setting of the pastes with 10% sludge occurs after some 21 hours of the production process, thus greatly exceeding the maximum end-of-setting time stipulated by standard EN 196-3: 96, which is 12 hours.

With the results obtained, we can conclude that additions of 10% sludge should not be used, unless we are planning to add a setting-accelerator additive in order to compensate for this delay.

The presence of mixes with 5% sludge also entails a delay in the end of setting, but as the time necessary to reach this point is rather over six hours, these results would be within the limits established by the standard.

HYDRATION PRODUCTS BY X-RAY DIFFRACTION

Qualitative analyses were performed with a Siemens D- 500 XRD equipment with Cu (λ = 1.5418 Å) radiation, using an angular velocity of 0.05° per 3 seconds over a Bragg angle (2θ) range of 4° to 70°. This technique allows the identification of the crystalline phases in the hydrating cement pastes, through the detection of ettringite and portlandite, and the disappearance of the anhydrous phases of the cement (gypsum, C_3S, C_2S, C_3A and C_4AF). [3]

The evolution in time of the crystalline phases of the pastes prepared was studied, at the moment when the end of setting occurs and at 2, 7, 14 and 28 days from this end, in order to make a qualitative assessment of their evolution in time.

In all the pastes, with both Portland cements, it is observed how the anhydrides disappear to form the hydrates. However, not all the mixes behave in the same way. In the mixes with greater percentage of sludge, the evolution is slower than in the mixes with less percentage of sludge. Therefore, the XRD results corroborate the setting speed results. The greater the addition of sludge in the mix, the lower the hydration speed and the greater the time necessary to reach the end of setting, as is observed in the evolution of the anhydride and hydrated phases.

It is also observed that in the pastes with only 1 % sludge the behaviour is similar to the pastes without sludge (0 % sludge).

The behaviour of the two cements is similar with regard to the formation and evolution of the anhydrides and hydrates: the principal difference is that more gypsum is detected in the pastes prepared with Portland cement CEM I 52.5/R, disappearing 7 days from the end of setting, while with the CEM I 42.5 there is less gypsum and this disappears 2 days from the end of setting.

HYDRATION PRODUCTS BY NUCLEAR MAGNETIC RESONANCE

From the pastes prepared for the determination of the beginning and end of setting, we selected those prepared with CEM I 52.5 R, without sludge, and the mixes with addition of 2.5% and 5% sludge, and we analysed them by MNR,[4] at the end of setting and at the ages of 2 and 28 days.

A Bruker AMX-300 MHz solid-state high-resolution spectrometer with thick-walled zirconia rotors, rotating at 3800Hz, was used to perform the ^{29}Si MAS (magic angle spinning) NMR analysis of the pastes. The spectra were performed at 59.6 MHz. This technique provides useful information about the state of the tetrahedral SiO_4^{4-} in the cement paste. In the process of silicate, polymerization, the individual tetrahedrons (called monomers, whose state is designated as Q^0) of the anhydrous silicate phases (C_3S, C_2S) of the cement are transformed through hydration. The tetrahedrons connect through oxygen atoms giving rise to other polymeric states, which are dimers (Q^1), polymeric chains (Q^2), lateral associations of two chains (Q^3) and three-dimensional lattices (Q^4). Each of these states, which reflect the degree of polymerization of the silicates in the pastes, is represented by a peak in the NMR spectrum (given as a function of the chemical displacement).

Since the peaks in the NMR spectra overlap, a semi-quantitative method is used to compare the curves obtained at different ages. The areas of the Q^0 and Q^1 peaks, denoted respectively as A_0 and A_1, are obtained for each spectrum.

If we compare, for each composition, the variation in the heights of the peaks corresponding to the monomer silicates Q^0 and the polymerised silicates of type Q^1, we observe that the peaks corresponding to the end of setting only present silicates of type Q^0 (Figure 1). At two days we observe the formation of peaks corresponding to silicates of type Q^1, (Figure 2), although in order to quantify the results we may encounter problems due to the overlapping in the bases of the peaks.

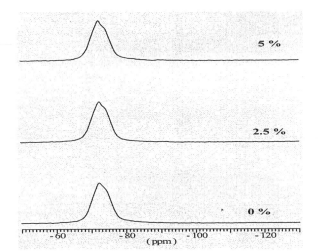

Figure 1 NMR Spectrum at End of Setting

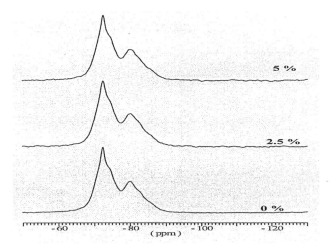

Figure 2 NMR Spectrum at 2 Days

At 28 days (Figure 3) the peak corresponding to the silicates of type Q^1 has increased noticeably, in correspondence with the advance in the hydration of the cement, and as in the case of 2 days there is an overlapping between the bases of the corresponding peaks.

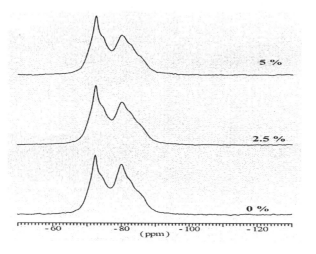

Figure 3 NMR Spectrum at 28 days

If we make a semi-quantitative analysis of the proportion of polymer Q^1 to monomer Q^0 (Table 7), we observe that at two days the ratio of areas A_1 (corresponding to the form Q^1) to A_0 (corresponding to the form Q^0) is of the same order of magnitude for the three pastes, while at 28 days there occurs a significant increase in area A_1 for all the pastes, and that this increase is more significant for the reference paste than for the pastes containing sludge, and that between the two additions of sludge there are no great differences.

Table 7 Rate between A_1/A_0

	REFERENCE	2,5 %	5 %
End of Setting	0	0	0
2 days	0,55	0,61	0,59
28 days	1,25	1,07	1,04

From these results it is deduced that at the moment of the end of setting, the reaction of hydration of the silicates, if it has taken place, is not detectable by means of this technique.

At two days the ratio between the areas of the hydrated silicates with regard to the areas of the anhydride silicates is of the same order of magnitude in all the pastes, which implies that the hydration is similar in all the samples.

At 28 days the areas corresponding to the hydrated silicates have increased considerably with regard to the anhydrides, and the reference paste presents greater hydration than those containing sludge, which implies a lower hydration speed of the pastes containing sludge.

DISCUSSION

This study evaluated the hydration process in a system of cement with addition of dry sewage plant sludge. The techniques used for this evaluation were XRD and ^{29}Si MAS NMR with various percentages of sludge in the mix, in order to optimise the maximum amount of sludge which can be added to a Portland cement without the latter being significantly changed.

In the ^{29}Si MAS NMR study, a lesser degree of polymerisation of the silicates was observed in the pastes with added sludge, and this was observed very well at 28 days from the end of setting. In the spectrums obtained there was a lesser proportion of the dimer (Q^1).

The XRD technique enabled us to qualitatively assess the tendency of the hydration in time, as the reduction of the anhydride components in the cement paste in favour of the increase in the formation of the hydrates, such as CH. The XRD analysis was more detailed, evaluating more time intervals (at end of setting and at 2, 7, 14 and 28 days from the end of setting).

Both techniques are valid to study the evolution of the hydrates formed in the pastes and to relate them to the setting speed of the different pastes.

CONCLUSIONS

The addition of dry sewage sludge entails a reduction in the hydration speed of the Portland cement, which manifests itself in the increase in the time necessary to reach the conditions of beginning and end of setting of pastes of normal consistency prepared with different additions of sludge, and it increases with the increase in the addition of sludge.

This variation tallies with the results of the XRD and ^{29}Si NMR-MAS study, in which it is observed that the speed of appearance of hydrated phases and the speed of disappearance of anhydride phases correspond to the amount of sludge added.

Except in the case of the addition of 10% sludge, the delays produced are relatively low. In any case, the addition of a setting accelerator could be considered, if necessary, in order to compensate for these delays.

In all the cases, it must be pointed out that the species detected are the same, in both the reference samples and those containing different additions of sludge. This leads us to believe that there are no significant changes in the mechanisms of reaction, other than the above-mentioned reduction in speed.

The variation in the requirement of water which is entailed by the addition of the sludge for the preparation of the paste of normal consistency is very small, and it is only significant for additions of 10% sludge, rising from 29.6% to 30.4%.

In conclusion, it does not appear that there are serious contraindications in the use of additions of up to 5% sludge, and if it is desired to use a proportion of 10%, consideration should be given to compensating for the delay produced with the addition of an accelerating additive.

REFERENCES

1. ASOCIACIÓN ESPAÑOLA DE NORMALIZACIÓN Y CERTIFICACIÓN. UNE 80301:96. EN 197-1:92

2. COMITÉ EUROPEO DE NORMALIZACIÓN EN 193-3:92

3. MATAMALA J.M Utilització de Llots Secs de Depuradora a la Fabricació de Morters amb Ciment Portland. Tesina de Grado. Barcelona 2000.

4. POWDER DIFFRACTION FILE SEARCH MANUAL. JOINT COMMITEE ON POWDER DIFFRACTION STANDARDS. International Centre for diffraction Data. 1601 Park Lane, Swarthmore, Pennsylvania 19081. USA, 1980.

5. ZANNI, H., CHEYREZY, M., MARET, V., PHILIPPOT, S., and NIETO, P. Investigation of Hydration and Pozzolanic Reaction in Reactive Powder Concrete (RPC) using ^{29}Si NMR. Cement and Concrete Research, Vol, 26, n° 1, pp: 93-100. 1996.

THE POTENTIAL FOR STRUVITE RECOVERY FROM DIGESTED SLUDGE LIQUOR

J D Doyle   S P Parsons   Y Jaffer   F Wall

Cranfield University

K Oldring   J Churchley

Severn Trent Water Ltd

T A Clark

Thames Water

United Kingdom

ABSTRACT.   Struvite in wastewater treatment plants was identified as early as 1939. Whilst studying digestion Rawn (1939) found crystalline material identified as struvite, in the digested sludge supernatant lines. Problems with struvite formation date back to the 1960s when it was noticed at the Hyperion treatment plant, Los Angeles (Borgerding, 1972). Operators at the plant noticed crystalline deposits on the underside of post digestion screens. The digested sludge stream was diluted and it was thought the problem was solved, until five years later when the normal gravity flow of digested sludge had decreased to such a stage that pumping was required. This paper reports the findings of a series of experiments have been undertaken to identify the potential of recovering struvite from sludge liquors. Eight STWs have been investigated including one detail. A number of the works has the potential to form over 100 mg/L of struvite. Recovery of struvite using chemical dosing has been investigated.

Keywords: Struvite, Phosphorus recovery, Magnesium balance, Modelling

J D Doyle, received BSc in Marine Biology from Queen Mary and Westfield College, University of London, in 1996 and completed an MSc in Water Pollution Control Technology at Cranfield University. He is currently researching Struvite Formation and Control in Wastewater Treatment.

S P Parsons, has a BSc and PhD in Chemistry from Leicester University. He joined Cranfield University in 1994 initially as a post doctoral research officer and from 1995 as a Lecturer in the School of Water Sciences.

Y Jaffer, studied for her first degree at South Bank University. Upon graduating, she joined Castrol International initially as a Development Microbiologist and later as a Research Chemist. After four years she left and returned to college, where she undertook an MSc in Water Pollution Control Technology, at Cranfield university and currently works for Thames Water Utilities Ltd.

F Wall, has a degree in Biochemistry at the University of York. She later undertook an MSc in Water Pollution Control Technology, at Cranfield University during which she undertook a 4 month research project at Severn Trent Water.

K Oldring and J Churchley, work for Severn Trent Water plc and have been involved in projects associated with struvite for a number of years.

T A Clark, studied Marine Chemistry as her first degree at Liverpool University, followed by a MSc in Water Pollution Control Technology (sponsored by Thames Water) and a PhD in Water Sciences (sponsored by Alcan Chemicals) at Cranfield University. She now works for Thames Water Research and Development in Reading.

INTRODUCTION

Since the implementation of the EC Urban Waste Water Treatment Directive, (UWWTD) 97/271/EC (21st May 1991) a number of fundamental changes in wastewater treatment have occurred. Two of the changes directly impact upon water companies' treatment of sludge produced from wastewater treatment facilities.

- Dumping of sewage sludge at sea is now prohibited.
- Nitrogen and phosphorus limits have been imposed to reduce the potential of eutrophication of sensitive inland and coastal waters.

The removal of compounds containing nitrogen and phosphorus is a key element of the UWWTD and is intended to reduce and prevent eutrophication of sensitive inland and coastal waters. Eutrophication can be defined in two ways, either the result of over fertilisation of aquatic environments, with anthropogenic inputs being the cause (Harremoes 1998).

Alternatively a natural phenomenon which increases the organic load in a lake due to increased nutrients. Currently requirements for the removal of nitrogen and phosphorus are based upon the population size and the minimum reduction required of nitrogen and phosphorus, Table 1.

Table 1 The removal of nitrogen and phosphorus from wastewaters as stipulated by annex 1.2b of the UWWTD

PARAMETER	POPULATION EQUIVALENT (p.e.)	CONCENTRATION (mg/l)	MINIMUM REDUCTIC (%)
Total Phosphorus	10 000 – 100 000	2	80
	>100 000	1	80
Total Nitrogen	10 000 – 100 000	15	70-80
	>100 000	10	70-80

With more stringent standards imposed regarding nutrient removal, processes have been developed to remove compounds containing nitrogen and phosphorous.

The result of removing greater concentrations of phosphorus from the wastewater is that the wasted sludge has a greater concentration of phosphorus, nitrogen and magnesium, Table 2. This combination of ions found in sludges produced from nutrient removal, specifically biological nutrient removal (BNR) processes, can result in the formation of a mineral called struvite.

Table 2 Comparison of BNR and activated sludges

PARAMETERS	UNITS	BNR SLUDGE	ACTIVATED SLUDGE
Total-COD	mgL^{-1}	15320	13640
Total Solids	mgL^{-1}	12620	11080
Total Nitrogen	mgL^{-1}	486	399
Total Phosphorus	mgL^{-1}	335	143
Soluble Phosphorus	mgL^{-1}	55	34
Total Calcium	mgL^{-1}	686	247
Total Magnesium	mgL^{-1}	108	39
pH	mgL^{-1}	7.2	7.4

Struvite in wastewater treatment plants was identified as early as 1939. Whilst studying digestion Rawn (1939) found crystalline material identified as struvite, in the digested sludge supernatant lines. Problems with struvite formation date back to the 1960s when it was noticed at the Hyperion treatment plant, Los Angeles (Borgerding, 1972).

Operators at the plant noticed crystalline deposits on the underside of post digestion screens. The digested sludge stream was diluted and it was thought the problem was solved, until five years later when the normal gravity flow of digested sludge had decreased to such a stage that pumping was required. The pipeline had diminished in size from twelve inches in diameter to six (Borgerding, 1972).

Whilst struvite can be a problem in wastewater treatment plants it has potential use as a fertiliser. Natural sources of struvite include guano deposits and cow manure and it has been shown to be a highly effective source of nitrogen, magnesium and phosphorus for plants foliage and soil applications. Struvite can be recovered from wastewater and sludges etc. if the chemical constituents of the sludge are such that the K_{sp} value is exceeded.

A number of processes have been used to recover struvite including fluidised bed reactors and pellet reactors, Table 3. In all of these processes the precipitation is achieved by either (i) pH changes or (ii) concentration changes. The pH is changed either by dosing base in the form of NaOH or $MgOH_2$ or by aeration of the liquors to degas the solution. The second method to initiate precipitation is to increase the concentration of one of the constituent ions, usually Mg, so that the driving force for precipitation in promoted.

This paper assesses the potential for recovering struvite at a number of sewage treatment works.

Table 3 Examples of P recovery at bench, pilot and full scale.

REFERENCE	SCALE	SOURCE	METHOD	P REMOVAL
Ohlinger *et al.*, 2000	bench FBR	digester liquor	Aeration + seed crystals	>80%
Kabdasli *et al.*, 2000	bench	landfill leachate	aeration	~90% removal of NH_3
Lind *et al.*, 2000	bench	human urine	Adsorption on to zeolite	65-80% removal of NH_3
Susckha et al.,2000	full scale	dewatering liquors	aeration	-
Battistoni *et al.*, 1998	pilot FBR	belt press liquors	aeration	80%
Battistoni *et al.*, 2000	full scale FBR	belt press liquors	aeration	-
Taruya *et al.*, 2000	full scale FBR	dewatering liquors	$MgCl_2/MgOH_2$ 1-2 Mg:P	>90%
Webb *et al.*, 1997	bench scale	piggery waste	$MgSO_4/NaOH$	-
Matsumiya *et al.*, 2000	pilot scale reactor	belt liquors	seawater	>70%

RESULTS AND DISCUSSION

Struvite Formation

Prediction of struvite formation

To assess the potential for struvite formation a computer model has been used. The struvite precipitation potential (SPP) for each sampling point was then calculated using a computer model called Struvite (Version 3.1). This model was developed for the Water Research Commission, South Africa (Loewenthal *et al.*, 1994).

A series of experiments were undertaken with real sludge liquors to test whether the computer software model could predict struvite formation. The masses of precipitate formed were calculated from the ICP data gained from the remaining magnesium and phosphorus concentrations in the real liquors (Figure 1). The formation of struvite based upon the data input into the computer model initially occurs at a pH of 7.1. In comparison struvite formation was not observed in both real and synthetic liquors until a pH of 7.5 is reached. The mass of precipitates formed appears to display a more linear relationship with respect to pH than the model predicts. The synthetic data generated from the previous jar tests regarding the mass of struvite formed displays a closer relationship to the data generated from the real liquors. The trendline plotted from the synthetic data had an R^2 value of 0.93. Trendlines plotted for the masses of struvite formed from real liquors based upon magnesium and phosphorus concentrations remaining in solution produced R^2 values of 0.75 and 0.82 respectively.

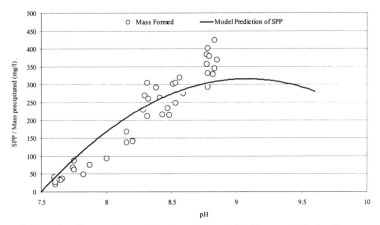

Figure 1   Comparison of the Struvite model with actual sludge liquors

The model whilst useful does tend to under predict the formation of struvite formation and this must be considered when looking at the potential for recovery. The potential for formation has been investigated at seven Severn Trent Water sites and in details at one Thames Water site.

Sites

Severn Trent Water
Seven sewage treatment works in the Severn Trent Water region have been investigated to identify the potential for struvite formation and hence the potential for recovery. A summary of the sites is given in Table 4. Data is presented as struvite formation potential (SPP). A positive SPP indicates there is a potential to form struvite (in mg L^{-1}), whereas a negative SPP denotes no potential for struvite to form. It is clear that all sites do not have the potential for formation but three of the sites reported here have the potential to form in excess of 100 mg of struvite per litre of sludge liquors.

Table 4 Struvite and calcite formation potential at all STW sites

SITE	STRUVITE FORMATION POTENTIAL (MG/L)	CALCIUM FORMATION POTENTIAL (mg/l)
Barton	72	-72
Coleshill	-126	-117
Mansfield	-142	-313
Milcote	-105	79
Oswestry	128	-120
Spernal	148	-54
Wanlip	32	-251

Slough STW : Thames Water

Slough STW treats a population equivalent (PE) of approximately 250,000, of which 114,000PE is industrial effluent.   The works consist of two treatment streams one consisting of conventional activated sludge and the other a Bardenpho BNR plant.

A mass balance of total phosphorus, TKN and magnesium through Slough STW is shown in Figure 2. When trying to predict the formation of struvite it is necessary to measure the levels of phosphorus, magnesium and ammonia through the works. The areas where the highest level of all three components occurs, should correspond to the area which has the most potential to form struvite.   The potential for struvite formation (SPP) is also included in the mass balance. The data used to obtain the SPP results is shown in reported in detail in Jaffer *et al.*, 2001.

The digested sludge, centrifuge liquor and centrifuge cake are identified by the model as streams which have the potential to form struvite. These streams all have high concentrations of soluble phosphorus.   The centrifuge cake has the highest SPP, as it has the highest magnesium concentration of any of the streams.   The digested sludge also has a high SPP which could due to the high concentration of phosphorus. The centrifuge liquor also has a positive SPP, though at 140 mg L^{-1}, it is not as high as the other two streams.   The magnesium concentration in the centrifuge liquors is more than 50% less than the magnesium concentration in the other two SPP positive streams.

The thickened SAS has the highest magnesium concentration of all the streams, but has a negative SPP. The pH of the thickened SAS is less than 7.0, so the potential for this stream to form struvite is low.   If the pH of the thickened SAS stream increased to 7.5, the SPP would increase from -21mgL^{-1} to 51mgL^{-1}.   The blended SAS also has a high soluble phosphorus and magnesium concentration but a low SPP. The pH of the blended SAS is relatively low at 7.0, but the pH would have to increase to 8.5 for the SPP to increase from -320 mg L^{-1} to 16 mg L^{-1}.

It is clear that a number of sewage treatment works has the potential to form struvite if the correct stream can be identified.   The next stage is to recover the product from the waste stream.

Recovery

There are a number of methods for recovering struvite scale as shown in Table 3. They all rely on either changing the pH or supersaturation level of a sludge liquor. Here are series of experiments were undertaken to look at possible recovery of struvite at bench scale.   The bench-scale reactor was constructed using a Water Research Council (WRC) porous pot apparatus (Bird & Tole Ltd, UK).   Two peristaltic pumps (Watson Marlow, UK) were used to feed centrate liquors and magnesium chloride into the reactor. The average influent flow rate was 20 ml/min (of which 63% was magnesium chloride) producing an HRT of 3 hours. Aeration was supplied at 220ml/min by an aquarium aeration unit, which consisted of a pump and two aeration stones.

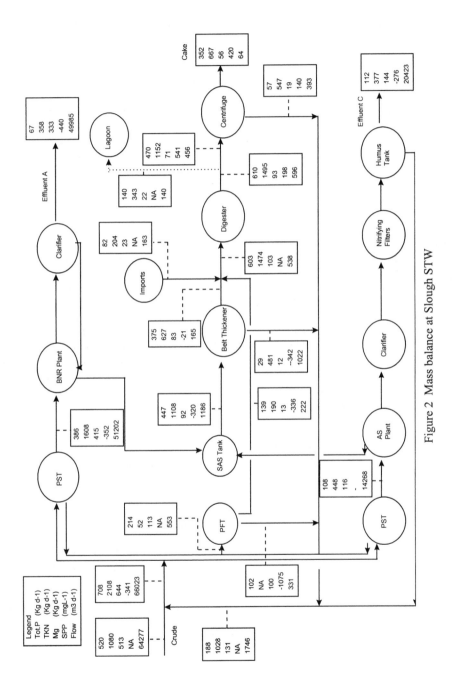

Figure 2 Mass balance at Slough STW

Centrifuge liquor was collected from Slough and stored at room temperature. The pH of the centrifuge liquor was raised to 9.0, using sodium hydroxide. A pH of 9.0 was found to be optimum for struvite precipitation by Siegrist *et al.*, (1992). Centrifuge liquor samples were analysed before and after pH adjustment.   Levels of soluble phosphorus, magnesium and calcium dropped after raising the pH to 9.0. Raising the pH must have caused the magnesium and calcium in the sample to react with phosphorus, forming precipitates. The ratio of calcium:magnesium in the centrifuge liquor was roughly 2 : 1. This decreased to a 1:1 ratio after the pH had been raised.   This reduction in the ratio indicates that more calcium is reacting with the phosphorus in the sample than magnesium.   The magnesium levels in the centrifuge liquor samples were too low to remove the remaining phosphorus as struvite. The pilot plant was therefore dosed with magnesium chloride ($MgCl_2$) to provide a source of magnesium ions and maximise struvite production.

After 24 hours operation, using centrifuge liquors and a dose of 252 mg L^{-1} of $MgCl_2$, crystals were seen on the surface of the porous pot. The crystals produced underwent X-Ray Diffraction (XRD) and were confirmed to be struvite.

Once it was established that struvite could be formed from the centrifuge liquors at Slough STW, the magnesium dose to the pilot plant was altered to determine an optimum dosing regime.   The removal of soluble phosphorus and ammonia increased with increased magnesium dose, up to 97% at a dose of 3.46 mM, Figure 3.   The relationship between magnesium dose and phosphorus removal indicates that at high dosages of magnesium, the phosphorus is probably removed as struvite. If struvite production is occurring, phosphorus removal and magnesium usage will be similar, this trend can be seen at higher doses of magnesium. At magnesium doses below 3.4 mM L^{-1}, phosphorus is still removed, but not solely as struvite. The molar removal of ammonia exceeds the molar removals of phosphorus and the molar usage of magnesium and was greater than the requirement for struvite. The surplus ammonium was probably being removed from the reactor by air stripping.

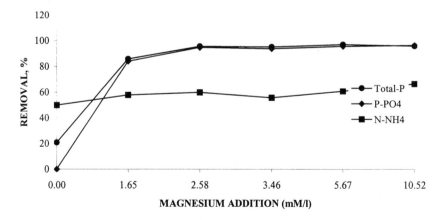

Figure 3 Percentage removal of phosphorus and ammonia with increasing magnesium dose

It was found that 95% of the total phosphorus could be removed from the centrifuge supernatant as struvite, by the addition of at least a 1.05:1 molar ratio of magnesium to phosphorus i.e. a magnesium dose of about 83 mg L^{-1}. The ratio of 1.05:1 was also found by Fujimoto et al., (1991) whereas Siegrist et al., (1992) found a higher ratio of 1.3:1 was required to guarantee phosphorus removal as struvite. The lower ratio necessary for struvite precipitation during this series of experiments was probably due to the lack of any competing reactions. When the pH of the centrifuge liquor was raised to 9.0 in the storage containers, 77% of the calcium was removed, before entering the reactor. On average 6 mg L^{-1} of calcium entered the reactor. At a dosing regime of 83 mg L^{-1} this equates to a 0.04:1 molar ratio of calcium : magnesium. Hwang and Choi (1998) found that for effective struvite formation, the ratio of calcium to magnesium should be less than 1. Musvoto et al., (2000) found that the ratio of magnesium : calcium should be greater than 0.6. In this case, the ratio of magnesium : calcium is 23:1. Before the addition of sodium hydroxide to raise the pH, the molar ratio of calcium : magnesium was 1.2:1. A soluble phosphorus removal of 7% was observed on raising the pH , before the centrifuge liquor was fed into the reactor. Most of this phosphorus was probably removed as calcium phosphates.

CONCLUSIONS

- Many STW in the UK have the potential to form struvite at reasonable concentrations (>100 mg/L).
- Digester sludge liquors typically have the highest potential to form struvite although this is usually limited by the magnesium concentration in the liquor.
- Recovery methods exist and are usually based on chemical addition.

REFERENCES

1. Battistoni, P., Pavan, P., Cecchi, F., MataAlvarez, J. (1998) Phosphate Removal in Real Anaerobic Supernatatnts:Modelling and performance of a fluidised bed reactor. *Water Sci. Technol.* 38 (1) 275-283.

2. Battistoni P., Pavan P., Prisciandaro M., and Cecchi F. Struvite crystallization: a feasible and reliable way to fix phosphorus in anaerobic supernatants. *Wat. Res.* 34 (11), 3033-3041. 2000.

3. Borgerding, J. (1972) Phosphate deposits in digestion systems. *J. Water Pollut. Control Fed.* 44 (5) 813-819.

4. Fujimoto, N., Mizuochi, T., Togami, Y. (1991) Phosphorus fixation in the sludge treatment system of a biological phosphorus removal process. *Water Sci. Technol.* 23 (4-6) 635-640.

5. Harremoes, P. (1998) The challenge of managing water and material balances in relation to eutrophication . *Water Sci. Technol.* 37 (3) 9-17.

6. Hwang, H. J. and Choi, E. (1998) Nutrient control with other sludges in anaerobic digestion of BPR sludge. *Water Sci. Technol.* 38 (1) 295-302.

7. Jaffer Y, Clark T A, Pearce P and Parsons S A. (2001). Assessing the potential of full scale phosporus removal by struvite renoval. *Wat. Res.* submitted.

8. Kabdasli, I., Gurel, M., and Tunay, O. (2000) Characterization and treatment of textile printing wastewaters. *Environ. Technol.* 21 (10) 1147-1155. 2000.

9. Lind, B.B., Ban, Z., and Byden, S. (2000) Nutrient recovery from human urine by struvite crystallization with ammonia adsorption on zeolite and wollastonite. *Bioresource Technol.* 73 (2) 169-174.

10. Loewenthal, R.E., Kornmuller, U.R.C., Van Heerden, E.P. (1994) Modelling struvite precipitation in anaerobic treatment systems. *Proceedings of the 7th annual international symposium on anaerobic digestion* 107-116.

11. Matsumiya, Y., Yamasita, T., and Nawamura, Y. (2000) Phosphorus removal from sidestreams by crystallisation of magnesium-ammonium-phosphate using seawater. *Water Environ. Management* 14 (4) 291-296.

12. Musvoto E.V., Wentzel M.C., Loewenthal R.E., and Ekama G.A. (2000) Integrated chemical–physical processes modelling–I. Development of a kinetic-based model for mixed weak acid/base systems. *Wat. Res.* 34 (6), 1857-1867.

13. Ohlinger K.N., Young T.M., and Schroeder E.D. (2000) Postdigestion struvite precipitation using a fluidized bed reactor. *J. Environ. Engineer.* 126 (4) 361-368.

14. Rawn, A.M., A.Perry Banta., Pomeroy, R. (1939) Multiple stage sewage digestion. *T. ASCE.* 105, 93-132.

15. Siegrist, H., Gajcy, D., Sulzer, S., Roeleveld, P., Oschwald, R., Frischknecht, H., Pfund, D., Morgeli, B., and Hugerbuhler, E., (1992) Nitrogen elimination from digester supernatant with magnesium ammonium phosphate. *Proceedings of the 5th Gothenburg symposium*, September 28th - 30th. Springer-Verlag, Berlin.

16. Suzuki, Y., Takahashi M., Haesslein M., and Seyfried, C. F. (1999) Development of simulation model for a combined activated-sludge and biofilm process to remove nitrogen and phosphorus. *Water Environ. Res.* 71 (4) 388-397.

17. Taruya, T., Ueno, Y., and Fujii, M., (2000) Development of phosphorus resource recycling process from sewage. IWA World Congress, Paris.

18. Webb, K.M., Ho, G.E. (1992) Struvite ($MgNH_4PO_4.6H_2 O$) solubility and its application to a piggery effluent problem. *Water Sci. Technol.* 26, 9-11, 2229-2232.

RECYCLING OF SEWAGE SLUDGE TO LAND: LEGISLATIVE, SCIENTIFIC AND PRACTICAL CONSIDERATIONS

W Towers　　　**P Horne**

E Paterson　　　**M Coull**

Macaulay Land Use Research Institute

United Kingdom

ABSTRACT. Sludge recycling to land requires that a number of environmental, legislative, agricultural, economic and social issues be considered. This paper outlines the use made of a number of spatial and aspatial digital datasets to help address some of these issues. In particular, they are of value in assessing the potential impact of regulatory changes concerning permitted heavy metal concentrations in soils. They have also been used to assess the suitability of land for sludge recycling and, when integrated with information on sludge quantities and sources, help determine whether a recycling strategy is sustainable. Sludge recycling should also be compatible with existing farming practice, in particular livestock farming and with specific cropping rotations; examples are presented to illustrate their potential impact.

Keywords: Recycling, Legislation, Heavy metals, Land suitability, Agriculture, Sustainability

Mr Willie Towers, is a research scientist within the Soil Quality and Protection Programme at the Macaulay Land Use Research Institute (MLURI). One of his main interests is the use and interpretation of environmental and related data in addressing issues of environmental concern, including the recycling of sewage sludge to land. This work, initially funded by central government, led to a significant amount of technology transfer to the water industry.

Ms Paula Horne, is a research assistant at MLURI, specialising in Geographic Information Systems technology, and provides computing support. She is responsible for devising and applying some of the scenario-generation techniques described in the paper.

Mr Ed Paterson, is programme manager for the Soil Quality and Protection Programme at MLURI. His research interests include the development of process-based indicators of soil quality. He was the lead MLURI contact in the SERAD funded 'Waste to Land' Project and has also been involved in a project assessing the potential of dried sludge granules as a forest fertiliser.

Mr Malcolm Coull, is a research assistant at MLURI. He currently provides computing and technical support within the Soil Quality and Protection Programme at MLURI, but was a key member in the 'Waste to Land' Project and has been involved in the National sewage sludge network experiment from its outset in 1994 until the present day.

INTRODUCTION

Two of the requirements of the EC Urban Waste Water Treatment (UWWT) Directive [1] - the ban on sea disposal from the end of 1998 and the increased volumes of sludge which will arise from the provision of enhanced waste water treatment - will have a profound effect on the future pattern of sewage sludge disposal/utilization throughout Scotland. Previously the main disposal option, accounting for approximately 75% of the total, was the convenient sea disposal route.

In their Waste Strategy, the Scottish Environmental Protection Agency [2] state that, based on information provided by the three Scottish Water Authorities, 52% of the projected sludge volumes (92300 tds by the year 2006) are likely to be recycled to agriculture land. This represents a four fold increase from the current 24000 tds/annum, but it is highly likely that the land area required will increase substantially beyond than this because of increasingly stringent limits for permissible sludge application rates.

Against this background, it is important that this increased recycling activity proceeds in a sustainable manner and that it does not compromise soil quality and function or water and air quality. It must also be compatible with the different farming systems throughout Scotland and be economically and socially acceptable. This paper demonstrates the use made of a number of digital environmental datasets, held within a Geographic Information System (GIS) and a relational database management system (RDBMS) in addressing a number of these issues and describes how these analyses provide a basis for assessing the security and sustainability of sludge recycling strategies.

DATA SOURCES

National Soils Inventory

The Scottish Soils Database [3] is held in a relational database with a 'flagged' subset termed the National Soil Inventory, taken on a 5km grid across Scotland. These are often called the National Inventory Point (NIP) dataset. It contains soil and site descriptions at all grid points (n = 2880) and standard soil chemical and physical analysis at the 10km points (n=720). Using archived samples from the NIP dataset, a geochemical dataset has been assembled using methods similar to those employed by McGrath and Loveland [4]. With the exception of mercury, all the metals which feature in the EC and UK sludge regulations are in this dataset.

The 1:250 000 Scale National Soil Map

The 1:250 000 scale national soil map comprises 580 soil map units, differentiated on geological (soil association), pedological (component soils) and physiographic criteria (landforms). Soils are classified into different 'types' on the nature and sequence of soil horizons within soil profiles. The system of soil classification used in Scotland [5] is typological rather than definitional in nature in that it relies on the recognition of central concepts of soil classes and comparison of soil profiles with them. The criteria for differentiating the soil types in the Scottish classification and the terms used in soil description can be found in the Handbook which accompanies the map series [5].

Land cover map (1:25,000 scale)

The Land Cover of Scotland 1988 (LCS88) database [6] is a full census of land cover captured by air photo interpretation and validated by field checking. It comprises 126 single categories and well over 1000 mosaics where land cover consists of two intermingled categories. It adds additional information to the soils map; in particular it identifies soils that have been cultivated and as a consequence radically altered from their original state.

Farm Census data (SERAD)

This dataset holds data on agricultural activity within every parish in Scotland and gives information on areas of arable crops, grassland and rough grazing areas as well as the types and numbers of livestock. Thus, it is complementary to the LCS88 dataset in that it adds detail on specific crop types as well as providing animal numbers from which estimates of waste volumes can be generated. Not all data are released because of data protection issues, and this is a particular weakness with crops on which waste utilisation is not advised and/or not allowed and for intensive animal enterprises.

THE LEGISLATIVE FRAMEWORK

Current Situation

Significant benefits may be derived from wastes through recycling of major nutrients, such as phosphorus and nitrogen, as well as enhancing the quality of mineral soils by increasing their organic matter content. However, these benefits must be balanced against potential adverse environmental impacts such as transmission of pathogens, the entry of potentially toxic elements and organic contaminants to the soil environment and the risk of water pollution. For these reasons, sludge utilization on land is a highly regulated activity, largely concerned with controlling the inputs of the potentially toxic elements (PTEs) contained in sludge to soil [7, 8]. Soils to which sludge is applied must meet certain pH and soil PTE concentration criteria and there are also statutory maximum permitted application rates.

In order to minimise the risk to health of humans, animals and plants, sludge application is precluded on certain crops, specifically growing fruit and vegetable crops. To help alleviate consumer concern over sludge recycling on agricultural land, the industry has reached a voluntary agreement with food manufacturers and retailers – the 'ADAS matrix' – which sets out which level of sludge treatment is acceptable for different crops [9]. This consultative process has also led to the use of untreated sludge no longer being acceptable for recycling.

Restrictions on sludge application rates based on nutrient content of the sludge and plant needs are less rigorous, but recycling must ensure that 'there is no conflict with good agricultural practice' [8]. A number of European countries already have annual maximum permitted application rates of phosphorus and/or nitrogen from sewage sludge. If pressure is increased in order to ensure phosphorus application rates match crop needs, it is likely that for most sludges, phosphorus would be the rate determining element [10].

Impact of Potential Legislative Changes

Impact of proposed soil metal levels

There are proposals from the EU to revise radically the maximum recommended levels of heavy metals in sludge-amended soils from the current limits [11]. These proposals are summarised in Table 1. They are complemented by similar large reductions in permitted metal levels in sludge, representing considerable shifts in policy and reflect the Commission's aim to reduce metal inputs at source.

Table 1 Proposed limit values for metals in sludge-amended soils (mg/kg dry matter)

METAL	EC DIRECTIVE (current limits)[1]	UK CURRENT LIMITS[2]	PROPOSED LIMITS		
			Soil pH 5-6	Soil pH 6-7	Soil pH 7-8
Zinc	150-300	200	60	150	200
Nickel	30-75	50-75	15	50	70
Copper	50-140	80-135	20	50	100
Lead	50-300	300	70	70	100
Cadmium	1-3	3	0.5	1	1.5

[1] Mandatory and recommended levels
[2] For soils with pH values between pH 5 and pH 7

If the proposed limits in Table 1 were invoked, the impact on sludge recycling in Scotland would be considerable. Previous work at the Institute has developed a rule-based approach to determine the suitability of land for sludge application where suitable land is identified using a combination of soil type, including soil pH and metal concentration, topography and land cover. When this rule-base is applied to the National Soil Inventory, 19.8% of the land area of Scotland was identified as suitable for sludge application [12].

Assuming that the NIP samples are representative of the agricultural soils across Scotland, less than half of the land which meets the existing UK regulations would meet the new proposed levels. Only 70 of the original 150 NIPS have existing metal levels below the proposed thresholds. This reduction of 53% approximates to 10 % of the land area of Scotland. The location of the points which meet the old and new criteria are shown in Figure 1.

This reduction is not uniform across Scotland. The Scottish water industry is structured into three publicly funded water authorities, the North (NOSWA), the East (EOSWA) and West (WOSWA) of Scotland Water Authorities. The NOSWA area would incur a reduction of 45%, compared to a 64 % reduction in the WOSWA area. In the EOSWA area, the reduction is close to the Scottish average. These figures are comparable to those areas in England and Wales where the greatest impacts are predicted (south-west England and Wales) [13]. However, the overall potential impact is considered to be greater in Scotland largely through the influence of the lower soil pH levels in Scottish soils. The proposed reduction in the nickel limit value for soils in the pH range 5-6 (15 mg/kg), has the biggest impact. Of the 80 sites that become unsuitable (Figure 1), 70 have a nickel concentration above the proposed new limit.

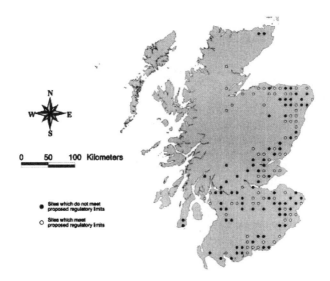

Figure 1 Impact of proposed soil metal limits

Rate of heavy metal addition to soil

Within the 1986 EC Directive [7] and the current UK regulations [8], there are maximum permissible average annual and 10 year additions of heavy metals to soil. Large reductions to these are proposed (Table 2). For example, there are ten fold reductions for nickel and lead and a fifteen fold reduction for cadmium. These reductions would have a considerable impact on the maximum permitted sludge application rate (Table 2). In the example shown, copper is the rate-limiting metal with an average annual application rate of 1.7 tds/ha/annum.

Table 2 Impact of current and proposed rates of permitted
PTE addition to soil on sludge application rates

METAL	MEAN METAL CONC IN SLUDGE (mg/kg ds)[11]	MAXIMUM PERMISSIBLE AVERAGE ANNUAL ADDITION OF PTE (kg/ha)		MAXIMUM PERMISSIBLE 10 YEAR ADDITION OF PTE (kg/ha)		MAXIMUM AMOUNT OF SLUDGE WHICH COULD BE APPLIED OVER TEN YEARS (tds)	
		current	proposed	current	proposed	current	proposed
Zinc	922	15	3	150	30	163	33
Nickel	65	3	0.3	30	3	462	46
Copper	574	7.5	1	75	10	131	17
Lead	201	15	1.5	150	15	746	74
Cadmium	5	0.15	0.01	1.5	0.1	300	20

It should be noted that the PTE sludge concentrations for zinc, copper and nickel in Table 2 are all below the proposed limit values for these metals in sludge although the 'long-term' target value for lead (200 mg/kg dry matter) is similar to mean existing levels in sludge. However the proposed long – term target for cadmium (2 mg/kg) is considerably below current concentrations in sludge (Table 2).

The potential impact of these proposals are also significant; if permitted sludge application rates are reduced, then more land will be required for the same volume of sludge. Based on information provided by the three Scottish Water Authorities [14], 52% of the projected sludge volumes (92300 tds by the year 2006) are likely to be recycled to land. Based on an application rate of 1.7 tds/ha/annum (the maximum rate allowed for copper, Table 2), a total land area of 543 square kilometres would be required annually. This compares to the recent land requirement of 40 square kilometres at an average application rate of 6 tds/ha [14]. This represents a 13 fold increase in the land area required annually for sludge recycling.

LAND SUITABILITY FOR SLUDGE RECYCLING

The underpinning rationale for a sludge recycling strategy is that it must be environmentally sustainable and operationally secure. To achieve this, it is important that an assessment of the amount of 'suitable' land is made, how much of the suitable land would be required on an annual basis and the compatibility of the agricultural land use with sludge recycling.

Land Suitability Assessment

Using a methodology based on land evaluation procedures and a number of decision rules with thresholds, the soils and land cover data were screened and areas of land considered suitable for sludge recycling were identified. The criteria used in the classification are soil type, slope, rockiness and land cover. These factors, either singly or in combination, influence the behaviour of sludge or components of sludge when applied to land, the accessibility of land for sludge application and the appropriateness of sludge application based on land use.

The classification has been applied to these national datasets and the amount and location of suitable land has been identified. The national picture has been broken down into the three Scottish Water Authorities, and also into the previous administrative structure which is embedded within it (Table 3). These national and regional area estimates become more relevant when they are related to the projected volumes of sludge which are to be produced within each area. Although many of the boundaries have less relevance since the establishment of the Water Authorities, they do serve to indicate internal disparities in relation to where the sludge is produced and where it can be recycled.

The main point illustrated Table 3 is the relative similarity between areas of suitable land (column 2) compared to the huge difference in the sludge:land ratios in column 4; the smaller this ratio, the more favourable is the sludge:land balance. The presence and impact of Glasgow (Strathclyde) and Edinburgh (Lothian) are obvious in these figures. The table also illustrates the mis-match between where almost half of the suitable land is (North of Scotland) and where approximately half of the sludge is produced (West of Scotland).

Table 3 Relationship between suitable land and sewage sludge production in Scotland

WATER AUTHORITY AREA (including *Former Regional Authorities*)	AREA OF SUITABLE LAND (km^2)	PROJECTED SLUDGE VOLUMES (tds) in 2010	RATIO of tds: km^2 (rounded)
North of Scotland	7731	39 600	5:1
Highland	*1331*	*4000*	*3:1*
Grampian	*4113*	*25 600*	*6:1*
Tayside	*2287*	*10 000*	*4:1*
East of Scotland	4210	43 800	10:1
Central	*623*	*5 500*	*9:1*
Fife	*920*	*9 000*	*10:1*
Lothian	*929*	*27 000*	*29:1*
Borders	*1738*	*2 300*	*1:1*
West of Scotland	4228	100 000	24:1
Strathclyde	*2641*	*95 000*	*36:1*
Dumfries &Galloway	*1587*	*5 000*	*3:1*
TOTAL	16169	183 400	12:1

Public Perception

GIS has also allowed us to investigate the potential 'bad neighbour' impact of sludge recycling, because of smell, unsightlyness or any other negative perception, in effect a social constraint. This has been recognised as an important issues [14]. If the 500 metres of land which is adjacent to built-up areas is excluded from recycling, the total suitable area in Strathclyde Region reduces by about one-third to 1857 square kilometres.

Impact of Transport Constraints

Some of the suitable land in Strathclyde (2641 km^2) lies at some distance (up to 100 km) from the sludge sources (dominated by the city of Glasgow) and it would be uneconomic to transport bulky liquid or cake sludge such distances. The analysis was taken further by generating a 30 km radius from Glasgow city centre (a surrogate for the sludge source) and excluding all suitable land outside this area. This has a dramatic effect on the size of the available land bank reducing it to 977 square kilometres, a reduction of almost two-thirds and increasing the sludge:land ratio to 97:1.

This approach of focusing on land in the near vicinity of sludge treatment works had a resonance with the West of Scotland Water Authority who commissioned work to estimate the suitable land within a 30 km 'crow-fly' distances from the Shieldhall and Daldowie sludge treatment centres, in Glasgow (Figure 2). The projected annual sludge production is 30000 tds and 18000 tds respectively. Suitable land was delineated using the methodology described, but account had to be made of the 'competition' for land between the two treatment works. This was done by apportioning the land within 30 km of both centres according to the relative volumes of sludge which each will produce i.e. approximately 3:2.

Table 5 demonstrates that both sludge treatment centres have unfavourable sludge:land ratios, whether or not the land outside the WOSWA area is included. Depending on which option is chosen, the annual percentage land requirement for Shieldhall is between 7.7 and 22.3% and for Daldowie between 5.0 and 16.7%. These land requirements, exceed a recent estimate (1% of agricultural land) for the national requirement of land for sludge recycling [15]. One of the companies, Severn Trent Water, which is in the forefront of sludge recycling to land in England applies sludge to about 1% of the land area available annually [16].

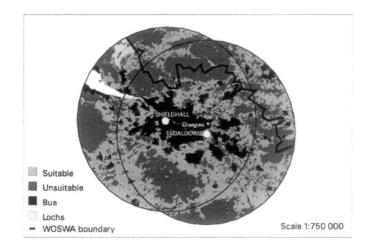

Figure 2 Assessment of land suitability for sludge recycling around Glasgow

Table 5 Assessment of sludge recycling around Glasgow

TREATMENT CENTRE	SUITABLE AREA[1,2] (square km)	SLUDGE:LAND RATIO	ANNUAL LAND REQUIREMENT (KM^2) AT APPLICATION RATE/HECTARE/ANNUM	
			2tds	5tds
Shieldhall	782[1], 672[2]	38:1[1], 45:1[2]	150	60
Daldowie	725[1], 538[2]	25:1[1], 33:1[2]	90	36

[1] includes suitable land outwith WOSWA area.
[2] suitable land within WOSWA area

Using this information along with other considerations including farmer and supermarket perception of sewage sludge reuse on land and the requirement of PFI schemes for a 25 year secure outlet, has led to a considerable change from the previous policy inherited from the former Strathclyde Region [17]. Recycling to land remains the policy in outlying and less densely populated areas of the WOSWA area, with the sludge from the Glasgow area being thermally dried and being used as co-fuel for combustion within a power station operated by Scottish Power [18].

Agricultural Constraints

Sludge recycling must be compatible with good agricultural practice and the agricultural systems carried out in different areas. The main constraints are land growing crops that are excluded from sludge use, livestock farming and the organic wastes which it generates and cropping rotations. These constraints differ across Scotland, but Fife provides an appropriate area to demonstrate these constraints [19]. The policy in Fife is to build sludge drying facilities at Dunfermline and Levenmouth (Figure 3), and offer the thermally dried product for recycling to agricultural land.

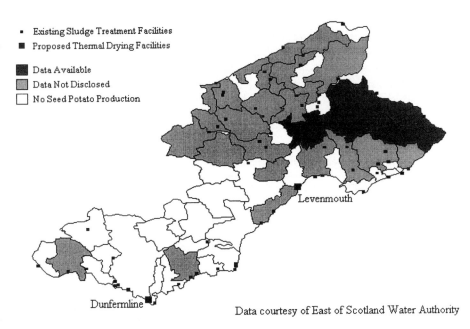

Figure 3 Sewage Treatment works and Seed Potato Production In Fife

Cropping constraints

If we assume a sludge P_2O_5 concentration of 35 kg P_2O_5 per tds, an application rate of 70 kg P_2O_5/ha/annum and therefore an application rate of 2tds/ha/annum, 4,500 hectares would be required annually. This represents almost 5% of the suitable area in Fife (Table 1). If a precautionary stance is adopted with regard to crops for human consumption, then approximately 22,000 hectares - 19,411 hectares of potatoes, including an allowance for rotations, 2,664 hectares of vegetables and 163 hectares of soft fruit - would be excluded. It should be noted that Hickman *et al* [9] suggest that thermally dried sludge could be used on these crops, but this assertion would need to be subject to rigorous testing.

One crop on which the use of sludge products is explicitly prohibited [8] is seed potatoes. This is concentrated in the northern part of Fife (Figure 3). Thus, it is likely that there will be greater difficulties finding suitable outlets for the thermally dried sludge product from Levenmouth than that from Dunfermline (Figure 3). Based on the limited information available, it is estimated that approximately half of the total area under potatoes in Fife (9-10 000 hectares, approximately 10% of the total land bank) would be excluded by this legislation.

The main windows for application of sludge to crops in Fife, and indeed on crops throughout Scotland, are February to April, and August to October. Additional limited sludge outlets will be available in May to July on grassland. However, storage will be required from November to January, and some storage in May to July in readiness for application during August to October. At present grazing is prohibited on grassland for three weeks after sludge application although this may be increased when the results of current research are available.

Estimate of allowance of nutrient contribution from animal wastes

It is important that nutrients from all sources are integrated and there is increasing evidence that phosphorus is the rate determining nutrient for sludge and other manures and fertilisers [10, A Sinclair, pers comm] and this has been acknowledged by Hickman *et al* [9]; permitted applications levels of N can lead to over-application of P. At the regional scale, estimates of the amount of land required for the sustainable utilisation of farm wastes are indicated on Table 6.

Table 6 Estimates of land requirements for animal waste utilization in Fife

LIVESTOCK TYPE	NO OF ANIMALS [21]	EST P_2O_5 PRODUCED (kg) [22]	AREA REQUIRED (ha)[1]
Dairy cows	9,761	204,981	2,928
Beef cows and bulls	18,817	301,072	4,301
1-2 yr beef cattle	14,661	146,610	2,094
Sows/gilts/boars	3,827	38,720	546
Fattening pigs	17,291	125,447	1,792
Fowls	1,986,181	1,072,523	15,322
Broilers	781,074	406,610	5,802
TOTAL		**2,295,063**	**32,785**

[1]Application rate of 70 kg P_2O_5 /ha/annum

The application rate is based on a high moderate (50-75 mg/l) P-status soil. The estimated amount of P produced (Table 6) represents almost 40% of Fife's annual requirement, based on the total area of crops and grass in the area. Even with adjustments for low-P status soils, i.e. using higher application rates, animal wastes would still contribute a significant proportion of the P requirements of the area. However this assumes that all the waste is used on agricultural land in Fife, and therefore represents a 'worst case' scenario for sludge recycling.

CONCLUSIONS

Sludge recycling to land requires a high degree of strategic planning from the outset, as there are a number of legislative, environmental, agricultural, economic and social factors to consider. These factors often interact with each other. The interpretation of appropriate data held within a Geographic Information System has proved to be a powerful tool for testing different scenarios and ultimately assessing the security and sustainability of sludge recycling strategies. More detailed work and analysis are required to make such a policy operationally secure.

ACKNOWLEDGEMENTS

This work was funded by the Scottish Executive Rural Affairs Department and the West of Scotland Water Authority

REFERENCES

1. COUNCIL OF EUROPEAN COMMUNITIES. Directive concerning urban waste water treatment. Official Journal L135/40, 21 May 1991. CEC, Brussels.

2. SCOTTISH ENVIRONMENT PROTECTION AGENCY National Waste Strategy, Scottish Environment Protection Agency, Stirling, 1999

3. LANGAN, S.J., PATERSON, E. AND TAYLOR, A.G. The Scottish Soil Resource: Its current status and future priorities for management In: Soil, Sustainability and the Natural Heritage (A. G. Taylor, J. E. Gordon and M. B. Usher eds), HMSO, Edinburgh, 1996, 69-91

4. MCGRATH, S.P. AND LOVELAND, P.J. The Soil Geochemical Atlas of England and Wales, Blackie Academic, Glasgow, 1992.

5. MACAULAY INSTITUTE FOR SOIL RESEARCH. Organization and methods of the 1:250 000 soil survey of Scotland. The Macaulay Institute for Soil Research, Aberdeen, 1984.

6. MACAULAY LAND USE RESEARCH INSTITUTE. The Land Cover of Scotland 1988. The Macaulay Land Use Research Institute, Aberdeen, 1993

7.   COUNCIL OF EUROPEAN COMMUNITIES Directive on the protection of the environment and in particular of the soil when sewage sludge is used in agriculture (86/278/EEC). Official Journal L181/6, 4 July 1986.

8.   DEPARTMENT OF THE ENVIRONMENT. Code of Practice For Agricultural Use of Sewage Sludge. HMSO, 1996.

9.   HICKMAN G A W, CHAMBERS, B J AND PIERREPONT P J (in press) Addressing customer concerns - development of the ADAS matrix for the sustainable application of sewage sludge to agricultural land. In: Proceedings of Agriculture and Waste: Management for a Sustainable Future. Edinburgh 1999

10. MINISTRY OF AGRICULTURE, FISHERIES AND FOOD/DEPARTMENT OF THE ENVIRONMENT (1993) Review of the Rules for Sewage Sludge Application to Agricultural Land: Soil Fertility Aspects of Sewage Sludge Use in Agriculture. MAFF Publications 1993.

11. ENVIRONMENTAL DATA SERVICES New EC sludge proposals. ENDS Report, 2000, 301, 46

12. TOWERS, W.   Towards a Strategic Approach to Sewage Sludge Utilization on Agricultural Land in Scotland. Journal of Environmental Planning and Management, 1994, 37, (4), 447-460

13. ENVIRONMENTAL DATA SERVICES. DETR slates EC sludge proposals ENDS Report, 2000, 303, 50

14. SCOTTISH ENVIRONMENTAL PROTECTION AGENCY Strategic Review of OrganicWaste on Land Scottish Environmental Protection Agency, Stirling, 1998

15. ROYAL COMMISSION ON ENVIRONMENTAL POLLUTION. Nineteenth Report: Sustainable Use of Soil. HMSO:London, 1996.

16. ENVIRONMENTAL DATA SERVICES Scottish study cautions councils over sludge strategies. ENDS Report 1995 No. 245

17. STRATHCLYDE REGIONAL COUNCIL Sewage Sludge Disposal Regional Strategy Study (1993)

18. WEST OF SCOTLAND WATER AUTHORITY Impact of the Waste Water Treatment Legislation, 2000.

19. TOWERS W, COULL M C, PATERSON E, STEPHEN N H, WATSON C A, DUNN S, AITKEN M A, LANGAN S J, SWAFFIELD R, VINTEN A AND WATT D. Waste to Land – Development of a Spatially Based Decision Support Tool. In: Proceedings of Agriculture and Waste: Management for a Sustainable Future. Edinburgh 1999

20. EAST OF SCOTLAND WATER AUTHORITY A Waste Water Sludge Strategy for East of Scotland Water, 1997.

21.   SCOTTISH OFFICE AGRICULTURE AND FISHERIES DEPARTMENT Economic Report on Scottish Agriculture. HMSO, Edinburgh, 1995

22.   MINISTRY   OF   AGRICULTURE,   FISHERIES   AND   FOOD   Fertiliser recommendations for agricultural and horticultural crops (RB209), pp8-11, HMSO, 1994

NITROGEN NUTRITION OF RYE GRASS UNDER LOW APPLICATION RATES OF SEWAGE SLUDGE

M Smith

M Tibbett

Bournemouth University

United Kingdom

ABSTRACT. Sewage sludge is an excellent soil conditioner and a renewable source of N, P and micronutrients. As part of a wider study to determine the nutrient dynamics of soils amended with different types of sludge from the same treatment stream at low amendment rates, an initial study focused on 'baseline' N fertiliser effects of different sludge types. In particular the N status of the amended soils and N uptake and yield of the crop was determined. The study showed that even at application rates as low as 4 tonnes per hectare of sewage sludge application can have a significant benefit and that this can last for beyond a single growing season.

Keywords: Biosolids, Immobilisation, Mineralisation, Nitrate, Nitrogen, Sewage sludge.

Mr M Smith, is a Research Student at Bournemouth University. He has been associated with the water industry for 18 years prior to commencing his research both in the scientific and IT disciplines, writing process control systems for water treatment plants.

Dr M Tibbett, is a Senior Lecturer in Soil Science at Bournemouth University. He has experience of heavy metal pollution in soils both inside and outside the water industry. Other research interests include soil microbiology, especially mycorrhizal symbiosis and plant nutrition.

INTRODUCTION

Sewage sludge is an excellent soil conditioner and a renewable source of N, P and micronutrients [1,2]. The beneficial effects of the application of sewage sludge to agricultural land include the ease and cost of disposal, and savings in fertiliser for the farmer. Conventionally, water utilities have supplied farmers with large quantities of sludge as an economic disposal option and in order to guarantee fertiliser benefit. Stricter constraints on sewage sludge utilisation, designed to protect watercourses from elevated nitrate levels and crops and soils from the deleterious effects of heavy metals require a change in traditional working practice, and hence lower application rates. At these rates heavy metals are unlikely to accrue to levels approaching legislative controls [3] but NO_3^- accumulation may be problematic.

The potential risks of nitrate-N (NO_3^-) leaching is addressed by the *European Council Directive Concerning the Protection of Waters Against Pollution Caused by Nitrates from Agricultural Sources* [4] which established mandatory controls on the timing and rate of sludge application in Nitrate Vulnerable Zones. These were implemented in England and Wales [5] and Scotland [6] by The Protection of Water Against Nitrate Pollution Regulations 1996.

N is present in sludge as both organic N and NH_4^+-N, the amounts depending on the method of sewage and sludge treatment [7,8]. N in liquid raw sludge is largely in organic form with only 5-10% being NH_4^+. Liquid digested sludge has a much higher proportion of NH_4^+ as much of the readily degradable organic matter will have been mineralised during anaerobic digestion. Cake sludges loose a large part of their inorganic N as soluble nutrients during the drying process. Therefore, the type of sludge, and hence the form in which the N is present in the soil, will effect the N-mineralisation dynamics of the sludge amended soil [9]. This is important for both crop nutrition and the potential for NO_3^- leaching.

Much work has been undertaken to determine the nutrient benefits of sewage sludge, a summary of which is beyond the scope of this communication. In particular, Smith *et al.* [9] categorised different types of sludge according to whether they showed high NO_3^- production potential (liquid digested and lagooned liquid undigested sludges), intermediate to low accumulation potential (dewatered digested, lagoon matured digested and liquid undigested sludge), initial immobilisation of native soil N followed by limited NO_3^- production (dewatered undigested sludge) or high resistance to mineralisation and NO_3^- production (air dried digested sludge). The rate and extent of NO_3^- production in amended soils was found to be dependant on sludge type, soil temperature and time from sludge amendment.

As part of a wider study to determine the nutrient dynamics of soils amended with different types of sludge from the same treatment stream at low amendment rates, an initial study focused on 'baseline' N fertiliser effects of different sludge types. In particular the N status of the amended soils and N uptake and yield of the grass crop was determined.

METHOD

A sandy loam soil of the Fyfield series from a previously unamended site was placed in 50 l tubs, allowed to equilibrate in a greenhouse over winter period and hydrated to approximately field capacity with distilled water.

Sewage sludge was obtained from three points in the treatment stream of a modern municipal sewage works - (i) Anaerobically digested and thickened liquid sludge (which had been lagooned for *ca.* 30 days), taken from a point immediatly prior to being applied to land (T series sludge), (ii) Lagoon settled liquid sludge (primary settled and surplus returned activated sludge mixture which has been lagoon settled for *ca.* 14 days) taken from the feedstock to the digester (R series sludge), (iii) Mechanically thickened/dried sludge cake (C series sludge).

The sludge was applied to the tubs at rates equivalent to 4, 8, and 16 tonnes per hectare (tds ha $^{-1}$) and incorporated into the upper 15 cm of the soil profile. These application rates were chosen to reflect current agricultural practice [2]. A further treatment (zero) received no sludge as a control. All 10 treatments were replicated 12 times and were randomised in a complete block design. The soil in the tubs was allowed to re-equilibrate for a further 8 days, prior to being sewn with perennial rye grass (*Lolium Perenne* cv Melle) at a rate equivalent to 24.3 kg ha $^{-1}$.

The rye grass yield was determined at 35d, 70d, 140d and 422d following sewing. The grass was harvested by cutting approximately 1 cm above the soil surface, washed in 0.01% Teepol (Merck) and rinsed twice in distilled water prior to being dried at 60 $^{\circ}$C.

The dried material was weighed to determine dry weight yield and a sub-sample was ground into a powder for total N analysis. Soil samples were also obtained from the top 15 cm of the soil profile at 5 randomly generated co-ordinates on the soil surface in each tub.

Total Nitrogen was determined for the sludge, soil and grass from the first (35d) harvest using a Carlo Erba Elemental Analyser model 1106 (Carlo Erba Strumentazione, Milan, Italy). Process control and data acquisition functions were controlled by an Emasyst software package (Elemental Microanalysis, Okehampton, Devon). The machine was standardised by the combustion of certified reference materials (BCR143R sludge amended soil for soil samples, BCR281 ryegrass for sludge and plant materials) and three replicate determinations were performed for each soil/plant sample. Data were analysed by two way ANOVA (SPSS).

RESULTS AND DISCUSSION

Carbon to N ratios of the sludges varied as anticipated with widest ratio in the undigested liquid sludge (R series) and the narrowest in the thickened digested cake (C series) [9] (Figure 1). Thirty five days after sludge amendment, N levels in the soil reflected application rate (Figure 2). Although total N in the sludge amended soils was greatest in the C series sludge, this was not show in the soil and at 35 days. The T series soils had the highest N concentration and the widest range of values across treatments.

Rye grass yield responded positively in relation to application rate of all sludges at each of the five harvests (Figure 3). Yield was significantly different ($p<0.05$) with differing amendment rates of the same sludge type. A fertiliser benefit was apparent in all sludges more than one year after initial application. The digested liquid (T series) outperformed the other sludges in terms of yield and long-term benefit. The undigested liquid sludges (R series) had the poorest yield at all comparable levels of application (Figure 3).

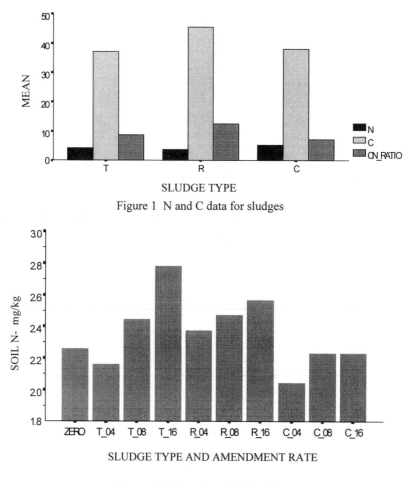

Figure 1 N and C data for sludges

Figure 2 N data for soil after 35d

Nitrogen concentration after 35 days in the rye grass shoots showed a clear pattern within each sludge type. In the T series sludges there was a large increase in leaf N concentration with higher application rate. In the C series sludges a similar pattern emerged but at lower levels. In the R series sludges an inverse correlation occurred, with lower levels of N in the shoot at higher levels of sludge application. This is an interesting result especially as N is thought to be related phosphorus uptake in plants. We assume that the wide C/N ratio of R series sludge has led to either a partial immobilisation, or reduced mineralisation, of labile N in the soil. The net result of this is slightly higher yield but reduced nitrogen in the plant. This has major implication for seed set if similar finding occur in arable grasses.

This study clearly shows that even at application rates as low as 4 tonnes per hectare sewage sludge application can have a significant benefit and that this can last for far beyond a single growing season. In this paper we have considered only nitrogen as a nutrient, however, their are a range of other macro- and micronutrients supplied by sewage sludge at these low levels that may contribute to long-term soil fertility.

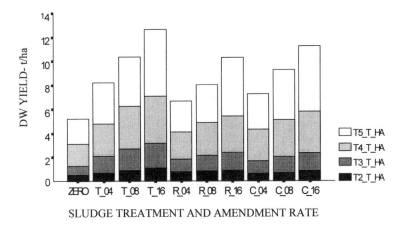

Figure 3 D.W. Yield data for harvests

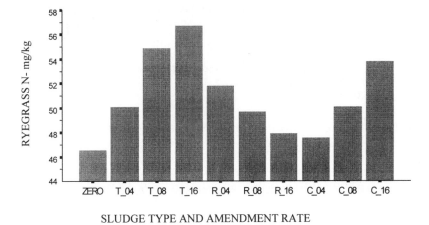

Figure 4 N data for 35d Rye grass harvest

FURTHER INVESTIGATION

Further investigation to determine the N dynamics of the soil in the period immediately following sludge amendment are in progress. The values for total P in the plants and available P in the soils are also being determined along with micronutrient status.

REFERENCES

1. CARRINGTON, E. G. DAVIES. R. D. PIKE. E. B.   Review of the Scientific Evidence Relating to the Controls on the Agricultural Use of Sewage Sludge (DETR 4415/3) Part 1 - The Evidence Underlying the 1989 Department of the Environment Code of Practice for Agricultural Use of Sludge and the Sludge (Use in Agriculture) Regulations. WRc, Frankland Road, Swindon. SN5 8YF 1998a

2. CARRINGTON, E. G. DAVIES, R. D. PIKE, E. B.   Review of the Scientific Evidence Relating to the Controls on the Agricultural Use of Sewage Sludge (DETR 4415/3) Part 2 - Evidence Since 1989 Relevant to the Controls on the Agricultural Use of Sewage Sludge. WRc, Frankland Road, Swindon. SN5 8YF 1998b.

3. GREEN, I. G. AND TIBBETT, M. Implications of the recycling of sewage sludge to the agro-ecosystem: zinc transfer in the soil-plant-arthropod system. Proceedings of the International Symposium on Recycling and Reuse of Sewage Sludge, Thomas Telford, London March 2001.

4. COUNCIL OF THE EUROPEAN COMMUNITIES   (CEC),   Council Directive of 12 December 1991 concerning the protection of waters against pollution caused by nitrates from agricultural sources (91/676/EEC).   Official Journal of the EuropeanCommunities. No. L 375/1-8 1991.

5. STATUTORY INSTRUMENT (SI),   The Protection of Water Against Agricultural Nitrate Pollution (England and Wales) Regulations 1996. Statutory Instrument 1996 No. 888 HMSO, London.

6. STATUTORY INSTRUMENT (SI),   The Protection of Water Against Agricultural Nitrate Pollution (Scotland) Regulations 1996.   Statutory Instrument 1996 No. 1564 (S.137), HMSO, London.

7. SMITH, S. R. Agricultural Recycling of Sewage Sludge and the Environment. CAB International, Wallingford, UK. 1996

8. SMITH, S.R. TIBBETT, M. EVANS, T.D. Nitrate Accumulation Potential of Sewage Sludge Applied to Soil. Nitrate and Farming Systems, Aspects of Applied Biology. 30, 1992, pp157-161

9. SMITH, S.R. WOODS, V. EVANS, T.D. Nitrate Dynamics in Biosolids-Treated Soils. I. Influence on Biosolids Type and Soil Type. Bioresource Technology. 66, 1998, pp139-149

PART FOUR:

WAY FORWARD AND DEVELOPING THE SUSTAINABLE USE OF SEWAGE SLUDGE

FACTORS OF VORTEXIAN ENERGY SOURCES

M W Youds

Newco Sewage Limited

United Kingdom

ABSTRACT. This paper relates to a technology applicable to biosolids processing. High speed photography has revealed reverse vortices within the apparatus. Disruption caused by the action within vortices and reverse vortices, in a cyclonic air-stream, together with the shearing action of an impeller's blades may alter the chemical structure of water. It may dissociate water, and release: ozone; N2; hydroxide ions; hydrogen radicals; hydrogen peroxide; oxidised hydrogen protons; and various oxygen compounds (with high and low Rydberg states). Hydrogen and negatively charged oxygen molecules could have their molecular structures altered by breaking their covalent sigma bond. (It will also comminute material containing oxygen.) This technology has processed and treated sewage containing 21% dry solids. The powdered product contained up to 95% dry solid.

Keywords: Atomic, Cavitation, Dissociation, Electron, Implosion, Quantum, Standing-wave, Torsion, Vacuum, Vortex.

Dr M W Youds Ph.D., B.A.TH (Hons)., is the Inventor of a non-commercialised fireproof product made entirely from waste material. His research interests include Vortexian physics and theological quantum cosmology. He is the granted Patent holder of a device for altering the crystalline structure of gypsum, with 4 on-going applications for other technologies related to this paper. In his capacity as the science officer for Lodestone Technology, he is currently working on 3 research projects centred around the Coal Research Establishment (CRE) in Cheltenham - 'Brite-Euram' (comminution of quarry fines), ECSC (coal and steel), and ETSU (investigating the resulting energy savings from this technology). In a personal capacity, and as a Director of Helix Comminutions and Newco Sewage, he has travelled widely in his investigation of vortex technology. This paper outlines his Vortexian theory.

INTRODUCTION

The apparatus consists of a high speed motor attached to an impeller rotor suction fan which rotates horizontally or vertically, contained in a housing, attached to which is a conical section. The conical section is attached to an inlet. This inlet tube is parallel, in line with the fan axis, and can be mounted horizontally or vertically. With a potential 'solenoid' field, a 25.4 mm metal ring, preferably made of brass, is located at the inlet to the rotor. The vanes and the ring can make mechanical energy from the kinetic and thermal energy stored in liquids. A rotor will preferably have a diameter of 612 mm - requiring a motor in the order of 200Kw, with impeller speeds up to 7222 rpm. A cyclone further enhances the process and may be used for controlling flocculation and precipitation, together with the effect of providing the necessary back-pressure required for optimum configuration of the invention.

Configuration of Apparatus

A formula is used to determine the rotor's RPM and the length of the inlet tube - outlined later. All parts of the invention have relative dimensions to the other parts when the required standing wave is obtained, together with the following: fundamental frequencies; dominants; diatonics; harmonics; enharmonics; or sympathetic resonating isochronous wave vibrations thereof : 1 - 3 Hz; 7.24 to 10.17 Hz; 13 to 990 Hz; 27,618 Hz to 45,696 Hz.

For the processing of material to be realised, the resonant acoustics of the medium must be ascertained - i.e. its ultra-sonic frequency value and sonic frequency value. This is neither 'Acoustophoresis' nor 'Electrophoresis', nevertheless those skilled in the art of Acoustophoresis could also identify the necessary values (representative - no external source actually creates the frequencies and in their terms the 'sonic value' would only be a three digit 'division' of the first acoustic). Indeed, NASA patented [1] an invention in which, ' ...the second acoustic wave can be tuned to a frequency different from that of the first (acoustic wave), and to a different amplitude thereby producing a high resolution "shearing" of the liquid into its separate species'. [2]

If a wide range of frequencies and vibrations are created within the conduit, a hexagonal (assumed shape) lattice of superconductive vorticles, which can create 'Cooper Pairs' of electrons within 'Soliton' waves when the correct frequencies are input (explained later, in the formula), and non-superconductive powerful vortices are created in the air stream. This sets up pulses without and within a standing wave configuration within the system. Vorticles containing quasi single pole quantum singularities could therefore be created in the cyclonic air stream.

EMPIRICAL

High speed video photography, taken by the IMC group, from inside the conical section / rotor, has successfully recorded the existence of the reverse vortices, whose growth and stability will depend upon the interrupter's peaks' gradient velocity.

Furthermore, after tests conducted at CRE, by IMC, the harmonic spectra data supplied by IMC proved that the apparatus generated ultrasonic frequencies.

The more energy that went into forming rock, the greater the comminution potential. However, the opposite is the case for dissociation. The greater the energy input to the sewage, the less the dissociation potential e.g. it is unlikely that many types of river-bed silt would dissociate adequately for commercial purposes and neither would heavily plasticised sewage. (The ideal sewage, known to date, would be centrifuged and transported without the aid of a screw-feed device.) Polymers, particularly in combination with other polymers, would also restrict the performance of the technology. The energy release from the electrons - outlined later - would be severely reduced because their spatial motion would be restricted by the polymer. This novel invention has processed and treated centrifuged sewage containing 21% dry solids, at a rate of between 3800 Kg and 4100 kg per hour. The powdered product was between 68% and 95% dry solid. (CRE have confirmed that cattle manure was pathogen free.)

Note: Conventional comminution energy costs are 5 times higher, by comparison, than this invention. When the apparatus, configurated according to my patent application, processed 25.4 mm lumps of rock at a rate of 18 tons per hour there was no significant wear on the steel rotor.

THEORY BEHIND THE PROCESSES

Cavitation

'When subject to intense sound waves, liquids can be stretched until they break and gas bubbles appear' [3]. During particle cavitation ionisation occurs, and certain electrons give up thousands of electron volts to produce heat. At this point, the apex of certain vortices are going faster, reducing frictional resistance, increasing the density, and reducing the temperature, therefore, the magnetic field strength will increase. An acoustic pressure amplifying oscillation and intensifying vibrational ultrasonic wave travelling through the ions produce an extremely large sound pressure level, increasing the temperature on a micro level by many thousands of degrees, but not more than 10 degrees overall. (This occurs in a 'boundary envelope', located in the 'boundary cylinder' - to be explained later.)

At this moment (of the 'critical frequency combination of pulsed wave intensity') of superposition between the 'sub-critical harmonic particles combination intensity' waves of phased and out of phase particles, either explosions and / or implosions [depending on the medium] take place together with an increase in heat. In this locality is situated a resonating two-dimensional (due to an ellipsoidal time harmonic function, relative to its dimension in space) convex complex pitch discharging 'corona' - hereafter referred to as the 'corona'. This is not sonoluminescence, although there are similarities (with Chemiluminescence also).

The 'corona', whose nearby electric field is a time harmonic solution of Laplace's equations in spherical co-ordinates which also interacts with a magnetic field, hermetically seals the high pressure sound level inside the 'boundary envelope'.

The 'corona' is situated at the apex of a leaning reverse vortex, whose convex base emanates from the interrupter. A vacuum is created between the concave part of the interrupter and the convex base of the vortex. The interrupter is another high frequency, high amplitude, resonating complex pitch generator. Whilst rotating at speed, the leaning reverse vortex creates a 'cylindrical boundary shape', with a resonating calibre base. The base calibre depends on the length 'C' of the 'cylinder', as the diameter of its base is exactly the length of the 'cylinder' divided by Pi. The resonating calibre also produces a complex feedback loop in the 'boundary layer' of the 'cylindrical shape', which assists in breaking down the anti-nucleation energy barrier. (The apex of a 'boundary envelope' is located inside the 'boundary cylinder'.)

Therefore, a great deal of potential energy is obtained from the high volume resonating complex pitch of the frequencies (when the cavitation heterogeneous [due to dopants] nucleation bubble expands) at the precise moment the kinetic energy is being concentrated (when the cavitation bubble explodes).

Dissociation

Dissociation of water, due to an electron flow vibration - to form hydroxide ions; negative hydroxyl ions; hydrogen radicals; hydrogen peroxide; positive hydronium ions; oxidised hydrogen protons; various oxygen compounds; the elimination of bacteria; and the initiation of the formation of micro floc, can occur, amongst other processes, through electrolytic processes. The harmonic and enharmonic frequencies and ion-acoustic oscillating vibrations, enhanced by an instantaneous sweeper wave-form, occurring within the invention, could provide the same impetus as the electrical pulsating signal that occurs during those processes.

In the magnetic field, positively charged hydrogen is compressed during cavitation, which results in it also heating up. The magnetic field also compresses the hydrogen which will emit ionising radiation. The frequencies focus on the weak hydrogen bonds rather than the oxygen molecule. The word 'dissociation' does not adequately describe the chemical activity which changes the hydrogen and negatively charged oxygen molecules into other structures by breaking their covalent sigma bond.

In electrolysis, an electrical pulse signal must be generated in the form of a square wave and in an inverse relation to the conductivity of the water. When correctly configured, the invention becomes a high-order harmonic complex wave form generating synthesiser, wherein the conduction angle has been fixed to maximise the output of the desired harmonic [4]. Pulses also release iron cations from iron in the fabrication. Iron cations form compounds which polymerise - on exiting the impeller - and initiate the formation of floc in the form of micro-floc, and metal hydroxides are also formed as precipitates. The cations could also destroy cyanide. [5]

Preferably, it would be more advantageous to ensure that the sewage had a pH value of 8 to 10, together with traces of a proteolytic enzyme, which brings the hydroxide ion concentration to a level which provides the most economic contaminant removal. The increase in pH will reduce hydronium concentration, thereby increasing electrocatalytic ion or couple cations.

A non-dissipating travelling electrical impulse is also located around the 'boundary cylinder' due to the fact that we have a high speed rotor, creating a constantly changing magnetic field containing some adiabatic electrons that move parallel to the magnetic field and at right angles to the electrical field. At this point it is worth referring to Mills' U.S. Patent (utilising a new atomic theory) which refers to a nickel cathode (the interrupter is preferably made of a high content nickel alloy), one of the preferred embodiments in that Patent being to use 'an intermittent square-wave having an off-set voltage of approx.' 1.4 volts'. with an applied frequency. [6]

Vacuum

Anyone familiar with homopolar generators will accept that the invention's high speed rotor will emit an intensified voltage.[7] This voltage assists the process when its oscillation becomes synchronised with the input frequencies. The reverse vortex carries frequencies from the axis, and contains a concave based vortex standing columnar wave 'boundary envelope'. This base is just below the 'zone of vacuum polarisation' produced by a plasma's acoustic mode - located at the boundary layer of the two-dimensional 'corona', at a hyper-spacial intersection between non space-time and space-time (this smaller 'envelope' has an apex angle equal to its angle of torsion vibration, from which a standing columnar wave is created). Presumably this particular boundary layer has no additional fermionic quantum dimensions. The plasma may be produced by quantum vacuum radiation. (To suggest a 'black hole' is being generated would be a fanciful and ignorant remark, as it is more likely to generate 'stars' from the helium and hydrogen than a quantum chromodynamic holographic matrix.)

This particular vacuum in the invention, although relatively small, is important with regards to the electrical induction phenomenon and its place in quantum electrodynamics. [8] When the frequencies are acoustically oscillating the ions at the same time as the electrical charge from the rotor core axis and / or further pulses out of phase are introduced, an implosion takes place inside the vacuum. The ions at this point act like photons on the crystalline structure by increasing the electrons conductivity. The 'cylinder' also acts as a wave-guide containment field for the electro-magnetic waves, and as a gatherer of electrons in the transverse direction - a process which amplifies the sound in the 'boundary envelope'.

Implosion / Explosion

Rocks can be 'comminuted', when oxygen inside the rock fissures is temporarily dissociated - e.g. into two atomic fragments, one of these fragments having a low metastable Rydberg state and the other a high Rydberg state - which are ionised as a result of thermal collision. This is because an explosion will take place when the oxygen associates, causing a massive generation of energy at a micro level. In addition, as a result of any H2O in the fissures, the acoustic waves would travel faster than those in the rock, thereby sending a shock wave through the rock.

Although implosion occurs within certain material, not without (due to degeneracy pressure), -except for dissociation in the 'boundary envelope' vacuum- nevertheless it is again both fanciful, and incorrect to say that rocks implode or 'disintegrate' - empirically it has been seen that they do not. The explosions and / or implosions do not always cause the rock to completely break apart, rather they weaken the rock and makes it brittle. The rock will impact upon the interrupter and break up -not spontaneous disintegration- the larger pieces bounce back within a reverse vortex surrounding the cylinder. This vortex is centrifugal, and so the pieces first impact against other pieces -creating smaller pieces, which move towards the inner wall of the conical section, impact against each other, and finally grind against the wall, before moving between the vanes. At all times, the material is within a flow of vortices, not travelling back and forth across a single vortex. (Both cannot occur at the same time.)

Space Vortex Energy

We should take note of Paramahamsa Tewari's (Kaiga Atomic Power Project, Karwar, India) opening abstract from his paper 'Phenomenon of electric charge generation by space rotation': 'The medium of space (absolute vacuum without matter) is defined as an incompressible, zero-mass, nonviscous, continuous and mobile entity which, in its rotation at the limiting speed of light as a submicro vortex, creates electrons. The property of electric charge of electron and its electrostatic field can be shown to be the effect of rotation of space around the electron's centre. The mass property of electron is seen to be rising due to the creation of a spherical void (hole) at electron's centre where space rotates at the limiting speed of light'. [9]

Under the right conditions, the 'corona' may also 'contain' slowed-down high-energy neutrons, with nuclei that are gravitationally and inertially confined. Anti-matter may be nothing more than an 'echo' from an alternative phase-space dimension caused by: the negative entropy effect from the 'corona'; and / or the incumbent torsion field. All of the inherent processes are interactive and depend upon one another for successful treatment of the material. This novel combination of processes occurs without a chronology. (This Nexus to be known as the 'Youds Factor'.) Its 'Fluence' is therefore immeasurable. This cannot be underestimated, when one considers the simultaneous knock-on effect of the infinite spiralling of processes, and its potential on the nucleonic molecular mean squared velocity. No time elapses between either implosion and / or explosion, cavitation, or the ranges in temperature and pressure etc (except for the vacuum created implosion that occurs at the 'boundary layer' of the 'cylinder' hyper-spacial intersection between non space-time and space-time).

PHYSICISTS OF NOTE

In the 19th Century, John Keely claimed he was, '... able to draw vibratory energy directly from space by the aid of special resonating expedients' [10]. He stated that this energy, 'is duplex, or has two opposed conditions, like positive and negative states of electricity' [10].

The name given to this 'space' has changed according to the individual scientist, e.g. 'scalar waves', 'tachyon energy', 'ether' or, 'negative-time-energy', according to Robert Adams [11]. Adams went on to quote Nikola Tesla who said that sound waves travel at the speed of light in the ether, however, it is really particles of sound, rather than the speed of compression waves, which travel at the speed of light within vortices. These accelerating charged particles would produce vorticles, therefore the electron spin in the vorticles would give off 'Synchroton' radiation when spiralling into the magnetic field [12] - and because material is moving through the invention, the material itself produces vorticles. [13]

Furthermore, Keely went on to say, '... what we call electricity is but one of the triune currents, harmonic, enharmonic, and diatonic' [14]. Although nothing like the current invention, Keely's devices utilised frequencies to create electricity and to dissociate water and matter. Indeed, the Keely motor created a standing wave with two polarisation zones within a resonator with two opposing pressure zones. The water inside the motor was subjected to impulses which caused the water to expand and therefore the pressure was increased. Readers of Keely's work will notice that he often referred to low atomic ether produced during dissociation.

According to Dan A. Davidson, pressure is placed on the nucleus of an atom when sound pressure is placed on a mass that has had a standing wave generated within it. Furthermore he states that, 'The wavelength of sound - Nuclear magnetic resonance (NMR) rattles the nucleus', when the frequencies are on the order of the nuclear particles, 'based on the proton spin which produces a small magnetic moment', because 'the speed of sound is much slower than EM so a relatively low frequency doesn't travel very far before it has gone through a complete cycle and that distance is on the order of the proton spin resonance frequency. Thus, it is easy to see that sound can resonate with the atomic level in as far as frequency is concerned.' [15]

THE FORMULA

The following formula is relative to the rotor speed being equal to 0.75 that of the air speed entering the inlet tube. In any machine where this is different, the 0.75 figure in 'U' should be amended. Speed is in millimetres per second. Lengths are in mm.

The key to the Abbreviations is as follows (See Figures 1 and 2 on page 11):

A = constant value 9;   B =   variable value B;
C = maximum 'boundary cylinder' length;
D = distance from the start of the sound wave to the back of the hub;
E = speed of sound value in millimetres per second;
F = ultra-sonic frequency value, in the range 27,618 to 45,696, to be input into the 'corona and vacuum polarisation zone';
G = distance from the back of the hub to the wider edge of the conical section;
H = combined length of the conical section length and the sound wave;
I = inlet tube length; (The interior of the inlet tube could have an aluminium lining.)
J = conical section length;
K = the sonic frequency value, in the range 103 to 359, to be input;
L = distance from the start of the inlet tube to the outside of the rotor housing casing;
M = length from the start of the sound wave to the outside of the rotor housing casing;
N = exterior distance from the wider edge of the conical section to the rotor housing;
O = optimum configuration for combined dissociation and comminution;
P = constant value 8;   Q = minimum length of the 'boundary cylinder';
r = radius of the inlet tube;
R = rotor tip speed - divide by the circumference and multiply by 60 for the RPM;
S = variable value;   T = air speed;   U = K divided by 0.75;
V = one-third of I;   W = one-third of X;   X = 3K;
Y = constant value 5; and, Z = optimum conditions for harmonic frequency precision.

The Main 20 Equations:

1.   F divided   by A = B
2.   E divided   by B = C
3.   2(A multiplied by C) = D
4.   D minus G   = H
5.   H minus J   = I
6.   I multiplied by K = R
7.   H plus N   = M
8.   M minus 0.6r   = L
9.   (H divided by 2) divided by P = Q
10. (E divided by 2H) multiplied by Y = S
11. T divided by I   = U
12. R divided by X   = V
13. I = T divided by U
14. W = R divided by I
15. Distance Q to C = The 'corona' and 'vacuum polarisation nexus zone'
16. When S = X, then Z
17. When C = Q, then O
18. Space is folded, rather than time reversal, when C is less than Q (explained later, in the section 'Heuristic Applications')
19. 3(R divided by S)+J+N-0.6r-'L'=degree of accuracy for 'L' in mm.
20. 3(R divided by S) multiplied by K, minus R, divided by the rotor's circumference, multiplied by 60 = the degree of accuracy in the rotor's rpm.

Additional Parameters To Be Considered

To estimate how much water will be removed from the sewage you can use the following guideline: ('C' divided by 2'P') minus the distance between 'C' and 'Q' = a variable. Divide this variable by ('C' divided by 2'P') = another variable. Multiply this new variable by the percentage of water in the sewage to find the number of percentage points that will be deducted ('PD') from the original percentage of water in the sewage. However, at cooler ambient air temperatures the actual percentage of water removed may increase because of increased conductivity transmission rates when the temperature declines. On a continuous basis, as a guide, the apparatus will process 0.65 kg per hour of sewage, for every 1 rpm of the rotor.

For every increase above the through-put guide figure, a proportional decrease in the amount of water dissociated will occur. For example, an 8% increase in the amount of sewage fed into the apparatus, above the 'guide' figure given above, would result in an 8% reduction of 'PD'. The very high centrifugal acceleration that is present assists in the stability of the 'boundary cylinder', despite the introduction of material to be processed. An excess of material, or a high inconsistent through-put, may cause instability within the reverse vortices.

Although the primary process takes place around the 'corona', the 'boundary cylinder' where the itinerant nucleonic dipolar field is excited, and the 'boundary envelope', other processes occur, other than these three areas - e.g., the reverse vortex that extends as far into the inlet tube as the length of the 'cylinder'.

Number of Blades (vanes)

An 8 vane is less likely to: square the wave-form; smooth the wave-form; or reach the required sub-critical decibel intensity ranges - although it is better than a 9 vane at producing heterodynes. Furthermore, the peak frequencies generated by the 8 vane can be five-sixths of the frequency input for the 9 or 10 vane impeller. The following equation can be used to establish the preferred number of vanes: ('F' divided by 6) divided by (The RPM established from 'R', divided by 10) = the number of vanes to be used on the impeller.)

HEURISTIC APPLICATIONS

Cold Fusion

If Randell L. Mills' atomic theory [16] is correct, then cold fusion (or 'Coulombic Annihilation Fusion' - ['CAF']) is obviously taking place inside the invention. The CAF process present would not be on-going, due to a lack of nuclei during the neutron flux which would occur after the spherical shock wave obtained a neutron split over neutron loss. When 'CAF' occurs, the 'corona' plasma's electrical resistance decreases.

Atomic Energy

The proof that cold fusion effects are limited is based on empirical evidence, namely the formation of Abrikosov vortices and temporary gamma-radiation that occur when the invention is correctly configured. This could mean that oppositely spinning pairs of photons would be present - John Griggs' 1954 'Unified particle theory'.

Instantaneously occurring sweeper wave-forms, referred to earlier, are often associated with thunderstorms, as are Abrikosov vortices, ball-lightning, electrical discharging plasma, and neutron formation. [17]

The technology could therefore create permanent 'storm' conditions, coupled with vortex energy. As such, the law of conservation of energy is maintained, together with no loss of quantum information. In the equation, C is less than Q, space is 'folded' due to a rapid increase in captured photons sympathetically vibrating with their counterparts at an immeasurable distance - rather than as a result of virtual photons being produced by the vacuum - assisted by the 'solitons' being squeezed - which also assists the refinement of the ultrasonic frequency and the creation of negative feedback, enhanced by the resulting action from the nickel ions, travelling back down the centre of the inlet tube, being surrounded by incoming aluminium ions.

When space 'folds' (not warps) dissociation reduces dramatically but implosions within matter, for comminution, increases dramatically. This is because the vacuum polarisation zone is now in front of the 'corona', rather than below it. The percentage of CAF taking place also increases. ('C' minus 'Q') divided by ('C' divided by 2'P') multiplied by 5.4617215 = the percentage of time that the CAF process takes place.

CONCLUDING COSMOLOGY

The duality of particles / waves should be viewed from the perspective of the vibration from the nucleus, acting as a protective barrier to its programming. Particles form themselves into waves through sympathetic attraction to the protective wave barrier. Therefore, the nucleus is dictating the wavelength to the electron.

From a theological cosmology, all matter is attracted in an effort to achieve consciousness. This 'ether' consciousness is beyond the 'Youds Factor' space vortex energy source - where neutral mass particles, of neither matter nor anti-matter, do not revolve until an external source activates them, in their potential fields, to produce matter. Prior to activation, there is no 'time' or Weyl curvature.

In a magnetic field, when particular external frequencies bombard the nucleus, the radiative electron particles are further excited and change their orbital movement. During self-polarisation, if you sufficiently alter the vibration from the nucleus, then solid matter may cease to be solid, together with an excess combination of electrons whose up / down equilibrium has now been destroyed. Although the out of phase waves cause interference and cancel each other out, the inward 'missing spin' dialectic particles remain and are attracted - making them susceptible to be dictated to from an external, quantum mechanically generated, matrix of standing waves.

The knowledge obtained theoretically and empirically, is limited to only altering the matrix of frequencies in order to control the processes herein. However, if you could accurately dictate the structure of the matrix (and its relationship to valence band electrons) you could therefore create any kind of matter you desire - only if the relationship between the particle spectrum (and its physical probability factor [as an imaginary number only]) and the nucleus' wave (and its matrix / matrices) is established. (I.E. particle to wave, not wave to 'superposed' wave.)

To the layman, the phenomenon described herein seems incredible because the process can't be easily 'visualised', or therefore easily understood. However, any enlightened physicist could see that no laws of physics have to be reinterpreted, or Higgs particles / fields included, in order to explain it - with no 'strings' attached.

ACKNOWLEDGEMENTS

The sound-wave chemistry of Philip Boudjouk, Chemist, North Dakota State University. The experiments in 1952 by Dr. Franz Popel, Stuttgart Technical University. Dan Davidson for his, 'Energy: Breakthroughs to Free Energy Devices', which, on page 33 and 34 shows how Keely could find the resonant frequency of a material. The section, 'Nature of excited states' by James A. Patterson, Ph.D. in his U.S. Patent 5,607,563. Randell L. Mills' atomic theory compounded in U.S. Patent No. 6,024,935. The atomic energy theory that recognises the energy in electron spin - John Ecklin, U.S. Patent No. 4,567,407.

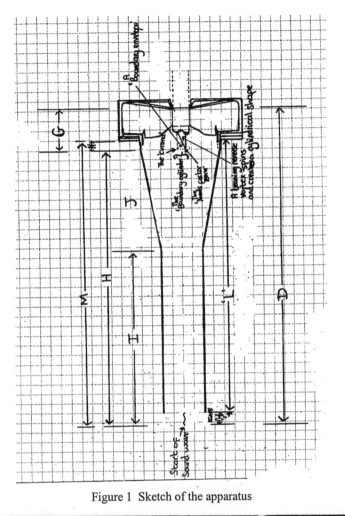

Figure 1 Sketch of the apparatus

Figure 2 Photograph of the apparatus

REFERENCES

1.   U.S. Patent numbers 5,192,450 and 5,147,562

2.   NASA tech' brief, January 1990

3.   Negative Pressures and Cavitation In Liquid Helium, MARIS, H., and BALIBAR, S.

4.   U.S. Patent No. 5,990,712.

5.   U.S. Patent No. 3,933,606.

6.   U.S. Patent No. 6,024,935

7.   Homopolar "Free-Energy" Generator', a paper presented on June 21st 1986 at the Society for Science Exploration in San Francisco, by KINCHELOE, R., Professor of Electrical Engineering at Stanford University.

8.   Macroscopic Vacuum Polarisation, KING, M. B.

9.   The Free-Energy Device Handbook: A Compilation of Patents and Reports, HATCHER CHILDRESS, D.,Adventures Unlimited Press, 1995, chapter 8, page 191.

10. Universal Laws Never Before Revealed: Keely's Secrets - Understanding and Using The Science of Sympathetic Vibration, Message Company, 1995 (Dale Pond).

11. Nexus Magazine, 30/4/1993.

12. Scientific American Feb. 1969, 56.

13. On The Motion of An Elliptic Cylinder Through A Viscous Fluid, RICHARDS, G.J., A.R.C.S., Bsc., P.I.C., PhD., London: Philosophical Transactions of the Royal Society of London, Series A., Vol. 233, pp 279 - 301; and Computer Experiments In Fluid Dynamics, HARLOW, F.H. and FROMM, JACOB., Scientific American, Feb. 1964.

14. Snell Manuscript, SNELL, C.W., Delta Spectrum Research.

15. On The Production of Aetheric Stress Waves Utilising Sound Vibration, or, Sonic Stimulation of The Aether, DAVIDSON, D.A.

16. The Grand Unified Theory Of Classical Quantum Mechanics, MILLS, R., Technomic Publishing Company, Lancaster, Pa., 1995.

17. Possible Natural Cold Fusion In The Atmosphere, HAWKINS, N., Fusion Technology, 19, 2212, July, 1991.

PROGNOSES ABOUT THE REUSE OF SEWAGE SLUDGE FOR AGRICULTURAL PURPOSES IN GERMANY

F von Sothen

Germany

Abstract. Due to German law, disposal of sewage sludge and other organics on deposits is forbidden from the year 2005 on. Therefore an important issue is whether it is possible to reuse sewage sludge for agricultural purposes (only long-term recycling path), or if it is necessary to make arrangements to burn more sewage sludge. The German waste act prefers recycling instead of deposal, if both methods are similar in terms of costs. Taking into account, that German law does not regard burning of sewage sludge as (energy-) recycling (due to it's low burning-value), it is of overriding importance for the development of new waste management concepts. The paper explores whether the agricultural sector will be able to use all this sewage sludge in future and if farmers, guided by monetary aspects, agree.

Different scenarios were considered with an agro-economic model system called RAUMIS, which is also used by the German Agriculture Ministry.

Keywords: Sewage sludge, Composts, Biosolids, Agriculture, Waste management, Northrhine-Westphalia, Germany, Germany, Scenarios, RAUMIS

Author: Dr. Florian von Sothen, Bonn/Germany; sothen@t-online.de

INTRODUCTION

Figure 1 shows the methods for distribution sewage sludge being used in Germany as a whole and in Northrhine-Westphalia in particular. The burnt tonnage is growing rapidly, while deposal is becoming less and less. This trend can be explained by the fact, that deposing organics, such as sewage sludge, will be forbidden from the year 2005 on, due to the German decree TA Siedlungsabfall [1].

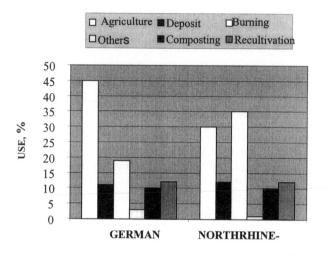

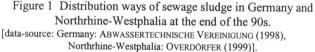

Figure 1 Distribution ways of sewage sludge in Germany and
Northrhine-Westphalia at the end of the 90s.
[data-source: Germany: ABWASSERTECHNISCHE VEREINIGUNG (1998),
Northrhine-Westphalia: OVERDÖRFER (1999)].

In general, waste needs to be recycled in Germany if other alternatives are not cheaper. In this context it is important to note, that burning of sewage sludge is not regarded as a form of energy recycling, because of its low heat value of <11 MJ/kg [2].

With regard to future trends, the year 2005 is of importance due to the above mentioned fixed time-limit. The federal state Northrhine-Westphalia was chosen for a detailed analysis concerning the use of sewage sludge for agricultural purposes, because if it's possible to use most of the sewage sludge produced in this federal state, it will be no problem in others.

CHARACTERISTICS OF NORTHRHINE-WESTPHALIA

Northrhine-Westphalia is one of 16 states in Germany, but 20 % of Germans live there. It includes the northern part of river Rhine, with cities like Cologne and Düsseldorf. Further large cities were founded due to coal-mining possibilities at the river Ruhr at the end of the 18th century. Today this area is characterised by industry, but the service-sector has also developed here.

Figure 2 Germany and Northrhine-Westphalia

The landscape in the north of Northrhine-Westphalia is dominated by the agricultural sector with a lot of cattle farming, producing manure. Taking the whole of Northrhine-Westphalia into account, nowhere else in Germany produces more manure per acre/hectar. This fact and the high population density raise the question of whether it is possible to use all sewage sludge from Northrhine-Westphalia for agricultural purposes within its boundaries. As shown in Table 1, Northrhine-Westphalia is, due to its bad benchmarks, a worst case scenario concerning the reuse of sewage sludge for agricultural purposes in Germany.

Due to the fact that most of the waste-water-treatment plants in Northrhine-Westphalia are eliminating phosphorus, the sewage sludge is characterised by quite high P_2O_5-concentrations. Heavy metals and other polluting components are low, especially if one compares the analysis with those of other industrialised countries. Furthermore the number of towns collecting biosolides separately in the households is increasing.

Table 1 Comparing Northrhine-Westphalia with other federal states in Germany

	POPULATION (in Mio)	FIELDS AND GRASSLAND (LF) (in 1000 hectar)	"CATTLE-MANURE-Units" per hectar LF*	MEN (per hectar LF)
Schleswig-Holstein**	3,55	1065,9	1,21	3,33
Lower-Sachsia**	9,86	2723,7	1,26	3,62
Northrhine-Westphalia	**17,68**	**1575,8**	**1,39**	**11,22**
Rheinland-Pfalz / Saarland**	4,96	798,2	0,65	6,21
Hessen	5,92	782,9	0,81	7,56
Baden-Württemberg	10,17	1484,7	0,99	6,85
Bavaria	11,77	3388,2	1,14	3,47
Thüringen	2,54	787,2	0,67	3,22
Sachsia	4,64	854,3	0,80	5,43
Brandenburg**	6,02	1298,5	0,56	4,64
Sachsen-Anhalt	2,79	1064,9	0,49	2,62
Mecklenburg-Vorpommern	1,86	1312,0	0,50	1,42
Germany	**81,76**	**17.136,3**	**0,96**	**4,76**

source: own calculation, data-base: AUSWERTUNGS- UND INFORMATIONSDIENST FÜR ERNÄHRUNG, LANDWIRTSCHAFT UND FORSTEN (1997, p. 14 - 16). [3]

*   calculated like described in the practicable-decree concerning the sewage sludge decree (MINISTERIUM FÜR UMWELT, RAUMORDNUNG UND LANDWIRTSCHAFT DES LANDES NORDRHEIN-WESTFAHLEN, 1995) [4]

** Berlin (3,48 mio. inhabitants) is added to Brandenburg, while Bremen (0,68 mio. inhabitants) is added to Lower Sachsia and Hamburg (1,70 mio. inhabitants) is added with half of its inhabitants to Lower Sachsia and Schleswig-Holstein. Saarland (1,08 Mio. inhabitants) is added to Rheinland-Pfalz. The population-number are based on data from STATISTISCHEN BUNDESAMT (Statistical Office; 1997, p. 24). [5]

RAUMIS - THE AGROECONOMICAL MODEL-SYSTEM

Farmers are not using sewage sludge for altruistic reasons, e.g. to help the society to get rid of the sewage sludge. Their motivation is money. If they can make more money out of animal production with it's "waste" manure, they will not use sewage sludge or composts (see for example reference 6). But other factors like time can prevent expansion of animal production on individual farms.

The produced composts are competing with sewage sludge and manure for land. Of course, composts in particular can also be used for recultivating deposits etc., but in the future these possibilities will decrease. Only the agricultural sector offers the possibility of a long-term recycling path in future. If this method is not possible, then other options like co-burning of sewage sludge in brown coal power station (an example for Northrhine-Westphalia is described by RHEINBRAUN [7]) must be set up.

All these facts show that an agro-economical model-system is needed to give detailed answers about suitable waste-management systems for these organic wastes in the future.

The computer simulation program RAUMIS was used to calculate the marketing possibilities for regional sewage sludge and biowaste-composts with regard to a reuse in the agricultural sector of Northrhine-Westphalia. RAUMIS is an agro-economic program, which is also used by the German Agricultural Ministery for scenario-calculations (for details about RAUMIS: see references 8 to 10). RAUMIS takes the common agricultural policy of the EU into account. In addition to this, the progress concerning the breeding of plants (for example wheat: 1,7 % each year) and fodder-technology (especially phytase concerning pigs and poultry $\rightarrow$ leading to a total reduction of 11 % P_2O_5 in the manure under c.p.-conditions in the year 2005; background information about phytase in references 11 to 13), the set-aside scheme and the use of land for road construction etc. is taken into consideration (recommended information in reference 14). During all calculations, RAUMIS maximizes the income of the farmers. This aim is of overriding importance.

It is assumed in all calculations that, at most up to 80 % of the total sewage sludge and up to 50 % of biowaste-compost in Northrhine-Westphalia can be potentially used for agricultural purposes, because some will always be used for others purposes or cannot be used by farmers due to heavy metal pollution etc. Within RAUMIS the farmers receive as much money for the sewage sludge as the owners of the waste-water-treatment plants have to spend otherwise for burning it (in most cases the cheapest alternative in Northrhine-Westphalia are brown-coal power stations). From this sum, the costs for the sewage sludge fonds (an obligate insurance for the farmers, paid by those waste water plants, which give sludge to farmers; for details see reference 15) and for the soil analysis (concerning heavy metals and nutrients) need to be deducted. The same method is used concerning the composts. RAUMIS also offers farmers the possibility to compost the biosolids (like described for the practise in references 16 and 17). If they do so, they receive extra money (for details see references 18 and 19) apart from the fee they get for spreading the compost on their fields.

LIMITING FACTOR: P_2O_5-CONCENTRATIONS IN THE SOIL

In the past too much manure and fertilisers were spread on the fields in Northrhine-Westphalia. Therefore the P_2O_5-concentrations in the soils are higher than necessary (50 % are higher than necessary; 20 % are extremely high). It is an environmental aim to bring these P_2O_5-concentrations back to normal level. Therefore, compared to the plants P_2O_5-demand, less nutrients than are needed by the plants will be spread within the next few years. This is a hard limiting restriction for the use of sewage sludge, compost, manure and other fertilisers for agricultural purposes. But it is an overriding environmental aim, plants reduce the P_2O_5-nutrient pool in the soil step by step.

Three major groups of scenarios were calculated by RAUMIS:

1. The P_2O_5-concentrations in the soils are all normal.
    This scenario shows what will be possible if todays P_2O_5-soil-concentrations will be reduced once. In that case more P_2O_5 from sewage sludge, compost, manure and other fertilisers will be needed, especially compared to the following two scenarios.

2. The P_2O_5-concentrations in the soils are too high. Only half of the plants demand is spread. The plants have to take the other 50 % of their P_2O_5-demand from the pool in the soil. Spreading compost, sewage sludge or manure on soils with a very high P_2O_5-concentration is forbidden (this scenario takes most of todays laws and decrees into account).

3. The P_2O_5-concentrations in the soils are too high. 75 % of the plants demand is allowed to be given. The plants have to take the other 25 % from the nutrient-pool in the soil. Soils with a very high P_2O_5-concentration are only allowed to receive 50 % of the plants demand from compost, sewage sludge and manure.

4. Reducing the P_2O_5-soil-concentration is still of overriding importance, but it takes more time. On the other hand there is not a hard cut between todays (2005) and the future (years after 2005) situation. This leads to the conclusion that sewage sludge - and compost-management-concepts will have a better long-term perspective, because the needed tonnage is not too much changing during the years.

LEASED AREAS

Most of the German landlords try to forbid the use of sewage sludge and composts on their land [20], due to the fear their land might get polluted with heavy metals as has happened in the past, when there were no strict rules like the German sewage sludge decree [21]. Due to this fact two kind of scenarios were examined.

1. Leased fields can be used to spread sewage sludge or biowaste composts on, but the landlords therefore receive an extra 20 % rent each year (the farmers have to pay).

2. Leased fields can definitely not be used for spreading sewage sludge or biowaste composts on.

TRANSPORT

Sewage sludge is sometimes transported up to 350 miles within Germany. Therefore it was also one of the scientific aspects of the work to find out, if it is possible to reuse sewage sludge and composts within the districts where it is produced. In this context, two scenarios were examined:

1. The sewage sludge is only allowed to be transported within the districts where it is produced.

2. Sewage sludge can be transported to all places within the federal state of Northrhine-Westphalia (higher transport costs are taken into account).

GENERAL THOUGHTS

Considering a simple mathematical example, the situation is quite easy. The total P_2O_5-plant-demand in the year 2005 in Northrhine-Westphalia is 88.862 t. Manure from animals will contain 56.178 t P_2O_5. Consequently 32.684 t are required. The rest can therefore be added by using sewage sludge, composts and/or mineral fertiliser.

The total amount of P_2O_5 in sewage sludge and compost available for agricultural purposes from Northrhine-Westphalia is 20.206 t. Even if all of it is spread, there is still a further demand. For some years, the plants can take it from the soils but finally mineral fertilisers will be needed again. But taking all limiting factors into account, the situation is much more difficult.

RAUMIS-RESULTS

Table 2 shows, that depending whether landlords agree to a use of sewage sludge and compost on their land, between 311.000 t of dry mass and 482.000 t of dry mass of sewage sludge will be used by farmers in Northrhine-Westphalia. This is between 58 % and 65 % of the total sewage sludge amount which is available to the agricultural sector.

Table 2 The use of sewage sludge in Northrhine-Westphalia in the year 2005; normal P_2O_5-soil-concentrations, no transportation of sewage sludge between different districts

USAGE	SEWAGE SLUDGE (in tons, dry mass)	(in %)	COMPOSTS (in tons, dry mass)	(in %)
Without leasehold-land	269.973	58	240.822	64
With leasehold-land	301.019	65	262.288	70

In case sewage sludge is transported between the different districts within Northrhine-Westphalia (higher transporting costs are also taken into account) nearly double the tonnage of sewage sludge can be used for agricultural purposes. Less compost will be used, but the total amount of recycled P_2O_5 and other nutrient is nevertheless increasing enormously (compare Table 2 with Table 3). The agricultural sector is asking for more sewage sludge than is available.

But taking the high P_2O_5-concentration in the soils into account by reducing the sewage sludge and compost tonnage, which is allowed to be spread per acre (minus 50 %) on soils which have high P_2O_5-concentration and stopping the spreading of these on soils with extremely high concentrations, RAUMIS is prognosticating the results as shown in Table 4 (no transport between the districts).

Table 3 The use of sewage sludge in Northrhine-Westphalia in the year 2005; normal P_2O_5-soil-concentrations, transport of sewage sludge between different districts

USAGE	SEWAGE SLUDGE		COMPOSTS	
	(in tons, dry mass)	(in %)	(in tons, dry mass)	(in %)
Without leasehold-land	525.185	113	160.232	43
With leasehold-land	652.381	140	140.080	37

Table 4 The use of sewage sludge in Northrhine-Westphalia in the year 2005; taking actual P_2O_5-soil-concentration into account (practicable-decree concerning the sewage sludge decree), no transport of sewage sludge between different districts

USAGE	SEWAGE SLUDGE		COMPOSTS	
	(in tons, dry mass)	(in %)	(in tons, dry mass)	(in %)
Without leasehold-land	191.674	41	252.819	68
With leasehold-land	260.641	56	252.806	68

Table 5 The use of sewage sludge in Northrhine-Westphalia in the year 2005, taking actual P_2O_5-soil-concentration into account (like described in the practicable-decree in relation to the sewage sludge decree), transport of sewage sludge between different districts

USAGE	SEWAGE SLUDGE		COMPOSTS	
	(in tons, dry mass)	(in %)	(in tons, dry mass)	(in %)
Without leasehold-land	251.121	54	250.674	70
With leasehold-land	349.064	75	227.332	61

Depending on the decisions of the landlords, between 41 % and 56 % of the sewage sludge from Northrhine-Westphalia, which are available for the agricultural sector will be used by farmers, even if there is no transportation between different districts. But if transportation between the different areas within Northrhine-Westphalia is allowed, between 54 % up to 75% will be used by farmers (see table 5). Another interesting fact, comparing the scenarios in Tables 4 and 5, that the used tonnage of composts in both scenarios is nearly the same.

COMPROMISE-MODEL

Of course the best alternative is to use sewage sludge in the region where it is produced. But if that is not possible, one has to transport it. If farmers do not use it, one has to transport the sludge in most cases to the brown-coal power-stations, which are situated between Aachen and Cologne in the south-west of Northrhine-Westphalia. Due to that fact, transportation for agricultural purposes is - from the environmental point of view - not a worse alternative. One of the results in this context is: Less miles will be driven, if the sewage sludge is transported to fields in other districts, compared to the situation, if the sewage sludge is transported to the brown-coal power-stations.

Consequently the alternative, taking transportation into account, seems to be a realistic exogen parameter for a waste management concept concerning sewage sludge and composts. But it is unrealistic to deny the problem of high P_2O_5-concentration in the soil. Therefore it is important to examine this problem in detail.

As mentioned nearly 50 % of the soils show high P_2O_5-concentration. But about 70 % of these are close to the level "normal P_2O_5-concentration". Therefore it might be an option to realize the following scenario: Soils with a high P_2O_5-concentration must reduce these concentrations. Therefore less nutrients are allowed to be spread compared to soils with normal concentrations. In the following scenario 75 % of the plants demand is allowed to be added. Consequently it will take more time to reduce the high concentrations, but the environmental aim will be reached.

Concerning soils with "very high P_2O_5-concentration", nearly the same situation is observed. Most of them are close to the "high concentration" level. Therefore in the new scenario in these areas, half of the plants demand can be spread as sewage sludge or composts. Table 6 shows that the farmers are questioning between 81 % and 125 % of the available sewage sludge.

Table 6 The use of sewage sludge in Northrhine-Westphalia in the year 2005, transportation of sewage sludge between different districts; looking on the P_2O_5-concentration in the way like described with the "compromise model"

USAGE	SEWAGE SLUDGE (in tons, dry mass)	(in %)	COMPOSTS (in tons, dry mass)	(in %)
Without leasehold-land	376.239	81	163.617	44
With leasehold-land	578.368	125	137.359	37

Due to the fact that only 100 % is really available, the farmers have to compete for the sewage sludge. Consequently the prices the owners of waste-water plants have to pay for getting rid of the sewage sludge will fall. The owners of the waste-water-treatment plants have a strong instrument to enforce this competition and - with this - their market position. It is "exporting" sewage sludge to other federal states in Germany. Predestinated are big towns on the river Rhine, because they can export much sewage sludge and they can also use the cheapest way of transporting goods: ships. First experiences have already been made.

CONCLUSIONS

The reuse of sewage sludge for agricultural purposes will continue to grow, because even in Northrhine-Westphalia, a federal state in Germany with quite bad benchmarks for a recycling of great amounts of sewage sludge in the agricultural sector, nearly the whole amount which is available for the agriculture sector can be used.

Summary

Due to German law, disposal of sewage sludge and other organics is forbidden from the year 2005 on. Therefore it is important to establish whether, if it is possible to reuse the sewage sludge for agricultural purposes (only long-term recycling path) or if it is necessary to make arrangements to burn more of it in the future.

Different scenarios were considered with an agro-economic model system called RAUMIS, which is also used by the German Agriculture Ministry. The results show, that todays high P_2O_5-concentrations in the soils are the most important limiting factor. But it is also of importance, whether the landlords are accepting the use of sewage sludge and biowaste-composts on their land, or not.

The quantity of both negative effects can be more than compensated, if sewage sludge is transported across the district borders within Northrhine-Westphalia. It is even possible, depending on the selected scenario, that the whole sewage sludge pool, which is available to the agricultural sector could become a rare good for the farmers, so that real market prices can be established. Because the density of the population in Northrhine-Westphalia is extremely high, this fact is remarkable. In order to reach this target, the big waste-water-associations will have to improve their logistic concepts. If these concepts are brought into action, all waste-water-associations and communities in Northrhine-Westphalia would be able to save a great deal of money.

REFERENCES

Non-english headlines are translated to give the reader information about the kind of source; the translation is not always close to the original German or Netherlands headline.

1. DRITTE ALLGEMEINE VERWALTUNGSVORSCHRIFT ZUM ABFALLGESETZ (TA Siedlungsabfall) - Technische Anleitung zur Verwertung, Behandlung und sonstigen Entsorgung von Siedlungsabfällen (German decree about recycling, treatment and deposing of municipal solide waste) vom 14.05.1993, BAnz. Nr. 99a.

2. GESETZ ZUR FÖRDERUNG DER KREISLAUFWIRTSCHAFT UND SICHERUNG DER UMWELTVERTRÄGLICHEN BESEITIGUNG VON ABFÄLLEN (Kreislaufwirtschafts- und

Abfallgesetz -KrW-/AbfG; German law about recycling and waste) vom 27.9.1994, BGBl. I S. 2705.

3. AUSWERTUNGS- UND INFORMATIONSDIENST FÜR ERNÄHRUNG, LANDWIRTSCHAFT UND FORSTEN E.V. (AID) (1997): Landwirtschaft in Zahlen (Facts about agriculture in Germany), Bonn.

4. MINISTERIUM FÜR UMWELT, RAUMORDNUNG UND LANDWIRTSCHAFT DES LANDES NORDRHEIN-WESTFALEN (MURL; Ministery of Environment and Agriculture in Northrhine-Westphalia) (1995): Verwaltungsvorschriften zum Vollzug der Klärschlammverordnung (AbfKlärV) (Rules about the way how to use the German sewage sludge decree in practise) , *Ministerialblatt für das Land Nordrhein-Westfalen - Nr. 39 vom 12.07.1995*, 674 - 687.

5. STATISTISCHES BUNDESAMT (Statistical Office for Germany) (Hrsg.) (1997): Datenreport 1997 - Zahlen und Fakten über die Bundesrepublik Deutschland (Data-report 1997 - facts about Germany), 2. durchgesehene Auflage, Band 340 der Schriftenreihe der Bundeszentrale für politische Bildung, Bonn.

6. BREUNINGER, E. (1992): Komposthof statt Schweinestall? (Compost plant instead of pigsty), *top-agrar*, H. 4, 30 - 33.

7. RHEINBRAUN AKTIENGESELLSCHAFT (Hrsg.) (1997): Klärschlamm-Mitverbrennung in der zirkulierenden Wirbelschichtfeuerung (Co-burning of sewage sludge in brown coal power station), *Rheinbraun informiert*, April, Köln.

8. HENRICHSMEYER, ET. AL. (1995): Stand der Arbeiten im Kooperationsprojekt zur Entwicklung des gesamtdeutschen Agrarsektormodells RAUMIS 96 (Status report about the cooperation-project concerning the development of a German agricultural sector model for whole Germany, RAUMIS 96), Bonn / Braunschweig.

9. HENRICHSMEYER, ET. AL. (1996): Endbericht zum Kooperationsprojekt "Entwicklung des gesamtdeutschen Agrarsektormodells RAUMIS 96" (Final report about the cooperation-project: Development of a German agricultural sector model for the whole of Germany, RAUMIS 96", Bonn / Braunschweig.

10. LÖHE, W., SANDER, R. (1997): The use of the RAUMIS modelling system to analyze regional effects on agriculture and environment in Germany by regions; in: EUROPEAN COMMISSION (Hrsg.): The effects of a worldwide liberisation of the markets on cereals, oilseeds and pulses on agriculture in the European Union, Luxemburg, 53 - 66.

11. JONGBLOED, A., KEMME, P., DELLAERT, B. (1990): Microbiel fytase in de voeding van varkens (Feeding pigs with microbiological phytase), in: JONGBLOED, A., COPPOOLSE, J. (Hrsg.): Mestproblematik: aanpak via de voeding van varkens en pluimvee (The manure-problem: Feeding pigs and polatry), Lelystad/Netherlands, 51 - 57.

12. DELLAERT, B. ET AL. (1990): A comparison of different techniques to assess the biological availability of feeding phosphates in pig feeding, *Netherlands Journal of Agricultural Sciences*, 38, 555 - 566.

13. COPPOOLSE, J. ET AL. (1990): De uitscheiding van stikstof, fosfor en kalium door landbowhuisdieren, Nu en Morgen (Todays and tomorrows N-, P_2O_5- and K_2O-concentration in manure from farm animals), Den Haag.

14. KOCH-ACHELPÖHLER, V. (1996): Landwirtschaft in Nordrhein-Westfalen, Analyse und Projektion des Agrarstrukturwandels 1980 - 2003 (Agriculture in Northrhine-Westphalia, Analysis and projection of the change concerning the agricultural structure between 1980 - 2003) , *Bericht der Forschungsgesellschaft und Agrarpolitik und Agrarsoziologie e.V.*, H. 304, Bonn.

15. BUNDESMINISTERIUM FÜR UMWELT, NATURSCHUTZ UND REAKTORSICHERHEIT (BMU; German Environmental Ministry) (1996): Entwurf der "Verordnung über die Verwertung von biologisch abbaubaren Abfällen auf landwirtschaftlich, forstwirtschaftlich und gärtnerisch genutzten Flächen (Bioabfall- und Kompostverordnung; Composting decree), Stand: 16.12.1996, Bonn.

16. DÖRPMUND, H.-G. (1993a): Bayerische Landwirte als Kompostprofis (Bavarian farmers are compost-profis), *Agrar-Übersicht*, Jg. 44 (1), 18 - 20.

17. DÖRPMUND, H.-G. (1993b): Hier entsorgen Bauern auch die Biotonne (Farmers are managing the biosolids from the separate collection in households), *Agrar-Übersicht*, Jg. 44 (1), 21 - 22.

18. KERN, M. (1989): Kostenstruktur der Mietenkompostierung - Arbeitswirtschaft und Betriebskosten (Cost-structure of composting) - , *Abfall- Wirtschaft* 3, Kassel.

19. KERN, M., WIEMER, K. (1990): Kostenstruktur der Boxenkompostierung - Arbeitswirtschaft und Betriebskosten (Cost-structure of box-composting)-, *Abfall-Wirtschaft 4*, Kassel.

20. AUSWERTUNGS- UND INFORMATIONSDIENST FÜR ERNÄHRUNG, LANDWIRTSCHAFT UND FORSTEN E.V. (AID) (1991): Pachten und Verpachten, Teilflächen und Betriebe (Leasing land), Bonn.

21. KLÄRSCHLAMMVERORDNUNG (AbfKlärV; German sewage sludge decree) vom 15.04.1992, BGBl. I , S. 912.

PRODUCT CERTIFICATION OF SEWAGE SLUDGE

A Carlson-Ekvall
M Sandström
The Swedish National Testing and Research Institute

Sweden

ABSTRACT. Traditionally about half of the produced sewage sludge is used as soil amendment in Sweden, either directly by using sewage sludge for soil improvement, or indirectly by the production of soil from sewage sludge. To effectively and safely recycle nutrients, third party quality assessment of waste products is crucial to avoid unwanted effects and to keep the confidence of users. Such a quality assessment could be the certification system developed by the Swedish National Testing and Research Institute, the P-mark. This system is described in this paper.

Keywords: Sewage sludge, Certification, Quality assessment, Soil improvement, Recycling of nutrients, Organic waste.

Dr C E A Carlson-Ekvall, has a MSc in chemical engineering and a PhD in Sanitary Engineering. Her research interests include environmental aspects of sewage sludge with a focus on leaching and bioavaliability of toxic metals. Presently, she works at the section for Building Materials at the SP Swedish National Testing and Research Institute, where she is responsible for the product certification of sewage sludge, compost and digestate from biowaste. She is also responsible for the development of quality criteria for soil and slag.

M Sandström, is head of the section for Building Materials at SP Swedish National Testing and Research Institute. His research is focused on microstructure of building materials and its impact on function and durability. He is project manager for a Technology Transfer project. The aim is to improve the development of small and medium sized enterprises (SME).

INTRODUCTION

Minimum requirements on products have traditionally been given in law and regulations, sometimes supplemented with regulations for maximum allowed environmental impact. Nowadays, requirements set up by trade associations or other organisations, such as environment organisations, seem to be more and more important. The fulfilment is demonstrated by certification by a third party.

In the 1980s, the Swedish National Testing and Research Institute developed a certification system for products, the P mark. Until this date, around 60 "Regulations for P-marking" have been issued.

INTRODUCTION TO CERTIFICATION

SP as Certification Body

The certification of SP The Swedish National Testing and Research Institute covers a number of fields, environment, quality systems, the working environment and products. Product certification confirms certain required characteristics or properties of a product, requirements that are set out in standards or that are specified by public authorities or in voluntary specifications. Certification covers a wide range of areas for various approval marking schemes, such as:

• The CE symbol required by about 15 EU directives

• P-marking, SP's own type-testing quality approval symbol.

P-marking in General

After permission from the Swedish National Testing and Research Institute (SP), manufacturers may use the P-symbol to mark their products. The certification normally includes both the process by which the product is manufactured as well as requirement on the product itself.

In order to be granted a P-marking permit, the manufacturer must be able to demonstrate the compliance of the product with the prevailing norm. The extent of the continuous quality control of the products is regulated in an agreement between SP and the producer.

The continuous quality control is made mainly by the manufacturer. The manufacturer's control is checked through inspections made by SP. These inspections are carried out in the plant and at locations for import. The main purpose with the quality control is to see that the requirements on the product are fulfilled.

Examples of products that can be P-marked are sewage sludge, lime, cement, nail plate trusses, windows and floorball equipment.

PRODUCT CERTIFICATION – WHY?

There are many reasons for choosing to certify a product, but most of them fall into four categories:

- To establish and maintain control over the product and the production requirements.
- To get a guarantee from a third party that the product fulfils certain requirements.
- To achieve a good-will in order to increase sales.
- Because someone else (i.e. the customer) demands a certificate.

A certified product has two advantages that can be helpful in marketing: it is controlled and the result of the control meets certain requirements. Many customers appreciate the possibility to choose a product with defined properties and a guarantee that it works for the proposed purpose. Many regulations for P-marking are the result of a wish from a whole branch, often in the form of a trade association, to establish and maintain a reputation for good quality, thus increasing the confidence in their products. Sometimes the desire for a quality guarantee, such as a product certificate, comes from another part rather than from the trade itself. This other part can be a customer, or an organisation of customers, but also others, such as environmental organisations.

There are significant advantages of having a product certificate. First of all, the manufacturer gets someone from outside the company who goes through the production with fresh eyes. This alone can be very valuable, especially since all inspectors are well acquainted with the actual trade. Secondly, the inspection from a third part gives credibility to the product and the manufacturer. This is particularly important when the demand for quality control is coming from the outside, i.e. an organisation of customers.

To receive a certificate, a quality system is necessary. This gives the manufacturer an opportunity to go through the different activities which together result in the product. Many manufacturers wish to build up a system according to the ISO 9000 standard. Product certification can then be a good starting point, since the demands on the quality system is harmonised with the ISO 9000 and ISO 14 001 standards, but the scope of the quality system is restricted to the processes which have a direct effect on the product quality. Other manufacturers may have problems with large variations in the quality. A thorough penetration of the processes together with the inspector from the certifying organ can be very helpful to pin-point weaknesses that can explain quality variations.

P-MARKING OF SEWAGE SLUDGE

P-marking rules no 89 applies to sewage sludge. The certification rules are available on the Internet at the address http://www.sp.se/cert/cert_prod/spcr/spcr089.pdf (in Swedish, but with a summary in English). To be allowed to use the P-mark on sewage sludge it must fulfil certain requirements with regard to organic pollutants and metals. To ensure this, the producer must build up a quality system similar to ISO 9000 for all processes affecting the sludge quality.

Product Requirements

A difference between an ISO 9000 certificate and product certification is that, to receive a product certificate, the product must fulfil certain requirements. Those requirements are decided by the certifying organisation, often in close contact with the concerned trade associations and authorities. The requirements are the same for all manufacturers and all products. In the case of sewage sludge, the same rules apply for raw sludge, digested sludge and limed sludge. The requirements have been discussed with representatives of the concerned trade associations as well as the authorities together with representatives for users, distributors and individual sewage treatment plants.

Table 1 Requirements for P-marking of sewage sludge in Sweden

PROPERTY	REQUIREMENT (mg/kg dry sludge)
Dry matter	Declared
Loss on ignition	Declared
pH	Declared
Total phosphorus	Declared
Total nitrogen	Declared
Ammonium nitrogen	Declared
Lead	100
Copper	600
Nickel	50
Zinc	800
Cadmium	2
Chromium	100
Mercury	2,5
Nonyl phenol	50
Sum PAH (6)	3,0
Sum PCB (7)	0,4

The requirements concerning metals in Table 1 are limit values decided by the Swedish National Environmental Protection Agency, which means that it is illegal to spread sewage sludge on farmland unless these requirements are met. The organic substances do not have limiting values. The values are characteristic recommendations and can be exceeded occasionally. However, the trend is not allowed to increase. The values for the organic substances originate from an agreement between the Swedish Water & Waste Water Associates, the Swedish National Environmental Protection Agency and the Federation of Swedish Farmers made in 1994. At that time, toluene was also included. However, two reasons made toluene an unsuitable substance for regulation. Most importantly, it was found to be formed naturally in the sludge. Since toluene was included to be an indicator for industrial pollution, this finding made the analysis of toluene pointless. Secondly, it turned out to be very difficult to measure toluene with reasonable reproducibility. In 1999, toluene was excluded from the requirement list.

It should be observed that these requirements do not prevent a sewage treatment plant with P-marked sludge from producing sludge with poor quality. What the regulations do stipulate is that the sludge cannot be marketed with a P-mark unless the actual sludge batch fulfils the requirements. This in turn means that procedures must be defined for how the controlled sludge is separated from the sludge that is not yet controlled, and also how the approved sludge is separated from the sludge that does not fulfil the requirements. Only sludge that is controlled and approved can be P-marked.

Demands on the Quality System

To ensure that the sludge fulfils the above requirements, and also to ensure that the sludge which in spite of all efforts does not fulfil the requirements is properly labelled and separated from the rest, a quality system is necessary. The quality system must contain the following parts:

Quality policy: The sewage treatment plant must have a quality policy where two features have to be included. Firstly, a statement of the quality ambitions not only generally, but specifically concerning sewage sludge. Secondly, there must be a commitment to continual improvement.

Responsibility and authority: The responsibility, authority and the interrelation of people who manage, perform and verify work affecting the sludge quality must be defined and documented.

Manufacturers representative: The manufacturer shall appoint a representative whose responsibility is to evaluate the quality of the product and to maintain contact with SP.

Management review: The management shall have documented meetings on a regular basis in order to review the quality system. Issues to discuss are, amongst others, internal quality audits, non-conforming products and the fulfilment of goals.

Quality records: Only valid documents shall be available for concerned staff. There shall be a list of all valid documents and an instruction for creation of new documents, updating of old documents and document storage.

Corrective and preventive action: The manufacturer should establish and maintain documented procedures for implementing corrective and preventive action, including non-conforming products and complaints from the public.

Note that, in order to obtain a P-mark for sewage sludge, only processes that directly affect the sludge quality are included. For example, processes involving clean water are not included, once the water stream is separated from that of the sludge.
Thus, if a sewage treatment plant is certified according to ISO 9000 or ISO 14 001, the above requirements can be considered to be fulfilled without further control.

Of course, the control of the product is crucial in product certification. Several items in the quality system concern this, such as;

Receiving inspection and testing: This concerns several parts of the process. Like many other manufacturers, the sewage treatment plant must control purchased articles, such as chemicals used as coagulants. However, the majority of the material that enters the sewage treatment plant comes through the sewer system.

To ensure a good sludge quality, and an early warning in case of quality problems, the incoming water must also be controlled. In the case of digested sludge, an alternative is to control the sludge before digesting. With normal time spans for digesting and a sufficiently quick analysis, the results from an analysis of incoming sludge should be available by the time the sludge has fermented, and in the event of poor quality, the sludge can be separated from the approved sludge.

Another source of pollutants can be solid or liquid material that enters the system in other ways. An example is the emptying of septic tank sludge in special receiving stations on the sewer system or at the sewage treatment plant, where instructions for what can be received and some kind of control of who has access may be necessary. Other examples include addition of organic materials directly to the digestion chamber, such as fat from fat separators at restaurants.

In-process inspection and testing: Should be performed when necessary, with care and sufficiently documented. Final inspection and testing: Samples should be taken from the sludge at sufficiently short intervals to ensure that a representative sample is analysed. The sub samples are mixed and sent to analysis according to the following scheme (Table 2)

Table 2 Sampling plan for sewage treatment plants of different sizes with dewatering equipment

SAMPLE TYPE	NUMBER OF CONNECTED PERSON EQUIVALENTS		
	200 - 2000	2001 - 20 000	> 20 000
Primary sample	1 sample every second week	1 sample/ week	1 sample/every day that the dewatering equipment is running
Preparation of bulk sample	1 sample/year	1 sample/6 months	1 sample/ month

Some small sewage treatment plants do not have dewatering equipment, but transports the wet sludge to another plant for dewatering. This sludge will then be impossible to distinguish from the sludge of the receiving plant, which means that it cannot be P-marked separately. One P-mark will then be valid for all sludge leaving a dewatering equipment.

Of course, the process of the smaller sewage treatment plant must still be controlled and approved according to the regulations for P-marking. A sub sample of the bulk sample is sent to analysis. The results of the analysis are then compared to the requirements in Table 1.

Equipment

To keep control over the process, it is necessary that the equipment works correctly. Examples of important items under this point are schemes for maintenance and correct and easily available instructions for use. All measuring equipment that can have any influence on sludge quality must be calibrated, for example the thermometer in the digestion chamber. Other important equipment are balances, flow meters and all laboratory equipment.

Control of non-conforming products: Products that do not fulfil the requirements may under no circumstances be launched as P-marked products, provided that the analysis results are known. As soon as the results from the analysis shows that the sludge is too polluted, all P-marks must be removed from labels, bags or wherever the manufacturer has chosen to display the P-mark.

If the quality is generally good and shows small variations, sludge can be P-marked and marketed before the results of the analysis is known. Should the analysis then show that a single batch is not approved, the customer should immediately be notified and necessary action be taken. To ensure this, it is of course necessary with procedures for labelling and traceability.

Labelling

Procedures for labelling of the product must be designed and implemented.

Traceability

It is important that every single analysis result must be possible to attribute to a defined batch of sludge A flow chart should be established to ensure traceability. Often, the sewage treatment plant divides the sludge according to month. This means that one analysis a month is enough. Of course, if the analysis shows results above the requirements, the whole month loses the P-mark. This can be avoided by analysing more often, but that is costly and is usually not considered necessary.

The sewage treatment plant must keep a register to keep record of where every single batch of sludge is spread. If the transport is outsourced to an entrepreneur, the register can be kept there. In that case, this should be regulated in the contract. This register must be available for the authorities, the customers and the certifying organisation for at least 10 years.

Follow-up of the Certificate

After issuing the certificate, follow-up inspections are carried out twice a year. The quality system is checked according to a check-list and all deviations should be amended promptly. SP annually takes sludge samples which are analysed both by the producer and SP. The analysis results at the sewage treatment plant must not deviate considerably from the results at SP.

All certificate holders are listed on an official Internet page, whereas everything else is subject to secrecy. Should it become necessary to withdraw a certificate, that also becomes official.

Other Certified Products in the Environmental Area

In 1991, "Regulations for P-marking of liming products for acidified lakes and water-courses" were issued. Today, there are seven certified products distributed amongst three manufacturers, who together cover almost the entire market. In 1998, RVF The Swedish Association of Waste management decided to launch their own certificate, "Certifierad Återvinning" for compost and digestate from biowaste. Although RVF has chosen to have their own label, SP Swedish National Testing and Research Institute has the commission to administrate the certificates as well as the performance of controls, excluding the laboratory analyses. This system is described in the Certification rules for compost and digestate from biowaste by the quality assurance system of RVF, SPCR 120, available on the Internet at the address http://www.sp.se/cert/cert_prod/kompost.htm (in Swedish, but with an English summary). The first certificate will probably be issues during the year 2001.

In 2005, it will be prohibited in Sweden to put organic waste on landfill. It is already very expensive to put waste on landfill. This had created an increasing interest in converting waste products to products. This is possible for many kinds of waste, provided that a quality system is developed to ensure that the waste products fulfil the requirements that can be set on products designed for a specific use. Of course, in the case of waste products, the environmental issues are crucial. Presently, quality criteria for two products are under development.

The current regulations for soil are inadequate, for example neither heavy metals or organic pollutants are regulated. Additionally, there are no requirements demanding that a soil contains nutrients. Many waste products are suitable for manufacturing of soil. Clear and all-embracing rules would simplify the use of waste products in soil and at the same time guarantee that material of poor quality does not enter the soil production.

Slag from metal industry is another material that can be useful for many purposes, for example as aggregates in road construction. The work of defining what properties, mechanical, physiological and environmental, are important to regulate has just started.

REFERENCES

1. SP Swedish National Testing and Research Institute, Certification rules for sewage sludge, SPCR 089 (Certifieringsregler för Biomull, SPCR 089, in Swedish), 1999

2. SP Swedish National Testing and Research Institute, Certification rules for compost and digestate from biowaste by the quality assurance system of RVF, SPCR 120 (Certifieringsregler för kompost och rötrest, SPCR 120, in Swedish), 2000

3. SP Swedish National Testing and Research Institute, Regulations for P-marking of Liming Products for Acidified Lakes and Water Courses, Björn Schouenborg, SP report 1991:35E, 1991.

4. EN 45 011, General criteria for certification bodies operating product certification

5. EN 45 012 General criteria for certification bodies operating quality system certification

6. EN 45 004 General criteria for the operation of various types of bodies performing inspection.

REVIEW OF STRATEGY FOR RECYCLING AND REUSE OF WASTE MATERIALS

B J Sealey

G J Hill

P S Phillips

University College Northampton

United Kingdom

ABSTRACT. Each year around 400 million tonnes of waste is produced in England and Wales. The UK government document "Waste Strategy 2000" identifies the need to curb the growing quantity of waste produced and sets out the changes needed to deliver sustainable waste management. In order to achieve sustainable waste management, it is not sufficient simply to concentrate on how best to reuse or recycle the waste that is produced, but to minimise the amount of waste that is produced in the first place.

The UK government has set challenging targets; by 2005 the amount of industrial and commercial waste sent to land fill is to be reduced to 85% of 1998 levels. While the issue of hardened concrete waste – as part of the construction and demolition waste stream – has received considerable attention, process waste arising from the manufacture of ready-mixed concrete is relatively unexplored.

It is apparent that initiatives such as the landfill tax have encouraged UK ready-mixed concrete manufacturers to substantially reduce the amount of waste they produce. This paper applies the current UK government waste strategy to this topic, analysing and evaluating current waste management methods.

Keywords: Waste strategy 2000, Waste minimisation, Ready-mixed concrete.

Mr B J Sealey, is a Research Assistant in the Waste Management Research Group at University College Northampton.

Mr G J Hill, is a Principal Lecturer within the Waste Management Research Group at University College Northampton.

Dr P S Phillips, is a Reader are all members of the Waste Management Research Group at University College Northampton.

INTRODUCTION TO WASTE STRATEGY 2000

The Rio de Janeiro Earth Summit in 1992 saw the formulation of the first series of sustainable waste management options. Sustainable approaches to managing waste in the UK were put forward in the 1994 UK Government publication, 'Sustainable Development: The UK Strategy.' [1] This was replaced in 1995 by the Government White Paper, 'Making Waste Work: A Strategy for Sustainable Waste Management in England and Wales.'[2] This document introduced the 'waste hierarchy' concept (Figure 1). Subsequent Government documents have refined the hierarchy concept, and the current waste strategy for England and Wales, is set out in 'Waste Strategy 2000.' [3]

A key principle of Waste Strategy 2000 is the selection of the Best Practicable Environmental Option (BPEO). Identifying the correct way to deal with particular waste streams is not a simple matter. BPEO will vary from product to product. Determining BPEO requires the consideration of both the waste hierarchy (Figure 1) and the Proximity Principle. The Proximity Principle requires waste to be disposed of as close to the place of production as possible [3]. At the top of the waste hierarchy is reduction (previously termed minimisation). While disposal is the least preferred option, it is important to realise that the most effective waste management decisions can be taken by adopting an integrated approach to waste management, and more than one waste management option from the waste hierarchy, in conjunction with the Proximity Principle, can be used to create the BPEO [4]. The BPEO for a particular waste may gravitate towards the bottom of the waste hierarchy due to the costs and impact of transporting that waste to a reprocessing facility. The BPEO for a waste stream will be a mixture of different waste management methods, as each component material of the waste stream will merit different waste management options. In this paper we consider the ready-mixed concrete plant waste stream.

Figure 1   Waste hierarchy

READY-MIXED CONCRETE

Concrete is the world's most important construction material. It is an essential part of modern life; our infrastructure depends on it. The UK ready-mixed industry grew rapidly in the 1950s and today the vast majority of concrete originates from a ready-mixed concrete batching plant.

Concrete is a mixture of sand, gravel, crushed rock or other aggregate held together by a hardened paste of cement and water.

One cubic metre of concrete has a mass of around 2400 kilograms. Around 80 per cent of this is aggregate, 12 per cent is cement and 8 per cent is water. Small quantities of chemical admixture may be incorporated.

The production of concrete at a ready-mixed batching plant involves accurately weighing the required quantity of each constituent material and mixing them together either in the drum of a mixer truck or in a static pan-mixer. There are currently 1200 ready-mixed concrete plants in the UK, producing 23.5 million cubic metres of concrete per year.

THE READY-MIXED CONCRETE WASTE STREAM

Process waste from ready-mixed concrete plants is distinct from the hardened concrete waste incorporated in the construction and demolition waste stream, which is said to comprise over 16% of total UK waste arising [5]. In the context of this paper, it also excludes the estimated £400 million of ready-mixed concrete that is dumped in the UK each year because construction sites inaccurately order quantities [6].

It is difficult to estimate accurately the quantity of waste generated by the ready-mixed concrete industry. There is no such thing as a typical ready-mixed concrete plant. Although the UK's 1200 plants are broadly similar, each plant will exhibit individual production practice as a result of local differences in plant design, market, geology, management and personnel. A plant with a large yard and extensive ground storage capacity, for example, may operate differently to a plant with a small yard and no ground storage facility. Estimating waste arising is further complicated by commercial secrecy.

The ready-mixed concrete industry is highly competitive. Producers who have successfully reduced the quantity of waste they produce by the introduction of new technology and management techniques will understandably want to reap the commercial advantage. There is also a prevalent climate of secrecy borne out of the culture of hiding true levels of waste. This is promoted by internal as well as external pressures.

However, a typical plant may create between 20 and 80 tonnes of waste per month. This would suggest that around 0.75 million tonnes of waste is created each year in the UK by the ready-mixed concrete production.

With the current cost of disposal to landfill at around £200 per 20 tonne load, disposal of waste arising from the production of ready-mixed concrete can be estimated to cost the industry around £7.5 million each year. This does not include costs associated with handling this waste at the plant or the loss of materials.

What is the Waste Produced by Ready-Mixed Concrete Plants?

Most ready-mixed concrete plant waste arises from two sources:

1. Washing out truck mixer drums at the end of each working day to prevent fresh concrete residue from setting in the drum overnight. Additionally, waste arises from washing down the yard and plant.
2. Occasionally unwanted fresh concrete is returned to the batching plant from site.

The wet waste consists mainly of water, with a variable proportion of coarse and fine aggregates, cementitious powders and chemical admixtures.

The production of ready mixed concrete is not an overtly wasteful process; the amount of waste produced is small in comparison to the quantities of material used. However, wet concrete waste is alkaline and hazardous. Traditionally this waste has been disposed of to landfill. Economic and environmental pressures make landfill an unsustainable option.

Ready-Mixed Concrete Plant Waste is Hazardous

Ready-mixed concrete plant waste has a pH of typically 11.5 or higher (Table 1). The Environment Agency Special Waste Regulations [7] state that any waste with a pH in excess of 11.5 is corrosive (and is therefore hazardous).

The active status of waste from concrete plants is acknowledged in the landfill tax regulations. Although hardened concrete waste is classed as inert and qualifies for the lower rate of tax, HM Customs and Excise Notice LFT1 'A general guide to landfill tax', specifically places "concrete plant washings" in the higher tax band [8].

Table 1   Typical chemical analysis of ready-mixed concrete plant waste

PROPERTY	VALUE
Mercury as Hg, dry weight	<0.05 Mg/kg
Arsenic as AS, dry weight	13.97 Mg/kg
Selenium as Se, dry weight	0.41 Mg/kg
PH	11.83
Cadmium as Cd, dry weight	<1.70 Mg/kg
Chromium as Cr, dry weight	19.20 Mg/kg
Copper as Cu, dry weight	11.20 Mg/kg
Lead as Pb, dry weight	18.75 Mg/kg
Nickel as Ni, dry weight	16.25 Mg/kg
Zinc as ZN, dry weight	118.80 Mg/kg
Boron as B, hot water soluble, dry weight	1.32 Mg/kg
Cyanide as CH, total dry weight	5.00 Mg/kg
Chloride as CL, water soluble, dry weight	836.17 Mg/kg
Sulfate Total as SO3 by ICP, dry weight	5172.00 Mg/kg

Alkaline substances, including fresh concrete, can cause serious burns to human skin [9].

Water discharged from ready-mixed concrete plants can pollute local watercourses. This can have serious repercussions for the surrounding environment and ecosystems.

CURRENT WASTE MANAGEMENT METHODS IN
READY-MIXED CONCRETE PRODUCTION

Description of the Traditional Method for Dealing with Waste

Most UK ready-mixed concrete plants have inherited a system for managing waste that dates from an era unaware of environmental pressures and the need to conserve resources.

This system, known as 'washing out', is summarized here (see Figure 2):

1. The empty truck mixer drum is filled with water.
2. The drum is rotated in an effort to wash residual concrete from the interior of the drum.
3. The entire contents of the drum (water and any solids) are discharged into a large pit.
4. Water discharged into the pit is allowed to drain into a separate facility where it may be recovered and recycled. The solids remain in the pit.
5. The pit is emptied periodically – the contents being transferred to a drying out bay.
6. The contents of the drying out bay are disposed of to landfill. The bay is emptied when it is full and when the contents are dry enough to be handled.

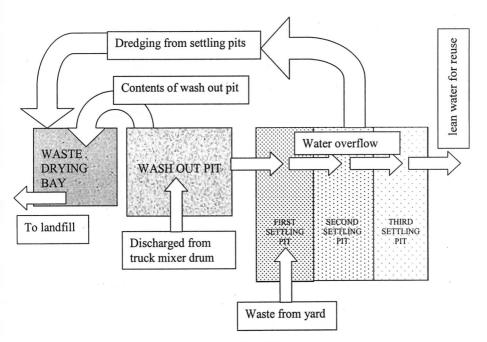

Figure 2 Diagram of traditional method

Washing out the mixer drum is undertaken whenever there is a risk that a residue of fresh concrete may 'set' if it is allowed to remain in the drum. This is usually necessary at the end of each working day.

Although the waste is cementitious, it does not 'set' or harden, as most of the cement has hydrated. The contents of the wash out pit are sludge like, while waste in the drying out bay is similar in consistency to that of a cheesecake base.

The wash out pit, the drying out bay and the settling pits are normally all emptied as one job, all the work being carried out during the course of one working day.

The drying out bay is emptied using a loading shovel and the contents are transported to a landfill site. The contents of the wash out pit are removed to the now empty drying out bay. The settling pits may also be dredged, again using a loading shovel, and the solids placed in the drying out bay.

Recycled Water

Recycling of process water is a common feature of UK ready mixed concrete plants. Water from washing out trucks is recovered from the wash out pit and stored in a settling pit. Run off water from the yard will also drain into this settling pit. The water in the settling pit is allowed to overflow into a second and possibly a third pit. The water in the third pit is relatively clean and free from solids, as most of the solids will have settled at the bottom of the first and second pits. The recovered water may be recycled and used in subsequent batches of concrete, or may be reused to wash out trucks.

Changes in Ready-Mixed Concrete Waste Management

The introduction of the Landfill Tax in October 1996 prompted the UK's ready-mixed concrete industry to evaluate its waste problem. Realising that the waste fell into the standard category and therefore attracted the higher tax rate, producers took the issue seriously. Management of waste – minimizing its occurrence - became a priority. New methods of cleaning mixer drums were sought. The two that have been most widely adopted are 'stoning out' and chemical wash systems. In addition to these new methods of washing mixer truck drums, fresh concrete reclaimers have been installed at a small number of plants.

The ever increasing cost of landfill – and it is clear from the Government's Strategy that these costs are set to increase and landfill will eventually cease to be a viable option – has encouraged ready-mixed concrete companies to continually develop and improve their waste management techniques.

Chemical Wash Out System

This method is relatively new to the UK, ready-mixed concrete companies are increasingly accepting it. The last ten years has seen its introduction, trial, modification and development such that the technique and equipment have been refined into a usable, effective and efficient system.

A significant amount of research has been published on hydration control admixture, evaluating its practical use, and economic viability [10 - 14]. The general consensus is that it does work and it is a practical and cost effective system. It has been demonstrated that hydration control admixture, when used appropriately, has no detrimental effect on subsequent batches of concrete.

The procedure involves spraying the truck mixer drum with the admixture and water at the end of the day. In the morning fresh concrete is batched directly into the drum. The amount of water used to 'wash' the drum is typically 300 litres as opposed to 3000 litres. A time saving of around 18 minutes is gained. The main advantage (Table 2) is the elimination of waste – the residue of concrete and water left in the drum at the end of each working day is simply incorporated into the first batch of the following day.

Table 2   Comparison of current methods of cleaning mixer trucks

METHOD	ADVANTAGES	DISADVANTAGES
Traditional Washing Out	• System already exists at most plants • Easy to operate • Low technology and low maintenance	• Produces a cementitious slurry which is increasingly expensive to dispose of • Requires extensive yard space • Takes a long time to drain waste
Chemical Wash Out	• Requires significant capital investment • Very little space required • Low maintenance	• Relatively high ongoing costs
Stoning Out	• No capital costs • All materials can be reused • Inexpensive	• Requires ground storage • Not suitable after a minority of mixes
Reclaimer	• Little space required • All materials can be reused • Efficient if well managed	• High capital costs • High maintenance costs • Requires good management • Requires a consistently high production plant to work efficiently

Stoning Out

This is a simple and successful method for cleaning concrete truck mixer drums. Typically two tonnes of coarse aggregate and 200 litres of water are placed in the mixer drum and the mixture brought to the point of discharge four to five times and either placed onto the aggregate stockpile or left in the drum overnight. The next day the aggregate can then be incorporated into a new batch with adjustments made to the mix for the contents of the drum.

Stoning out is the cheapest, simplest way to reduce waste at ready-mixed concrete plants (Table 2), as unlike the chemical wash out system, there is no requirement for new equipment to be installed and maintained and no ongoing admixture costs.

Reclaimers

Washing through a sieve can reclaim the constituent ingredients of fresh concrete. The coarse and fine aggregates can be reclaimed into individual stockpiles and the water and hydrated cement recovered and stored for reuse. Although the principle is simple, the equipment can be quite complex in design and requires careful management and maintenance, the capital cost is prohibitive for ready-mixed concrete plants (Table 2). This system eliminates wash out waste and has the advantage of reclaiming returned concrete. Plants that have managed to get systems working reliably report savings in waste disposal costs of seventy five per cent.

OBSTACLES IN THE WAY OF WASTE MINIMISATION

The Need to Change the Attitude of Ready-Mix Producers

Recent years have seen waste become a major issue for ready-mixed concrete producers and has been instrumental in initialising a change of attitudes.

The next few years should see a change of emphasis in ready-mixed concrete production with respect to waste management, as a producer will no longer be able to leave waste as an afterthought in the production process. Producers currently put great effort, control and documentation into the technical aspects of concrete production – monitoring the quality of constituent materials and the batched product. A similar level of care, documentation and control of waste – in terms of minimising its creation and its disposal, is required. The Environment Agency, currently novices in monitoring and policing this waste, are gaining expertise and awareness of this waste stream, this in turn will prompt ready-mix companies to improve their performance.

Concrete plants should be properly designed and maintained in order to prevent spillages, unwanted discharges and loss of materials. It seems obvious but it is all too evident at many UK plants that this elementary requirement for effective waste management is ignored. Whilst the UK's main suppliers of ready-mixed concrete have a number of modern, well designed and maintained plants in their portfolio, which they are proud to promote and advertise. For every modern, well designed concrete plant there is an ageing, out of date, badly maintained plant, designed in an era when environmental violations and concerns were given scant consideration.

There is no excuse for a batching plant that spills materials onto the yard floor every time a truck is loaded, or discharges wastewater into the surrounding environment. It is this lax attitude and management that will be punished severely as the Environment Agency gathers experience, expertise and power. It is apparent that there is an economic and commercial advantage in a proactive approach to waste management. Ready-mixed concrete producers should anticipate the impact of these new, increasingly stringent, regulations and by doing so, save money. Savings are to be made through reduced consumption of water, reduced time to wash out and handle waste, reduced waste disposal costs, reduced wastewater discharge costs, reduced build-up in mixer drums and reduced exposure to substantial environmental fines and liabilities.

The attitude of ready-mixed concrete producers needs to change now and the real test of determination will be shown through levels of investment.

The Role of Regulators in Ready-Mixed Concrete Waste

Ready-mixed concrete producers report ambiguity in the requirements to classify their waste. Once the waste has been dried does it represent the same hazard as waste in the wet condition? Does the dried waste require different handling to the wet waste? Producers find that the response of the Environment Agency varies between regions and between plants.

Integrated Planning Pollution and Control (IPPC) is designed to 'reduce pollution by means of integrated processes based on the application of best available techniques' [3]. The IPPC regime is one of the key levers for change identified by the government in Waste Strategy 2000 and will require that waste be recovered unless technically and economically impossible.

The stated primary goal of IPPC "is to achieve integrated prevention and control of pollution in order to secure a high level of protection of the environment taken as a whole." [15]. The intention is to move away from an approach based on "end-of-pipe" technology (i.e. reacting to pollution once it occurs), and adopt an approach where environmental considerations are given greater priority at the design of an installation [16].

The IPPC regime will limit the impacts of concrete batching plants, as it requires the protection of the soil, air and water and the restoration of the site to a clean condition on closure.

Plant Design

Many of the UK's existing ready-mixed concrete batching plants are constrained by their size and locality. Ready-mixed concrete has a very short shelf life, and plants tend to be located within one hours travelling time of customers. Plants are often therefore located in or near urban areas, with associated planning restrictions and constraints. The economics of ready-mixed concrete production do not promote high capital spending. A large proportion of plants were designed and constructed many years ago, and require significant investment to enable effective waste minimisation. However, new, modern plants are greatly improved. It is felt that further advancements in concrete production will be sought and adopted. It seems certain that future years will see the production of ready-mixed concrete become a waste free process.

THE FUTURE

Achieving Waste Minimisation and Reuse

Disposing of waste from ready-mixed concrete plants to landfill is now more expensive and more tightly controlled. These costs and controls will become more prohibitive as disposal resources diminish. Discharges of wastewater not only requires a costly permit, but also opens itself to the possibility of fines for breaching permitted levels.

Therefore there is a need to identify a production process which:

1. Minimises the creation of wet concrete waste
2. Reuses constituent materials

Encouraged by initiatives such as the landfill tax, UK ready-mixed concrete manufacturers have already taken steps to minimise the amount of waste they produce. These methods, including the use of chemical admixtures to wash out, recycling wash out water and the use of concrete reclaimers, have reduced substantially the amount of ready-mixed concrete waste being sent to landfill.

However, all of these methods and operations still result in the creation of a quantity of waste that is not reused or recycled at the concrete batching plant. It is current practice, therefore, to dispose of this waste to landfill.

A zero waste production process is already possible. As Huat [10], has recognised, a combination of chemical wash out and positive reuse of slurry solids waste, for example as sub-grade material for the construction of roads, eliminates waste from ready-mixed concrete production.

It would be preferable to adopt a system of waste management that enables the concrete plant to become totally self contained. As soon as a product, in this case waste, has to be transported from the plant to another location, the costs increase dramatically. In the spirit of the waste hierarchy (Figure 1) and BPEO, therefore, a truly efficient concrete plant would minimise waste by adopting a chemical wash out, stoning out or reclaimer system to wash out trucks. This combined with management practices to limit the amount of returned concrete and a system to recycle water will satisfy the priority of minimising waste. The inevitable, albeit reduced, waste which does arise, would then been reused in a process while remaining on the concrete plant site. This can be achieved by manufacturing a product at the plant that reuses the waste. It seems reasonable to promote the controlled reuse of ready-mixed concrete plant waste in selected concrete mixes, including foamed concrete. There are a number of technical issues that need to be addressed when considering reusing concrete plant process waste in fresh batches, however research is underway to investigate and quantify these factors [17 - 19].

CONCLUSIONS

Most ready-mixed concrete producers strive to improve their materials reuse and recycling capabilities for financial benefit, however the governments 'Waste Strategy 2000' has given greater emphasis on reducing the waste that is created. This initiative has assisted ready-mixed concrete producers in accelerating their search for improved methods of waste reduction.

As the cost of disposing of waste becomes more expensive, methods of reusing and recycling waste, previously thought to be uneconomic, will require revisiting.

It is hoped that the experiences, discussed in this paper, of ready-mixed concrete producers will offer guidance, by example, of the strategy that has been implemented by one sector of the UK industry.

REFERENCES

1.   DEPARTMENT OF THE ENVIRONMENT.   Sustainable Development: The UK Strategy. HMSO, London, 1994.

2. DEPARTMENT OF THE ENVIRONMENT. Making Waste Work: a Strategy for Sustainable Waste Management in England and Wales. HMSO, London, 1995.

3. DEPARTMENT OF THE ENVIRONMENT, TRANSPORT AND THE REGIONS. Waste Strategy 2000 for England And Wales. HMSO, London, 2000.

4. GRONOW B, PHILLIPS P AND READ A. East Midland countrywide waste minimisation initiatives: are they successful? IWM Scientific and Technical Review, April 2000

5. ENVIRONMENT AGENCY. The Management of Waste [online]. Available from: http://www.environment-agency.gov.uk/s…es/5waste-arisings/2disposal/5-2a.html [Accessed 26 September 2000].

6. FLEMING D. Concrete waste costs UK firms over £400m a year. Construction News, July 20 2000, p18.

7. ENVIRONMENT AGENCY. Special Wastes: A Technical Guidance Note on their Definition and Classification. 1999.

8. HM CUSTOMS AND EXCISE. Notice LFT1: A General Guide to the Landfill Tax. HM Customs and Excise, 2000.

9. PETERS W. Alkali burns from wet cement. Canadian Medical Association Journal, Vol. 130, April 1984. pp902- 904

10. HUAT L S. Recycling with hydration control admixture. Advanced Concrete Technology Diploma Project, Institute of Concrete Technology, 1998.

11. WILKINS T AND HODKINGSON L. Washout elimination from ready mixed concrete plants. Grace Construction Products, Warrington.

12. BORGER J, CARRASQUILLO R AND FOWLER D. Use of recycled wash water and returned plastic concrete in the production of fresh concrete. Advanced Cement Based Materials, 1, 1994. pp267-274

13. NEWMAN J. Reducing concrete waste. 21st Annual Convention of the Institute of Concrete Technology, Coventry, April 1993.

14. OKAWA Y, YAMAMIYA H AND NISHIBAYASHI S. Study on the reuse of returned concrete. Magazine of Concrete Research, 52, No.2, April 2000. pp 109-115

15. Council Directive 96/61/EC of the 24th September 1996 concerning integrated pollution prevention and control.

16. O'MALLEY V. The Integrated Pollution Prevention and Control (IPPC) Directive and its implications for the environment and industrial activities in Europe. Sensors and Actuators B-Chemical, vol. 59, 1999. pp 78-82

17. CHILSHOLM D. Cement and Concrete: Green research. Build. Oct 1996

18. HOLLAND T. Batching with recycled process water – What should be the allowable limits? The Concrete Producer, 1999.

19. PISTILLI M, PETERSON C AND SHAH S. Properties and possible recycling of solid waste from ready-mix concrete. Cement and Concrete Research, Vol 5, 1975. pp 249-260

BARRIERS TO INNOVATIONS IN CONSTRUCTIVE USES OF RESIDUALS

E H Bryan

Environmental Engineer

United States of America

ABSTRACT. The utilization of residuals as resources was a strategy used by the U.S. National Science Foundation's Environmental Engineering program to support research directed toward eliminating the pollutional impact that residues have on environmental resources of land, water and air. Topics addressed included use of wetlands for removal of plant nutrients remaining in effluents from secondary wastewater treatment processes to avoid their pollutional impact on receiving waters, agricultural and aquacultural uses of residual heat in water that had been used to condense steam produced to generate electricity, applications of sequencing batch reactors as an alternative to continuous flow processes for treatment of water and wastewater, refining of used lubricating oil for potential reuse as a lubricant, and uses of sludges derived from wastewater treatment processes for manufacture of topsoil and to manufacture bricks. The context within which this research was initiated and conducted and experiences relating to the adoption of concepts that emerged are presented and discussed to assist in the identification of barriers to the constructive uses of residuals.

Keywords: Wastewater treatment residuals, Sludge, Biobrick concept, Innovation barriers, Appropriate technology.

Dr E H Bryan, is certified as a Diplomate by the American Academy of Environmental Engineers. He was Program Director for the U.S. National Science Foundation's Environmental Engineering Program when he retired on January 29, 2000. Other program responsibilities for the Foundation since 1973 included the Waste Management Strategies element of the Regional Environmental Systems program in the Division of Environmental Systems and Resources and the Engineering Directorate's Appropriate Technology Program. His research at the University of Wisconsin from 1950-53 was on bio-utilization of chlorate as a source of respiratory oxygen for determination of the biochemical oxygen demand of wastewaters. With the Dow Chemical Company from 1953-60 his research and development assignments included synthetic media for fixed-film bioreactors and synthetic polymers for water and wastewater treatment. As a Professor of Civil Engineering at Duke University from 1960-70 he resumed research on use of chlorate to satisfy the biochemical oxygen demand of wastewaters and conducted research on non-point/diffuse sources of pollution to surface waters. As Manager of Technical Marketing for the Ecology Division of Rex Chainbelt, Inc from 1970-72 he coordinated the Division's work leading to development and evaluation of a responsive system for spills of hazardous substances.

INTRODUCTION

In his final report to the National Science Foundation for research on the potential use of sludge in manufacture of bricks, Alleman [1] included a copy of the patent issued in 1889 to Thomas Shaw for his "Improvements in Utilizing the Waste Product from Sewage Works for the Manufacture of Bricks, Tiles, Quarries, Building Blocks, Slabs, and the like" whose address was stated as being No. 46 Mode Wheel Road, Weaste near Manchester in the County of Lancaster [2]. As Alleman noted, "Research on this project was started in 1979 with a scholarly sense of innovative advancement in sludge management practice" and "...the concept appears to have lingered in obscurity until it was unknowingly resurrected by this project...again demonstrating the inescapable fact of historical repetition." Repetition of this research by Dr. Alleman and his graduate students Mark Prouty, who thought of the idea and conducted preliminary research on it, and Neal Berman, who also assisted in its conduct [3] was made possible by the quality of the idea, its relevance to objectives of the National Science Foundation's program to which it was submitted for support and absence of references to it in recent literature, current textbooks or those of Thomas Shaw's contemporaries including texts by Kinnicutt, Winslow and Pratt [4] in 1910, Fuller [5] in 1912, and Metcalf and Eddy [6] in 1915. Absence from these texts suggests that if these authors were aware of Thomas Shaw's concept, they did not considered it to have been of sufficient significance to warrant being included.

Regarding possible application of Shaw's concept following its disclosure, it is possible that sludge management was not a sufficiently significant problem to justify licensing its use. A section of Fuller's text on patent experiences notes reluctance of engineers to recommend payment of royalty or license fees on "one patent where there are other patents that are alleged to be infringed" and that "With unadjudicated patents it is difficult to forecast validity."

The production of sludge was significantly increased by the invention of the activated sludge process for treatment of wastewater and its rapid adoption without apparent regard to its patent status but responsiveness to public health needs. The panic that must have been associated with establishing the causative relationship between contaminated water and epidemics of typhoid fever and cholera seems evident from the rate at which the process was installed in full scale following its discovery. In only 13 years after Fowler had communicated results of research at the Lawrence Experiment Station to Ardern and Lockett, there were full-scale activated sludge wastewater treatment plants operating in Milwaukee, Indianapolis, Chicago and Houston in the United States; and in Manchester, Reading, Sheffield, Birmingham and Glasgow in the United Kingdom [7].

Regarding management of resultant sludges, the work of Ardern in England at Manchester on use of activated sludge as an agricultural fertilizer was cited by Fuller and McKlintock in their 1926 text and also mentioned similar research underway in Milwaukee, Chicago and Houston [7]. While its potential use as a fertilizer-base was identified as a likely concept to manage the sludge produced by the activated sludge wastewater treatment process they concluded that " The present outlook, however, is, except in the case of certain large cities which are favorably situated, that it may cost more to dispose of sludge as a fertilizer than by other means." Even if Shaw's concept had been considered, it is unlikely it would have been accepted over application to land and disposal in the ocean.

A review of the process that led to re-discovery of this concept and experiences associated with its adoption and acceptance may lead to insights into how this and perhaps other 19th and 20th Century innovations can be more aggressively applied to constructive management of residuals derived from treatment of wastewaters during the 21st Century

BACKGROUND

Relevant Research Characterized

The U.S. National Science Foundation (NSF) was originally authorized to support only basic research and education in the sciences and engineering. It did this by allocating funds that were appropriated to it by the U.S. Congress to colleges and universities on behalf of their faculty who initiated proposals for support of their research. This charter was amended in 1968 to authorize support of applied research relevant to solving problems involving the public interest. Initial implementation of its approach to supporting applied research was through a Research Applications Directorate that administered research programs addressing National needs. Its basic philosophy was expressed by DuBridge [8] when he suggested that "...the day is past when scientists and other scholars can sit quietly in their ivory towers unaware of and unconcerned with the world outside their laboratories, libraries, studies and classrooms.

Science is now a part of politics, is a part of the social and economic system. Scientists must carefully ponder the relevance of their work to the problems of human beings and they must ponder the ways in which this relevance can be clearly explained to the public at large. They must ask the question of whether the scientific work in which they are engaged is of sufficient importance to the progress of knowledge and its application to be worthy of public support." The original characterization of research in the Research Applications Directorate as Interdisciplinary Research Relevant to Problems of Our Society (IRRPOS) became Research Applied to National Needs (RANN).

Program Management

Proposals that requested support from programs in the Directorate for Research Applications were required to include a plan for utilization of the results of the proposed research, explanation of the relationship of the proposed research to the program's objectives, techniques proposed for conduct of the research and qualifications of the research personnel. The Utilization Plan frequently involved formation of a Project Advisory Committee with membership including representation from potential users. It was felt to be more likely that the results of the research would be utilized if potential users were included in the process by which the investigators conducted their research. Investigators were also encouraged to conduct seminars and workshops during the course of their research to provide suggestions for its conduct and to identify further research needs their work had identified.

Programs managers assisted in identification of issues to be addressed by the programs they managed. Submission of proposals was encouraged by publication of program announcements and use of other appropriate techniques such as participation in and support of conferences and workshops that addressed issues that had been identified as being addressed. When an issue addressing a particular topic had been sufficiently well defined to warrant conduct of a Proof of Concept Experiment (POCE), an experiment the conduct of which could lead to development of the concept or to identification of any further research that would be needed to establish its readiness for development, a plan was developed for its conduct. While further needed research was eligible for NSF support, support for the development stage of a concept was not within the scope of activity that was authorized for support by NSF. The time-scale between conduct of preliminary research and the POCE varied with respect to the amount of time that was needed to properly define its nature. Program management also involved conduct of seminars by researchers at the Foundation's location in Washington, D.C. if the projects involved matters of considerable immediate interest to other Federal agencies.

Waste Management Topics

The manner in which the NSF/RANN program element on waste management was planned to be conducted was presented in 1973 at a symposium on Ultimate Disposal of Wastewaters and Their Residuals [9]. The premise that guided the Waste Management Element of NSF's Regional Environmental Systems Program in its Division of Environmental Systems and Resources was that wastes are potential resources and recovery of their resource values could have economic benefits while simultaneously reducing the pollutional impact of their discharge into the environment and/or costs associated with managing them as wastes. Background research was conducted on a wide-range of topics in waste management that had relevance to environmental quality on a regional scale. Examples of topics included barriers to recycling of used lubricating oil, regionalization of waste collection systems, use of sequencing batch reactors for water and wastewater treatment, alternatives to single-purpose water systems, use of wetlands for advanced treatment of municipal wastewater, use of waste heat from generation of electricity for culture of aquatic animals of commercial value and management of sludges derived from wastewater treatment processes.

Proof of Concepts

Examples of concepts that successfully moved from the basic and applied stages through the POCE included one that started in 1972 with ecological modeling of a wetland near the Community of Houghton Lake, Michigan to explore the role it could play in removal of nitrogen and phosphorus from domestic wastewater as an alternative to capital and energy intensive systems. This led to a small pilot scale research project and then to a full-scale POCE. The effluent from the community's secondary wastewater treatment pond system was discharged into the existing, natural wetland where plant nutrients that would have otherwise caused eutrophication of the lake are utilized by the wetland's vegetation to increase its productivity. This project is now approaching its third decade of operation and was one of 17 case studies documented by the U.S. Environmental Protection Agency in a recent publication on use of wetlands for wastewater treatment [10]. .

Another concept that successfully moved through the POCE stage was the use of sequencing batch reactors for wastewater treatment as an alternative to continuous flow systems. Background bench and pilot scale research at the University of Notre Dame by Dr. Robert Irvine was followed by a POCE at Culver, Indiana where with the support of the U.S. Environmental Protection Agency, a conventional, continuous-flow activated sludge wastewater treatment plant was modified to be operated as a sequencing batch reactor [11]. Since then, the sequencing batch concept has been widely adopted as an alternative to continuous flow systems.

A concept for management of sludges derived from treatment of domestic wastewater that emerged for which a POCE was planned but not conducted involved use of an electron beam for disinfection of the sludge, its transport by pipeline to a site dedicated for use in its stabilization and then injection into topsoil. The research projects that led to this planned POCE were described in the Proceedings of the 8th U.S./Japan Conference on Sewage Treatment Technology that was held in 1981 [12]. A site had been selected for preliminary design to establish guidance for a the planned POCE [13] and a film was produced to brief potential contractors who would indicate an interest in submitting proposals for its conduct [14]. When the host program was terminated in 1979, research on sludge management was shifted to NSF's new Appropriate Technology Program [15].

APPROPRIATE TECHNOLOGY

NSF Program Defined

The definition adopted for implementation of the NSF Program in Appropriate Technology (AT) characterized it as seeking approaches to solving problems that did not require large investments of capital resources, used locally available resources, would be capable of being managed by their users, would be conserving in use of resources, and would be in harmony with the environment. As implemented by NSF, the AT Program excluded research on alternative energy sources and energy conversion and closely related topics because of potential overlap with the U.S. Department of Energy's Appropriate Technology Program.

During the two years that it functioned, more than half of all proposals received and awards made in the Appropriate Technology Program addressed some aspect of recycling, resource recovery and conservation. This direction of interest may have been strongly influenced by perceptions of the research community that recovery of resource values from agricultural, industrial and municipal wastes was a fundamental linkage between diminishing resources and potential solutions to environmental problems and this linkage was one amenable to being scientifically addressed by the research community served by the National Science Foundation. Sludge management proposals that received support included research on composting of sludge[16], agricultural benefits from application of sludge to farm land [17, 18], use of sludge for soil stabilization [19], stabilization of sludge [20] and the potential use of sludge in manufacturing ceramic products such as bricks.

The Biobrick Concept

The preliminary proposal for support of research that had already been initiated at the University of Maryland to study the potential use of sludges derived from treatment of domestic wastewater for manufacturing bricks was submitted to the NSF Appropriate Technology Program in May of 1980. The investigator proposed to vary the ratio of sludge to clay prior to firing and to determine the effect the ratio has on the structural properties of the product using procedures recommended by the American Society for Testing Materials (ASTM). After review of its quality and program relevance, the proposal was recommended for support [1].

During a two year period of research, a total of about 300 bricks were produced at bench-scale using clay and shale being used by Maryland Clay Products, Inc., a brick manufacturing firm in Laurel, Maryland for their regular production of bricks. Seven different types of sludges were used for producing those bricks from five wastewater treatment plants in the metropolitan area of Washington, D.C. Details of experimental procedures used, experiences in conduct of the research and its results were published in the Environmental

Engineering Journal of the American Society of Civil Engineers [21] and in Interbrick, an international journal that addresses manufacture of tiles, pipes and bricks [3][22]. Results from this research relating the effects of sludge to structurally significant properties of bricks produced during the laboratory scale production process were also presented in a paper given in 1989 at the Institution of Civil Engineers World Water '89 conference as illustrated in Figures 1,2,3 and 4 [23]. The cooperative relationship that had been established by the investigator with Maryland Clay Products, Inc. led its conduct of a full-scale production run during which 50,000 sludge-amended bricks were produced using 30 tons of well-stabilized sludge from the community of Bowie, Maryland. The bricks were used to construct a small playhouse at one of its parks.

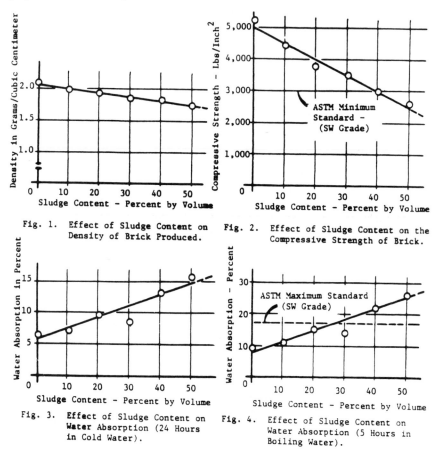

Fig. 1. Effect of Sludge Content on Density of Brick Produced.

Fig. 2. Effect of Sludge Content on the Compressive Strength of Brick.

Fig. 3. Effect of Sludge Content on Water Absorption (24 Hours in Cold Water).

Fig. 4. Effect of Sludge Content on Water Absorption (5 Hours in Boiling Water).

Figure 1-4 Effects of sludge content on properties of bricks

Large-scale Production

The successful experimental production of a limited number of bricks by Maryland Clay Products, Inc. led to a much larger production run of bricks in cooperation with the Washington Suburban Sanitary Commission when 600,000 bricks were produced using 120 tons of sludge from the Commission's Parkway Wastewater Treatment Plant, located a short distance from the brick-making firm. The sludge used was a centrifugally dewatered, digested sludge containing residual sludge from the Commission's water treatment plant located upstream on the Patuxent River.

The bricks produced in this large-scale production run were used by the Commission in the construction of several structures, notably Biobrick I, a picnic shelter at the Brighton Dam Park in Montgomery County, Maryland, and an electrical/mechanical maintenance building at the Parkway Wastewater Treatment Plant and a building at the Commission's Patuxent River Water Treatment Plant. The sludge provided all of the water needed to plasticize the clay and shale used in making these bricks and some of the energy needed to operate the kiln.

Fate of Metals

Further research was conducted at bench-scale to determine the fate of metal residues in sludges containing them. The sludges were obtained from the Belmont Advanced Wastewater Treatment plant in Indianapolis, Indiana and from several other locations in Indiana and Ohio. Shale and clay were obtained from General Shale, Inc. of Mooresville, Indiana. Fates considered were emissions from the kiln during production of bricks and potentially resulting from weathering.

Metals studied included arsenic, cadmium, chromium, iron, lead, nickel, selenium and zinc. The investiator concluded in his final report [24] that "standard municipal sludges laden with normal metal levels can be satisfactorily incorporated within commercial brick manufacturing processes without risk of metal loss." These results suggest the Biobrick Concept may be especially applicable for sludges that contain organic and inorganic contaminants that are not feasible to be restrained from entry into the wastewater collection system by regulation and are at a level that is not acceptable for placement on land or incorporation into soil.

Acceptability

Residuals are sometimes called "secondary materials." Products made from them compete for acceptability with products in current usage with a proven record of good performance that are made from materials sometimes described as "virgin." This implies their possession of superior quality not measurable by objective criteria used to establish quality standards such as those of the American Society for Testing Materials (ASTM).

Acceptability and marketability of products may also be adversely affected by their production from or associative relationship during the manufacturing process with substances of unclean origin. New concepts must also compete with alternatives including those with a those with a proven record of performance, the use of which involves little or no risk of failure. A factor that is slowly being overcome is the long-term, field verification of the durability of biobricks as was predicted by their having met acceptable standards of quality.

A recent photograph of the electricall/mechanical maintenance building at the Parkway Wastewater Treatment Plant is shown in Figure 5.

Figure 5 The building housing electrical/mechanical equipment and associated offices at the Parkway Wastewater Treatment Plant in Laurel, Maryland.

Acceptability in environmental engineering practice is also influenced by the process leading to design of pollution abatement facilities. Consulting engineers are not usually rewarded for placing their clients into situations involving risk of a project failing before completion of its useful life, often defined by the period needed to recover costs and especially to repay any debt incurred in facility design and construction. Finally, a significant barrier to adoption of an innovation or its product is the availability of alternative ways of accomplishing its objective at lower cost. Regarding sludge management, direct placement into the ocean has been largely foreclosed as a sludge management option but its aggressive application to land has not where sufficient land is available and application is permissible at a cost-effective distance from sources of sludge. For example, the five private firms processing and managing disposal of sludge from New York City now are distributing it to sites in Florida, Texas, Virginia, West Virginia and Pennsylvania [25].

CONCLUSIONS

We are facing challenges in addressing the environmental problems of the 21st Century especially as they relate to the management of wastewater and residuals derived from the treatment of wastewater. As the capacity of locations to which residuals can be acceptably transported and stored become exhausted, public pressure will increase toward requiring their management where they are produced. While the use of residuals as resources is a good strategy for coping with environmental pollution and survival within the limits of our ecosystem, sustainability of life in our ecosystem depends on identification of those limits and then undertaking the process to insure they are not exceeded.

Experiences summarized in this paper suggest a major barrier to adoption of innovative concepts for treatment and management of wastewaters that emerge from research is adequate appreciation of the important role that development plays in this process. While research can provide knowledge of potential solutions to problems, development evaluates potential solutions at a sufficiently large scale to obtain confirmation of their technical base and knowledge of economic factors that are needed to determine acceptability.

Acceptability of products produced from or by the use of residuals may be negatively influenced by perceptions of inferiority when compared to products made from primary sources or because of their associative relationship with materials of an unclean origin.. Trends toward privatization of water supply and wastewater processing and management systems coupled with merging of companies that provide goods and services to the environmental industry may provide the economic bases and associated motivation for supporting the development stage of technologies that emerge from research.

REFERENCES

1. ALLEMAN, J E. Beneficial uses of sludge in production of building components. Final Report to NSF, Grant 80-21357 to the University of Maryland, NTIS PB 84-179498, 1982..

2. SHAW, T. Improvements in utilizing the waste product from sewage works for themanufacture of bricks, tiles, quarries, building blocks, and the like. UK Patent 12,623, AD 1889, copy of patent in Reference 1, 1982. p 9.

3. ALLEMAN, J E. Beneficial use of sludge in building components, Part I: Concept review and   technical background. Interbrick, Vol 3 (2), 1987, pp 14-16.

4.   KINNICUTT, L P, WINSLOW, C-E A, AND PRATT, R W. Sewage Disposal. Chapman & Hall, Ltd, London, 1910.

5. FULLER, G W. Sewage Disposal. McGraw-Hill Book Company, New York, 1912.

6. METCALF, L AND EDDY, H P. American Sewerage Practice, Vol III, Disposal of SEWAGE. McGraw-Hill Book Company, Inc., New York, 1916.

7. FULLER, G W AND MCCLINTOCK, J R. Solving Sewage Problems, Chapter XL, Activated Sludge as a Fertilizer. McGraw-Hill Book Company, Inc. pp 494-497, 1926.

8. DUBRIDGE, L A. Federal research problems. American Scientist, Vol 57 (4), 1969, pp 546-552.

9. BRYAN, E H. Research needs in the context of our goal to restore and maintain thechemical, physical and biological integrity of the Nation's waters. Proceedings of Research Institute, University of North Carolina, 1973. pp 4-12.

10. CONSTRUCTED   WETLANDS   FOR   WASTEWATER   TREATMENT   AND WILDLIFE HABITAT. U.S. Environmental Protection Agency, EPA832-R-93- 005, 1993, pp 19-34.

11. IRVINE, R L AND BUSCH, A W. Sequencing batch biological reactors-an overview and related papers. Journal of the Water Pollution Control Federation, Volume 51 1979, pp 235- 304.

12. BRYAN, E H. Research supported by the National Science Foundation relating to treatment of wastewater and management of residual sludges. Proceedings of the 8th U.S./Japan conference in 1981 on sewage treatment technology, , U S EPA 600-/9-84-021, Office of Research and Development, Cincinnati, Ohio, 1984, pp 907-818.

13. SMITH, J L, LUTKIN, M H, LATHAM J S and DEHASI, A. Land management of subsurface-injected liquid residuals. Reports to NSF for Grant 74-08082 to Colorado State University and subcontract with Black & Veatch, Consulting Engineers. NTIS PB-267135 in 1977 and PB-280162 in 1978.

14. SLUDGE MANAGEMENT - AN INTEGRATED APPROACH. Film Produced by Media Four Productions under NSF Contract GPP 76-82708. National Audio-Visual Center, AO4783/CK (16mm Film) and AO4784/CK (Videocassette), 1978.

15. BRYAN, E H. The National Science Foundation's Experimental Program in Appropriate Technology, Session 14, 148th National Meeting of the American Association for the Advancement of Science, 1982.

16. GOLUEKE, C. Benefits and problems of composting mixtures of municipal sludges and solid wastes. NSF Grant 79-17407 to Cal Recovery Systems, Inc., 1979.

17. HAAG, R. Agricultural utilization of sludges derived from treatment of community wastewater. NSF Grant 79-17739 to Rickel Manufacturing Corporation 1979.

18. KIRKHAM M B. Productivity of land and quality of wheat grown using sludges as organic sources of plant nutrients. NSF Grant 80-14715 to Kansas State University 1979.

19. WARD G. Susceptibility of Mount St. Helens volcanic ash to stabilization by the use of organic sludges. NSF grant 80-20281 to George D. Ward and Associates 1980.

20. LOEHR R C. Stabilization of organic residues derived from treatment of selected industrial and municipal wastes. NSF grant 80-16764 to Cornell University 1981.

21. ALLEMAN J E AND BERMAN M. Constructive sludge management: Biobrick. American Society of Civil Engineers Journal of Environmental Engineering, Vol 110, 1984. pp 301-311.

22. ALLEMAN J E. Beneficial use of sludge in building components, Part II: Full scale production of sludge-amended bricks. Interbrick 1/89, Vol 5. 1989. pp 28-32.

23. BRYAN, E H. Appropriate technological innovation in constructive management of sludges derived from treatment of wastewaters. World Water '89, Proceedings of the Institution of Civil Engineers Conference, 1989. pp 117-124.

24. ALLEMAN, J E. Containment of metal contaminants within sludge-amended construction products. Final report to NSF for Grant 86-07019, 1989.

25. QUINN M. New York City experience. Presented at the Seminar in Richmond, Virginia on Wastewater Solids Processing and Reuse: A Survival Guide, Virginia Water Environment Association, Inc., November 2, 2000.

MANAGEMENT OF A LAND BANK FOR RECYCLING SLUDGE DERIVED FERTILISER (SDF) USING NORTH OF SCOTLAND WATER AUTHORITY GEMINI SOFTWARE

S Wright

North of Scotland Water Authority Board

A H Sinclair

SAC

United Kingdom

ABSTRACT. The paper describes Gemini, (North of Scotland Water Authorities) NoSWA custom-built sludge management system, which has proved to be a valuable tool in helping to provide a cost-effective service for recycling biosolids. Gemini is a computer software program designed to operate a fully computerised control system to monitor and record the transport and processing of biosolids. As well as playing a major role in providing a quality service to farmers, the system maintains a QA audit in line with the Scottish Environment Protection Agency requirements. To facilitate auditing and to provide the regulator with an official yearly/part yearly document, an Authority wide or area by area Sludge Register can be output.

Keywords: Gemini, Computer software, Recycling biosolids, Agriculture, QA Audit.

Mrs S Wright, is part of the management team responsible for wastewater quality and regulation with North of Scotland Water Authority. She is the corporate Recycling Team Leader and provides scientific, technical and legal advice to operational managers. She is also representative for Scottish Water Authorities on various research steering groups focussed mainly on projects to demonstrate that land recycling of wastewater sludge is environmentally sustainable.

Dr A H Sinclair, is a Soil and Fertiliser Specialist with SAC Aberdeen. He currently advises NoSWA on the rates and timing of their sewage sludge, which is applied to agricultural land. He was a member of the MAFF/DOE Independent Scientific Committee on Soil Fertility Aspects of Sewage Sludge Use in Agriculture, 1993 and co-author of the MAFF/DOE (1993) report "Review of the Rules for Sewage Sludge application to Agricultural Land. Soil Fertility Aspects of Potentially Toxic Elements." He is team leader of various commercial projects aimed at the development, management and maintenance of an agricultural outlet for reuse of wastewater sludge and other industrial wastes.

INTRODUCTION

To date, North of Scotland Water Authority (NoSWA) has followed a sludge utilisation strategy, based on Best Practicable Environmental Option (BPEO) which seeks to select the best environmental option, consistent with economic, finance, social and political realities. This methodology has identified that recycling sludge is considered the BPEO in most circumstances and is accepted and supported by national and international governments and regulators.

For many years it has been widely recognised by farmers and environmental bodies that managed correctly, sewage sludge (biosolids) is a valuable source of nutrients for crop uptake and can provide organic matter to improve soil structure.

Over the past few years, new, more advanced, sludge treatment processes have been introduced across the NoSWA area and this now provides farmers with a wider choice of safe, high quality products. Traditionally, demand has been from the farming community but biosolids are now also being used in land restoration, forestry, horticulture and many other land improvement schemes.

GEMINI *i*

Quality Controlled Recycling Service

The operation of a cost-effective, all embracing recycling service is a complex business, dependant on many factors and at the same time, the water industry has to deal with statutory and environmental requirements and reporting obligations that are becoming more numerous and complicated.

NoSWA has introduced *Gemini* a custom built sludge management system that has proved to be a valuable tool in helping to provide this service. It is a computer software program designed to operate a fully computerised control system to monitor and record the transport and processing of all wastewater sludge. Modules include a septic tank emptying service and an agricultural and advisory service linked to soil and sludge quality data.

The software package forms part of a quality control system that incorporates three major components:

1. Procedures based on Hazard Analysis and Control at Critical Points (HACCP)

2. The agronomic expertise of the Scottish Agricultural College (SAC) and

3. *Gemini* linked to:

   - a Geographical Information System
   - a sludge movement data logging information system
   - Department of Agronomy, SAC Aberdeen.

Information is gathered for transfer to SAC – soil data, product data, cropping patterns and details of other fertilisers used. After assessment, recommendations are made by SAC to the farmer on the quantities of sludge product required for the crops to be grown, together with advice on additional rates of lime, nitrogen, phosphate and potash which may be needed.

QA audit

As well as playing a major role in providing a quality service to farmers, the system maintains a QA audit in line with the Scottish Environment Protection Agency requirements. To facilitate auditing and to provide the regulator with an official yearly/part yearly document, an Authority wide or area by area Sludge Register can be printed out.

Sludge and Soil Databases

A pre-requisite when designing the system was the ability to monitor compliance with the Sludge Regulations and the Code of Practice on the use of sewage sludge to agricultural land. The system records all movement of sludge, while the results of sludge and soil analyses are imported from laboratory systems to give a comprehensive database on sludge products, soil history and composition. The total quantity of biosolids applied to each field can be retrieved along with the addition of nutrients NPK and potentially toxic elements (PTEs) for each application. Part of an audit report of the status of a field, which has recently received biosolids, is given in Table 1.

Table 1 Sludge addition and field status

	COMPARISON WITH SOIL CONCENTRATION LIMITS (Using audit sample taken on 15/10/1998)			
	Soil sample, kg/ha	Subsequent additions, kg/ha	Current status, kg/ha	Maximum allowed, kg/ha
Zinc	145	2.00	147	500
Copper	36.6	0.82	37.4	250
Nickel	76.1	0.07	76.2	150

Advice to Farmers

A module on the system incorporates the advisory service supplied to farmers by SAC on the fertiliser values of sludge products, application rates and fertiliser supplements required for different crops.

An example of a typical Sludge and fertiliser Report is given below:

SOIL ANALYSIS FOR FIELD Next crop   S.Barley
                         Sludge source   NO146220L4
                                         (Perth lime pasteurised cake)

ANALYSIS	VALUE (mg/kg)	STATUS
pH	5.8	
Nitrogen N	-	Low
Phosphorus P	4.4	Low
Potassium K	120	Moderate
Magnesium	183	Moderate

RECOMMENDED SLUDGE (fresh tonnes)

PER HECTARE :   25

PER FIELD :   228.5

RECOMMENDED FERTILISER APPLICATION (after sludge has been applied)

APPLICATION RATE (kg/ha)	FERTILISER	TIMING OF APPLICATION
300	20.8.14	at sowing
100	34N (ammonium nitrate)	soon as tramlines are visible

COMMENTS

The recommended application of sludge cake will supply 115 kg/ha total P_2O_5 (92 units/acre). As the soil P is low, P has been included in the seedbed fertiliser to help early growth. After application of sludge cake this field will not need to be limed for at least 3 years. The nitrogen recommendation is for feed barley. If you are aiming for the malting market do not apply N top dressing.

SUMMARY

SAC (Aberdeen) is linked to the Gemini server in North of Scotland Water Authority's Information Technology Centre (Dundee) to give direct access to the relevant databases. This allows SAC to carry out the advisory service to farmers which is required by the Sludge (Use in Agriculture) Regulations 1989 in order that account is taken of the nutrient requirements of crops and the quality of the soil is not impaired when SDF is applied.

REFERENCES

1. DOE. Code of Practice for Agricultural Use of Sewage Sludge, HMSO, 1996. 6pp

2. HM GOVERNMENT. The Sludge (Use in Agriculture) Regulations 1989. Statutory Instrument No. 1263. London, HMSO, 1998. 12pp.

DEVELOPMENT OF A SEMI-INDUSTRIAL ESCALE EXPERIMENTAL ORGANIC WASTES BIODEGRADATION REACTOR

R Plana   **C Pérez**   **J Domínguez**   **S Mato**

University of Vigo

F Aguilera

Informatic and Agricultural Engineer

Spain

ABSTRACT. An important problem in composting research is the aplication of the results of the laboratory-scale datas to industrial-scale operations. This invention is about an experimental organic wastes biodegradation reactor, caracterized for his size that lets an indutrial escale interpretation of the results, and his great utility to scientific research for all the degradative process variables that are controlled. The reactor's size is 3 metres long, 1,20 metres height and 1,20 metres wide. Made in iron, the walls are 2 cm wide with thermal isolation inside, and has two doors. There are nine temperature probes that also took an air sample in the same point where they take measures and O_2, CO_2 and NH_3 are analyzed. The ventilation system permits an aspiration or blow action inside the vessel. The air is moved by a high-pressure centrifugal fan, and the temperature and relative moisture of the air that comes in and out of the vessel are recorded. A programmed automat controls and register all the data.

Keywords: Composting process, Biodegradation reactor, Semindustrial size, Process variables, Temperature-gases probes.

Mr R Plana, is a Research Student at the University of Vigo. He did his degree about composting and vermicomposting of biowastes from wastewater treatment plants of the milk industry. He is cunrrently completing his doctoral thesis on the subject of composting biowastes of urban wastewaters treatment plants with the BIO.RES.OR.

Mr F Aguilera, is an Informatic and Agricultural Engineer. He works as Counsellor to differentes companies and city halls about waste management, specially composting techniques, in Spain.

Mr C Pérez, is the Director of the I+D department at ROS-ROCA, S.A.. He has been working about waste treatments since years, being an authority about composting in Spain. His research interests are about the composting problems at the industrial level.

Dr J Domínguez, is a Research/Teacher at the University of Vigo. He has many works about composting and vermicomposting. His research interestes are focusing about earthwomrs biology to improve their degradative activity at different organic wastes.

Professor S Mato, is Director of the Environmental Biology Research team at the University of Vigo. He specialices in composting and vermicomposting techniques, both others waste treatments. His interests also include the technique adviser of differents companies and city halls about their waste management problems.

INTRODUCTION

The origin of using a closed vessel with certain characteristiques to compost organic matter comes from the mushrooms industry (Gerrits, 1987). That vessel, that would be called "tunnel" by his form and dimensions, used to have the capacity to recirculate the inner air or introduce new one from outside, depending of his temperature measure and his composition, basically the proportions of CO_2 and NH_3.

Later, when it was seen the convenience of composting industrially the organic materials that the modern society produces in a massive way, like biosolids from urban wastewaters treatment plants and the organic fraction of the urban solid wastes to use them in agriculture, the tunnels makers hurried up to adapt them to these new finalities (Lokin & Oorthuys, 1994).

Although is true that almost any organic waste can be composted, it is also true that not always it is possible to do it in the more adequate conditions due to:

a) the disturbances that it generates

b) the final product quality

c) the effiency of the consumed energy and time

There has been a lot of experiences to improve the process (Longsdon, 1992; Stentiford et al., 1985; Strom et al., 1985; Youngberg, 1990) varying the moisture, particles size, C/N, temperature, oxygen presence, etc... But transfer these results to the actual industrial tunnels with a capacity higher than 100 m^3 and even closer to 1000 m^3, has lots of difficulties. First they are not really versatile and they do not have the needed instrumentation to could obtein precises conclusions. And in the other hand it would suppose an excessive energetic, material and work cost to experiment with those volumes.

That is why there have been doing several investigations in small laboratory reactors with not many liters of volume, with any exception of 200 liters (Marugg et al., 1993), and the mass losses and CO_2 production (Mato, 1994), even the behaviour of many different wastes (Finstein *et al*, 1983) with differents particles sizes (Domínguez, 1996). But there is a big problem to extrapolate these researches to the industrial tunnels because the conditions and mass sizes are different.

MATERIAL AND METHODS

The parts of the reactor are a vessel of 3 meters length, 1,20 meters width and 1,20 meters height; with iron walls ("sandwich" type) with poliurethane filled up 2 cemtimeters width. The structure that gives form and consistence to the vessel is builded in iron. It has two doors: an upper one to load, and other at the side to unload. Inside the vessel has a false floor made with strips of wood with conical holes that creates a lower ventilation chamber.

Inside the vessel there are 9 temperature probes that also took a gases sample in the same point where they measure. These samples are conducted until a box with multiplexates electrovalvules in an unique exit to the closet where the O_2, CO_2 and NH_3 analyzers are. All these measurements are taken for a programmed automat that controls the process and register all the data (Figure 1).

The ventilation system is composed by a tubes circuit that with a combination of six valvules can establish an aspiration or blow action inside the vessel. Depending if we open three valvules and close the other three we establish an action or other, through two holes to the inner of the vessel, an upper and a lower one. The air is moved by a high-pressure centrifugal fan (Figure 2). The automat controls the fan, and it records the temperature and relative moisture of the air that comes in and out of the vessel.

A computer connected to the automat permits to program and to control it, and save the data to a disk.

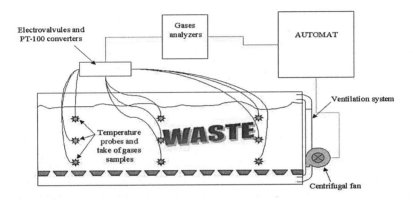

Figure 1 Scheme of the reactor with the differentes parts of it

The waste used in the first experiment with this reactor was cow manure from a big farm sited in Leon (Spain) (9000 cows) produce meat, fed on corn, barley and straw. The chemical characteristiques of the waste are shown in Table 1.

The manure is mixed with straw because it is used to cover the floor where the cows live. Although the material tended to form particles of big size that induce anaerobic problems, it was not used any other bulking material than the straw that was in it. That straw is not a good bulking agent because it has not the estructure needed to maintain a porous structure of the material. Nevertheless it was wanted to test the capacity of this reactor to composting a waste that is not adequate to be composted in tunnels in bad conditions like are a non-optimal initial structure.

A bulldozer was used to load and remove the bioreactor with the manure using the upper door. The ventilation rate (centrifugal fan frequenzy and the period of time it was working) was selected everyday, depending of the development of the process. The same was done with the flow or aspiration action.

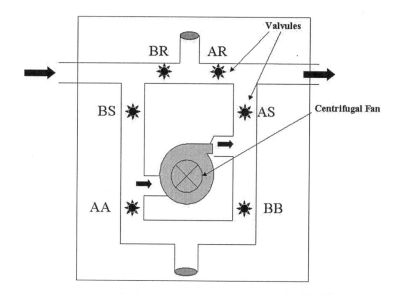

Figure 2 Scheme of the ventilation system at one of the vessel's sides

At the same time a traditional composting pile was made with the same material in order to compare the results of the process and the resulting material with the two composting methods. The pile had a dimensions of 1,60 meters height and 2 meters width at the base. Temperature was measured everyday in six points inside of it. The pile was removed every week during the time of the experiment.

Samples were taken after a month from the material inside the reactor.

RESULTS

The experiment was runnig during a month. During this time the reactor was opened once to moisture the material again in order to reactivate the process, reaching the 69,99% of moisture. It was done the fifteenth day of the experiment.

The results (Table 2) show an important loss in organic matter (in three points inside the vessel and in the pile) founding differences depending in which place of the reactor the sample were taken, having the lesser organic matter values in the points near the unload door, and the highest values near where the ventilation system connects with the vessel.

The pH value at the end of the experiment was the expected after a composting process, reaching alkaline values, with a maximum of 9,04.

Table 1 Initial cow manure characteristiques

CHEMICAL CHARACTERISTIQUES	%
Moisture (%)	65,41
Organic matter (%)	82,13
pH	8,46
CE (mS · cm^{-1})	2,86
DOC (g · kg^{-1})	14,15
NH$_4^+$ (g · kg^{-1})	3,78
C tot (g · kg^{-1})	380
N tot (g · kg^{-1})	28
P tot (g · kg^{-1})	14,5
K tot (g · kg^{-1})	32,7
Mg tot (g · kg^{-1})	8,16
Na tot (g · kg^{-1})	8,58
C/N	13,57
Respiration rate (mg O_2 consumed · kg^{-1} · h^{-1})	2,14

The data registered by the computer allows to check the process development attending to temperature and gases values, even know the temperature and moisture of the air who comes inside and outside the vessel.

The temperature values saved from the probe sited in the center of the bioreactor shows that the composting process was maintained in feedback almost all the time (Figure 3). The waste reached the mesophilic phase in only 12 hours. The program used had to be adjusted to keep the temperature in the wished range. The great fall at the fiftheen day was caused because the reactor was opened and unloaded and the waste was moisture to continue the process for a longer time.

Attending to the oxygen data (Figure 4) only during the first days there were reaches low values that could be limitants for the bacteria, but the time was not enough to affect the process.

The other gas, CO_2, reached high values in certain moments of the process and at the last days there is a big difference between the samples taken at the places near the unload door and those in the rest of the vessel, being the last ones who reached highest levels of CO_2. The NH_3 samples exceeded the ranges of the analytic sensor in different moments during the process.

Table 2 Final cow manure characteristiques. 1-2-3 correspond to samples from the first three probes; 4-5-6 are samples from probes sited in the middle of the vessel and 7-8-9 are samples from the part of the vessel closed to the ventilation system holes.

COW MANURE CHARACTERISTIQUES	1-2-3	4-5-6	7-8-9
Moisture (%)	49,66	36,33	47,54
Organic matter (%)	67,69	68,81	72,92
pH	9,04	8,9	9,01
CE (mS · cm^{-1})	2,76	2,36	2,34
DOC (g · kg^{-1})	6,61	12,5	28,17
NH$_4^+$ (g · kg^{-1})	4,38	4,31	4,23
C tot (g · kg^{-1})	350	350	270
N tot (g · kg^{-1})	24	26	24
P tot (g · kg^{-1})	18,1	17,5	21,2
K tot (g · kg^{-1})	40,9	38,3	45
Mg tot (g · kg^{-1})	9,69	9,27	11,1
Na tot (g · kg^{-1})	10,5	10,2	11,4
C/N	14,58	13,46	11,25
Respiration rate (mg O$_2$ consumed · kg^{-1} · h^{-1})	0,21	0,38	0,35

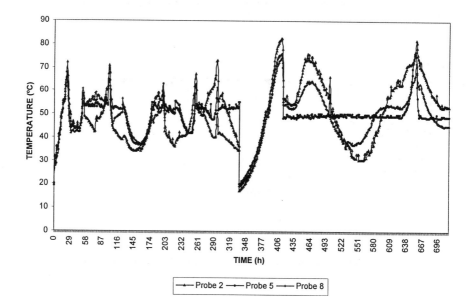

Figure 3 Temperature data registered in the central probes along the vessel

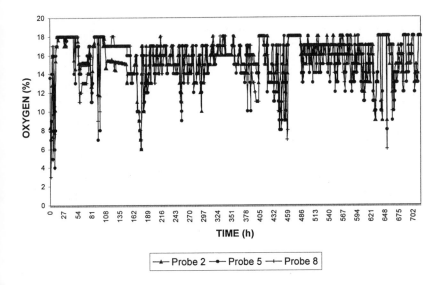

Figure 4a Gases data registered in the central probes along the vessel.

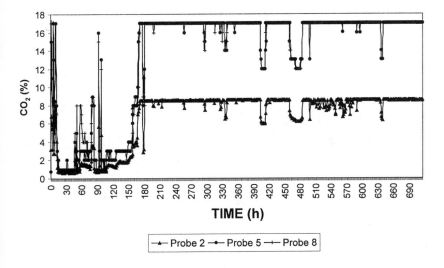

Figure 4 b Gases data registered in the central probes along the vessel.

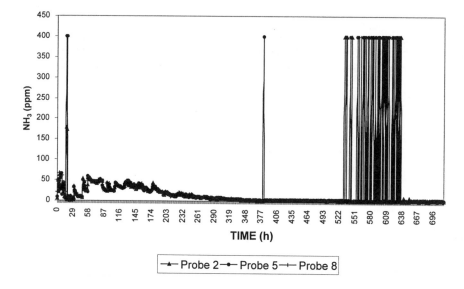

Figure 4 c Gases data registered in the central probes along the vessel.

DISCUSSION

Even when the waste used in this experiment presented a great energetic potential, the bioreactor design permits to control the process and avoid the problems that it would exists in other static systems. The manure was not mixed with any structural element before to introduce it in the vessel. It only had a little quantity of straw that is not enough to allow a correct ventilation inside the waste, so there were differents temperatures in the vertical way. The posibilty of change the air flow blowing or aspirating gives us the chance to maintain all the material at the same temperature range.

The O_2 consumption did not reach limit values because the fan had to been working very often to control the temperature, nevertheless the points of less O_2 values coincides with moments of high microbiological activity.

The high CO_2 production shows the great activity of the waste, specially during the first hours after the beginning of the experiment how it was expected. The NH_3 values reached the highest points almost a day after the beginning, reflecting the degradation of proteins, nitrogenated bases,. (aminas) following the next reaction:

$$R\text{-}NH_2 \Rightarrow \Rightarrow NH_3 + H_2O \Rightarrow \Rightarrow NH_4^+ + OH^-$$

It indicates that the organic matter easiest to degradate has been used almost in its totality by the microorganisms and now more stable organic compounds begins to be degradated.

The analytics results shows an organic matter loss in the expected limits. It was more important during the first fifteen days that at the end, after that the waste was moistened again to extend the biodegradation in time. It could happened because the waste has a very low content of easily biodegradable carbon, because the carbon that the straw has is very hardly used by microorganisms due to the strong celulosic structures that it presents. That caused that the high ammonium levels could caused negative effects to the microbian activity altering the result of the competition between potents and less potents decomposers through the ammonium metabolite repression.

It can be the cause that the loss of organic matter in the last fifteen days was lower that at the beginning. The comparison of the total carbon values at the begining and at the end of the experiment shows that too, cause the decrease was not important. And it happened too with the nitrogen. It shows the difficulty of the microorganisms to degradate correctly the material. The alkaline pH values at the end reflects the important ammonium, as we can see with the increase of those values at the end of the experiment.

The decrease of the conductivity values corresponds to the volatility of ammonium and although having a high production of it. The loss of water for evaporation (as we can see at the final moisture values) helped to that decrease of conductivity, because the quantity of ammonium dissolved in it was lesser.

Figure 5 Image of the bioreactor when it was being unloaded

CONCLUSIONS

The experimental bioreactor that we designed and built allowed us to degradate big quantities of waste even those that presents bad conditions at the beginning. The capability of change the flow direction permits to confront those wastes with a structure very compact that has problems to let the air pass through it.

Measuring the temperature and gas values at nine different points of the material we have a perfect control of the development of the process at every moment. And permit us enquire the kind of problems that the experimented waste would have to be biodegradate in an industrial composting tunnel.

The experiment with this cow manure that is not very adequate to be composted in a industrial tunnel (without any bulking material to conditioned it), demostrated that even when it was possible to compost it because is a very energetic waste, it would present problems that we already know and that with a experimental reactor at laboratory scale would not be know. In those reactors the waste mass variable is not take in consideration during the experiment.

REFERENCES

1.   DOMINGUEZ, J. Estudio y comparación de los procesos de compostaje y vermicompostaje. Aplicación práctica al tratamiento de los purines de cerdo. Doctoral thesis. University of Vigo. 1996.

2.   FINSTEIN, M.S.; MILLER, F.C.; STROM, P.F.; McGREGOR, S.T. & PSARIANOS, K.M. Composting ecosystem management for waste treatment. Biotechnol., 1: 347-353. 1983.

3.   GERRITS, J.P.G. Compost for mushroom production and its subsequent use for soil improvement. Compost: production, quality and use. Edited by De Bertoldi, M. Proceed Symposium Italy. April 1986. pp: 431-439. 1987.

4.   MATO, S.; OTERO, D. & GARCIA, M. Composting on 100 mm fraction on municipal solid waste. Waste Mang. Res., 12, 315-325. 1994.

5.   STENTIFORD, E.I. & PEREIRA NETO, T.J. Simplified systems for refuse/sludge composts. Biocycle, 85: 46-49. 1985.

6.   STROM, P.F. Effect of temperature on bacterial species diversity in thermophilic solid-waste composting. Appl. Environ. Microbiol. 50 (4):899-904. 1985.

CLOSING
KEYNOTE
PAPER

CURRENT STATE OF BIOSOLIDS REUSE IN THE UK AND WAY FORWARD

A Johnson

TERRA ECO.SYSTEMS

United Kingdom

ABSTRACT. Biosolids production in the UK is increasing as a result of the cessation of sea disposal and implementation of the UWWT Directive. The principal route for disposal of biosolids in the UK remains beneficial re-use on land. However, this route is coming under increasing pressure from environmental regulation and in some respects negative perceptions still dog application to land. A considerable amount of work is being done to explore novel uses for biosolids but energy recovery and incineration still present the major alternatives. This paper seeks to outline the drivers effecting biosolids recycling to land from the perspective of a producer (Thames Water/TERRA ECO.SYSTEMS)

Keywords: Biosolids, UWWT Directive, Recycling to land.

Mr A Johnson, is an Applied Biology graduate with over 20 years experience in the Water Industry. He has worked in fisheries biology, river pollution control and trade effluent control. From 1989 he has been involved exclusively in biosolids recycling including a major contract to empty sludge lagoons at Thames Water's Perry Oaks site at Heathrow, the site of the proposed Terminal 5. He has had first hand experience of selling most biosolids products and has a particular interest in marketing issues. Currently he is occupying a general support role in TERRA ECO.SYSTEMS, the recycling arm of Thames Water, with specific responsibility for technical aspects of the production of TERRA compost and to Thames Water International on recycling feasibility and strategy studies for a number of projects.

INTRODUCTION

World population continues to increase hand in hand with increased urbanisation and economic growth. The issue of dealing with the corresponding increase in waste materials is high on the agenda of many nations but working together globally is inevitably difficult given the political and financial differences between nations. Many of the advances in sewage treatment and sludge technology have been developed in Europe and the USA and at the present time, many nations are adopting a regulatory regime for beneficial re-use similar to USA or European Union but much useful work is being carried out around the world on biosolids reuse in a range of applications. The global requirement for the development of waste water treatment facilities offers major commercial opportunities and in Europe alone there is enormous investment in sewage treatment facilities.

The state of sewage treatment in some east European countries is poor. In Romania for example, many treatment works are in a state of disrepair and sewage is polluting tributaries of the Danube but it is hard to see from where the investment for improvement will come. Elsewhere, in the west, many improvements to sewage treatment facilities are taking place, often with significant funds from the EU. In particular new schemes serving coastal communities are underway to replace sea disposal of sewage. These new schemes often involve treatment to high standards and include a requirement to recycle quality biosolids in a way which meets ever more stringent standards. In Eire many coastal schemes are being developed, involving full treatment for the first time and the resulting biosolids will be required to meet Code of Practice standards which equate broadly to Advanced Treated or US Class A product.

In the UK biosolids recycling to agriculture is well established and the producers respond to new environmental requirements and legislative change in an evolutionary manner. The rate of change has quickened significantly in recent years and here too the development of many new coastal treatment works has introduced biosolids recycling to new agricultural areas. One such example close to home is the construction of the new facility at Seafield in Edinburgh which has ensured biosolids are now available to farmers in the Lothians region.

The need for continuous improvement and prospects of ever increasing restrictions has ensured that many individuals involved at the sharp end of the recycling business in the UK are becoming increasingly pessimistic about the sustainability of biosolids recycling in the medium term. At present there is a lack of viable acceptable alternatives and beneficial recycling is likely to remain BPEO in most instances for some time to come.

PRODUCT AND MARKET DEVELOPMENTS IN UK

In those areas of the UK where biosolids reuse in agriculture is well established, product and market development is an ongoing process responding to the demands of the stakeholders within a framework of financial and regulatory constraints. In SE England, Thames Water and it's predecessors have a long history of recycling to land, with a wide base of farmers who recognise the benefits of biosolids use . From the early 1990s and maybe before, issues concerning odour and costs for haulage of liquid product, tended to result in increased treatment (by MAD) and more dewatering. Reduced opportunities for surface application of liquids on grassland has further favoured dewatering (or drying).

There has been a continuous improvement in the quality of service offered to the customer and an increased awareness of the need to address the concerns of the public. The importance of Quality Management is now widely accepted by the UK producers.

Whilst alternative treatment strategies and markets have been explored, cost considerations and a confidence in proven technology has ensured that agricultural recycling of digested liquid and cake remain the principal routes. Lime stabilisation and composting are becoming increasingly popular whether for the production of a Treated or Advanced Treated product. As existing disposal or recycling routes become more expensive or difficult then new processes and routes will undoubtedly become viable. For example there has been considerable interest in production of energy crops such as short rotation willow coppice (and Miscanthus may also provide opportunities in the future) but the economics have not been correct so far. Biosolids utilisation in land reclamation or in the production of soil forming materials has proved a useful route for the producer and may become increasingly important into the future; supplies of good quality top soil are becoming scarce. However such outlets rarely provide the continuous opportunities which agriculture has provided to date. Reuse in forestry is another option which the producers are aware of but the location of the forestry is often a considerable distance from major biosolids production centres and there are major practical difficulties in application into established forests.

With the establishment of The Safe Sludge Matrix the opportunity to recycle untreated liquids in agriculture almost closed but TERRA ECO.SYSTEMS, the recycling arm of Thames Water have sought to utilise the sludge beneficially before non-foodchain crops. Although perhaps only a short term measure, the savings from the avoidance of intersite haulage and treatment has allowed TERRA to offer farmers certain guarantees around income from non-food crops, which in previous years would not have been a viable approach.

In the 90's TERRA developed a range of bagged compost products, based on untreated sludge, which sold exclusively into the domestic market. The income stream from this route was sufficient to warrant the process but if the end product had proved suitable only for agricultural use then the process would not have continued. The composting is now housed in a purpose built building and the product has been further improved and relaunched this year at GLEE (Gardening and leisure industry exhibition). The TERRA product performs well, the market is expanding and increasing pressure to reduce peat extraction all bode well for future expansion. On the negative side copper levels are such that the products cannot meet the UK Compost Association standard and future European standards may also prove difficult. In trials, however, it has been clearly demonstrated that copper toxicity is not an issue and the levels of plant available copper are comparable to other brands with far lower total copper content! Clearly there is a need to influence those who set the standards and ensure that the main driver is "fitness for purpose and environmental protection". Also recently launched on the gardening market in the UK is Biogran; this thermally dried granule has been used widely in land reclamation and agriculture for some time but is now also sold in plastic tubs for home use.

Research into the beneficial re-use of biosolids continues through numerous avenues in the UK and the benefits of nutrients and organic matter are now firmly established. One of the major areas where more work is required is the study of the impact of biosolids on soil microbial populations and especially crop disease suppression.

A wealth of information is available confirming disease suppression characteristics of composted materials and some of the mechanisms are well understood. For biosolids much of the evidence remains anecdotal.

In the Thames Water region, the evidence for suppression of Take-All (Ophoibolus graminae) in second wheats on biosolids treated land is compelling and recent TERRA case studies are allowing farmers to communicate this benefit to one another. It would be valuable to understand the mechanism behind this effect which may relate to soil microbiology or some aspect of soil chemistry, possibly related to phosphate levels. Whatever the reason, benefits which may allow a reduction in the use of fungicides (or any other agrochemical input) would be looked upon favourably by most stakeholders.

The metals content of Thames Water biosolids continue to decline with improved control of industrial discharges but metals derived from domestic sources remain a potential problem for the future. Ironically treatment processes which serve to minimise sludge production tend to concentrate metals and this may present difficulties if future control switches from soil concentration and rate addition limits to include maximum biosolids metals concentrations.

REGULATORY CONSIDERATIONS

Revised Sludge (Use in Agriculture) Regulations and Code of Practice are imminent in the UK and a new Sludge Directive is also expected from the EU. This legislative change is largely focused on pathogen reduction in biosolids and further restrictions on metals applications to soils. Whilst this will have a significant impact on recycling other regulation transposed from the Landfill Directive, Waste Management Regulations and forthcoming European regulation of biowastes may have an equally significant impact.

The UK has been less reliant on waste incineration and recycling than much of the rest of the EU. By 2005 the quantity of industrial and commercial waste to landfill will be reduced to 85% of 1998 levels. In the coming years it has been estimated that composted and anaerobically digested biowastes available for beneficial reuse on land may equate to five times the quantity of biosolids. Unlike farm wastes (FYM, slurry) much of this material may be produced close to major population centres and therefore be competing for the same landbank as biosolids. However, the availability of new soil enhancement products may raise awareness and acceptance of the benefits of recycling in general. Opportunities for co-treatment of waste streams will increase. Farm waste management plans are now common and there is increasing pressure to offer some form of treatment before land application. Hopefully in the future the various product types will be specifically targeted to particular soil types and needs (e.g. low nitrogen products into NVZ's). Overall these developments may lead to a more integrated approach to the recycling of organic beneficials and more responsible soil management.

The Safe Sludge Use matrix has proved useful in establishing ground rules for biosolids application to agricultural land in the UK. The matrix defines the acceptable applications before crops in a number of categories for Untreated, Treated and Advanced Treated sludges with latter considered generally suitable for all crops (Subject to DoE Code of Practice restrictions).

Each producer must consider the local market and determine whether the landbank available will accommodate treated biosolids or whether the additional expenditure required to produce advanced treated biosolids is warranted. Advanced Treated biosolids are often drier (compost, thermally dried, lime stabilised) and of reduced volume compared to Treated alternatives. These features improve opportunities for handling and storage, reduce haulage costs (on a dry solids basis) and tend to allow the exploitation of niche markets, such as use in golf course maintenance and construction. Reduced odour is also a potential additional benefit for some advanced treated biosolids.

Some buyers of farm produce are unprepared to accept the assurances of the matrix. TERRA ECO.SYSTEMS biosolids area managers in both England and Scotland report numerous instances where farmers' are citing buyers misgivings or plain refusal to buy produce off biosolids treated land irrespective of compliance with the matrix. It is essential that the industry influence public perception such that the over-riding view is that responsible biosolids recycling is safe and generally beneficial in the support of UK Agriculture. Concerns over the impact of nutrients (N, P) on surface water and groundwater quality has resulted in tighter control over direct additions of these nutrients to soil and nutrients discharged in sewage effluent to watercourse.

The requirement for removal of phosphates from effluent streams may result in an increase in phosphate in biosolids (and where iron dosing is employed sludge production may also be increased). As the P:N ratio in biosolids is high for most agricultural applications this is likely to have a detrimental impact on recycling opportunities, although the plant availability of the phosphate may be reduced. This is a clear example of transferring a problem from one area to another. There is some evidence that iron dosing for nutrient removal also impacts detrimentally on the stackability of dewatered sludges reducing it's acceptability for recycling. One option for the future may be complete removal of some of the phosphate from the process in the form of struvite.

Nutrient considerations are generally leading to reduced biosolids application rates and 10tds/ha now represents the likely maximum. The potential reduction in supposed environmental hazard gained through these reductions does however have a downside for those involved in recycling. Reduced application rates require more land to be treated in any one year with a resultant increase in movement of plant and equipment between farms. To the farmer a lower rate of treatment represents reduced value both in terms of nutrient supplied and soil structural improvements. With reduced rate applications, a return to the same land year on year may be possible but this involves increased trafficking across the land, more potential disruption to the farmers' work programme and is more likely to reach the notice of the public, who may be prepared to accept a one year in four operation but not an annual event.

For TERRA ECO.SYSTEMS compliance with Code of Practice recommendations on the rate of addition of phosphate to soils from organic manures has resulted in the short to medium term loss of farm land at soil phosphate index 3+ (ADAS) from the landbank. However this has lead to a better focus by our customers on the use of biosolids. Hitherto many have accepted the nitrogen benefits and soil conditioning benefits but largely ignored the phosphate or simply adopted the attitude that it will boost soil reserves. Now many customers are much more considerate of the phosphate in biosolids and by eliminating bagged phosphate inputs, see an additional benefit on the bottom line.

CLIMATE CHANGE

Recycling opportunities vary dramatically throughout the UK. Climate and topography influence the nature of agriculture and clearly the relatively dry, flat, south, east and to some extent the midlands regions are suited to arable production and present widespread recycling opportunities. Even in SE England however, the excessively wet weather in late 2000 resulted in major problems and significantly increased costs for some recycling operations. Some on-farm stockpiles of dewatered biosolids (cake) required containment as rewetting occurred and the cake reverted almost to a slurry consistency. For lengthy periods the land lay too wet to access for stockpiling biosolids and storage areas on the production sites became full; even there, on uncovered storage sites, straw amendment of the digested cake occasionally proved necessary in order maintain the biosolids in a stackable condition. Whether or not global warming was the major factor behind the extreme weather events in 2000 the experience should act as a warning; most climate scientists believe such events will become more commonplace in coming years. This may be yet another reason for the Industry to move towards advanced treatment processes which reduce volumes and generally produce dry materials more resistant to rewetting.

It has been suggested that cropping patterns will change significantly within twenty to thirty years in response to climate change and it remains to be seen whether this widens or narrows seasonal opportunities for biosolids application. Certainly wetter winters and drier summers would invite us to reassess the value of biosolids (organic matter in general) in respect of both improved soil moisture retention and reduced susceptibility of soils to erosion. As ever changes in crop subsidies and other farming practices, including the expansion of organic production, will have an impact on recycling in coming years.

RECYCLING CONTRACTORS

The profile of Recycling Contractors in the UK is also changing and will probably continue to do so. Haul and spread contractor has developed a better understanding of customer service, improved environmental awareness and some now offer a full service to the producer including marketing and environmental assessment.

Some have become involved in the production or operation of treatment plant. It is probably true, with notable exceptions, that more contractors are dedicated to the recycling of biosolids (avoiding other materials) but this may change again when increasing quantities of other acceptable organic materials enter the market. Thames Water's strategy has been to develop long term partnerships with it's main contractors enabling them to invest adequately in high specification plant and equipment which in turn helps to ensure an efficient and reliable service.

STAKEHOLDERS, PERCEPTION AND DRIVERS FOR CHANGE

"Stakeholder" and "Perception" are words widely used amongst those involved in biosolids re-use! Perhaps they are overused. It's not possible to list all stakeholders but Table 1 below identifies some of the key players. Column 3 indicates whether biosolids recycling might be seen as an advantage/positive activity or a threat/negative activity. In many cases there are arguments either way and in these instances the stakeholder attitude may be open to changed perception.

Table 1 Stakeholders and interests in bioosolids re-use

STAKEHOLDER	AREA OF INTEREST/PERCEPTIONS	POTENTIAL IMPACT ON LAND USE
Farmer	Improved profit margin	+
	Acceptability to buyer	+/-
	Acceptability to community	+/-
& Landowner	Land Value	- ?
Fertiliser manufacturers	Preservation of market	-
	Sustainability of farming in UK	+
	Integrated farm management	+
Agronomist	Reputation	+/-
Water Utility Customer	Lowest sewage related charges	+ (for now)
Water supply company	Drinking Water Quality	- +?
Producer	Continuation of cost effective disposal route	+
BRC/Supermarket	Acceptability and safety of produce to customer	-
	Green credentials	- +?
Environmentalists	Water Quality	-/+
	Soil Quality	-/+
	Organic farming	-
	Air Pollution	?
Farming	Financial benefit to the Industry	+/-
	Deflect focus from farm waste issues	?
	Public perception / PR	+/-
Scientific Community	Funded projects	+
	Reputation	+ -?
Plant and Process Developers	Commercial Opportunities	+/-
Public	Safety to health (General)	+/-
	Food Quality	+/-
	NIMBY	-
	General Nuisance - odour dust vehicles	-
Legislators	Protecting Environment	+/-
	Public safety	?
	National Interests/Politics	+/-
	Impact on/relation to other waste disposal activities	+/-

INFLUENCING THE STAKEHOLDERS

The discussion above has hopefully served to catalogue and highlight some of the developments and changes in the recycling of biosolids in the UK. There are new opportunities ahead but also pressures to improve biosolids quality, reduce application rates and increased competition from other treated biowastes. Many of those involved in the business meet to exchange ideas and discuss the latest scientific developments and new legislative proposals; developments which will make life harder for some and introduce new commercial opportunities for others. There is a wealth of information categorising the potential benefits of biosolids in both agriculture and other markets and it is vital to the sustainability of re-use that this information is made available to the stakeholders in a meaningful way.

Some stakeholders, and particularly many of the public, are sceptical of the claims of the scientific community and are unlikely to be convinced of the benefits of "putting sewage on the land" by the presentation of scientific data and statistics. Perhaps with the exception of David Bellamy, there are few media celebrities interested in promoting biosolids recycling. The power of such people cannot be overestimated. TERRA regarded Alan Titchmarsh's 15 second endorsement of the TERRA compost on a television gardening programme in 1997 as a major coup. In Scotland Hugh Pennington is perhaps becoming a household name and his views on the health dangers of "washing-up bowls and tea towels" reached a huge radio audience one day in November last year. Earlier in 1999 a debate on national radio about Iceland's (The Frozen food chain) plans to purchase only organically farmed produce threw up a potentially damaging and unchallenged remark about the spreading of "sewage" on farm land.

Some would suggest that biosolids re-use is not a subject which should be discussed in the mainstream media, potentially doing more harm than good to the cause. It is important however that some of the very positive aspects are related to the appropriate stakeholders in a meaningful and consistent way and that misconceptions are addressed whenever possible.

As a major player in biosolids recycling TERRA ECO.SYSTEMS has tried to be influential in establishing an understanding of the benefits of biosolids recycling amongst farmers, agronomists, landowners, local Authorities the public and various Regulators. It is also important to seek the views of stakeholders and not to assume what they think; it came as something of a surprise to TERRA that most gardeners were quite prepared to utilise a compost derived from sewage sludge and only an estimated 5% of gardeners seemed to have any serious misgivings.

The discussion below outlines how TERRA went about establishing confidence in a market and sustainability of a recycling route for a major PFI contract here in Scotland

SEAFIELD AND ALMOND VALLEY PFI CONTRACT

This DBO contract was let over a term of 30 years and the main element of the contract was construction of a new STW to serve Edinburgh. At the time the Contract was out to tender a report had been produced for Lothian Regional Council indicating that there would be insufficient land availability and farmer acceptance to allow biosolids recycling as a viable option for the Edinburgh sludge.

Indeed planning permission had previously been determined for the construction of an Incinerator to handle the sludge. As part of one of the bidding consortia (Stirling Water), Thames Water (and therefore TERRA) had an excellent track record in recycling and were reluctant to accept the necessity of incineration without further exploration.

It was unfortunate that during the bid stages the very serious outbreak of food poisoning due to E. coli 0157 occurred in Wishaw. That, together with BSE, had the farming community on the back foot and highly reluctant to contemplate the use of "human sewage" on their farms. One potential customer described it in these terms - " we need this stuff like a hole in the head". Even arable farmers who were generally most receptive to the recycling proposal were concerned that the public in general, their neighbours in particular, and their buyers would have a very negative view of the activity. Many also had concerns about heavy metals additions to the soil, pathogens in general, soil damage during application and pollution risk.

TERRA carried out interviews with individual farmers to understand their views on "sewage sludge" recycling and then set out a strategy to address the negative aspects and demonstrate that with farmer acceptance the landbank available within reasonable haulage distance of Edinburgh was sufficient.

Working with the locally recognised experts in agriculture, the main activities comprised the following stages:

1. Demonstrated the **potential** landbank utilising soil and cropping statistics.

2 . Identified seasonal factors affecting spreading window available.

3. Determined appropriate spread rates and assessed the percentage of the landbank which would be required annually.

4. Presented our proposals at farmer meetings.

    - Scottish Agricultural College presented on the potential benefits and disadvantages of utilising biosolids.
    - TERRA explained their working philosophy, the mechanisms for delivery and spreading and environmental monitoring
    - Existing TERRA customers spoke of their experiences over a number of years in the Thames Region

5. Sought the views of farmers subsequent to the meetings through questionnaires designed to identify their concerns and willingness to consider biosolids use in future.

6. TERRA, along with other groups within the Consortium, were involved in numerous meetings with other stakeholders where our proposals were presented.

7. Options for biosolids use in other markets including forestry and land reclamation were also assessed and other fallback solutions identified.

By comparing the situation to the circumstances in the Thames region TERRA were convinced that recycling was a realistic and sustainable option and ultimately presented our findings to East of Scotland Water.

Notably it has become clear since that the greatest value of the farmer meetings came from the involvement of TERRA customers from the Thames region. In essence the farmers spoke the same language - even though the accents were different! The reassurances of those existing biosolids users were more persuasive than the technical information presented at the meetings.

TERRA continue to run trials on a farms in East Lothian and in particular exploring biosolids application prior to spring sown barley to determine whether biosolids derived nitrogen might impact on malting quality. In particular farmers in the region should appreciate the benefits of the organic matter and sulphur content of the biosolids.

CONCLUSIONS

Agriculture remains the biggest market for biosolids recycling in the UK but this route is coming under ever more restrictive regulation and faced with the prospect of increased competition from additional organic soil conditioners and fertilisers. Nevertheless there are precious few alternative disposal routes and agriculture can continue to benefit significantly from the well managed, integrated use of biosolids for some time ahead. In order to ensure the route remains available for as long as possible it is vital that the Industry and in particular the recycling practitioners continue to highlight the positive aspects of the activity and offer a high level of service to the customer. More can be done to influence public opinion on the acceptability and general safety of biosolids in agriculture. It is also vital that we continue to explore and exploit new sludge treatment technologies and seek out alternative beneficial use markets.

INDEX OF AUTHORS

SUBJECT INDEX

This index has been compiled from the keywords assigned to the papers, edited and extended as appropriate. The page references are to the first page of the relevant paper.